Dis

MW00454391

UPPER
ROOM BOOKS®
NASHVILLE

AN OUTLINE FOR SMALL-GROUP USE OF *DISCIPLINES*

Here is a simple plan for a one-hour, weekly group meeting based on reading *The Upper Room Disciplines*. One person may act as convener every week, or the role can rotate among group members. You may want to light a white Christ candle each week to signal the beginning of your time together.

OPENING

Convener: Let us come into the presence of God.

Others: Lord Jesus Christ, thank you for being with us. Help us hear your word to us as we speak to one another.

SCRIPTURE

Convener reads the scripture suggested for that day in *Disciplines*. After a one- or two-minute silence, convener asks: What did you hear God saying to you in this passage? What response does this call for? (Group members respond in turn or as led.)

REFLECTION

- What scripture passage(s) and meditation(s) from this week was (were) particularly meaningful for you? Why? (Group members respond in turn or as led.)
- What actions were you nudged to take in response to the week's meditations? (Group members respond in turn or as led.)
- Where were you challenged in your discipleship this week? How did you respond to the challenge? (Group members respond in turn or as led.)

PRAYING TOGETHER

Convener says: Based on today's discussion, what people and situations do you want us to pray for now and in the coming week? Convener or other volunteer then prays about the concerns named.

DEPARTING

Convener says: Let us go in peace to serve God and our neighbors in all that we do.

Adapted from *The Upper Room* daily devotional guide, January–February 2001. © 2000 The Upper Room. Used by permission.

THE UPPER ROOM DISCIPLINES 2024
© 2023 by Upper Room Books®. All rights reserved.

Upper Room Books® website: upperroombooks.com
Cover design: Left Coast Design, Portland, Oregon
Cover photo: Shutterstock.com

At the time of publication all websites referenced in this book were valid. However, due to the fluid nature of the internet some addresses may have changed, or the content may no longer be relevant.

Revised Common Lectionary copyright © 1992 Consultation on Common Texts. Used by permission.

Scripture quotations not otherwise identified are from the New Revised Standard Version Updated Edition. Copyright © 2021 National Council of Churches of Christ in the United States of America. Used by permission. All rights reserved worldwide.

Scripture quotations marked CEB are from the Common English Bible. Copyright © 2010 Common English Bible. Used by permission.

Scripture quotations marked KJV are from the King James Version of the Bible.

Scripture quotations marked NIV are from the Holy Bible, New International Version®, NIV®. Copyright © 1973, 1978, 1984, 2011 by Biblica, Inc.™ Used by permission of Zondervan. All rights reserved worldwide. www.zondervan.com.

Scripture quotations marked MSG are from THE MESSAGE. Copyright © by Eugene H. Peterson 1993, 1994, 1995, 1996, 2000, 2001, 2002. Used by permission of NavPress Publishing Group.

Scripture quotations marked AP are translations or paraphrases by the author.

The week of November 18–24 originally appeared in *The Upper Room Disciplines 2015*. Reprinted and used by permission.

Editorial note: The named contributors wrote the daily meditations and prayers. For some weeks the editors supplied the scripture overviews and the questions and suggestions for reflections.

Writers of various books of the Bible may be disputed in certain circles; this volume uses the names of the biblically attributed authors.

ISBN: 978-0-8358-2012-7 (print)
978-0-8358-2013-4 (enlarged-print edition)
978-0-8358-2014-1 (epub)

Contents

Foreword

I have begun a new race. When Beth A. Richardson, Dean Emeritus of The Upper Room Chapel, handed me the baton recently, it reminded me of my days running track in junior high school. Those stories are not triumphant. I was not a strong runner! But I loved the coaches, my teammates, the thrill of competition. And I ran hard with the baton in my hand. If history remembers, it will note that, though usually behind the other runners, I never gave up. I always showed up for practice. In practice, the coaches helped me understand the strategy of a relay and how to care for the brutal pain of shin splints. And in practice, I learned that though winning my events mattered, track was ultimately a team sport. Despite my lack of natural ability, our team was usually very successful.

The spiritual practice of the regular reading and study of scripture is also a team sport. While carving out personal time to read, pray, and wrestle with ideas is important to us individually, our practices bind us together in faith. They expose each of us to religious language, like *covenant, exile, transgression, oppression, supplication, redemption,* and *forgiveness.* The regular spiritual practice of study and prayer forms us in a story that we are a people, ancient and set apart. Moses, Abraham, Sarah, Hannah, Deborah, Ruth, Mary, Amos, Micah are our people, a part of our spiritual identity, our religious heritage. I remain grateful to my mother, father, aunts, and uncles for inspiring me to listen to these stories. I learned to sing, read, pray, color, quiz, and perform these stories because I knew them through family devotion, Vacation Bible School, Sunday school, lectureships, youth conferences, baptism, Communion, choirs, revivals, and through my own prayer and study time. Those stories and those names became as near to me as Harriet, Sojourner, Coretta, Martin, Malcolm.

I am fresh from an Academy for Spiritual Formation retreat (Academy 42), and I can say that spiritual practice remains as important to me now as it was in my formative years. In fact, now I am more intrigued by communal life and what it might mean for us to have a common ethical vision rooted in the beatific vision of a liberated, just, and peace-filled eternity. The practice of reading the lectionary and listening for divine truths as they were revealed through a covenantal exchange, listening for divine truths through the prophets, the Wisdom Literature, the parables, the Letters, and now through devotional writers, artists, theologians, and poets, I recognize that the field of spiritual practice is alive. When we contribute to the field of knowledge, when we read or listen to it, when we engage in spiritual disciplines, the Spirit of God is at work renewing us and redeeming the earth.

The Upper Room Disciplines provides us a guide to daily practice that shapes us individually. Following the Revised Common Lectionary gives us the opportunity to be shaped collectively, to journey together through the Christian year. As we read together, may we once again note the mystery of our existence and the way in which God's grace beckons us to remember that "the earth is the Lord's and the fullness thereof" (Psalm 24:1, KJV). We belong to God. And our race, less about winning than about running and playing, calls us to prioritize our ends—unrestrained loving for the healing of the world.

AMY E. STEELE
Executive Director of Programming
and Dean of the Upper Room Chapel

Let's Get Started . . . Again

JANUARY 1–7, 2024 • JOY J. MOORE

SCRIPTURE OVERVIEW: The beginning of the year marks several occasions for the people of the book to remember God's works to set right all that is wrong in the world. This week we will remember the original Creation project that exposes God's intention to form a people—communities of faithfulness. It's a disrupting claim when we move from the Advent season of expectation into the season of Epiphany where we see clearly that our hopes are not yet realized. Each reading reminds us of God's provision of opportunities to take the next leg of the journey toward the promised peace of God made known in Jesus.

QUESTIONS AND SUGGESTIONS FOR REFLECTION

- Read Ecclesiastes 3:1-13. Consider what season of life you (and your community) find yourself in as we begin this new year.
- Read Genesis 1:1-5. How might this year begin a season of seeing through the chaos so that your actions show others the beauty God continues to create?
- Read Psalm 29. Choose a word that you will hold throughout the coming year that enables you to acknowledge God presence in all things, every day.
- Read Acts 19:1-7. What relationships hold you accountable for demonstrating God's presence among those who are not members of your community?
- Read Mark 1:4-11. How does your life reflect that your primary identity—one baptized with the Holy Spirit—is a witness to God made known in Jesus?

Professor of Biblical Preaching, Luther Seminary, St. Paul MN; ordained elder in the Michigan Conference of The United Methodist Church.

New Year's Day

Let's begin again. As always, every beginning is in the middle of what has already happened. Enter memories.

As far back as I can remember, whenever someone in my family dies, Ecclesiastes 3 is read at the funeral. You might think that would be a negative association for me, but it is just the opposite. Whenever our family gathers to celebrate the life of a loved one, we acknowledge the passing of a season. We pause together to recognize that we are not the first or the only people to experience these emotions. We focus on our shared memories. Sometimes we laugh. Sometimes we cry. Always we are reminded of God's presence with us.

One preacher made a clear claim of the majestic sovereign presence of God through this text. The preacher focused on Solomon as the traditional writer of these words. Solomon seemed to have it all: riches, relationships, and reason. And still it wasn't enough. Missing was the yet unfulfilled promise of the glory of God where justice is practiced wisely. Missing, as the seasons come and go, is the performance of life as promised by God. Jesus tells us to perform that promise by feeding the hungry, sheltering the homeless, trusting that God's provision for some does not create lack for others (see Matthew 25). Trust means our actions are an expression of God's faithfulness.

The new year is the appropriate time to remember that we have the opportunity to start again. The reset does not have to begin with our failure but rather with focusing on the God-given opportunities to begin again. This, truly, is the season!

Sovereign God, in moments of disappointment enable us to glimpse where your promises have been kept. Amen.

In the beginning . . . God. Can there be a more disruptive idea? Consider that this is not a journal entry by Adam on the eve of his creation (no pun intended—really). This idea—that the one, true, living God was in the beginning—was conveyed by Israel while they lived among the Babylonians who had their own stories of gods.

Familiarity can cause us to linger in the poetry and miss the actual promise. I ask my students in preaching class to show how a passage of scripture is a window to the presence, power, and promise of God. In a culture that has lost its imagination to believe in God as Spirit, we speak a narrative of the world that begins with the Creator God whose Spirit hovers over the deep.

How disruptive it is to suggest there is a God, and this God indeed is good, even when we are in Babylon. And yet the Resurrection and promised return of Jesus show that the beginning is not over. God has not given up on the original intention of forming a community that makes the whole world say "In the beginning . . . God."

It is hard to overestimate the importance of beginnings. Each new year, each new week—even each new day—offers a reset for us to keep our promises to ourselves, God, and others. Rather than recount our failures and shortcomings, we can consider possibilities and promises to be kept—especially the promise of God.

Today we read a significant proof of promise. God's promises are words offered by the very one who spoke, and stuff happened. Into the chaos, God spoke creative beauty. Into the darkness, God spoke light. Into nothingness, God spoke something-ness. The promises made by the Creator who brings this kind of life are worth holding to.

Creator God, enable us to move through the chaos into the new creation you alone have promised. Amen.

It's midweek already. We began with God's voice and God's promises. Today the psalmist assigns words for our voice.

The best vantage point for hearing the philosophy of this generation is from the earbuds connected to their phones. Reading the psalms is like scrolling through ancient Israel's royal playlist. This beta version of Israel's top 150 best loved hymns could be a predecessor of Casey Kasem's American Top 40 countdown. We learn much about groups of people from the poetry and songs they compose. Consider what the lyrics of country tell us about the working-class rural communities or how rap and hip-hop expose the ills of urban existence.

Just as we replay our favorite lyrics through our earbuds or hum the tune during our workouts, the psalmist is calling for the people of God to say what they believe. Here, we are invited to speak what we know of God's presence in human history. Recognize how the lyrics testify to the majesty of God. Israel is doing a little canny competition here. All the other nations had gods and songs. But in the midst of all the attributes assigned to those gods, Israel declares none holds sway over the One who framed the universe, stirs the wind that strips bare the trees, and shakes the wilderness.

The psalmist remembers and the lyrics glorify God, acknowledging the great things God has done. In order for our generation to write a song of praise, we must remember the God who is worthy. So let us sing through this midweek day with words that acknowledge God's presence and power.

God whose voice brings peace, may our words credit you as the source of all that is good. Amen.

Today's reading shows that Paul did more than start new churches; he also brought people into full understanding of the gospel. Before going out to create a new community, Paul met people who were already believers. But they had never heard of the Holy Spirit.

Paul was not in such a hurry to move on that he would allow any to miss the full promise of God's presence. It's not enough for the name to go on; the quality must go in. As if in a moment of confirmation, Paul baptized them in the name of Jesus and laid hands upon them. What happened next was made possible not because of the gestures but because Paul was able to explain that John was a witness to the God who came to dwell among us. And then Paul got out of the way so that God could do what God alone can do. The Spirit who hovered over the waters descended upon these twelve disciples and they spoke in tongues and prophesied.

Envision this moment not merely as a joyful frenzy of grace but as the moment described at Pentecost. The people ascribed to God the things that God had done in a way that all could understand. They spoke words of truth about what God is yet doing in the world.

Paul left this group to go among the Jews and then he went to speak of God among the Gentiles. As in the previous chapter, Paul is forming friendships across whatever divisions have been assigned. Whose disciple are you? To what geography, genealogy, or government are you aligned? Like Paul, we are invited to speak to our religious heritage, and our practices testify to what God has done in Jesus.

Spirit-sending God, in this our season of division, help us form friendships as a testimony to what you are doing to form communities of faithfulness. Amen.

We return to Paul on the road to Ephesus and his encounter with the disciples who are so close to getting it right. In proper Paul fashion, Paul gathers them in, redirects their focus, and sets them loose to experience the fullness of God's grace.

This scene is a perfect metaphor for new beginnings in the middle of our current mess. We are a people who like to begin with the end in mind. Indeed, it's a good place to begin, but it's not always possible. We do not know what tomorrow will bring, and while we have much capacity to direct the world we live in, it's ending is not up to us. And, anyway, the excitement occurs on the journey. I confess, as much as I want the fullness of God's peace, I'm not ready for this journey to end.

At this point in Paul's ministry, Christ-followers were still believing that Jesus would return any moment. We are 2000 years in waiting. And—I hope I'm not the only one—we don't want to die to experience the peace of God. We want to experience the fullness of Christ here, and that means we have to be glimpses of the promise of God for others to see in this world, right now, until Christ returns. We are invited to begin again, just as these baptized believers were. Paul did not bring a new gospel. He brought clarity of the faithfulness of God to complete what God had started in the very beginning.

When the people of God embody God's faithfulness toward others, the world sees a demonstration of what it will look like when Christ returns. The promise of God, yet unfulfilled, can be powerfully evident in communities that gather as witnesses to the God who became human to dwell among us.

Speaking God, may we be willing to become what we pray for—evidence of your presence here on earth among us. Amen.

EPIPHANY

God likes to do things by sending us another way. Ancient Israel had long expected a glorious reign of a promised king from the line of David. But for most of the time since their Babylonian exile, the kings were not close to anyone's hope for a good leader. And they weren't related to David. Herod the Great, the king we meet in the story of Jesus' birth, wasn't even fully Jewish. He was an opportunist military commander, placed into leadership by the Romans to further their own Middle Eastern agendas.

But everything is about to change in our reading. Wise men recognize this change and make the trip from Babylon, foreshadowing that God's rule means peace and prosperity for every nation, tongue, and tribe.

From the middle of the story, we are back at the beginning. A star was the catalyst that beckoned travelers from the East, calling them to journey long distances because the Creator of the universe was spending the night in a stable. After the seasons had come and gone, and the hope of the scandalous promise was almost forgotten, one star would be the beacon confirming the promise. "God with us" was to come in the form of an innocent infant. And when God's word is heard and heeded by the wise, innocence is in jeopardy because the wicked see only a threat.

This story, like all of the witnesses to God, comes from a light pointing another way back home.

Light of the world, give us eyes to see paths not yet taken that bring us past wickedness to arrive in the places where you have shown up. Amen.

BAPTISM OF THE LORD

Already it's a new week. A new season of the Christian year (again). In this season of Epiphany, we will move between God speaking, first at the Baptism of the Lord and then at the Transfiguration, the last Sunday of Epiphany. After the season of Advent, expectation and celebration of the Incarnation, it's important for the moment of Epiphany to focus us on the sovereign majesty of God. Christians believe this is most clearly demonstrated in Jesus Christ. As we begin (again), our reading pauses us at the baptism of Jesus.

This is more than performing a ritual. Jesus here demonstrates radical submission to God's agenda. A hint that it is more than a ritual is that it does not make sense to John the baptizer (or us) that the one who is without sin, the one who was to come as God's anointed, would need a baptism of repentance. In a counter-intuitive move, Jesus surrenders to God's will at the beginning of his ministry just as he does at the end. Before the trials, Jesus humbles himself before the one he calls Father. And, at the end of his earthly mission, at the greatest trial of all, Jesus will again surrender to God's will.

It's a radical display of allowing God to set the agenda that will fulfill God's promise of peace in Creation. John, maybe still not fully understanding (or agreeing?), submits to Jesus' request. And two thousand years later we still eavesdrop on Jesus hearing himself identified as the child of God the Creator.

As children of God, we can seek in all we do to be Christlike demonstrations of the presence of God in the flesh. To a listening and watching world, it will not always make sense. Still, let's get started . . . again.

Creator God, animate us by your Holy Spirit so that all we do is undeniably a Christlike demonstration of your image in the world. Amen.

To Be Known and Called

JANUARY 8-14, 2024 • RONALD BELL

SCRIPTURE OVERVIEW: We read the stories of Samuel and the calling of Jesus' disciples in John, and it's easy to feel jealous. God spoke so directly into their lives that they should have had, it seems to us, full and unwavering confidence in their callings. Didn't they have an unfair spiritual advantage over us? However, the psalmist reminds us that God knows and sees us individually just as well as God knew Samuel and Jesus knew his disciples. God has plans for us, even if they are revealed in less obvious ways. The reading from First Corinthians is quite different in its message. Perhaps we can at least recognize that even if we never hear God's audible voice, through scripture God still provides guidance for our lives.

QUESTIONS AND SUGGESTIONS FOR REFLECTION

- Read 1 Samuel 3:1-20. Think of a time when you failed to hear God calling you. What helps you to listen to God?
- Read Psalm 139:1-6, 13-18. How does the knowledge that all humans are "fearfully and wonderfully made" inform the way you regard and care for others?
- Read 1 Corinthians 6:12-20. Paul writes, "All things are lawful." What does that mean to you? What are the responsibilities inherent in such freedom?
- Read John 1:43-51. Who are the people who invited you to "come and see" Jesus? Is there someone around you to whom you could extend that invitation today?

Director of Healing and Resilience for The Upper Room; pastor, teacher, lecturer, author, and regular guest columnist for several publications; passionate about emotional formation and the intersection of faith and mental health and has written on topics such as race, trauma, empathy, and grief.

I am a lover of all things jazz and grew up playing first the alto and then tenor saxophone. The first time I told my uncle, who also loved jazz, that I was going to be playing the saxophone, he brought me into his living room, told me to close my eyes, and then played John Coltrane's "Giant Steps." It was an experience I will never forget. He played that one song over and over again, charging me each time to keep my eyes closed and to "see" the notes. From that day forward, the sound of John Coltrane's saxophone has been seared in my mind. It's been decades since I have played the saxophone, but I am still certain that I could recognize John Coltrane's music if I heard it.

In this passage we see Samuel at a time when the voice and presence of God had gone silent for a while. The God who had once moved with clouds of fire and whose voice had compelled lightning was no longer presenting in such grand forms. Eli, however, hadn't forgotten the voice of God. Eli remembered God's sound. It was because Eli had a relationship with God and knew God's voice that he was able to confirm that it was God who was calling out to Samuel.

God's voice and presence in our lives change as we get older and our faith matures. In some seasons God's voice and presence can feel larger than life, consuming and all powerful. In other seasons God's voice and presence can feel like a gentle breeze or distant whisper. The ability to recognize the voice of God is critical for us and also essential for our ability to share with others who are searching to hear God.

God, help us to recognize your voice again. Help us to hear your whisper even when life seems too loud. Remind us, O God, of your sound, your tone, your warmth in our lives. Amen.

I have a peculiar diet. I cannot eat red meat or pork products, and I am severely lactose intolerant. As a result, I often prefer eating out at restaurants over visiting homes of family or friends for dinner. The exception to this is a visit to my mother-in-law's house. Like my own mother, my mother-in-law is an excellent cook. When visiting her house I do not have to worry about offending the host or not being able to eat any of the items prepared. My mother-in-law knows my dietary needs and always prepares something special just for me.

This moment that the psalmist invites us into is sacred. It is a beautiful recognition. In life many people will know us. They will know us based on our relationships with them. Some will know us as child, sibling, lover, parental guardian, friend, foe, neighbor, co-worker, or even "venti dark, single shot, honey." All of those are different relationships filled with unique expectations, personal stories, and authentic connections. No one relationship will know us as all of those things at once—except the Lord. God knows us in our entirety, beyond the parts of us we are cognizant of and those yet to be uncovered.

When I visit my mother-in-law's home, I experience a small piece of this knowing: the comfort and safety of being in the presence of someone who takes care to know what I need. The psalmist helps to shape this understanding that, in God, we are known. We can take comfort in knowing that God knows us. We can rest in the revelation that God is aware and attuned to all our needs, desires, fears, humors, and thoughts. It is good to be known by God.

God, thank you for knowing us. Thank you for thinking of us and caring for our needs. Amen.

My wife and I are "swim parents." Our oldest son is the swimmer in the family. Most of our weekends are spent in stuffy, non-air conditioned, chlorine-smelling gymnasiums surrounded by hundreds of kids and other parents. At each swim meet we show up with a big bag filled with our padded chairs, snacks, extra goggles, towels, water, and our son's heat sheet.

Heat sheets are a listing of all upcoming races with each swimmer's previous times recorded next to their name. The sheets are helpful because you can see who beats their previous times and who doesn't. From the moment our son gets out of the car to walk into the gym, we are watching him. We wonder if he stretched, if he warmed up, if he is ready, if he is in the right lane, if he is pushing, on and on. With every race we check his heat sheet, signal to him his progress, and check in to see what his coaches have to say.

I see in Psalm 139 a perspective of parental love. As strenuous and meticulous as being a swim parent sounds, it is nothing compared to how much care God has for us as conveyed in this psalm. God is constantly thinking of us, checking our progress, measuring our development by the dreams and desires laid out for us prior to our birth. God has plans for us and brings along the supplies and support we need. As with my child, it's up to each of us to ultimately choose to swim, but it is God who is thinking of us, rooting for us, and supporting us every stroke along the way.

Thank you, Lord, for always thinking of me, for rooting for me, and for supporting me every day. Your care for me is a daily source of encouragement. Amen.

A few years ago my wife and I were looking for a new home. We enlisted a real estate agent who set up appointments and guided us as we visited a number of houses before settling on one that we loved. I remember that season of visiting homes with the real estate agent very clearly. Often when we arrived at a showing to see a home, there were specific instructions prior to entering that we had to follow. We were asked to wear special shoe coverings or to take our shoes off in order not to track dirt in the home. We were asked to close what we opened, turn off any lights we turned on, and not touch the walls if possible. While trying to assess whether or not this place would become our home, we had to treat it gently and follow the rules laid out by the current owner.

I often think about that experience of house hunting when I read 1 Corinthians 6. Paul invites us to consider the way we treat our physical bodies and how that reflects our unity with Christ. It is a great reminder that our bodies are not temples we own but temples that belong to God. We, like potential homeowners, get access to these temples to tour, but not to own.

Our task is to care for the temples we have access to. We follow God's rules to honor our temples and care for them. We must be careful where we step and what we track in with us. There are a variety of ways to understand how one cares for one's own body, even several that Paul writes about in our scripture. Our job is not to judge how others take care of their God-given temples but to work on our own care for what God has given, all the while honoring that gift.

God, help us. Give us the strength, the consistency, and the patience to be good stewards over these temples you have given us access to. Amen.

As a United Methodist preacher's kid, most of my childhood was spent moving around a lot. I attended three different middle schools, two different high schools and lived in two different states before graduating and going off to college. As an adult that nomadic lifestyle stuck. In the first twelve years of our marriage, my wife and I lived in four different states and six different houses. Moving around often gives you a different perspective on what "home" means. For me home is not a place, a town, or a particular building. Instead home is a people. Home is my family.

When Nathanael asks if anything "good" can come from Nazareth, what he is subtly making a claim about is that the people of Nazareth, Jesus included, are suspected to be no good. I love this text because Philip does not refute him. Instead, he tells Nathanael to "come and see."

Jesus calls the disciples away from what they know of as "home," from their towns and houses, and even from their communities and families. But he invites them to come and see a new family, a new way of being in community: the family of God. By accepting this invitation, the disciples experience an entirely new way of living.

"Come and see." What a beautiful illustration for our faith and the role of discipleship. We are called to invite others through our relationship with God to "come and see." What would it look like to reshape all our interactions with that imaginative proposition, "Come and see"? How would it transform all our definitions of "home"?

Lord, give us the childlike joy of sharing with others your goodness and your works in our lives. Give us hope as a language and love as an action. Amen.

Twice a year every year—usually around New Year's Day and then again at the beginning of summer—I get this bold idea that I am going to start working out and get in shape. I buy a bunch of new clothes, fill the fridge with fruits and vegetables, and order powders, proteins, and energy bars to fuel this new initiative. Then I head to the gym.

At the gym, styled in my crisp, color-coordinated gear, I always go to the free weights first. The long rack of weights stretches out along the wall, offering weights from one pound to over one hundred pounds. I've learned not to stand near the professional bodybuilders as I work out. Watching them lift super heavy weights has an effect on me, and not a good one. It makes me think that I can lift that same weight, but, as you can imagine, I cannot.

In the gym there are no limits to the types of weights and machines you can try to use. Everything is available, but not everything is useful for everyone. Maturity and a deep sense of self are our only guide for measuring the amount of weight we choose. That is what I believe Paul was saying to the Church at Corinth. Everything is lawful, but not everything is a good idea.

We have to use our wisdom, based on our relationship with Jesus Christ, to judge what is beneficial and acceptable for our lives and for those in our community. Like those weights in the gym, we can grab any of them at any time, but doing so has a cost. To be free from the pain or embarrassment of lifting weights too heavy for us, leaning on our relationship to Christ is key.

Lord, help us to pause, stop, breathe, wait, and listen. May we hear you clearly in all that we do. Help us, Lord, to surrender our will to yours and walk joyfully in the freedom you provide for us. Amen.

Between my nephews and my own children, I have been blessed to be a part of a birthing team five times. On five separate occasions, I have been handed the scissors to cut the umbilical cord and welcome fully into the world a precious baby. Like most folk, every time I first held a new family member, the first thing I did was count. I counted the toes, fingers, eyes, and ears. I cannot think of a more precious and sacred moment than the birth of a child. And yet, just as I was eager to count body parts to mark such an occasion, so God also counts.

Jesus tells us that God even counts the hairs on our head. What is incredible to me is that the response to our creation at the conclusion of God's counting is that we are fearfully and wonderfully made. That we, each of us, are marvelous in God's sight.

Those affirmations are easy to say over a newborn baby. I remember pouring endless affirmations over my nephews and my sons when they were first born. All of the beauty and hope for a bright future are wrapped up in tiny clothes and blankets. But God isn't looking upon us as newborn infants. When the psalmist talks of our being fearfully and wonderfully made, marvelous and precious to God, the psalmist is indicating that God has seen the totality of us. God sees the fullness of our creation from our innocence and perfection at birth through the trials and struggles of life. God sees our flaws, our imperfections, our secrets, and even our wickedness. Yet, in God's mercy, we are still identified as fearfully and wonderfully made, marvelous and precious in God's sight.

O Lord, help us to see ourselves the way you see us. Help us to live into your vision of ourselves. Guide us, Lord, to trust that your thoughts and words over us are enough. Amen.

God's Time and God's Call

JANUARY 15–21, 2024 • ANNE CUMINGS

SCRIPTURE OVERVIEW: There are two strong themes in the scriptures for this week—God's call on our lives and the ways in which God's time is not our time. Jonah attempts to resist God's call, but finds himself in the belly of a great fish. He gets a second chance to follow the call, and a whole city responds in repentance. The psalmist reminds us that life is but a breath and the things that humanity places value on are not what God values. Paul also reminds us that time on earth is short and we should focus on the things of God. Finally, Mark offers us the call story of the first disciples. Jesus meets them where they are in their lives, and they drop everything to follow in a sense of urgency.

QUESTIONS AND SUGGESTIONS FOR REFLECTION

- Read Jonah 3:1-5, 10. Think of a time when you resisted God's call or have judged other people or groups of people as being beyond help.
- Read Psalm 62:5-12. How can you put your trust in the steadfast love of God?
- Read 1 Corinthians 7:29-31. Reflect on an experience that changed your perspective on what is important.
- Read Mark 1:14-20. How have you responded to God's call on your life? When have you experienced God's voice in the ordinary moments of life?

Ordained elder in The United Methodist Church; licensed clinical social worker; author of *My Body is Good: Embracing Body Positivity and Giving Up Diet Culture for Lent*; working for body justice and promoting embodied spirituality.

I was in the passenger's seat of my friend's red, late 90s Pontiac Grand Prix when he ran a red light and pulled directly into oncoming traffic, resulting in another vehicle T-boning into the passenger side door. While no one was injured, this was one of the few moments in my life when I felt a close call with my mortality. Time seemed to have been altered. I watched other cars drive past and wondered how they could just go about their everyday life. Didn't they realize that life was so fragile? For some time after the accident, it felt as though all the priorities I had been so caught up in just a couple of days before were foolish.

In the broader section that encompasses today's reading, Paul is responding to questions from church members in Corinth about marriage and divorce. But in the few verses that make up this reading, it's as if Paul pauses and says, "You guys are asking the wrong questions! Christ is risen and is coming back! Everything is different!" You can feel how Christ's resurrection and impending return has bent time for Paul. I imagine him, like me on that sidewalk years ago, asking the Corinthians, "Don't you realize life is fragile and short?"

Paul reminds us that anything we are engaged in on earth is relative in Christ's timeline. These words from Paul remind us to focus on what truly matters: the love of Christ that lives within us. When we view our lives from the perspective of life in Christ, things that seemed so important just moments ago carry a lighter weight, and the things that really matter come into focus. Time is growing short. Let's spend it focused on the things of Christ.

God of eternity, help me to live on your timeline. When I get caught up in worries and cares, remind me that the things of this world are passing away. Draw me back to Christ and the things that are truly important. Amen.

Yesterday we read Paul's words to the Corinthians urging them to put our time here on earth into perspective in the light of Christ. Today we turn to the Psalms for a very similar message. We are encouraged not to put our hopes in riches or in our position but to hope only in the power and love of God. The psalmist proclaims that, after all, our lives are but a breath.

It's hard to believe the onset of the COVID-19 pandemic was almost four years ago. The pandemic quickly became one of the most divisive concerns of our lifetime. But if you recall, those first few weeks after our country shut down brought out the best in so many of us. This virus that was literally taking breath away from so many inspired some truly breathtaking acts of generosity, creativity, compassion, and beauty. Artists were offering free online concerts and art classes. Neighbors were creating scavenger hunts and birthday parades for stir-crazy children. We were finding new and creative ways to stay in touch with one another through video-conferencing and socially distanced outdoor gatherings. For a brief time, the world saw life as both fleeting and infinitely valuable, and it changed the way we treated one another.

Psalm 62 reminds us that this is the perspective we should live our lives with. When we remember that our lives are nothing but a breath, each breath becomes more precious. Not only our own breath, but the breath of all those around us. Living in this way allows us to see all the stress and worry, division and hatred in our lives as delusion, and we can breathe in freedom. Take some deep belly breaths today. Let them remind you that you are sustained by the very breath of God. May this reminder calm your spirit and ground you in the eternal love of the God who created you.

Holy God, you are my refuge, my strength, and my hope. Help me to see each breath I take as a holy opportunity to love you and love others. Amen.

The immediacy of Mark has always been startling to me. With no birth story to ease us into the life of Jesus, we are thrown right in with a wild character from the wilderness dressed in camel's hair, eating locusts and honey. John the Baptist introduces us to Jesus by "proclaiming a baptism of repentance" in preparation for Jesus' arrival. Then just a few verses later, John has been arrested and Jesus has taken up his own message of repentance. Mark moves fast!

The first half of this passage tells us that Jesus' ministry was about proclaiming the "good news." And in true Markan fashion, the good news is brief. His sermon consists of this one sentence: "The time is fulfilled, and the kingdom of God has come near; repent, and believe in the good news." That's all we have at this stage of the story. Jesus proclaims that God has drawn near, and this little headline was enough to get people to change the way they were thinking and start to live in a different way.

I don't think the urgency and brevity we feel in Mark's writing is by chance. Mark uses the word "immediately" forty-one times in just sixteen chapters. There must have been something powerful about Jesus' presence that caused his earliest followers to change their entire lives with a simple encounter. My own Jesus encounters have been more like a subtle, gentle wooing. But there is something inspiring to me when I meet someone with the kind of zeal that Mark's Gospel depicts. They have experienced God in such a way that they can no longer live the way they lived before. Whether or not your Jesus encounters have been quiet nudges or powerful impacts, let these words from Mark create some urgency in you to change the way you think and live.

God of new life, move me to change my thinking and the way I live. Fill me with holy urgency. Amen.

When Jonah first hears God's voice calling him to go to Nineveh, he does not drop what he's doing and follow God's lead like the disciples in Mark's Gospel. He does the opposite. He heads in the other direction, trying to get as far as he can from God's call. Of course, this leads to him spending a cozy three days and nights in the belly of a great fish only to be spat out on the beach in a soggy heap of fish spew.

Our passage picks up with God trying again after Jonah has wiped off some of the fish goo. Jonah hears God's voice, saying, "Get up, go to Nineveh, that great city, and proclaim to it the message that I tell you." This time Jonah listens.

When it comes to God's call on our lives, we can be pretty thickheaded sometimes. There was a time after I had been called to ministry when I decided to head in the other direction. My rebellion was not as deliberate as Jonah's. I just decided to prioritize starting a family instead of following through with my ordination process for a few years. But I ended up drifting further away than I had planned, until the work environment I found myself in was so toxic and harmful that I felt I had landed in the belly of a beast. I left that position feeling physically and emotionally like I had been spat out in a messy pile of fish guts.

The good news of Jonah's story is that God's call doesn't dry up when we get lost in the waves of our own fears or egos. When we turn away from God's call on our lives, it results in a loss of peace; but that isn't the end of the story. God is always ready for us to get back on the path God has called us to.

Longing God, you call to me in so many ways, but I do not always answer. Sometimes I even turn around and run the other way. But you remain there, longing for me to return to you. Thank you for continuing to call, even when I stray. Amen.

If there is a perfect season to wait for God in silence, it must be winter. During this time of year all of creation seems to slow down and cozy up.

When I lived in Chicago, winter was a season of paradox. The weather could be extremely brutal and exquisitely beautiful at the same time. My favorite winter times in the city were early mornings after a good snowfall. The thick snowy blanket would cover everything, causing the cacophony of the bustling city to fall under a deep hush. Walking down the snowy sidewalks in the unusually quiet city, the crunch of my footsteps in the snow was my morning prayer. But eventually, that peaceful walk led me to my car, which would inevitably be buried by the dutiful snow plow in several feet of snow and ice. My prayer would quickly turn to muffled cursing as I worked to dig out in time to make it to work. Paradox indeed.

This psalm also elicits a sense of paradox in us. So often we put our hope in the things our society tells us will give us a firm foundation—wealth, position, power. Yet these are a delusion. The very things we think will bring us security end up letting us down.

The psalmist offers us a sturdier alternative—the steadfast love of our God. Five times in this psalm, the writer uses the Hebrew word ʾak, which is translated as *alone* or *only*. This emphasis is a drumbeat reminding us that it is God alone who gives us hope, salvation, and refuge. Trusting in anything else is fruitless.

God of quiet seasons, forgive me for trusting in temporary things for my security. Help me remember that only you can give me true hope and salvation. This winter, help me slow down and allow your love to warm my heart. Amen.

Though Mark's writing is concise, this scene from the Galilean seaside is evocative. Jesus is walking along the water's edge watching the fisherman in their boats a little way off shore, casting their nets in hopes of drawing in a hardy catch. He finds two disciples fishing along the shoreline. He finds two more in their boat, sitting in the sunlight mending their intricate nets.

Jesus met the disciples right where they were every day, out by the sea, doing their jobs. Sometimes we are guilty of listening for God's call only in special places. We think we will meet God only at a special retreat, during a revival service, or on the top of a picturesque mountain. We might expect to hear from God during a powerful worship service, but we don't think to listen for God in the ordinary moments of everyday life. This passage reminds us that God is calling to us right here and right now. God shows up in the work we do every day. Jesus even uses familiar language when he calls the first disciples. He doesn't strip them of their entire identity as fishermen. Jesus uses what they already know and understand and shows them that they can use those skills to bring a new kind of life into the world.

Right now God is calling to you. You don't have to go anywhere or do anything special to hear God's call. God will meet you right where you are. And you don't have to abandon your identity and become a different person to follow Christ. Christ will transform you along with the gifts and graces you have developed throughout your life. God will use your uniqueness as you choose to follow Christ's way.

God of this present moment, thank you for meeting me right where I am. Open my ears to your call. Show me the ways I can use my gifts to follow your way. Give me the courage to get up and go when I hear your voice. Amen.

The division that emerged over how to respond to the pandemic has only highlighted the deep divides that were already present beneath the surface. There are times when I wonder if our society even wants to overcome the divide. It seems like we relish in pointing our fingers at the other side. During the last presidential election, a wise and kind friend of mine decided to bring cookies to everyone on her block who had a sign in their yard for the candidate she opposed. It resulted in some beautiful conversations and even a neighborhood service project. But when many of her friends heard of her project, they scoffed and said they would never do such a thing. Even the thought of a conversation with someone they disagreed with was off-limits.

Those friends remind me of Jonah. Jonah didn't believe that the people of Nineveh could change. He perhaps even liked the idea of God punishing them for their evil ways. He definitely didn't consider that he himself could be part of the problem. It took getting swallowed up by a great fish to rattle Jonah out of that kind of thinking. But when we find him in this passage, he is ready to consider God's call to knock on the door of these neighbors he considered evil.

When Jonah follows through with God's call, something amazing happens. Change breaks through. The people of Nineveh repent. In response, God spares them. Because Jonah crosses the divide, a whole city is reconciled to God.

Let Jonah's story inspire you to cross some divides. Consider ways you can open yourself up to those you have written off as lost causes. Spend some time reflecting on how you might need to change your perspective in order to follow God's call. Let God use you to break down the walls of division in our world.

God of unity, show us the places where we can find common ground. Use us as instruments of reconciliation. Give us the courage to cross the great divide. Amen.

The Grammar of the Divine

JANUARY 22–28, 2024 • VICTOR JUDGE

SCRIPTURE OVERVIEW: Grammarians study the behavior of language. When a writer places one word beside another, a behavior is constructed that stimulates our faculties of reason, sense, and imagination. Language is the medium through which God's desires are expressed, and the grammar of God's holy will for us is revealed in this week's readings through the prophetic words spoken by Moses, the lyrics of praise written by a psalmist, the correspondence of Paul to the church in Corinth, and the Gospel according to Mark. These four grammars share a common antecedent in Divine Mystery, the grammar of God's covenant that no person can diagram definitively. When reading these passages from Holy Scripture, hear and hold the words for the ways they stimulate your faculties and the textures of meanings they have acquired through the ages.

QUESTIONS AND SUGGESTIONS FOR REFLECTION

- Read Deuteronomy 18:15-20. To whom or to what setting do you turn when you yearn to hear God's voice?
- Read Psalm 111. For what are you praising God today? How have you experienced God's steadfast love recently?
- Read 1 Corinthians 8:1-13. What do you think of Paul's statement, "Knowledge puffs up, but love builds up"? Can you think of examples of this in your everyday life?
- Read Mark 1:21-28. How do you react to the concept of authority? How does the authority of Jesus differ from the authority we may encounter in the world?

Assistant dean for academic affairs and lecturer in literature and religion at Vanderbilt Divinity School; holds baccalaureate and graduate degrees in English from Peabody College of Vanderbilt University; poems published in *The Habersham Review* and *The Orchards Poetry Journal*; parishioner at Christ the King Roman Catholic Church, Nashville, TN.

Moses himself was an example of one who was selected to reveal the extraordinary. And in today's reading, we hear through Moses that God declares, "I will raise up for them a prophet . . . I will put my words in the mouth of the prophet, who shall speak to them everything that I command."

Note that God speaks in imperatives, not in the subjunctive mood (a tense that implies an imagined future) or in metaphors. There is a seriousness in God's voice that is conveyed in God's admonition for the false prophet: "Anyone who presumes to speak in my name a word that I have not commanded the prophet to speak—that prophet shall die."

This passage shows the care and respect God asks us to give to language. God speaks creation into existence, and then the monologue becomes a dialogue when God "raises up" prophets from among the people to proclaim God's will for the greater good of the human condition.

The prophets summon us to listen, discern, and question words whenever God's name is invoked. By heeding God's commandments and praying to unite our wills to God's holy will, we participate in the conversation with God and God's prophets.

Gracious God, the words of your holy prophets call us to embrace your mystery; grant us the courage to listen to their voices that call us to ponder your unfathomable depth. Amen.

The psalmist calls us to join our voices celebrating God's divine attributes. The "works of God's hands," the psalmist proclaims, should be "studied." At four intervals in the hymn of praise, the psalmist employs the noun "work(s)": the handiwork of God is "great," "full of honor and majesty," "power[ful]," "faithful and just." Throughout this psalm is the recurring present tense of the infinitive "to be." The work of God's hands will never be recounted in the past tense; the psalmist transports the reader into a different understanding of time where we find ourselves in the historical-present tense of the Great I Am.

We speak and write of art and of the Divine in the historical-present tense: The works of the artist and the works of God are conceived, created, and manifested in physical space and time. Art, such as the poetry of the psalmist, and God's artistry transcend our traditional understanding of chronological time that is generally understood in our more traditional use of verb forms. There is potency arising from sacramental time that defies the past tense: *As it was in the beginning, is now, and ever shall be.*

In our reading of the verses, we endow the text with life beyond the particularities of dates and composers. The hands of the mortal artist will be claimed by time, but the works of those hands become liberated from chronology. As our voices breathe life into the syllables of praise, we prove and experience the sacramental efficacy of a mystery that renders us breathless.

Merciful Lord, may the words I speak each day become verses of gratitude for your goodness. Amen.

When we place ourselves humbly at God's feet and seek to learn, we find that we receive wisdom. The psalmist has experienced delight while observing "the faithful and just works of God's hands." Such delight inspires study, and the psalmist distills in verse 10 the lesson received from contemplating God's fidelity to the covenant: "The fear of the LORD is the beginning of wisdom."

This "fear" is not synonymous with terror or angst but is rather akin to a sense of awesomeness, an experience that ultimately defies reason. By acknowledging this holy fear as the igniting point of wisdom, we remain humble, perpetual students who delight in the creative artistry of God's hands.

Psalm 111 is cyclical in its litany of praise for God's gracious and merciful deeds. The delight that descends upon the psalmist inspires a description of the awesomeness of God. This awesomeness and the writer's exploration of it start to build God's divine wisdom in the writer; consequently, God's awe begets awe; God's wisdom begets wisdom.

We find in this psalm a model for our spiritual and intellectual formation. To fear the Lord is to desire to discern the will of God and to imbue humility in our actions. This holy reverence is to be practiced. Yet our embracing of the practice is merely the *beginning* of wisdom. To study the works of God's hands, we remain in a *posture of beginning* because God "has commanded his covenant forever," and when encountering the mystery of God's infinite wisdom, we are forever beginning.

Our Redeemer and Fount of Hope, send forth your Holy Spirit to dream within us and inspire us to follow your commandments. Amen.

In the eighth chapter of Paul's first letter to the church in Corinth, he addresses whether it is lawful for a Christian to eat food that has been consecrated to an idol. Rather than giving a simple yes or no, he digresses by contrasting knowledge and love. Whereas knowledge "puffs up," love "builds up."

Paul reminds us that the knowledge that "all of us possess" is limited. Our knowledge is acquired and interpreted by our fallible, imperfect faculty of reason. When he refers to our not possessing the "necessary knowledge," Paul is saying that knowledge alone cannot sustain us. We are sustained by our love for God and from God for whom we exist. To love God is to be known by God, who alone is capable of knowing us as fully as we can be known.

Love that builds up is a love that is constructive, regenerative, and divested of puffed-up egotism; a love that builds up is predicated on the grammar of benevolence and good will toward humankind. By conducting our lives according to the principles of love, we build up and usher in the kingdom of God on earth. Committing our lives to this principle will guide us in making progress toward discovering the "necessary knowledge."

Our God of infinite love, grant me wisdom and courage to divest myself of self-interest so I may be a conduit for your love to build up each person I encounter today. Amen.

Paul describes Christians who believe that it is sinful to eat the meat of animals sacrificed in the temples dedicated to idols as "weak in conscience." But he also says that Christians who eat such meat without regard for the conscience others are being sinful.

The unnamed but implied idol among "the so-called gods in heaven or on earth" is the idol of intellectual superiority, the belief that the "possession of knowledge" is a license to regard oneself apart from the community of Christians. Paul reminds us that Christ died also for the weak believers.

Declaring oneself free from superstition does not make one stronger in conscience or elevated above the community. To act in such radical independence is to worship implicitly the idol of autonomy that Paul says is a "sin against members of your family," a transgression that is also a sin against Christ. "Family" in this letter is the church in Corinth.

When guided by the principle of love, we renounce self-interest. Perhaps the greater sacrifice Paul is encouraging us to make is the sacrifice of self, to become divested of self-interest and become invested with love for our community. A renunciation, an emptying of self allows one to assume a posture of humility. God created life from *humus*, the Latin word for "ground," and when we conduct our lives in humility, we remain close to the ground traversed by the feet of the community. Humility is essential to our spiritual and intellectual formation. We depend on relationships in the greater family of humankind and on love from our God.

God of wisdom and enlightenment, help me to discern your will so that I may walk humbly with you and not stray from the path of righteousness. Amen.

We meet Jesus in Capernaum teaching in the synagogue on the sabbath. Mark does not tell us about the lesson because the lesson was not the point. The emphasis was on the power of Jesus' words. The people were astounded because he taught as one with authority and not as the scribes.

The teaching authority of the scribes came from their knowledge of the traditional interpretations of the Torah; their authority came through the transmission of interpretations throughout the successive generations of scribes.

As we imagine the formative years of Jesus when he would have attended synagogue, he would have become well-versed in the grammar of tradition represented and imparted by the authoritative teachings of the scribes. The "new" authoritative voice of Jesus must not be interpreted as a dismissal of the scribes' authority—though they appear to have heard it that way (see Mark 2:6-7)—but as a variation that invites us to hear the lesson differently and to imagine how the tradition may breathe and extend into our contemporary lives.

As God incarnate, Jesus brings power and authority into his teaching. By the reactions of the people in the synagogue, we see that Jesus has inspired them to pay attention and to question teaching—a behavior that is essential as we open ourselves to Mystery.

God, I want to be a follower of your teaching authority. Hear my questions, comfort me in my uncertainty, and guide me deeper into your mystery. Amen.

Jesus' teaching authority is demonstrated concretely when a man possessed by an unclean spirit interrupts the lesson and asks, "What have you to do with us, Jesus of Nazareth? Have you come to destroy us? I know who you are, the Holy One of God."

Jesus does not dignify the disruption with an answer; instead, he rebukes the unclean spirit in an intolerant voice, commanding, "Be silent, and come out of him!" The unclean spirit yields to the directive, and the expulsion inspires questions among the congregants. As witnesses to the "new teaching," they are astounded and amazed by this authority even over unclean spirits.

Jesus' lesson on the sabbath is not theoretical or conveyed only by words. The new teaching authority is enacted, embodied, incarnated by the Word. An event that begins as a disruption becomes an incarnational exercise; the teacher's authority is demonstrated through application.

The teaching authority represents the convergence of word and deed, and the demonstration of the authority results also in an act of healing. The authoritative words are not meant to assert power over the hearers but to liberate the afflicted from suffering and to restore the man to health. Jesus exercises the new teaching authority not to garner attention for himself but to serve humankind.

This story is a portrait of the servant-teacher whose authority is not manifested merely by imparting acquired knowledge to a generation of followers; the servant-teacher's words are enfleshed in a deed motivated by love.

O Lord, our great healer, may my words and deeds be a balm for those who are discouraged. Guide me to words that will comfort their spirits. Amen.

God's Mission—My Priority

JANUARY 29–FEBRUARY 4, 2024 • COLLINS E. AKO

SCRIPTURE OVERVIEW: The passages for this week emphasize the rewards that come with discovering God's good purpose for us. We read about how God gives power to the faint and increases the strength of those who wait on him. Psalm 147 presents God as the author of creation and as a very active agent in the restoration of the world. The passages in First Corinthians and Mark warn against distraction from God's good purpose for all of creation once we come to engage in the *missio dei*. Mark also invites believers to constantly spend time in the presence of God as they engage in God's mission.

QUESTIONS AND SUGGESTIONS FOR REFLECTION

- Read Isaiah 40:21-31. How have you felt God renewing your strength when you have felt weak?
- Read Psalm 147:1-11, 20c. With reference to any personal challenges that you might be encountering at this point, what would the hallelujah look like for you?
- Read 1 Corinthians 9:16-23. What are some of your personal privileges and how do you use them to serve others and the gospel?
- Read Mark 1:29-39. Where and how have you seen God at work during your wilderness moments?

General Board of Global Ministries (of The United Methodist Church) missionary; lecturer in missiology and ecclesiology at the United Methodist University in Kindu, Maniema Province, Democratic Republic of Congo.

Since June 2018, I have been serving as a Global Ministries missionary in a post-conflict community and church reconstruction context with the East Congo Episcopal Area of The United Methodist Church in the Democratic Republic of Congo (DRC). The area I serve is shaped by the scars of war. The first and second Congo wars (October 1996 to May 1997 and August 1998 to July 2003 respectively) caused great trauma to communities here. Millions of people were killed, as many if not more sought asylum in surrounding countries as refugees, rape was used as a weapon of war, and most of the country's infrastructure was badly damaged.

During my very first meeting with Bishop Unda of the East Congo Episcopal Area, he shared with me his hopes for the region. It was easy to tell that the conversation was an invitation for me to join him in dreaming of a bright future for the East Congo Episcopal Area. We discussed his joys but also some serious challenges encountered by the church and local populations under his leadership.

As the bishop shared with me his dream for the restoration of parts of the eastern DRC devastated by long years of violent conflicts, he would occasionally slip in parallels from the book of Nehemiah, trying to get me to understand my biblical mandate for this missionary assignment. I would later learn that "Levons-nous, et bâtissons!" ("Let us rise and build"), a phrase from Nehemiah 2:18, had been proposed by Bishop Unda after his election in 2012 and adopted by the East Congo Episcopal Area as a slogan and rallying call.

I left the meeting feeling faint, weary, and exhausted, but hopeful that God who had called me to serve with the church in the DRC would surely renew our strength.

Great is thy faithfulness, O Lord, and your goodness is forever.
Teach me to trust in you. Amen.

Sometimes we ask questions—in our minds or audibly—to clarify a situation or subject, to gain knowledge, or to generate new ideas. At other times we ask questions to guide a conversation in the direction we want it to go, to influence or alter someone else's view on a matter, to gain a person's attention, or to reach an agreement.

The questions at the beginning of today's passage are guiding the conversation. They are reminding the hearers of what they already know about God. It is an invitation for the people of Israel to turn away from their sins and to put their trust in God's power and care. It is a call for the Israelites to wait on the Lord who alone can renew their strength, so they can soar on wings like eagles, run and not grow weary, and walk and not faint.

I remember asking lots of questions about the violent conflicts in parts of Eastern Democratic Republic of Congo (DRC) during my first visit with the bishop. I asked about the weather, the food, the people and their culture, transportation, and life in parts of the church in the DRC under his supervision. I also talked about my previous work in peace and development in a context of war as an attempt to justify my new assignment with his episcopal area.

Nonetheless, there were some questions that I did not dare to ask out loud for fear of expressing weakness, confusion, and doubt. Some of my non-audible questions would later find answers as I have seen God at work within communities and with individuals here at my missionary placement site. When I let them, the answers to my questions inspire me to remain strengthened by God.

God of power and might, reveal yourself in my weakness, confusion and doubt, and grant me divine direction. Amen.

In some parts of Eastern DRC, traveling by road, air, or river can be challenging, as some areas still have pockets of active violent conflicts, remnants of these long years of civil wars. More than eighty percent of the road infrastructure was destroyed during the two Congo civil wars, and any existing paved road is poorly maintained. Boats on the Congo River serve as a means of public transportation. They have scheduled departure times but often have no idea when they will arrive at their destinations. Local flights are canceled with often little or no information about the reason for the cancellation or a proposed time for the next available flight. You learn very quickly that every trip will last longer than planned, and you must imagine worst-case scenarios and plan accordingly.

Psalm 147 is the second psalm in what is referred to by some theologians as the "Hallelujah chorus" that ends the book. It is part of the final triumphant response of God's people to their difficult experience with God in a hostile world, a reminder that there still could be a hallelujah moment at the end of a difficult journey.

You would think that in the context of communities traumatized by the violence of armed conflicts people would have little or no reason to sing praises to God, would have no faith in a God who did not stop all these atrocities from happening, would be cursing God for the challenges encountered in gaining access to the few hospitals and schools that are still functional in the area, and would be discouraged by the slow pace of reconstruction and healing. It's been a difficult experience for the people in the East Congo area, but their courage and faith in God, you will hear them say, has kept them going as they continue to sing a hopeful hallelujah chorus.

Merciful Lord, grant me the strength to stay faithful in your mission. Help me feel your presence even in challenging times. Amen.

According to statistics from the General Board of Global Ministries, United Methodist missionaries serve in professional careers as educators, health workers, pastors, evangelists, church coordinators, agriculturists, development specialists, community organizers, and peace builders in about 60 different countries. Since the founding of the first denominational Methodist missionary society in 1819, training, commissioning, assigning, and supporting missionaries in the United States and around the world have been at the heart of mission.

During training, missionaries are encouraged to follow the example of Jesus Christ by setting aside their personal preferences so that they can serve others at their place of assignment. These newly recruited missionaries are taught adaptability skills and knowledge that will equip them for success in missionary service.

In today's reading, Paul says that adaptability is the basis for successful mission. He was obligated by the law of Christ to set aside his personal preferences so that he could serve the Corinthians and lead them to Christ. Paul shares how he uses his freedom in Christ to adapt his behavior to the context and situation in his missionary field. Paul explains how his main goal is not to uphold tradition. It is not to fight tradition, nor to side with one ethnic group or another, but to preach Christ.

As a follower of Christ, Paul's example of making the gospel a priority and attractive to potential converts is an example worthy to emulate. Paul does not want to disqualify himself (see 1 Corinthians 9:27) by living a self-centered life. So Paul goes out of his way to renounce his personal privileges all for the sake of the gospel.

O Lord my God, lead me to that place where I can make the gospel a priority for my life. Amen.

Church people commonly assume that God favors church people over "unchurched" people. This kind of mentality leads us to act in ways that ensure that those "unchurched" people will stay the way are. Very often, we make those outside of the Christian faith feel unwelcome.

Paul's statement, "Woe to me if I do not speak the gospel!" speaks helpfully to a present-day society that often approaches church life through the lens of self-centered and self-protective entitlement. Woe to us if we are not concerned about how our attitudes and practices keep people from a relationship with God through Christ Jesus. We forget the commission Christ set for us, not to turn inward to build up our own power and desires but to go out into the world and share God's love with the world.

How often do we stop and take a moment to check if our attitudes and practices are representative of the Christ we present as Lord and Savior in our sermons? This passage is also an invitation for church people to practice what they preach, a reminder for us to walk the talk. If the lives we live throughout the week do not model the speech we engage in on our day of worship, we are missing the point of living as followers of Christ.

It is important for us to put our words into action, showing that we mean what we say by actively living the life of a beloved child of God. This is an invitation to align our attitudes and practices with the gospel.

God, help me to be mindful of my practices and attitudes and their effect on how I invite others to experience your love. Amen.

I teach courses in missiology and ecclesiology at the Methodist University in Kindu, Maniema Province in the Democratic Republic of Congo. My students are mostly student pastors who are assigned to local churches in the area as part of their pastoral training. These students are often already very engaged in the life of a local church and involved in programs aimed at making disciples of Christ. In both courses, I spend considerable time with the students exploring the concept of *missio dei,* a Latin theological term translated as "mission of God" which refers to the work of the church as being part of God's work of restoration of all of creation. I invite them to reflect on the dangers of not creating space for God while engaging in God's mission.

In today's reading, well before sunrise and after a long day of preaching, healing, and exorcism, Jesus gets up while it is still very dark and goes to a deserted place to pray. The deserted place mentioned in this passage is not a desert, but a place void of distractions where Jesus could give himself unreservedly to prayer. This was the place where he could pray without distraction, a place where he could find strength from God in whose service he had been called.

As we engage in God's mission, this passage is an invitation and reminder to find that deserted place where we can talk to God without distraction. We cannot be about God's work without the strength that only comes from prayer.

God, thank you for inviting me to be a part of your mission. Help me to always seek your continuous presence throughout the journey. Amen.

As I read about Jesus departing into a deserted place, I wonder if there is any relationship between it and the deserted places mentioned in other passages in the scripture. In John 1:23, we see John the Baptist is calling the people to repentance from a deserted place. In Matthew 4:1-11, Jesus triumphed over Satan's deadly temptations in a deserted place. And it was a deserted place that shaped the Israelites and made them into the people of God.

The Greek word for "deserted" is *eremos* and is often used to speak of the wilderness. Referring to the passages mentioned above, it is fair to say that much of God's work is done in the wilderness. This truth should be a source of hope as we experience wilderness moments when we feel hopeless and the horizon seems to be bleak. God might be using our wilderness moment to redeem and reshape us for God's purpose.

At the end of today's reading, Jesus comes out of this quiet place with a clear perspective on his mission. He invites his disciples to go with him to the nearby villages to preach, affirming that preaching, healing, and exorcism are the reasons he had been sent by God.

Moments in the wilderness should not be times when we get bitter and turn from God. Rather we should seek the face of God and create more room for God's will to be done in our lives. It should be a time when we redefine our priorities and fine-tune our focus on our role in the *missio dei*.

God, lead me to that deserted place where I can meet you, and help me to discover your purpose for my life. Amen.

Being Seen, Seeing God

FEBRUARY 5–11, 2024 • KRISTIN G. STONEKING

SCRIPTURE OVERVIEW: In the week leading to Transfiguration Sunday, the texts all deal with holy, transforming light; but they also speak to the awkwardness of waiting for and finally experiencing that light. Elisha's is a stop-and-go pilgrimage before he sees the chariots of fire. The psalmist proclaims the march of the sun across the sky while also waiting for the eschatological arrival of God's justice for God's people. Paul empathizes with the believers in Corinth who are having to wait and work to "give the light of the knowledge of the glory of God." Jesus leads Peter, James, and John up a mountain where they wait and are terrified by the cloud of glory that overshadows them.

QUESTIONS AND SUGGESTIONS FOR REFLECTION

- Read 2 Kings 2:1-12. Think of a time when you waited for a blessing from God. How did the waiting feel? How did you experience the blessing when it came?
- Read Psalm 50:1-6. What helps you to be aware of God's presence with you from "the rising of the sun to its setting" each day?
- Read 2 Corinthians 4:3-6. What are the areas of your life where God is shining a light? Are there any areas where you need God's light, or may not see God's light?
- Read Mark 9:2-9. Identify a spiritual "mountaintop experience" you have had. What was the lasting impact of that experience on your life as a follower of Christ?

Superintendent of the Bay District centered in San Francisco in the California-Nevada Conference of The United Methodist Church; adjunct faculty of United Methodist Studies at Claremont School of Theology in Los Angeles, California.

The story of Elijah the prophet and Elisha his successor is one of mentorship. Elijah's earthly life is ending. He has prepared Elisha to receive his mantle. Having a mentor is a blessing, not only for the support and encouragement provided but also because it is an experience of being seen. To be effective, mentors must see what grace God has given to their mentee and then nurture and encourage these special talents and capacities.

How often does our mentoring or parenting seek to remake those who come after us in our own image rather than to help develop their God-giftedness? The mentor's gifts are not necessarily the mentee's talents. Each person has a God-given role to assist in accomplishing God's purpose.

Or conversely, when we have guides we greatly admire, do we seek to become exactly like them rather than embracing what God has entrusted us to contribute? God has so ordered creation that without each person's unique contribution, the world will be impoverished. Our task is to see ourselves with God's eyes, becoming more who God created us to be.

Elijah says to Elisha, "Tell me what I may do for you, before I am taken from you." Elisha responds, "Please let me inherit a double share of your spirit." Elijah, in his wisdom, knows that the blessing Elisha is asking for can only come from God. He responds, "If you see me as I am being taken from you, it will be granted you; if not, it will not." For Elisha to see Elijah as he is would be to see that they are distinct and differently gifted. If Elisha is able to see this, he will receive his blessing.

Generous God, may I see others as you created them and celebrate their giftedness. May others see me for all of who I am, knowing the spirit you have placed in me is what I most need to proclaim your glory on earth. Amen.

The need to be seen is a basic human need. The desire to be recognized and known is intended to be met in the community of the church. We are greeted by those we love and are called by name. But beyond being recognized, we also want to be understood in all of our complexity.

The prophet Elijah is one of the greatest prophets in the Hebrew scriptures. He caused miracles to happen and foretold important events in Israel's story. He was well and widely known. He helped others understand the meaning of what was happening to them. He interpreted God's voice and message, making visible what was veiled.

Later, in the Transfiguration scene on the mountaintop with Jesus, Elijah appears with Moses. To those who knew the Hebrew scriptures, their appearance was a representation that the power and authority of the Law and all the Prophets were present. Elijah had become a metaphor.

What does it mean that Elijah's last words were about "being seen as I am"? Too often we believe we know all there is to know about a person based on the narrative around them, their outward appearance, gender, background, or physical ability. The Vietnamese poet Ocean Vuong has written about how his life as an Asian-American gay man is often not "legible" to others. Preconceived notions of who he should be based on his appearance do not fit his lived reality and experience.

To be legible is to be seen as we are in all of our complexity. We grow, change, have seasons of external thriving and seasons of internal cultivating. Some of this is visible; some is not. Even what is visible can be misinterpreted. There is always more to understand about what we are seeing.

Visible and invisible God, guide my sight and my understanding. Help me to eschew the facile narrative of "what we all know" and embrace your revelation. Amen.

As the psalm opens, the psalmist declares praise for the God of Israel. "Praise" may call to mind light and upbeat music, pure happiness and joy. But to offer praise, particularly in a mixed theological setting such as was present in ancient Israel and in many places today, takes risk, specifically three risks. First, in praising we acknowledge a distinct authority—God. Second, in praising we make ourselves vulnerable. And third, in praising we express a commitment to the One who is being praised. These risks give praise its power.

To praise is to express a vertical relationship with a higher power in and over our lives. We are telling the world who we love, appreciate, honor, and on whom we rely. Now, as then, many authorities compete for our loyalty, and adherence to the dominant authority can offer safety. The ancient Hebrews were aware of the risk they were taking by saying God alone is God and worthy of praise. Yet they still proclaimed the power and authority of Yahweh, the one God.

In praise, we accept vulnerability. Hold the image of someone you love in your mind and feel the warmth of love in your heart. Would it be possible not to express this feeling? Yet, is it ever possible to express it fully? Still we must try. How much more, then, must we express our delight and joy in our ultimate Love, our God, even though it makes us vulnerable to do so? We leave ourselves exposed as we attempt to fully express our praise for God.

Finally, when we lift a psalm of praise, we communicate that we stand in the goodness, grace, and mercy of God. And yet to fully receive these good gifts, our commitment to our relationship with God is necessary. We express this commitment through our loving obedience to God's word and will for our lives.

Great God, no matter the cost, we praise you! Amen.

It feels good to focus on the glory of God and the beauty of God's creation. The God of unconditional love is popular. But what of God the judge? Life can be challenging, and in our struggles, we may want to hide from God. We may feel defensive at our sense of inadequacy or about times when we have not been our best selves.

The paradox is that God does not judge our struggles but our hiding. God knows that with which we struggle. God knows when we have fallen short of the glory of God. We are seen at all times, at our best and at our worst. God asks us to continually bring all before God in humility and reverence.

The psalmist reminds ancient Israel of their covenant with God. A covenant is not like a contract. In a covenant, the participants uphold their commitment, seeking unbroken relationship in spite of the behavior of the other. However, God is not silent when the covenant is broken. God calls us back into covenantal relationship at all times.

How are we upholding our covenant to bring all of our lives before God? Do we trust God enough to be seen in all of our humanness? Do we accept that we are not God and therefore are always fallible? In God's continual calling out to us and seeking to enfold us in covenant we find the grace of unconditional love. God the judge is necessarily also the God of unconditional love.

Abiding God, thank you for never giving up on our covenant. Thank you for not staying silent when I hide from you. In being seen, I see your forgiveness, grace, and love. Amen.

Paul's opening words, "Even if the gospel is veiled," suggest that Paul is defending against some attack. It sounds as though he's answering a charge that the good news is obscured or that he and those around him have not made it plain to others. Apparently, people may be saying they cannot "see" the gospel. As often happens with defensiveness, Paul becomes wrapped up in his argument of why the gospel might be veiled.

How many church meetings have you been to that focus on why others are not receiving the gospel or why we are not able to make the good news visible to those who need it? Sometimes we leave these meetings depressed, feeling that even our best efforts are not reaching people. But other times, someone speaks a word of hope and faith, reminding us that we share the gospel because it has been good news for us! We have been changed. We have experienced a way that is not just life-giving but life itself.

John Wesley wrote, "Love cannot be hid any more than light; and least of all when it shines forth in action, when ye exercise yourselves in the labour of love, in beneficence of every kind." If the gospel is veiled, it could be because we are not making our love visible. Are we focusing on scarcity and conflict? Or are we proclaiming Jesus Christ and rendering love visible through our actions? As the scripture says, "For we do not proclaim ourselves; we proclaim Jesus Christ as Lord and ourselves as your slaves for Jesus' sake."

Unveiled God, reorient us toward your visible presence in the world, and help us to make it plain to others. Grant us the strength and grace to keep shining light on your love and good news. Amen.

Emily Dickinson wrote, "Exultation is the going / Of an inland soul to sea— / Past the houses—past the headlands— / Into deep eternity! / Bred as we, among the mountains, / Can the sailor understand / The divine intoxication / Of the first league out from land?" Today's scripture begins with another moment of exultation. But as Mark's mountaintop exultation changes, literally "transfigures" in the person of Jesus, the meaning and message of the moment shift from exultation to something else.

Jesus goes up to the mountaintop to pray with Peter, James, and John. While praying, Jesus becomes infused with energy, glowing as if from inside. We see this same phenomenon later, after the Resurrection when Jesus is on the road to Emmaus. Present but transformed, he says to the disciples, "Don't touch me!" In these moments, the divine energy of God is on display in Jesus in the fullness of his humanity and divinity. At the same time, we are reminded that we cannot contain, control, or hold the power and being of God.

Yet we are connected to the power of God. God came to us as a human and showed us that though we are not God, we are constantly being invited into relationship with God. The flow of God's energy is present. In Jesus, we see that God loves us so much that God came to us as one of us to affirm this essential interrelatedness.

On the mountaintop, Moses and Elijah also appear, representing the Law and the Prophets. In one sense their appearance in this scene shows that Jesus is the culmination of their hope and faith. But in perhaps a more important sense, in standing with Jesus they represent the power of community and our essential interrelatedness.

Energetic God, may I act in ways that affirm the interrelatedness of all creation and your people through the ages. Amen.

TRANSFIGURATION SUNDAY

Human beings have strong impulses to maintain pleasure and avoid pain. Peter is a human being. As a part of the electrifying, life-changing public ministry of Jesus, Peter has been on a high. And then, when Jesus begins to talk of his impending suffering and death, Peter enters a state of frantic denial.

Elijah and Moses appear with Jesus and signify the height of sacred power. Peter sees an opportunity to hold on to a high moment and avoid the pain that is to come.

How often do we deny what is difficult, seeking just the mountaintop moments? But Jesus calls us to face reality. Through Jesus' ministry, many people have answered his call to love all without exception. But others have not accepted Jesus' invitation. Rejection of Jesus' message stems from that same impulse to avoid pain—loving all in an imperfect world and standing with the most vulnerable means suffering.

In refusing to face pain, we become trapped, holding on to static definitions and identities. But God enters into this clinging, becoming visible in transformative and redemptive ways. God speaks from the cloud, "This is the Messiah. Whatever you have been running from, he is here to walk with you. Whatever you suffer, he is with you in the depths of your pain. Do not doubt the lengths he will go for you. You will emerge from this journey together, transformed" (AP). Then Jesus touches the disciples and says, "Get up and do not be afraid."

The uniqueness of Christian faith isn't that God was born; other traditions have made the divine human. The miracle of Christianity is that God suffered, died, and then conquered death. Our arrival at that place where pain is no more is real, but it doesn't circumvent the Cross.

Jesus, strengthen me to follow wherever you lead. I know that in rejoicing and suffering, in life and death, God is with me. Amen.

Hiking into Lent

FEBRUARY 12–18, 2024 • JONATHAN F. HARRIS

SCRIPTURE OVERVIEW: The season of Lent is now upon us, a time of inward examination that begins on Ash Wednesday. We search ourselves and ask God to search us so that we can follow God more completely. This examination, however, can become a cause for despair if we do not approach it with God's everlasting mercy and faithfulness in mind. Although the Flood was a result of judgment, God also saved the faithful and established a covenant with them. The psalmist seeks to learn God's ways, all the while realizing that he has fallen short and must rely on God's grace. For Christians, baptism functions as a symbol of salvation and a reminder of God's covenant faithfulness. It is the means by which we accept and receive God's love and mercy.

QUESTIONS AND SUGGESTIONS FOR REFLECTION

- Read Genesis 9:8-17. When have you, after a season of loss, experienced new life? What was the sign of that new life?
- Read Psalm 25:1-10. How are you experiencing God's steadfast love and faithfulness in your life? How do you offer thanks?
- Read 2 Corinthians 5:20–6:10. What negative consequences have you experienced as a result of your servanthood?
- Read Mark 1:9-15. Recall a "wilderness" experience in your own life. What helped you to move through that experience? What were the spiritual gifts of that experience?

Hiker of the Appalachian Trail and Canon to the Bishop in the Episcopal Diocese of Southwestern Virginia.

On long hiking trails, such as the Appalachian Trail, one finds people who go out of their way to help the hikers, offering food and drink at a trail head, a ride to the grocery store, or a free tenting spot in their backyard. They are known as "trail angels." They don't belong to any formal organization, but up and down the trail one finds them. Paul describes how God calls us to do a remarkably similar thing. While for many of us being a member of a church mostly means spending our time in the church building, here we are called to be "ambassadors."

Ambassadors are sent out to another land for some purpose. In the case of trail angels, they don't just stay at home and wait for the hikers to come to them—they go out to find them. Trail angels feel that they get as much in return as they give. They draw inspiration and companionship from the hikers, and a true community forms.

One time I was hiking in the Smoky Mountains and a trail angel gave me a ride into town. She said, "I like to drive, and I get to see all this beautiful scenery and wildlife. Down in Gatlinburg the tourists all complain about the long lines and the prices, but I pick up the hikers and they're just glad to get out of the rain and are grateful for the ride. I meet all kinds of different people. I sold my soul to the devil in retail for years—this gives me my soul back."

I believe trail angels model for us Christians what God calls us to do. We aren't called to sit in our churches and wait for people to come to us. We are Christ's ambassadors, sent out into our neighborhoods, not only because we have something to give but also because we have much to receive.

God, send us out to discover who you are to all the world. Amen.

Hiking into Lent

For many American Christians, living one's faith is more a matter of appreciating the benefits of being a member of a congregation than it is an enterprise that makes spiritual and physical demands on us. Yet the experience Paul shares reminds us that following Jesus isn't just a walk in the park. "Troubles, hardships, beatings, imprisonments, sleepless nights and hunger" are a few of the conditions that beset Paul and the early cadre of Christians.

Because of my interest in hiking, I regularly follow accounts of hikers embarking on long journeys. I was struck by the observations of one hiker who recounted a particularly difficult day trudging amidst cold and wet conditions in Shenandoah National Park in Virginia. It was a moment when he was not enjoying hiking. Yet at the end of the day he came to a conclusion that surprised him. He recalled how he had come to the Appalachian Trail at least in part to discover true happiness and realized that he had found it on this difficult day "in a way that sunny skies and rolling hills just could not deliver." "Happiness," he said, "requires contrast, not mere contentment. My formerly comfortable, well-fed, air-conditioned life had left me content. But now I know that true happiness has to be earned."

Paul's account reminds us not only that Christian living has not always been easy, but that often God asks for more. Indeed, if we're diligent and courageous "in truthful speech and the power of God," our Christian witness may challenge us in ways we haven't faced before. That might cause us discomfort, yet it also may leave us "always rejoicing" as servants of God.

God, help me to understand your larger purpose when challenges weigh me down. Amen.

ASH WEDNESDAY

On Ash Wednesday Psalm 51 launches us into a Lenten journey that seeks to recover the identity God has given to each of us. Lord knows in the course of settled habits and daily rhythms we have a way of getting off track from the people God has created us to be. Movingly, the psalmist pleads, "Wash me," "Cleanse me," "Restore in me," "Create in me a pure heart, O God, and renew a steadfast spirit within me." The desire for restoration is strong.

In recent years I've begun to explore hiking and backpacking. I have observed with interest individuals attempting to hike the entire Appalachian Trail, which passes near where I live in Virginia as it winds approximately 2,200 miles from Georgia to Maine. Everyone who approaches the feat of hiking the entire Appalachian Trail arrives with their own motivation, but strikingly common among them all is a desire to change in some significant way: to recover something that was lost, to make amends, to take stock of their lives, or to discover a new purpose. One such hiker put it this way: "You're so tired. There's so many ups and downs that you have no energy to just not be one hundred percent yourself. And I think that was the biggest gift—I don't have to pretend for anyone. I'm not trying to be someone who I think I should be, I'm just being me, and who that is . . . is not who I was before."

I find the Lenten journey to be remarkably similar to that of the long-distance hiker embarking on his or her journey. We know it may not be easy, and we know there are unforeseen twists and turns ahead. But we open our hearts, yearn with a strong desire for change, and ask of God, "Restore to me the joy of your salvation."

Lord, lead me on a journey where I become more fully yours. Amen.

Many people find spending time outdoors peaceful and rejuvenating. Hiking is a way I have found to engage in nature and spend time in prayer. Not all long distance hikers are religious, but many discover that their journey takes on a spiritual dimension. The hours and days spent walking make way for ample time to think and reflect and, for some, to converse with God. One hiker in his twenties recently shared his experience of praying as he walked: "I very seldom spoke out loud as I was praying, but I just found being in the woods by myself listening to the birds and the water and everything to be very therapeutic."

Jesus' words today urge us to do spiritual actions not to impress others, but God alone. Prayer is a private conversation with God: "And whenever you pray, do not be like the hypocrites, for they love to stand and pray in the synagogues and at the street corners, so that they may be seen by others. . . . But whenever you pray, go into your room and shut the door and pray to your Father who is in secret, and your Father who sees in secret will reward you." Similarly, giving and fasting are activities that should be done in private, not in an effort to receive praise from others who see us doing them.

Praying and walking outdoors helps me to pray—for God alone. There aren't the distractions of chores to complete, media vying for my attention, or preoccupations with other people for whom I may be tempted to perform. It truly is a time for me to be alone with God. Outdoors apart from the clamor of daily life, I more easily give myself over to God "who sees in secret."

Next time you pray, try going outdoors. It can be in the woods, at a park, or just around the block. Being outside has a remarkable way of settling us into focus.

For many the season of Lent provides a framework to work out a spiritual goal, such as establishing a more regular prayer life, giving oneself in service, or choosing to fast.

In Psalm 25, the goal is to present oneself before God for pardon. "Do not remember the sins of my youth or my transgressions; according to your steadfast love remember me, for the sake of your goodness, O LORD!" In addition, the psalmist asks God to provide instruction in the new way of life: "Make me to know your ways, O LORD; teach me your paths . . . All the paths of the LORD are steadfast love and faithfulness, for those who keep his covenant and his decrees."

A hiker will notice that the guidance God gives comes in the form of traveling a path. The world of a hiker, of course, is defined by a pathway, a continuous long ribbon of dirt traversing meadows, forests, and mountaintops. The beauty of a trail is that it is always leading you forward. There may be days you don't feel like walking, or when the only thing you can physically or mentally muster is putting one foot in front of the other; but not to worry, the trail leads you on. The trail experience is always the same and yet always different. The two-foot-wide pathway pointing the way is the same as always. At the same time, through the focus of the footpath much becomes visible that before lay hidden, leading to unexpected newness. Choosing a pathway to travel through Lent can keep us on pace to our goal and open a self-understanding heretofore undiscovered. Along with the psalmist, following a spiritual path keeps us in forward movement toward deeper union with God.

This Lenten season choose a pathway that can keep you focused and lead you into deeper union with God.

For me the most joyful moments of hiking are walking along the ridgelines of the mountains that surround where I live in southwestern Virginia. They often follow sheets of rock outcropping that crest the high elevation points on the mountains. To straddle those ridgelines and look out across the valley below makes you feel as if you are in outer space looking down on planet earth. The barns look like dollhouses and the country roads like pencil lines. It is an otherworldly experience.

The mythic story of the Flood in Genesis presents its own cosmic perspective. When God finds the earth full of violence, God decides to remake it, sending a flood to cover the earth for 150 days, save for the people and animals in the ark. The story is all-encompassing, touching the lives of every living creature, and leaving even the highest mountains under water.

Hiking in the Appalachian Mountains calls to mind the great epochs of history when the Appalachians were as high as Mt. Everest, were subject to successive waves of crumpling, cracking, and uplift, and ancient rivers carved out steep gorges. The historical perspective of millennia upon millennia of activity imparts a sobering humility when we consider the short span of our lives. Such a consciousness could deflate us into indifference, or even sheer fatalism, especially if one considers that the violence God sought to wash away in the flood is still with us. But God's statement here spurs us on otherwise, to take to heart the promise that God will never cease to guide us. "When the bow is in the clouds, I will see it and remember the everlasting covenant between God and every living creature of all flesh that is on the earth."

Help us, Lord, to trust your redemptive hand in the long arc of history. Amen.

First Sunday in Lent

As Christians, we each need to make a conscious effort to discover what God calls us to do. God's call isn't the same for everyone, and it is only through prayerful consideration that we can discern what exactly God calls forth from the deepest place from within each of us. And even if we do identify a calling, it doesn't necessarily mean smooth sailing ahead.

When Jesus is baptized, the Spirit "immediately" drives him into the wilderness to face attempts to push him off his call. No honeymoon period here—Jesus is put to the test straightaway.

Each year certain individuals set out to hike the entire 2,200-mile length of the Appalachian Trail from Georgia to Maine. Of course, much is required to complete the feat. Amidst the beauty are many challenges such as rain, cold, bugs, boredom, cost, and risk of injury, to name a few. But what is noteworthy is that those who complete the trek often aren't the ones in the best shape, with the most money, the best equipment, or the most experience. Rather, what defines them is that, at some level, they feel called. Despite the soggy shoes, nights sleeping on the ground, and eating the same mundane food day after day, something within them carries them the distance. There is a hunger that supersedes the discomforts. There is a drive to complete the journey that isn't thwarted by obstacles. Their call urges them on. Likewise, as Christians we follow God's call not because it is the easiest path for us but because God sends us that way for God's loving, liberating, and life-giving purposes.

Lord, help me to keep pace with your loving purposes even when obstacles come into the way. Amen.

When Things Seem Impossible

FEBRUARY 19–25, 2024 • SANDRA STOGSDILL BROWN

SCRIPTURE OVERVIEW: We cannot earn God's love. Going back to the time of Abraham, God's blessing has been based on faith. God chose Abraham for a covenant not because Abraham was perfect but because he believed God. The psalmist reminds his audience of their ancient relationship with God and expresses the hope that it will continue through future generations. In Romans, Paul reinforces the centrality of faith. Following the law was not bad, but no one should believe that following the law could earn God's favor. Some of Jesus' disciples share with him an experience that mystifies them. Trusting God means surrendering everything in faith.

QUESTIONS AND SUGGESTIONS FOR REFLECTION

* Read Genesis 17:1-7, 15-16. What is the basis of your relationship with God? How comfortable do you feel in it?
* Read Psalm 22:23-31. Where do you find hope in troubling times?
* Read Romans 4:13-25. How easily do you live in God's grace? In what areas do you find yourself "reckoning" your righteousness?
* Read Mark 9:2-9. When have you found it difficult to believe in things you may not fully understand? What helps you to trust in God?

Pastor of First Presbyterian Church of Topeka, KS; M.A. in Religious Education from the Claremont School of Theology; M.Div. from Central Baptist Theological Seminary; is passionate about education, stewardship, team building, creative worship and radical hospitality.

Like many Presbyterian pastors, I lead a congregation where older members far outnumber the younger ones. Some of them need canes and walkers to navigate their way to worship now. Others no longer worship in person because they do not drive anymore, or because sitting in a wooden pew for too long simply hurts. People look at the average age of our members and wonder about our future. I have lost count of how many times I have heard the question, "What are we doing to attract younger members?"

Abram was 99 years old when the Lord gave him the name "Abraham," meaning "father of nations." Sarah was ninety. They are painfully aware of their ages and the limitations that come with them. Yet God calls and chooses these two older adults and promises to make them not just fruitful but "exceedingly fruitful." They see their ages as an obstacle (understandable), but God sees an opportunity.

Instead of viewing old age as a liability, what if we viewed aging as an opportunity to let God make us more fruitful? Rather than fret about where the young people are, why not focus on celebrating the people who are already with us? What if we treated older adults like the asset they truly are? Older adults have tremendous power to uniquely bless others. My congregation—and my own life—is much richer because of the prayers, stories, wisdom, acceptance, words of encouragement, brave questions, financial gifts, artistic talents, hospitality, and life experiences of saints in their 80s and 90s.

The story of Abraham and Sarah invites me to let go of the idea that "old" means "less than" and to trust that God is working in me and in the churches I serve to make us "exceedingly fruitful."

God, thank you for calling people of all ages throughout the ages. Make me fruitful my whole life long, for your sake. Amen.

My all-time favorite novel is Jane Austen's *Persuasion*, first published in 1818. It tells the story of 27-year-old Anne Elliot, the daughter of an English baronet. When she was nineteen, Anne had been persuaded to break off an engagement to a man she loved because of her youth and his lack of family and fortune. Years go by, and Anne never stops loving her former fiancé, who soon becomes successful and wealthy as a sea captain. When circumstances throw them back into one another's lives again, Anne must stand by silently as the man she loves seemingly pursues another, younger woman, while he watches Anne being wooed by someone of whom her family thoroughly approves. Eventually the two are joyfully reunited, but it is poignant to read of Anne's perseverance in loving someone so faithfully for so long, when all hope seemed gone.

What was it like to be Abraham, who first received God's promise to make him the ancestor of many nations when he was 75 years old? At age 99, the promise had still not materialized. By the time Isaac is born, Abraham is 100 years old. He waited a quarter of a century! What kind of doubts, fears, impatience, and frustration did this "ancestor of nations" experience during those twenty-five years? Did he ever feel "gaslighted" by God?

In today's world, we can get what we want faster than ever. We order a gadget online, and 48 hours later it arrives on our doorstep. In these times of nearly instantaneous gratification, the story of God's call to Abraham is more relevant and challenging than ever. When what we are seeking is slow to arrive, it helps to remember that God keeps God's promises on God's timetable, not ours.

God, you are sometimes slow, but you are never late. Help me to trust in your divine timing and rest in the assurance that you always keep your promises. Amen.

It's astonishing how easy it is to forget the amazing things God does for us. Not long ago I was doing some reorganizing and came across a shoe box filled to the brim with beautiful greeting cards. People had sent them to me during the first year of the pandemic, when I was diagnosed with breast cancer. The message of those cards boils down to: "We love you. We are praying for you." Two and a half years later, I had already forgotten the outpouring of support I had received during the time of my treatment.

I attribute my current cancer-free status to early diagnosis, excellent doctors, effective medication, and my own good habits, all of which are valid contributors to my health. But I have completely overlooked all the prayers offered on my behalf. I am back to taking my good health for granted and forgetting to praise God for the healing I experienced. Praising God for our healing can be challenging: What about those who prayed and were prayed for but did not experience the same healing? I don't know the answer, but I do know that struggle does not let us off the hook for expressing our own gratitude and praise.

"You who fear the LORD, praise him," says the psalmist. The act of praise turns our attention toward God who heals and helps us. Praise reminds us that we do not generate our own blessings or engineer our own rescue. It is God who works through the doctors, nurses, first responders, teachers, neighbors, and others who help us. The psalmist refers to God more than twenty times in these verses. The continual reference to God calls the people's attention back to God, who keeps delivering them.

During this season of Lent, this portion of Psalm 22 not only reminds us to praise God from whom all blessings flow; the psalm's persistent call to "praise him" leads us in doing just that.

God, I praise you for all the blessings in my life. May I never forget that my help and healing come from you. Amen.

Recently I officiated the funeral of a 96-year old man. He and his wife had three children, eight grandchildren, and twenty-two great-grandchildren. It was necessary to block off at least five pews in our sanctuary to seat all the family members who attended this man's service. "Isn't it amazing?" marveled the husband of one of the man's children. "Without this man, none of these people would be here."

With the echoes of Genesis 17 still reverberating in our ears, Psalm 22 takes on an additional layer of comfort and assurance. By addressing "all you offspring of Jacob" and "all you offspring of Israel," the psalmist subtly reminds us that God keeps God's promises. God had kept God's promise to Abraham and Sarah with the birth of Isaac hundreds of years before, or there would be no offspring now for the psalmist to address.

With that assurance in mind, the psalmist makes one outrageous claim after another: The poor will eat and be satisfied, seekers will find, and everybody everywhere will worship the Lord! But in my 21st-century, Midwestern American context, perhaps the most outrageous claim of all is that "future generations will be told about the Lord and proclaim his deliverance to a people yet unborn." In my presbytery, churches are closing every year, and those that remain are declining in numbers or holding steady at best. It's tempting to see this trend and feel overwhelmed with discouragement. If our churches keep closing, who will tell future generations about the Lord?

All I know is my anxiety about the future crumples like dried autumn leaves in the face of God's centuries of faithfulness. That might be the psalmist's point.

God, thank you that you are the faithful God who always comes through for your people. When I get anxious, remind me that it is safe to trust you. Amen.

As a pastor—as a professional "person of faith"—I am keenly aware that I am expected to set a good example not only in my congregation but also for the people I encounter in my community. Though nobody has explicitly told me what that involves, I interpret it as the need to avoid profanity, give generously, be kind/welcoming/friendly and caring towards others, pray before meals, read scripture, listen attentively, overlook the well-meaning but thoughtless comments of others (or gently call them on it), dress well (but not too well), show up on time, and other virtuous acts. A "good example" might vary from community to community, from job to job, but it generally involves a list of mutually agreed-upon desirable or "righteous" behaviors.

In today's scripture reading, Paul points to Abraham as a good example of someone who was righteous. Yet as Paul goes to great lengths to explain, Abraham was not righteous because of his good behavior; he was righteous because of his faith. He continued to believe God's promise that he would become a father of many nations, even when his body "was already as good as dead."

Centuries later, we still struggle with wanting to earn, deserve, and behave our way into God's good graces. It's almost too much to take in that by believing that Jesus Christ is Lord, we are already there. Righteous action—"being kind," etc.—is the grateful, heartfelt *response* to the delighted approval we already have from God, not how we get that approval. Such news is too good to be true, too ridiculous to trust. That's exactly why we share in Abraham's righteousness when we, too, believe.

God, thank you for the example of Abraham, who believed the promises you made to him even when they looked impossible to fulfill. Help me to believe in you too, and help my life to reflect my belief to everyone I meet. Amen.

After becoming the first disciple to declare that Jesus is the Messiah, Peter turns around and rebukes Jesus for saying that he must suffer, be rejected, and be killed. Some interpret this encounter to show that Peter wants Jesus to be a different kind of Messiah—the kind who would get rid of the Roman occupation of Israel and accomplish a great military victory. Peter wanted Jesus to come out on top in THIS world. He could not bear to think of the Messiah as being a loser or being humiliated.

I wonder if Peter had different motivations. Peter loved Jesus. Jesus was his dearest friend. Maybe Peter rebuked Jesus because he couldn't bear to think of Jesus going away. By teaching the disciples about his upcoming death, Jesus was clearly preparing them for exactly that, and Peter was not yet ready to hear it.

After Jesus, in turn, rebukes Peter, Jesus says to his disciples and the larger crowd that "those who want to save their life will lose it, and those who lose their life . . . will save it." What does it mean to lose one's life? We might better ask what it means to save one's life, and looking back to Jesus' rebuke of Peter may give us our answer. We are called to set our mind on divine things, not human things. This is Jesus' call to Peter, and to us. At the time of Mark's writing, Christians were faced with actual persecution, physical harm that would come if they chose to follow the Way of Jesus. To follow Christ today, we may not face the same physical threats as the early Christians, but we still must pursue the things of God's kingdom, which are often contrary to the things of the world.

In Peter's case, he must deny his desire to keep Jesus close and his idea of who the Messiah truly is, and instead support Jesus as he fulfills God's plan for the Messiah.

Jesus, thank you for the call to lose my life for you and to set my mind on God's kingdom. Give me courage as I choose to follow you. Amen.

SECOND SUNDAY IN LENT

Some things are just counterintuitive. For example, if we want more energy, expending it through exercise generally gives us more energy than resting too much. If we want to steer a canoe to the right, we paddle on the left. Or to protect ourselves against a disease, we inject ourselves with a tiny bit of it in the form of a vaccine.

It seems counterintuitive that the Son of Man must undergo great suffering, rejection, and death. Shouldn't avoiding all that be one of the perks of being the Son of Man? And it definitely seems counterintuitive that those who save their life will lose it, while those who lose their life for Jesus' sake and the sake of the gospel will save it. But that seems to be the way God loves to work. After all, this is the same God that brought forth the entire Jewish population from one elderly man and his elderly wife when they were decades past their childbearing years.

When we hold up this passage next to the other readings we have looked at this week, it's as though God is trying to reassure us. "When things seem most impossible, don't worry. This is my specialty. I am setting things up so that when it all works out, there will be no doubt that I am the one who is responsible" (AP).

Over and over, we see this pattern. David the shepherd boy defeats Goliath the giant. The Virgin Mary has a baby boy. What other examples can you think of? How has this been true in your life? How have you experienced your life being saved even as you have lost it?

God, thank you for all the surprising, often counterintuitive ways that you work in our lives. Give us the courage to lose our lives for your sake. Amen.

Rules and Freedom

FEBRUARY 26–MARCH 3, 2024 • JUSTIN COLEMAN

SCRIPTURE OVERVIEW: As we continue in the season of Lent, we remember another important chapter in salvation history. Just as God established covenants with Noah and Abraham and their descendants, so did God renew the relationship with the Israelites by giving them the law. Obedience to the law was not the means of earning God's love but rather a response of love by the people to the love God had already shown them. The psalmist understands that God's law creates a cause for rejoicing, for it is more valuable than gold. Both Paul and John address situations in which some had distorted the worship of God. Either they considered themselves too good for the gospel (1 Corinthians), or they had violated the covenant by altering proper worship for the sake of profit (John).

QUESTIONS AND SUGGESTIONS FOR REFLECTION

- Read Exodus 20:1-17. How do you keep God as the central focus of your life? What draws you away from that focus?
- Read Psalm 19. In what ways do you experience God's laws as "sweeter . . . than honey"? When do you find yourself trying to resist God's laws?
- Read 1 Corinthians 1:18-25. What does it mean to you that "God's foolishness is wiser than human wisdom"?
- Read John 2:13-22. How do you respond to Jesus' anger and actions in this reading? Do his actions fit with the way you generally picture Jesus?

Senior Pastor of University United Methodist Church in Chapel Hill, North Carolina; former Chief Ministry Officer for the United Methodist Publishing House in Nashville, TN; former Lead Pastor of the Gethsemane Campus of St. Luke's United Methodist Church in Houston, TX; author of *Home for Christmas: Tales of Hope and Second Chances* (Abingdon Press, 2018).

I was in a conversation once with a teenager about freedom. The teen defined freedom as the ability to do what you want. This teenager is not alone; many people define freedom in this way. No rules. No regulations. Complete autonomy and ability to do or express what you want, when you want, and how you want. But is this truly freedom?

Without rules we are prone to chaos. Looking back at the book of Genesis and the way God created the world, we see that God sought to bring order out of chaos. The rules God set were meant to promote flourishing in the world, to create the space in which the beings God created could grow and thrive. In order to think outside the box you actually *need* a box. The box acts as a container that can release creativity.

Not all rules create freedom. Some rules are coercive and harmful. Healthy rules, however, create space for human flourishing. Healthy rules help us relate to one another and, in the instance of the Ten Commandments, help us relate to God in ways that build up rather than tear down.

The Ten Commandments were a wonderful gift to a community of people that had just exited an oppressive system. In the Egyptian system, many of the rules that governed the Hebrew people were rules that led to their marginalization and harm. Then the Hebrew people found themselves in that teenager's version of freedom: wandering with no rules or regulations and wondering what would constitute them as a people. Just at the moment when the people found themselves on the edge of chaos, God offered them commandments to help them flourish. The Ten Commandments became the basis for the holy imagination that generated how they would live in community with one another. Out of this structure, the Hebrew people grew and flourished in freedom.

God, thank you for the rules that give framework to my life and community. Amen.

Rules and Freedom

The structure of the Ten Commandments is important to note. The first three commandments focus on loving God, and the next seven commandments focus on loving neighbor. I find it interesting that the same pattern is used in the Lord's Prayer. The first three petitions of the Lord's Prayer are about God and the next four petitions are about the daily needs of community.

In seminary, I was taught to ask three basic questions when beginning to interpret a passage of scripture: What does the passage say about God? What does the passage say about humanity? What does the passage say about the relationship among God, humanity, and the world?

We begin with God. We center God and God's will in our lives, a process that decenters ourselves and other things that vie for our attention. The first three commandments warn us against the dangers of idolatry. Many people do not have any difficulty being the center of their own worlds, and others do not have any difficulty making someone or something else the center of their attention. But when something or someone other than God is the central focus of our lives, they become an idol—nearly or clearly an object of our worship in every practical sense. When we make God the center of our attention, it helps to re-center us and adds clarity to our priorities.

Next come the commandments about others. In them, we learn how to exercise loving care for our neighbor and community. Remember, it is all about relationship among God, us, and the world. This notion shapes Jesus' prayer for us in John 17. It turns out that as we adore and cherish God and discover that God adores and cherishes us, we are quickly turned toward cherishing one another. For a people who desire to cherish one another in healthy ways and become one people, the Ten Commandments provide healthy rules for living.

God, help us to grow in kinship with you and one another as we seek to follow your ways. Amen.

Have you ever been in a setting that absolutely took your breath away? Many of us experience this sensation out in nature. On one such occasion for me, I was with a church group approaching Victoria Falls at the border of Zambia and Zimbabwe. Victoria Falls is one of the largest waterfalls in the world. As we were walking toward the falls, we navigated what seemed like a dense rainforest. With each step the volume of the falls became louder and louder. Then we broke through the rainforest and there it was—Victoria Falls in all its might and magnitude. It simply took my breath away.

When I come to a majestic scene that takes my breath away, I am often moved to thank God because it is a sign of God's goodness and testifies to God's glory. This is exactly where Psalm 19 begins. God's creation gives testimony even when we fail to do so. This is why so many people say they encounter God through nature in a wholly different way than they encounter God within a community of people. The natural wonders of our world cry out praise of God and leads us to praise God as well.

The second half of the psalm considers God's words that instruct and guide us. While this may seem like a shift in direction, the psalmist is moved from praise of God's glory as seen in creation to praise of God's glory as seen in God's instruction, that which orders creation. In all aspects of our experience, God's majesty is on display. May we all be moved to delight in God's word and world.

O God, let the words of my mouth and the meditations of my heart be pleasing to you, Lord, my rock and my redeemer. Amen.

As a pastor, teacher, and leader, I spend a good amount of time trying not to be thought of as foolish. I'd venture to say that, unless you are in a particularly comedic profession, the last thing you would want to hear someone say about you in a performance review is that you were foolish. We want to be thought of as wise. But what does it mean to be wise, and who determines the characteristics?

Paul's message to the Corinthians begins with this contrast between wisdom and foolishness. The message of the cross just might be received as foolishness for those who are on a path leading to their own destruction. Paul suggests that people can be confidently stepping toward an abyss and be completely clueless about the dangers of the direction they are taking in life. In fact, these people can believe they are being wise. Paul offers this caution because any of us can fall prey to the foolishness of this world that masquerades as wisdom. Conversely, there is the message of the cross that seems like foolishness for those who are not directing their lives toward Christ.

Paul will pick up this theme of foolishness and wisdom again when he says: "Don't fool yourself. If some of you think they are worldly-wise, then they should become foolish so that they can become wise. This world's wisdom is foolishness to God. As it's written, *He catches the wise in their cleverness*" (3:18-19, CEB).

We are called to be the ones who drink deeply from the well of wisdom that is the way of Christ. This wisdom may look like foolishness to the world, but it is the very power that is saving our souls. It is the very power that is renewing the world.

God, help me to gain wisdom from the way of Christ. Amen.

For some reason, more and more people ask me to prove the Christian faith these days. Prove that God is real. Prove that Jesus is more than a historical figure but is also the Son of God. Prove that miracles happen. Prove there is a heaven. I understand the desire for certainty, but this kind of proof doesn't get us very far. One of my pastors used to say if you can argue someone into the faith then someone else can argue them out of it. I do not mean to say that we should abandon reason, but reason alone is not our only way of knowing God or pursuing the truth about God.

In addition to our reason, scripture, and the broad tradition of the Christian church, we add our *experience*—specifically our experience of God's Holy Spirit in the community of believers—as a way to know God and God's truth. After all, Jesus tells us in John's Gospel that the Holy Spirit will remind us of everything that Jesus has taught us. God's Holy Spirit becomes our tutor in the ways of Christ. God's Holy Spirit helps us to receive and understand the proclamation about Christ crucified.

The wisdom of God is no secret revelation. God desires to reveal God's self to us. God desires that we know God's ways and God's truth deeply so that we understand the wisdom of it. This wisdom of God shapes the way we live, move, and have our being in the world. Has anyone, sensing God's grace in you, ever asked why you are the way you are? Sometimes the way we forgive one another, offer compassion, make peace, and reconcile with one another makes no sense given the wisdom of the world, but this wise living "is the power of God for those of us who are being saved."

God, help me to be foolish in the eyes of the world for the sake of the gospel. Amen.

In the 1970s, a theory was promoted that humans have six basic emotions: happiness, sadness, fear, disgust, surprise, and anger. I've heard—and preached—a lot of sermons on happiness, sadness, fear, and surprise. I've never heard one on disgust, and we are going to continue to ignore that one. I have preached a few on anger, but never at great length. We tend to avoid discussions of anger. Where I come from, being nice is nearly thought to be a spiritual gift. Being angry is something that many people feel almost ashamed to talk about. After all, you go to classes to manage things like anger. So being angry—especially being angry often—is not something people are eager to admit.

But anger is an emotion, sometimes identified as a secondary emotion that is masking another deeper emotion. And we can't really control the emotions we feel. What we can control is our response to our emotions.

In scripture, we find that God gets angry. In today's passage, Jesus makes a scene. He uses a whip and flips over some tables in the Temple. Ephesians 4:26 encourages us to be angry without sin, and this points to the distinction between the emotions we feel and the way we act in response to those emotions.

One of the prayer practices that I engage in is the daily Examen. As a part of the process, I think about all the emotions I can remember from the day and then ask how God was present during those emotions. If I was angry, asking questions around God's presence or lack of presence amid my anger helps me to see if this anger was born of a holy discontent that is encouraging me to act with love in response or if it was born out of more sinful inclinations. Some tables need overturning. When we are connected to God's heart, we learn to be angry at what angers God and pleased with what pleases God.

God, may my anger be your holy discontent working in me. Amen.

THIRD SUNDAY IN LENT

Some people are unsettled by Jesus' overturning of tables. We tend to imagine Jesus as always meek, mild, and kind. That Jesus could become angry reminds us that God in God's Trinity can be angry, and it follows that God might be angry with me from time to time, and I sure do not want that.

Jesus seems always to be at work to dismantle barriers that marginalize and exclude. The tables Jesus overturned and the animals he drove away were essential for the Temple systems. Without them, the system of tithes and sacrifice would not work. Jesus was challenging the whole Temple system that regulated access to God. Jesus was angry that his Father's house was a marketplace and he began to bring about the day promised in Zechariah 14:21, "And there shall no longer be traders in the house of the LORD."

I wonder what barriers need to be overturned in our houses of worship so that others can fully participate. Perhaps those barriers are around access for those who have a disability. Perhaps there are barriers for those who are neurodiverse. Perhaps there are barriers around age, or race, or a number of other areas that we could name. I wonder in what ways our communities of faith can proclaim and demonstrate that God's doors are open to all.

In a divided and ever dividing world where margins seem to be increasing rather than decreasing, we could all use a dose of holy discontentment such that we become unwilling to maintain the status quo. In the midst of the dizzying display in John 2, Jesus' disciples remember Psalm 69:9 which says, "Passion for your house has consumed me." May zeal for God's house so consume us that we become passionate about God's house becoming what it was intended to be—a house of prayer for all.

O God, may passion for your house and your people consume me. Amen.

Look Up!

MARCH 4–10, 2024 • AMY VAUGHAN

SCRIPTURE OVERVIEW: Sometimes we get ourselves into trouble by our words and actions. It's okay to admit it; it happens to all of us. The Israelites experienced this when their constant grumbling provoked God's wrath in Numbers 21. Yet even in this story, God provides the means of salvation. The psalmist echoes the refrain that when we put ourselves in bad positions, we may cry out to the Lord for deliverance. We read in Ephesians that all of us were living in disobedience to God, but God has done all the work of reconciliation by grace given through Christ Jesus. John ties all this together, gesturing to the story in Numbers 21 to teach us that Christ is the means of restoration and salvation for all who believe in him.

QUESTIONS AND SUGGESTIONS FOR REFLECTION

- Read Numbers 21:4-9. When do you complain to God? Does your complaining ever interfere with your sense of God's presence with you?
- Read Psalm 107:1-3, 17-22. What practice helps you to thank God each day for God's steadfast love?
- Read Ephesians 2:1-10. How does your sense of God's salvation and grace move you to do good works?
- Read John 3:14-21. How do you act as a creature of light in the world? What are your "deeds that have been done in God"?

Ordained deacon in The United Methodist Church; serves an emerging faith community in the Western North Carolina Conference; previously directed a vocational arts program for adults with intellectual disabilities; enjoys writing and sharing poetry.

Does anything good ever come from impatience? Impatience makes us less likely to be kind. Impatience feeds negativity into the inner spaces of our minds and bodies. Impatience sees scarcity, not abundance.

The very people God brought out of actual slavery did not respond with gratitude but with impatience. From the beginning of the story of their wandering in the wilderness, the people complained. They complained about bitter water; the lack, quality, and type of food. They were free from bondage in Egypt but imprisoned by their own negativity. Focusing on what they did not have—what they wanted—made them miss what was right in front of them. How does God respond to those shallow complaints? Perhaps those venomous snakes were the physical representation of their own complaining, coming back to bite them—literally!

How often do our own actions, our own grinding complaints, mire us more deeply in misery? Whining and complaining bites us the hardest and often doesn't affect the target of our complaints. Wouldn't it be better to be grateful instead? And if change is needed, working to make those changes instead of complaining about them leads to better outcomes for everyone.

God offers us abundant life, even if it seems not "made to order" according to our desires. The people who spoke against Moses and complained to God were given a second opportunity for new life. Look up! See the poisonous negativity for what it is, and give thanks for life, nourishment, and the sustaining power of God. The healing begins when we realize that we have all we need not only to survive, but to thrive.

Gracious and giving God, forgive me when I complain because what I have is not what I want. Help me to see all that you have given me and respond in gratitude. Turn my words of complaint into songs of joy. Amen.

This passage from Numbers reminds me of the suffering of Jesus, lifted high on the cross at Calvary. In John's Gospel, the writer makes this comparison in verse 14 of chapter 3. Here in Numbers, Moses intervenes on behalf of the people, and God tells him to lift the serpent on the pole to alleviate the suffering of those who had been bitten by the "fiery serpents." What does it mean that the snake is both the pain and the cure? How can the source of pain also be the source of healing?

Have you ever had to have a broken bone set, or required extensive dental work to correct a problem so your mouth could function as it should? Surgery often requires the cutting of tissue or bone, and those curative remedies hurt. We undergo these procedures with local numbing or complete anesthesia and often take pain medicine for days afterward. We know that the suffering we experience is part of the process that allows us to get to the healing.

Our spiritual healing works in a similar way. In the season of Lent, we may feel like we are "suffering" by giving up something or taking on a challenging new practice. Whether it is going without chocolate or some other favorite food, or giving up screen time in front of a TV, computer, or phone, we may feel a sense of loss even when we willingly take on the Lenten practice. But that loss isn't intended to make us suffer. The loss is intended to provide an opportunity for healing to occur.

Christian expression of repentance makes redemption possible. Confessing our sin, although it may be painful, provides the first step to healing our brokenness, our separation from God.

Lord, may any suffering I experience draw me closer to your redemptive love. Amen.

What is it that God desires of us? God desires we recognize God's good gifts and tell the story, share the wealth, share in God's great abundance with others. We are called to recognize God's action in our lives and tell the story. Even when our lives are transformed through God's hand, when God gathers us in like wayward children, we rebel. We look at the very food provided for us as not good enough. Like a toddler spitting out good and nutritious baby food, we reject what is life-sustaining and prefer to be hungry rather than flourish, even to the point of starvation and death. God provides time and again a chance to come back, to rejoice in God's great gifts. God rescues us even when we look the gift horse in the mouth.

The good news is this: Even when we make foolish decisions that result in bad outcomes, God hears our cries. What a comfort to know that even as we fail to discern wiser ways, even then God does not abandon us. So, then, what does "telling the story" mean? Perhaps we come across others who, like us, have made foolish decisions. Perhaps we unwisely choose the wrong partner, who leaves us and dependent children when the going gets rough. Maybe we spend unwisely, and when the rainy day comes, we are left with nothing but an umbrella with holes in it. Even so, our God gathers us in, cleans us up, and loves us as we are. Perhaps the telling of our rescue should manifest in showing the same kind of grace to our neighbors, even the ones we think make decisions that lead to bad outcomes.

O Lord, help me remember your rescue, your enduring love, and extend it to neighbors and strangers who need me to look beyond their choices, as you have looked beyond mine. Amen.

Growing up in the shadow of an over-achieving older sister, I tried to earn the love of my parents through my achievements and good behavior. I found areas to excel different from my sister, even though in many ways we had some of the same gifts. I tried to twist myself into being uniquely deserving of my parents' love. I tried to make good grades, tried to be agreeable and kind. Even when out shopping for new shoes or clothes, I tended to make it easy on them by liking the first thing I tried on, especially if it was on sale.

I also wanted God to love me, and I carried some of that people-pleasing into my early relationship with God and with the church. Not until I was much older did I understand that my parents loved me without my having to earn it. I didn't have to be as smart as or smarter than my sister. This realization didn't mean that I could give up trying at all. It just meant that no matter my actions, my parents would love me. I didn't have to work to earn their love; it was there from the beginning.

Today's reading reminds us of this fact regarding God's love: "For by grace you have been saved through faith, and this is not your own doing; it is the gift of God." My parents loved me even when I had a messy room, when I wrecked the car, when I forgot what time it was and missed my curfew. While my parents wanted me to be the best me I could be, they understood and moved past any transgressions, especially if I was honest about them and worked to improve. I was fortunate that my parents exemplified this facet of God's love for me. But no matter what our relationship with our parents, we can come to know that God wants us to be the best version of ourselves possible and loves us even when we fall short. God prepares us to do good work, but we don't have to earn God's love.

Gracious God, help me to recognize that even when I fall short, I am more than the worst thing I've ever done and still your beloved child. Amen.

What does it mean to "be dead in your transgressions and sin?" We know that we humans tend to live into patterns. Patterns are comfortable ways to avoid making decisions. We just do the same thing over and over. Routines are important for us. It is how we structure our daily lives. For many people, Monday through Friday, we get up, take a shower, have breakfast, and head out for a day of work or school. We come home, cook supper, perhaps do some household chores or some homework, relax a little with a book or a TV show, and go to bed. Patterns are comfortable. But patterns can also be dangerous if we fall into habits that are not good for us. Unhealthy life choices sometimes develop through patterns of behavior. Some start harmlessly with occasional practices and develop into a problem, like drinking heavily, failing to exercise, always going by the fast food drive-through rather than eating healthier options. We fall into patterns. Sometimes these patterns distract us from seeing a situation clearly. God's holy disruption of our patterns comes when we are open to transformation.

This passage from Ephesians affirms what other readings this week tell us. We are flawed humans. We are also redeemable. We are a "work of God." Verse 10 says that we are God's handiwork, created to do good works. The Greek word used here is *poiēma*, meaning poem. We are God's poem, a poetic act created for good works. We are created to create goodness, in our words of worship and our deeds of service. We are made for this, as we shed the bad habits, bad patterns, and find healing and wholeness through God's gift of mercy. How does it feel to be God's work of art?

God, may I be alive in Christ. May I sing God's praises with my words, with my worship, and with my acts of mercy and service. Amen.

I once knew a young man who had been raised going to church and even attended a Christian elementary school. When invited to attend church with my husband and me, he complained that he just didn't get it—all that preoccupation with blood and broken bodies. He was talking particularly about Communion. He was thinking about it literally, and, in his words, he thought it was "gross." He had been taught about the sacrifice of Jesus, but when he was in his late teens, he couldn't make sense of it and wondered why anyone would want to talk about it every week.

Perhaps Nicodemus felt that way too. In the verses just before today's passage, Nicodemus, a Jewish leader, comes to Jesus at night to ask some questions. Perhaps he came at night because he was busy during the day. Or perhaps he didn't want to be seen and risk his reputation as a religious leader by meeting with this controversial Jesus. Nicodemus asks Jesus what it means when he says one must be "born again." Jesus tells him: "No one can enter the kingdom of God unless they are born of water and the Spirit. Flesh gives birth to flesh, but the Spirit gives birth to spirit" (John 3:5-6, NIV). Later in their conversation, Jesus refers to the Numbers passage we read earlier this week about the poisonous snakes.

For the Israelites in the wilderness, looking up at the very thing that threatened their lives brought them to recognize their own sins of disobedience. Without God's mercy, the snake— their sin—would kill them. Do we think it odd and difficult to think of the crucifixion of Jesus? While it may be uncomfortable to "see" Christ suffering, without Christ's act of sacrifice being lifted on the cross, we too would be left without hope.

God of life, may I remember the mystery of faith: Christ has died; Christ is risen; Christ will come again. May I look up and embrace the mystery of my own salvation. Amen.

Fourth Sunday in Lent

John 3:16 often appears on people's foreheads at ballgames, on placards, bumper stickers, or in pamphlets left in public restrooms. To grow up in a Christian church means that you know, or know of, this famous verse some call the foundational scripture for the entire Bible. Many who have never read a Bible know this verse.

However, many don't know the next verse, John 3:17. "Indeed, God did not send the Son into the world to condemn the world, but in order that the world might be saved through him." What kind of love is offered here? Is it without limit? Who is included? What does it mean to "save the world"?

"The world" includes the spotted leopard, the hummingbird, the humpback whale, the golden grains of wheat, and every living creature, every tree and flower and insect. Who in all of creation has within them the ability to be God's hands to cultivate the seeds, the intellect to clean oceans and streams, the heart to preserve and restore the rainforest which serves as a home for so many creatures? Who is made in the image of God, saved in order to be the light of the world? Of course, it is you and me. Every human being is created and crafted with God's own hands to protect and reconcile all these competing interests. Within each beloved person, the power of God's love breathes and empowers us. We alone of all creatures and forms of life can be used for this holy purpose, the salvation of the world God spoke into being, the world that God loves so much.

Lord, may our hands and hearts be used by you as your instrument of salvation for the world you so love. Use us to reconcile and restore all of creation. Amen.

Learning to Walk in the Way of Love

MARCH 11–17, 2024 • JONATHAN WILSON-HARTGROVE

SCRIPTURE OVERVIEW: We can maintain outward appearances for only so long. At some point what is in our hearts will come to the surface. God understands this, of course, which is the reason for the promise in Jeremiah. God promises a day when God's law will no longer be an external standard that we are trying to follow but will be written on our hearts. In the aftermath of his sin with Bathsheba, David cries out in Psalm 51 for God's forgiveness and a new heart. The New Testament readings begin to focus our minds toward the end of Jesus' life. God's transformative work comes at a cost to God through the death of his Son, who suffered in obedience but through his death was glorified.

QUESTIONS AND SUGGESTIONS FOR REFLECTION

- Read Jeremiah 31:31-34. What are the covenant relationships in your life? How do you fulfill your part of the covenant with God?
- Read Psalm 51:1-12. What are the things that clutter your heart, limiting your availability to fully love?
- Read Hebrews 5:5-10. When have you offered your prayers "with loud cries and tears" as Jesus did? How does knowing Jesus' vulnerability impact your life of faith?
- Read John 12:20-33. How does this example of the grain of wheat help you to understand Jesus' crucifixion and death?

Associate minister at St. John's Missionary Baptist Church in Durham, NC; assistant director at Yale Divinity School's Center for Public Theology and Public Policy.

The worst part about being a prophet, Jeremiah knew, was having to tell God's people what they did not want to hear. The false prophets of his day—as in ours—loved to tell of the great and wonderful things God was going to do. (Think, "God wants you to be happy! God wants you to be rich! God wants to give you the best parking space in the grocery store parking lot, if only you have the faith to believe!") But Jeremiah, who loved God's people, knew he had to tell them the hard truth, even though he didn't want to. When he tried to stay quiet, God's truth burnt him up on the inside. Eventually, he had to let it out.

Lent is about taking the time to listen to the truth we do not want to hear. Each of us has our ideas about how the world ought to be, how people around us should think and act, the choices our children should make, the person we each want to be. And most of us would like a god who could muster some cosmic force to make other people and our own stubborn selves conform to those ideas.

But Jeremiah knows no such god. Jeremiah is captivated by the Creator God who has tried and tried again to show Jeremiah's people what God's good life looks like, even though they will not have it. They keep ditching God for their own ideas. But God does not give up.

The one who made us will not take "no" for an answer from us either. This God promises to do a new thing: to meet our failure to live the good life with the gift of the way to the good life written on our hearts—so close to the center of ourselves that we cannot forget it.

Gracious God, order our steps today from the true center you have given each of us. Amen.

S hame is the feeling that comes from believing, whether we admit it or not, that we really aren't worthy of love and respect from our family, our neighbors, our God. It's not only a distortion of how we see ourselves, it's also a misperception about others, often rooted in a painful experience of rejection. "If they knew this about me, they could never love me," shame says. It is a lie—and one that religion has often bolstered.

But the psalmist is not bound by shame. With open honesty, the psalmist says something like this: "Look, I know these things about me. You do, too! I don't have the power to change them. I've tried. But you do, God."

When we don't know the freedom the psalmist teaches, we often only acknowledge the problems in our lives that we think we can fix. I can admit I struggle with mental health issues if I think my therapy is helping. I can talk about hard times in the past if I feel secure that I'm in a better place now. But the challenges we've overcome or are managing are not the problems sin names. Sin is about the troubles I was born into—the powers that had me in their grip before I even knew it.

The Psalms teach us we don't have to hide or be ashamed. We can face the shadow side of ourselves and the systemic evils of our society because our lives have been claimed by a God who has the power to remake us—to give beauty for ashes and make justice where inequality has persisted one generation after another. To confess that I was a sinner from the start isn't to play into the lie of shame. It is to reject it, rejoicing in the mercy of a God who both knows me and knows how to make a way out of no way.

God, you knit us together in our inmost parts, but we have distorted your creation. Give us hope that we can be made new. Amen.

The work of repentance can seem burdensome, but its true aim is joy. Martin Luther King, Jr. did not go to Montgomery, Alabama, to lead the civil rights movement. A graduate student who had not yet completed his Ph.D. dissertation, King took a pastorate where he could preach on Sundays, lead a congregation, and get some writing done in the evenings. The movement found King when Rosa Parks went to jail and her friends organized a bus boycott. They needed a spokesperson. King was drafted for the job.

Looking back at the Montgomery Bus Boycott in American history, it's possible to understand the campaign King led as a public call for penance. White supremacy campaigns across the South had implemented Jim Crow segregation, a separation of people in public spaces based on the lie that Black people were inferior to their White neighbors. This was, as King articulated clearly, a rejection of what God says about human beings. Segregation was a sin that required public penance.

When, after more than a year, the Supreme Court ordered Montgomery's buses to desegregate, the young preacher who had led the campaign gave a celebratory speech. The court's order was a win, but it was not the end. The end, King insisted, was "beloved community." It was a city where Black and White people could not only ride the bus together but also know one another as God knew them and enjoy being together in community.

Many citizens of Montgomery never believed beloved community was possible. In a similar way, we often avoid the work of repentance because we don't think the joy it promises is possible for us. The psalmist interrupts our assumptions and connects with our heart's cry. We want to know the joy of salvation. And it is ours when we are willing to receive it.

Make us willing, merciful God, to pursue the joy that comes on the other side of repentance. Amen.

Lent's practices of penance have parallels in the monastic vocation. Fasting, prayer, and almsgiving are ways of practicing the poverty, chastity, and obedience that monks and nuns take on as a way of life. For St. Benedict of Nursia, who wrote the rule of life that has shaped Western monasticism, nothing is more important than the listening that is at the heart of obedience. To grow in the Way of Jesus, we must learn to listen.

The author of the letter to the Hebrews knows this is true because Jesus has shown us the Way. Jesus learned to listen by what he suffered, Hebrews says. No doubt, Jesus the human being—made of flesh like you and me—had to learn how to listen to the love that led him to the cross. But maybe he learned to listen from every suffering person he met along life's journey. The friends who had lost their brother and couldn't believe he hadn't come sooner. The widow who had lost her only son. The mother who hadn't been able to buy enough wine for everyone who came to her child's wedding. To love them was to hear them, and for it Jesus suffered. Such is the Way of Love.

None of us has mastered the Way, but Jesus did. And Hebrews proclaims that Jesus is our salvation—our Way to Love—if we can learn to listen to him. But where do we hear Jesus today? Maybe we can hear him in the people through whom he promised to be present with us—in the hungry person who asks for the food or the stranger who seeks welcome, the incarcerated person we visit or the thirsty soul to whom we offer a cup of cold water. To listen, no doubt, is to enter into suffering we might rather avoid. But this is how Jesus invites us to grow in the Way of Love.

Dear Jesus, open our ears that we may hear the stories that invite us into the struggles where you are present. Amen.

John's Gospel opens with a proclamation that would have shocked any of its original audience: "We have seen [God's] glory," John says (1:14). But this is impossible! No one can see God and live. Moses saw God's backside in the midst of a storm on Mt. Sinai, and even that was enough to make his face glow so bright that no one could stand to look at him. How could anyone see God's glory and live? It's a question that readers of John's Gospel would have carried with them from the opening prologue.

In today's reading, the one whom every sign and wonder in the story has pointed our attention toward speaks for himself. The time has come, he says, for the Son of Man to be glorified. But what does God's glory look like when God takes on human flesh?

We often want to see God's glory—God's healing power or a decisive victory for the causes we believe in and know are right. As we look ahead to the victory of Easter morning, we hope and pray that our own efforts will be infused with the power of God who can overcome even death.

But John's Gospel says that Jesus is glorified in the moment when he is betrayed by his friend Judas. We see God's glory when Jesus loves the one who cannot love him back—the one who would rather sell him out than follow him on the Way of Love. It may not be the glory we always want, but it is the glory we need. Jesus does not promise we will be successful. He promises that if we follow him we will learn to walk in the Way of Love.

Jesus, teach us to see your glory and know its good news for each of us. Amen.

For Florence Jordan, a White woman who grew up in early 20th-century Kentucky, Jesus was someone she learned about in Sunday School—the Son of God whom everyone she knew honored. But not everyone thought Jesus could be taken seriously in matters of their daily life.

In the early 1940s, Florence's husband established what he called a "demonstration plot for the kingdom of God" in South Georgia. Clarence Jordan was a New Testament scholar and a follower of Jesus. He was also a farmer, and he heard the teachings of Jesus with a farmer's ear. The Way of Love wasn't simply an ideal. It was a new way of living that could be put into practice, just as the agriculture extension office might set up a demonstration plot for a new kind of melon or variety of chickens.

While the Jordans worked to set up an interracial farm where Black and White people could fellowship, work together, and serve their local community, they joined the local Baptist church. For years they were welcomed as members, even serving in leadership positions. But then one day at a called business meeting after Sunday morning worship, the Jordans and their friends at Koinonia Farm were accused of bringing a Black person to church. The moderator of the meeting called for a vote on their removal from the church. After some moments of awkward silence, Florence Jordan stood to second the motion. If fellowship across race lines was a violation, she was guilty as charged.

Following the Way of Love got the Jordans kicked out of church. It nearly got them killed in 1950s Georgia. But they lived into today's reading. In losing their membership in the local Baptist church, they gained welcome into the beloved community that Jesus' Way of Love makes possible.

God, give us grace to give up what we cannot keep in order to gain what cannot be lost. Amen.

FIFTH SUNDAY IN LENT

Perhaps the greatest gift teachers can offer their students is their own love for the subject they aim to teach. Details matter, and there are pedagogical devices that set some teachers apart. But ask people about their favorite teachers and you'll almost always hear some version of, "You could just tell how much she loved literature" or "I knew the first time I saw him hold a guitar that it was the love of his life."

To be a disciple of Jesus is to know the God who took on human flesh as a teacher. Jesus is, of course, many other things as well. But the Gospels make clear that he was a teacher—and a good one at that. In the debates that happen among professors of any age, Jesus gave memorable replies, leaving his interlocutors speechless on more than one occasion. In the more intimate setting of the disciples' circle, he asked probing questions, helping students name and confront assumptions that prevented them from getting the main point. With a metaphor or a story, Jesus could make the message plain and unforgettable.

But Jesus didn't simply teach a subject or a craft. Jesus invited us into the Way of Love and showed us how to live it. This is the new covenant spoken of in the thirty-first chapter of Jeremiah. Like all the great teachers, Jesus moves us with his passion for a life with God, lived in beloved community. But as the prophet Jeremiah foretold, his aim wasn't simply to inspire. It was to get the Way inside of us, to somehow make it possible for us to live the life that Jesus lived among us. When that happens, Jeremiah says, there's really no need for teachers anymore. We will embody the law—the love—of God, fully being God's people.

Loving God, grow us up to become people who live your Way because we love it. Amen.

What a Way to Walk

MARCH 18–24, 2024 • WILL WILLIMON

SCRIPTURE OVERVIEW: "When Jesus and his followers approached Jerusalem . . ." (Mark 11:1) All of the gospels depict Jesus and his disciples on a constant road trip. By the time this week ends, their destination will at last be reached. Jerusalem, center of national hopes and pride, the great Temple, heart of the faith of Israel. Although he is welcomed into the capital with crowds crying "Hosanna!" the adoration will cease as Jesus is taken to his cross. To be with Jesus is to follow Jesus, go where he goes and move in the world as he moves. It's a narrow way, as we shall learn in this week's scriptures, a way that not many wish to go. Here is the scripture we must read in order to prepare ourselves for the holiest week of the Christian year, journeying with Jesus to the very heart of our faith.

QUESTIONS AND SUGGESTIONS FOR REFLECTION

- Read Isaiah 50:4-9a. How does your faith community reflect the servant in this reading?
- Read Psalm 118:1-2, 19-29. How are you rejoicing in this day that the Lord has made? How are you blessing "the one who comes in the name of the LORD"?
- Read Philippians 2:5-11. How does this hymn of the early Christian community speak to you as you prepare for Holy Week?
- Read Mark 11:1-11, 15-18. Spend some time imagining the scene of Jesus entering Jerusalem as described in the reading. Where are you in the scene? What do you see? What do you hear around you? What do you feel as you watch this event?

Professor of the Practice of Christian Ministry, Duke Divinity School and a bishop (retired) of The United Methodist Church; one of his most recent books is *Preachers Dare: Speaking for God in the Sermon* (Abingdon Press, 2020).

Jesus told his friends, "We are going up to Jerusalem" (Mark 10:33). Surely his disciples knew he was leading them into the storm. Their journey with Jesus was about to become difficult.

He could have stayed out back in Galilee where his movement began. Sure, there was opposition, but many of the rural folk heard him gladly. They warned him not to go (see Luke 13:31). But Jesus, determined to complete his mission, refused to detour and headed into the city in spite of the peril.

While I'm as conflict-averse as any pastor, as we see Jesus set his face toward Jerusalem, we must ask ourselves, "Where did we get the idea that journeying with Jesus is safe?"

In a heated confrontation with one of my parishioners after my sermon, I finally said, "I'm not going to continue to argue with you, George. I'll never persuade you."

To which George replied, "Humph. Glad that our Lord didn't have your attitude. Never saw Jesus back down from an argument. If I'm wrong, seems like you would want to convert me."

Ouch.

"What's the most important thing a pastor can do to help a languishing church go forward?" I asked a church consultant.

"Pastors must be courageous enough to begin difficult, potentially painful, often contentious conversations that their churches have been avoiding for decades. But because most pastors see themselves as peacemakers and caregivers, that's tough."

"When Jesus and his followers approached Jerusalem" (CEB), Jesus surely knew the death-dealing conflict he would encounter there. And yet there he goes. So here's the question as we begin this week before Jesus' last week: Will we go with him?

Go ahead, Lord, and show me where I'm avoiding possibly painful, difficult journeys that you want me to take. Amen.

Anxious? Stressed? Fearful? Jesus can fix that. Problems? Jesus will deliver you. Where does it hurt? Jesus will heal.

While gladly received by a therapeutic, self-help culture, this message makes the life, death, and resurrection of Jesus incomprehensible. If Christ's mission is solely comfort, relief, and care for us, why did the church connect Jesus with Isaiah's "servant" who "gave my body to attackers" and didn't hide "from insults and spitting" (CEB)?

The good news of Christ didn't sound like good news to all. The way Jesus walked and talked evoked constant opposition. We know where this journey leads by next Friday, don't we?

The good news of Jesus Christ is not first and foremost healing, caregiving, or release. True, Christ often comforts and cares. But a main way he cares is by calling, "Follow me." Our salvation connects to our vocation. And if we dare to follow, the world sometimes deals with us as it dealt with him. Jesus was upfront that cross-bearing is part of the journey.

"Having had a hellish week, I came this morning seeking comfort and reassurance," she said to me at the door after worship.

"I hope my sermon was helpful," I said, nervously.

"Not particularly," she responded. "I came here seeking comfort, only to have Jesus give me an assignment!"

Jesus thinks nothing of calling others to serve him, some of whom may be afflicted with pain of their own. Suffering for him and with him is part of his salvation of the world.

That is strange good news. Anxious? Stressed? Fearful? Jesus will call you to follow him anyway. But as you walk, be sustained by Isaiah's testimony, "The LORD God will help me" (CEB).

When was the last time you suffered because you are walking and talking like Jesus?

Heroic martyr Dietrich Bonhoeffer said that to pray a psalm is praying along with Jesus. "Have mercy on me, LORD . . . I'm depressed . . . My life is consumed with sadness . . . groaning . . . suffering . . . I'm a joke to all my enemies . . . I scare my friends . . . like I'm dead . . . out of mind" (CEB).

Surprised to consider our Lord praying like this? You'll be disappointed if you must have your saviors high and lifted up, untouched by human finitude or misery. Jesus Christ is not only fully God but also fully, unreservedly human. In every way, he was one of us—including sadness, suffering, anguish, and death. Betrayed, forsaken, ridiculed, and hanging from a cross (a joke to his enemies), he completely embraced our full humanity.

The good news never claims that Jesus delivers us from all unhappiness; it says that God promises always to be with us. God promises to be merciful, even in times of inevitable depression and groaning—especially there.

"Unfortunately, I'm at a 'happy church,'" a woman once told me. "Our preacher bounces on stage each Sunday, grinning, so pleased to be there, so thrilled with himself. The music is upbeat. The joy relentless. Sermons are always positive and uplifting. It's . . . depressing if you happen to come to church unhappy." Where's the good news in that, in never acknowledging the darkness?

God wasn't content to love from afar. Because of the path that Jesus walks, even when the world gives us its worst, we can still say with the psalmist, "'You are my God.' My future is in your hands" (CEB).

Lord, no matter how difficult my circumstances are, it's good to know you've been there and are there with me. Amen.

It's hard enough to understand that in Christ, God "emptied," took the form of a "slave," became "like human beings," and obeyed "to the point of death, even death on a cross." The Almighty Creator, Lord, "humbled" (CEB)?

But then Paul takes the already challenging—God was in the crucified, despised, servant Jesus—and makes it even more demanding: "Adopt the attitude that was in Christ Jesus" (CEB).

Who, us?

It is a strange way of salvation: emptying ourselves of ourselves. In humbling ourselves, we rise. In suffering, we are saved. In dying, we live. Jesus not only walked this downward way, he invites us to go with him.

The other day, someone said something most hurtful to me. By the grace of God, these words came to mind: "Adopt the attitude that was in Christ." And I, even I, reacted to another's wounding not as I usually do—full of myself, quick to take offense—but somewhat (though not perfectly) adopting the self-emptying way of Christ.

Remember when Jesus predicted to his disciples that he would suffer, be rejected, and killed (see Luke 9:21)? It was a jolt. Jesus followed that with an even greater offense, "All who want to come after me must say no to themselves, take up their cross daily, and follow me" (Luke 9:23, CEB). Who, us?

It is bad enough that the Christ—Son of God, Lord of all—must suffer the cross. But for the crucified, suffering Jesus to predict that a cross will be daily laid upon our weak backs too? Us?

It makes it all the more amazing that when Jesus called your name, in spite of your inclination to build yourself up, to look out for Number One, you followed him anyway.

Jesus, give me your servant attitude. No matter how much it may hurt. Amen.

Jesus' opponents "were searching for a way to arrest Jesus and kill him" (CEB). You suspected that the authorities would eventually put an end to the Jesus commotion. What you didn't know is how they would do it: "Judas Iscariot, one of the Twelve, went to the chief priests to give Jesus up to them . . . they were delighted and promised to give him money" (CEB).

Why? Why would one so close, chosen by Jesus for his inner circle, collaborate with the authorities to silence Jesus? What motivated Judas? Scholars have speculated that Judas might have been a zealot who hoped that Jesus would be the expected Messiah, raise a righteous Judean army, and vanquish the Romans. His bitter disappointment that Jesus was not the revolutionary he expected led Judas to do the terrible deed.

There is no need to speculate, says Mark. Judas did it for the money. Thirty pieces of silver is a hefty sum, but surely not enough to justify the betrayal of your friend. Mere money led to the murder of the Son of God? Still, there you have it. Money is exchanged; Jesus is crucified.

What preacher talks as negatively about money as Jesus? Jesus never suggested that property is private or a sign of superior piety, intelligence, or hard work. While he called all to walk with him, he turned away many by insisting that his disciples travel light.

I once was asked, "What's the greatest threat to marriages and families in your church?"

"Money," I replied. "Our claim that we're working to provide for our families is often a cover for our greed."

It is a battle as old as the story of human history. But Jesus' message is clear: We can only serve one master (see Matthew 6:24).

Lord, forgive me when I turn away from walking your way for no better reason than money. Amen.

At last our journey with Jesus has led us to Jerusalem, two days before Passover. The walk has not been easy, but in spite of the difficulties and misunderstandings the disciples have trudged behind Jesus. Now they will celebrate together in the Holy City.

Then the horrible truth: "Judas Iscariot, one of the Twelve, went to the chief priests to give Jesus up to them" (CEB). Along the way, Jesus has been dogged by fierce opponents. But the most hurtful blow is dealt not by one of Jesus' enemies; the final, deadly betrayal will be by one of Jesus' twelve best friends.

Judas was no fake disciple. Called by Jesus at the first, Judas was there every step of the way as an eyewitness in the front row for all of Jesus' teaching. And yet, for nothing more than money, he conspired "to give Jesus up to them."

"I wish I could have been present when Jesus walked the earth," a parishioner said. "Following would be easier if I could have seen and heard him myself." If there's an eyewitness advantage, what do we say about Judas? From the first, all the way back to Judas, the problem was not the gap between our time and Jesus but rather between who we are and what he demands of us.

And though Judas's betrayal is noteworthy, when Jesus was arrested, most of the other disciples fled into the darkness.

Infidelity to Jesus didn't end with Judas. He betrayed Jesus for money; I do it daily for others' approval, to avoid ridicule, or because the cost of following Christ is more than I want to pay.

That's why I'm glad that Judas was there at the table, one of Jesus' twelve best friends who are also his betrayers. If Judas had not been there, close to Jesus in spite of his forsaking Jesus, what hope would there be for me in my multiple betrayals?

Lord, have mercy on your betrayers. Amen.

Palm/Passion Sunday

As Jesus ends his journey and enters Jerusalem, you'd think Mark would give us a lofty summary of his work or a stirring sermon to prepare us for the climactic spectacle to come. Instead, Mark opens Holy Week's high drama with mundane details of how Jesus gave two disciples a task to rent a donkey, specifying a "colt that no one has ridden" (CEB). If anybody questions the disciples, they are to reply, "Its master needs it" (CEB).

The disciples do as they are told. Then the Palm Sunday parade begins and crowds welcome Jesus. Hosanna!

Yet here's what's curious: Holy Week begins—Christ enters Jerusalem to claim his throne—but only after a couple of unnamed disciples are given a task, the unspectacular role of securing transportation because Jesus "needs it."

Here's a great wonder that you might miss because it's clothed in such humble garb. Whatever Christ, Messiah, Savior of the World wants to do *for* us, he chooses to do *with* us. In Christ, God Almighty needs the likes of us. To ordinary, unnamed disciples (like us), Christ assigns a role in his saving work. Often, we don't know why the task needs doing, and rarely do we know why he picked us. But we have faith that if we are obedient, he condescends to work with us and through us to save the world.

All you did was bake and take cookies when you heard of their loss. You gave her a ride to the doctor's appointment. An afternoon at the nursing home in conversation was nothing much. You arranged a pot of palms for the altar for this morning's service. That was all. And yet, through such humble tasks performed by ordinary disciples, Jesus saves.

Jesus is on his way to accomplish the salvation of the world. Guess whom he needs to work with him?

What tasks have you assigned to me, Jesus? Amen.

Choosing the Way That Leads to Life

MARCH 25–31, 2024 • TRACY S. MALONE

SCRIPTURE OVERVIEW: This week's readings take us through the depths but then into the eternal light. We walk each step with Jesus, who suffers betrayal, abandonment, and death. But it is more than that. In his suffering, Jesus also enters into the brokenness of our human condition and feels our pain, such that on the cross he even feels abandonment by God. He walks through the valley of the shadow of death because of God's amazing, reckless love for us. This is the power of Holy Week. But that is not the end of the story. Jesus' steps do not end at the cross, for he walks out of the tomb! Now we can follow in his steps and participate in his new life. He is risen indeed!

QUESTIONS AND SUGGESTIONS FOR REFLECTION

- Read Isaiah 42:1-9. How is God calling you to be a light? How does God empower you to follow God's call to you?
- Read Psalm 70. What is prompting you to reach out for God's help today? In what ways do you ask for that help?
- Read John 13:1-17, 31b-35. What acts of service does Jesus' example in this reading move you to perform? Choose one act you will do today in remembrance of Jesus' humility.
- Read John 20:1-18. When have you, in the light of God's love, let go of the way you thought your life would be in order to live a different reality that God intended for you?

Resident bishop of the Ohio East Episcopal Area of The United Methodist Church; President-Designate of the Council of Bishops.

I was taught as a child never to question God's presence and always to look to the Lord as my source of help and strength. As I've matured into adulthood, however, I have discovered that no matter how deep and abiding one's faith and hope is in Jesus Christ, we all find ourselves asking God at some point, "How much more can I be expected to bear?" or "How much longer will I endure this struggle?" Every one of us will experience times in our lives when we feel overwhelmed by difficult circumstances and daunted by painful conditions in our world. How many of us have prayed to God and found that we had no words of praise or faith but only questions?

As I read this passage, I can imagine the Israelites asking many questions. They have found themselves in exile and must be feeling defeated and abandoned. The prophet Isaiah proclaims a message of hope, reassuring the people of Israel that despite their present circumstances and conditions, the Lord is with them and is upholding them, even in the middle of their suffering. Isaiah declares that God will send a servant who will bring justice and healing to the nations. This servant will not be defeated by sin and darkness. God will redeem God's covenant people and will empower them to be God's agents of love, light, justice, and hope to the world.

When we feel far from God's presence, let us remember that Jesus is our strength, our deliverer, and our hope. Jesus is right here with us in the middle of our circumstances. Our doubts and questions can never separate us from this promise or from God's presence.

God, help us always to place our trust and hope in you, even—especially—when you feel far away. Remind us that you always hear us when we pray. Amen.

In September of 1995 my mother called our family together to tell us that we needed to start preparing for her death. She knew that it was just a matter of time before she would go home to be with the Lord. I can remember sensing how troubled my mother's spirit was and also being amazed at her unwavering hope and trust in the Lord. No matter what she faced in those difficult days leading to her death, she focused on her faith and shared her joy in Christ Jesus. Many that came to visit her to say their good-byes said that while they were in her presence it was as if they had been in the presence of Christ.

Jesus' soul was troubled as he shared the news that the time had come for him to be "glorified." The disciples had heard him talk about his death before, but now it was imminent. Jesus was not expecting them to feel sorry for him. He needed them to understand how his death would impact them and have eternal impact in the world. It was in this moment that the disciples had to make a choice. Are they willing to follow wherever Jesus led them? There was no turning back. Jesus said, "Whoever serves me must follow me; and where I am, my servant also will be. My Father will honor the one who serves me" (NIV).

During this Holy Week we are invited to examine ourselves. We must ask ourselves the same question the disciples faced: are we being faithful in following Jesus wherever he leads us? Who are the people we are called to serve? Where are the places we are called to go?

Lord, give us the courage to follow wherever you lead us. In Christ's name. Amen.

What does it really mean to let go of all that which weighs us down and makes us feel trapped? What will it take for us to keep our eyes fixed on Jesus as we run this race called life?

We find in this passage words of encouragement that teach us that we can look to the examples of disciples of Christ—in the Holy Scriptures and in our own lives—who went through trials and yet kept the faith. The apostle Paul, for example, knew something about being entangled with sin. He had done some things in his past that he was not proud of. Paul had a life-changing moment with God, and the Holy Spirit came upon him and transformed his life. Paul began preaching the good news of Jesus Christ.

And even more than looking to disciples and apostles, we can keep our eyes on Jesus, the foundation and sustainer of our faith. Jesus is our ultimate example of faithfulness, revealing to us what steadfastness looks like as he endured the Cross. Jesus never lost sight of God's divine plan and purpose for his life.

We all have a race to run and will encounter stumbling blocks along the way. Sometimes these are circumstances we have no control over, and sometimes they are situations that we create for ourselves. Hear the good news! No matter what your condition is and whatever your case may be, keep your eyes fixed on Jesus! Do not become discouraged and do not grow weary in your faith. God has an amazing way of showing up in our lives when we least expect it, and the Holy Spirit moves in life-changing ways. Stay the course!

Loving God, when things get hard or when we feel helpless, give us eyes to see Jesus. Help us find his strength through the power of your Holy Spirit. Amen.

Maundy Thursday

Maundy Thursday, or Holy Thursday, is the day we tradi- tionally remember the last meal Jesus had with his dis- ciples, when he instituted the Lord's Supper and, according to John's Gospel, washed their feet. When I was growing up, every year on this day my home church observed these traditions in a worship service. Everyone who attended the worship service, no matter their position, status, or title, was invited to wash the feet of someone and to allow someone to wash their feet. We were each given a bowl of water and a towel. We were invited to kneel and take turns serving each other. As we poured the water on each other's feet, we said, "Jesus loves you, and you are a beloved child of God." After washing one another's feet, we celebrated the Lord's Supper together and again had the oppor- tunity to serve each other.

Washing someone's feet and allowing them to wash yours is a sacred act of humility and service. Being able to be vulnerable with one another reminds us of our own humanness and how fragile we really are. Serving others and allowing others to serve us helps us recognize our own needs and to see Christ in each other. How would we serve and treat people differently if we saw all people as God's beloved children? How might we serve or receive from others differently if we considered the acts of love, kindness, and compassion as sacred acts of humility and service?

Jesus said, "No servant is greater than his master, nor is a messenger greater than the one who sent him." On Maundy Thursday, we remember our call to serve with humility and grace. As we follow in the footsteps of Jesus, we learn the way of love and the way to becoming a beloved community.

Holy Spirit, grow in us a desire to love and serve with grace and humility so we may reflect your goodness in the world. Amen.

Good Friday

I've talked with many Christians throughout my ministry who've said they avoid Good Friday because they find it to be too funereal. The sorrow and gloominess of the day is too much for them to handle. Some of them ask the age-old question, "What is good about Good Friday?" This is a question every Christian should ponder. How do we find good in the suffering, crucifixion, and death of Jesus Christ? Truth be told, it is hard to reconcile suffering and death with what we call "good." We know that suffering and death are universal experiences, but we do not ordinarily refer to them as being good.

But I would argue there is much good about Good Friday. We celebrate the goodness of God and the radical love of Jesus who willingly suffered and sacrificed his life. Jesus loved God with all his heart, with all his soul, with all his strength, and with all his mind—and he loved all his friends so much that he bore the weight of their guilt and shame. Jesus' relentless faith set us free, and through faith in Jesus Christ we can experience life in all of God's abundance.

What happened on Good Friday isn't just about what happened to Jesus; it is also about what happens to us. We witness how God's redemptive love and power can transcend even the darkest hour of suffering and death. If God can redeem suffering and death, we know that God can redeem any hardships we face. We can wait on God because we know that God always has the last word. And that is *good* news!

Lord, thank you for the good news that we proclaim on Good Friday. May the somberness of this day remind us of your radical love for us. Amen.

HOLY SATURDAY

When I was younger, I looked forward to Holy Saturday because I knew it was the last day I was expected to fast from the things that I said I would give up for Lent. At the beginning of the Lenten season each year, my parents made us write down what we were choosing to fast from. I would often put on my list the things I needed to do less of, like eating sweets and chips. As I matured in my faith, I gained a deeper understanding of the meaning of Lent. I began to list not only the things I wanted to give up and let go of, but also the things I wanted to take on and add to my life. I started adding to my list things like being more patient with others and becoming more disciplined in prayer.

The season of Lent is a journey of surrendering our will to God. It is a journey of transformation. It is a time for us to gain more of Christ and for our faith to be renewed in Christ.

Jesus came to love and to serve. He gave his life to set us free from sin and from the burdens of life. He knows temptation. He knows discouragement. He knows loneliness and betrayal. He knows pain and suffering. He knows grief and death. And he knows the power of resurrection. Jesus knows us and cares about all that concerns us.

What are the struggles or sin in your life that you need to give up and let go of? What are you missing or seeking to add to your life? Though this is the last day of this Lenten season, maybe this is the first day of a new beginning for you. Peter encourages us not to dwell on our past or focus on who we once were but to choose to live a life fully surrendered to Jesus Christ.

Almighty God, help us surrender all our past, our worries, and our needs to you. May your will be done in our lives. Amen.

EASTER

The tomb is empty! Jesus has conquered the grave! Christ is risen! These facts remain the same and the promise is true yesterday, today, and all our tomorrows. The Easter story reveals how God is always working for good in our lives and in the world, bringing light into the darkness, making hope out of despair, and turning tragedy into triumph. There is nothing impossible for God! No matter how dark, tragic, or hopeless a circumstance or situation might be, the worst day or the worst thing is never the last thing.

As Easter people we must decide every day not to shrink in fear and doubt. We must choose not to succumb to the suffering we experience and the evil and injustice that pervades the world. We must have the faith to claim Christ's resurrection power in our own lives and choose to live victoriously, embodying and proclaiming God's love, compassion, justice, peace, and hope. We do this by relying on God's endless supply of grace and mercy and resting in the knowledge that nothing can separate us from the love of God in Christ Jesus. Every day we must proclaim that we are more than conquerors through Jesus Christ, who is our hope and salvation and through whom all things are possible. Why? Because this is a fact and a promise!

Jesus tells Mary Magdalene not to hold on to him but to go and share that she has seen him. We give witness to the power of the Resurrection by sharing testimonies of our faith in Christ and by living as Resurrection people. Who will you go and tell that Christ is risen? How will you live differently knowing you follow a resurrected savior?

Almighty God, help us to experience the joy of Easter today and always! May our lives be a testimony to your power and love. Amen.

Creating Caring Communities

APRIL 1–7, 2024 • THEODORE HIEBERT

SCRIPTURE OVERVIEW: The earliest followers of Jesus faced the challenge of creating communities unlike any that had existed before. This was an amazing opportunity because they had the chance to build communities from the ground up, creating more open, intentional, and caring fellowships than they had known before. But it was also daunting. They sought to build their new communities in a politically, socially, and religiously hostile world where they were not guaranteed success. Each of the New Testament texts this week reveals early Christians struggling to form new communities, make them whole and healing spaces, strengthen them to survive the harshest threats, and build them to endure. Because of their courage, we still live in Christian communities of all kinds, and we continue to find ways to make them caring communities.

QUESTIONS AND SUGGESTIONS FOR REFLECTION

- Read Acts 4:32-35. In what ways does your Christian community extend generosity to those within and those beyond the community?
- Read Psalm 133. How do you experience God's extravagant love for you? What is your response to this love?
- Read 1 John 1:1–2:2. What experience of Christ have you "heard . . . seen . . . looked at . . . touched"? How do you share your experience of the risen Christ with others?
- Read John 20:19-31. How do you relate to Thomas's desire for tangible proof of the Resurrection?

Francis A. McGaw Professor Emeritus of Old Testament at McCormick Theological Seminary; editor and translator of the Common English Bible; member of the Mennonite Church and has served as pastor of the Boston Mennonite Congregation.

The first Christians were, above all, intentional about living together. They were so intentional about their relationships with one another, in fact, that they brought their credit cards to the table. When the author of Acts describes these early Christians as being "one in heart and soul," we shouldn't take this to mean that they all looked alike or thought alike. Rather, we should understand that they were completely committed to one another, sharing the kind of loyalty best friends or marriage partners share with one another (see Philippians 1:27).

"One in heart and soul" recalls the Old Testament charge to Israel: "You shall love the LORD your God with all your heart and with all your soul and with all your might" (Deut. 6:5). By choosing to echo this phrase, the author of Acts portrays the early Christians as not only devoted to one another but wholly devoted to God. Only by being completely committed to God and to each other could the early followers of Jesus "bear powerful witness to the resurrection of the Lord Jesus" (CEB).

Including economics in this commitment is expecting a lot! Especially for those of us who've grown up in a very individualistic society and who've learned a very individualistic kind of faith. I have friends within my Mennonite tradition who have taken this vision of the caring community so seriously that they have established intentional communities like this one in Acts, sharing even their economic resources in common to live out the mission of the church together.

We may not choose to join or to create such a first-century community in the twenty-first century, but we can't lose this vision of how intentional a caring community should be. Intentionality is the foundation on which we continue to create caring communities.

God, remind us how much intention it takes to care for others in our lives and in our communities. Amen.

The first step early Christians took to create their intentional, caring communities was to do something serious about the economic inequalities among themselves. As soon as the church was born at Pentecost (Acts 2:1-41), its members began to share their resources: "They would sell pieces of property and possessions and distribute the proceeds to everyone who needed them" (Acts 2:44, CEB). As today's text makes clear, sharing their wealth is a hallmark of the first Christian communities. They redistributed their wealth to eliminate poverty, so "that there was not a needy person among them."

Such radical behavior has deep roots in our religious heritage. The Old Testament prophets continually preached against the rich who "trample on the needy and destroy the poor of the land" (Amos 8:4 CEB). Jesus, like the prophets before him, took economics as a religious matter, instructing a Jewish leader who asked how to express fully his commitment to God: "Sell everything you own and distribute the money to the poor" (Luke 18:22, CEB).

You may agree with me that our differences in wealth—our pocketbooks, our paychecks, and our economic fortunes—are one of the hardest topics to talk about openly and frankly in our Christian communities. We've come to believe this is an individual matter. Meanwhile, the economic gap between rich and poor in the United States is increasing rapidly and painfully. Between 1965 and 2018 the typical corporate CEO's pay rose from twenty times a typical worker's pay to 278 times their pay.

The first Christians knew that this was not God's vision for community, and they tried hard to do something about it. They learned from their prophets and from Jesus that caring meant economic caring. And they followed through. They created caring communities that aimed to take economics seriously.

God, may the first Christians remind us that caring includes wealth as well as words. Amen.

When we read this ancient psalm, we are distracted, maybe even amused, by the precious oil running down Aaron's beard, and then we may wonder why it is paired with the image of dew covering the slopes of Mt. Hermon, the highest peak in ancient Israel. To us, these are unusual images, but for the psalmist they are extravagant images of the beauty and well-being of community solidarity.

This short psalm celebrates healthy communities: "How good and how pleasant it is for brethren to dwell together in unity!" (KJV). The psalmist uses the word "brothers" because he lived in a kinship society built around its male members. "Brothers" therefore signified all members of his kinship community (NRSVUE: "kindred"; CEB: "families"). Old Testament communities were kinship communities: nested communities of individual and extended families, clustered into villages, then into tribes, and ultimately into the whole people of Israel itself.

In such kinship communities, just as in our less kinship-oriented communities in the United States today, conflict is inevitable. We know this from the stories of family conflict in the book of Genesis—the stories of Cain and Abel, Isaac and Ishmael, Jacob and Esau, and Joseph and his brothers. This psalm and these Genesis stories know how fragile families and communities are, how susceptible they are to conflict and disintegration, and how crucial it is to find ways to mediate conflict and seize opportunities for resolution and rebuilding in order to preserve them.

It's easy to take revenge and destroy families as Cain did. It's much harder to find ways to resolve conflict and to rebuild relationships, as did Isaac and Ishmael, Jacob and Esau, and Joseph and his brothers. That's why the psalmist is so extravagant with his images celebrating community solidarity. Creating caring communities is hard, but it means everything.

God, remind us of the extravagant beauty of the caring communities to which we belong. Amen.

A colleague and I taught a workshop about caring communities in the summer of 2021 with ten men at the Cook County Jail in Chicago, sponsored by McCormick Theological Seminary. We wanted to learn about caring communities like the one the psalmist celebrates in this psalm "when brothers live together as one" (AP). So we studied together the stories of families and their conflicts in Genesis, the stories of Cain and Abel, Isaac and Ishmael, Jacob and Esau, and Joseph and his brothers.

We called the workshop "Community, Conflict, and Restoration." We wanted to understand better how fragile even the best communities can be, how badly conflict can damage them, and how essential it is for their members to find ways to heal and rebuild damaged relationships. I had read and studied these stories for years. But I had never quite grasped one essential fact about them until our conversations at Cook County Jail.

We asked the participants to consider the following questions as they studied these four stories of brotherly conflict: Who causes the conflict? Whom does the conflict harm? Who restores the relationships and rebuilds the community? I had always thought of these stories with a single villain, a single victim, and a single savior. But in our conversations, we came to realize that each member of the community in their own unique way is implicated in the conflict, is victimized by it, plays some role in rebuilding relationships, and is healed when community is restored. When it comes to community, we're truly all in it together.

There are no single villains in caring communities, and there are no single heroes. Caring communities remain alive and enduring when we recognize how we are all capable of contributing to the conflict, capable of being harmed by it, capable of rebuilding relationships, and capable of being healed.

God, remind us how much we rely on one another to build caring communities. Amen.

We've already been reintroduced to the Pentecost community in Acts as an intentional community sharing economic resources. And we've learned from the ancient kinship communities in Psalms (and Genesis) about conflict and restoration. The community in today's text is a unique community of early congregations who connect themselves with the apostle John, churches who themselves face the threat of internal conflict (see 1 John 4:1; 2 John 7; and 3 John 9).

In the face of such conflict, this letter, this "announcement," aims to promote true fellowship within these early churches. "Fellowship" here translates from the Greek word *koinonia*, which means "partnership" or "joint ownership" in pursuit of a common calling or mission. Just how such partnership can be accomplished is the key concern at the beginning of this letter. And it starts by calling out those who say they have no sin, who claim innocence, and who refuse to acknowledge their shortcomings.

The church I grew up in taught that sin was an individual matter. Acknowledging my sin meant that I, as an individual, should look inside myself to see where I might have gone wrong, then confess my sins to God and ask for forgiveness. If I was sincere, I could then expect my relationship with God to be restored. It was a personal matter.

But if the real aim of this advice about sin is *koinonia*, the kind of fellowship that builds true partnership in Christian communities, then the sin in question cannot be only individual. Our individual sins are relevant, but so, too, are our collective sins as a community. We must recognize that we aren't perfect, look for the ways we have undermined true fellowship, and acknowledge our own collective failures. Both our individual work and our collective work in addressing our sins are important in creating a community that cares.

God, teach us humility as the beginning of building caring communities. Amen.

Our story today goes back to the very beginning of the community that would become the church. Only ten followers of Jesus are present: Judas has betrayed Jesus to the authorities and is no longer with them, and Thomas is absent. It is the night of the Resurrection, though the disciples have only heard what has happened from Mary. Understandably, they are behind closed doors, locked off from the world, fearful, afraid to come out of hiding, endangered, uncertain, directionless. Their prospects don't look good. Frankly, they look disastrous.

This is the perilous beginning of the community that would become the church. Their teacher and mentor has just been convicted of subversive speech, has been executed by a dishonorable crucifixion, and has been buried. They wonder whether they'll be next. Their future looks darker than dark. Then, against all odds, that same Jesus is in the room with them. And Jesus gives them new life.

This is the Gospel of John's most important story about the resilience of caring communities. These first ten followers of Jesus stuck together when they were under the gravest of threats. Facing their end and the end of their community, they didn't abandon one another. But, really, they only came to life when Jesus appeared. They were overjoyed! This is the true meaning of the Resurrection. When the future of a community of Jesus' followers seems humanly lost, the risen Jesus reappears among them—over and over—and makes hope possible again.

Many early Christian communities, doing the best they could but facing life-threatening forces, saw themselves in this story. It gave them the strength to go on. It happened once, at the very beginning, and it can happen again. Caring communities rely on something—and Someone—bigger than themselves.

Spirit of God, keep showing up to give us and our communities hope. Amen.

And then there was Thomas. For whatever reason, he wasn't there when his friends huddled behind closed doors, fearing for their lives, trying to keep their little community together. And then, when they told him what had happened, how Jesus had appeared and given them life, he wouldn't believe them. Thomas the doubter. Thomas: not the model member of a caring community.

The thing is, for all of us later hearers of this story, Thomas represents us! In the Gospel of John, Thomas stands in for all of us who were not there in the room where it happened, who were not part of that first little group of followers fearing their end, who doubt that Jesus will reappear, who lose confidence in our own Christian communities and wonder if they are worth it.

Thomas was not convinced he should commit to his new community. But he got a second chance. A week later, when he was back together with Jesus' followers still hiding behind closed doors, Jesus appears to him, too. Jesus shows him the scars of his execution, and Thomas finally believes. Then, Jesus speaks to all the rest of us, all of us who may at times doubt the presence of the Spirit and the resilience of the Christian community to which we belong: "Do you believe because you see me? Blessed are those who don't see and yet believe" (CEB).

The earliest followers of Jesus faced the challenge of creating communities unlike any that had existed before. And they accepted that challenge under the harshest threats. Because of their courage born of their faith in the risen Lord, we still live in Christian communities of all kinds, and we continue to find that Jesus Christ is the source of our own courage to build and sustain them.

God, give us the continuing courage to build up the Christian communities of which we are a part and for which we deeply care. Amen.

A Beautiful and Broken Mess

APRIL 8-14, 2024 • DAWN MARTIN

SCRIPTURE OVERVIEW: A repeating theme in scripture is our failure to recognize God's work among us. In Acts, Peter declares that the death of Jesus happened because his fellow Israelites acted in ignorance. The psalmist decries the fact that so many people follow lies, yet God's blessings for the faithful continue unhindered. John tells his audience to expect that the world will not recognize them as God's children because the world did not recognize God to begin with. In Luke, Jesus appears to his doubting disciples. He proves the reality of his resurrection by allowing them to touch his body and by eating food in their presence. Only then do they feel certain that they recognize him. In what places in our lives do we not recognize God's work?

QUESTIONS AND SUGGESTIONS FOR REFLECTION

- Read Acts 3:12-19. Recall a moment when you felt the presence of Christ in your life in an unexpected way. How does that moment stay with you when you feel overwhelmed?
- Read Psalm 4. What inhibits you from crying out to God when you are in distress?
- Read 1 John 3:1-7. How does your identity as a child of God empower you to deeds of love in your daily life?
- Read Luke 24:36b-48. What story of the risen Christ do you have to share with others? How will you share your story?

Director of Program Ministries, Hinton Center; ordained deacon in The United Methodist Church; lives in the mountains of Southwestern North Carolina with her husband, Aaron, and their three dogs; loves creative dabbling, coffee, animals, and books.

Sometimes it's easy for me to relate to the disciples and those we read about in scripture. At first glance, Peter seems to be admonishing the Israelites in these verses, reminding them of how they betrayed and rejected Jesus, and how they seemed to doubt and are amazed at the healing of the man they knew had previously been unable to walk.

Thankfully, though, that's not all we read in today's verses. Peter doesn't stop there. There's a pattern here: *You denied and rejected Jesus, but yet . . . God raised him from the dead. You are shocked at this man walking, but yet . . . there is power in Jesus' name.* How many times have I needed the "but yet" side of the story? In God's amazing power, evident through Jesus, we are offered the "but yet" moments:

You've messed up, but yet . . .

You've lost your way, but yet . . .

You've turned your back, but yet . . .

You're afraid, but yet . . .

You've had doubts, but yet . . .

But yet, Jesus! There is still power in his name! Our relationship with Jesus isn't stagnant, and it's not just full of things we read about that happened back then. It's alive and breathing today.

Consider the "but yet" moments you've had, not to rehash the things you did or didn't do but to recognize that we serve a risen Savior who offers us love, peace, joy, kindness—even on the "but yet" side of things. It's not a free pass to do whatever we want whenever we want. It's an assurance that God loves us in our humanness, with all the ups and downs and bumps along the way.

But yet, Jesus!

God of love, help us cling to the hope we have in Jesus, who offers us the "but yet" side of the story. Amen.

Most of the time, I'm a rule follower. I'm the one who will walk the extra steps to go in the actual "in" door, even though the "out" door opens and will allow you to go through. Fewer than ten items? I have two of the same thing—some small, insignificant item—that makes my item total eleven, so that's not the aisle for me. A parking space reserved for parents with children? No kiddos in my vehicle . . . will not park there.

One time while traveling to a conference a few hours away from home, I was following my GPS when I came upon a sign indicating the road I was directed to take was closed ahead. My GPS gave no indication that the road was closed. It was a pretty significant route. So I paused and thought, *that road can't be closed*, and I kept driving. A few more miles down the road—yep, you guessed it—the road was blocked off. I had to turn around, retrace my steps, and find another way. The rule follower side of me shook her head, muttering, "See, this is why you follow the rules!"

In today's reading, Peter instructs, "Change your hearts and lives! Turn back to God so that your sins may be wiped away" (CEB). How many times have I made a not-so-great decision and had to turn back around? Certainly more than I'd like to admit. How many times have I made a mistake and had to ask for someone's forgiveness? Can you relate?

The good news is that even in those moments when we ignore the signs—literal or figurative—and mess up, we can still turn to God. What a comfort it is to know that we can turn back around.

Reflect on a time you've had to turn back around. Write some notes, draw a road with a "road closed" sign, whatever speaks to you. Then thank God for the opportunity to change your heart and life and turn around and try again.

I'm intrigued by art forms that take brokenness and make something whole. One such form is the Japanese practice of *kintsugi*, repairing broken pottery with lacquer that's dusted or mixed with gold, silver, or platinum. Another is creating mosaics, where small, often broken pieces are put together to create an image or pattern.

A few years ago I had an opportunity to make a few pieces of mosaic art. I hadn't given it much thought until I started sorting through bits of broken glass. Some had beautiful colors and some were oddly shaped, but on their own they all appeared disposable and unimportant. Yet as the picture began to form in my mind, I realized just how important each piece I chose was for the larger whole. The variety of pieces was essential to the full picture. I needed various colors, sizes, and shapes. Each piece contributed to the whole of the mosaic image.

Just like those pieces of glass, our lives are made up of messy, broken parts. God has the ability to take what's broken, messy, and maybe even ugly and make it more beautiful and whole. The psalmist reminds us that God "takes personal care" of us. God hears us when we cry. When "we can't find goodness anywhere," God fills our hearts with joy.

What pieces of yourself do you think are unnecessary or disposable? What parts of your story do you wish you could put back together without any blemish or hint of a crack? We can offer those things to God and allow the Creator of the universe to create something new in and through us.

God, we are your works of art. Help us to give you all the pieces of ourselves so that you can put us back together. Amen.

Several years ago, I experienced a time of disorientation. After thirteen years in a place I loved, I relocated for a new ministry role. I had grown up in my call to ministry in the place I left. It was a place ingrained in who I was. So when I moved, I struggled for a while. I could no longer identify myself by my former title or the organization where I had worked. It made me wonder, *Who am I now?* To complicate matters even more, not long after relocating, I had another major life change that caused me to further question my identity and place in the world.

So much of our lives can be defined by our situation or our relationships. We introduce ourselves with our job title, legitimize ourselves by the organizations with which we are associated. We're someone's child or sibling, spouse or parent. There are numerous titles that we wear and share to define who we are.

Those labels/titles are important, but today's scripture reminds us that ultimately we are children of God. No matter what other ways we identify ourselves, when we remember who we are by remembering whose we are, we can live with peace, love, and hope. It won't magically make all the pain and worry disappear, but it grounds us with a deep understanding that we belong to God. That is who we really are.

According to Henri Nouwen, "Self-rejection is the greatest enemy of the spiritual life because it contradicts the sacred voice that calls us the 'Beloved.' Being the Beloved constitutes the core truth of our existence."

As we struggle with and grow to embrace our many identities, may we always remember the most important one: We each are a beloved child of God.

Craft a prayer to God that includes who you are. Maybe it's the labels/titles you have, maybe it's the dreams and hopes you hold dear. Thank God for all these pieces of you. Thank God that you are called a child of God.

Today's reading left me considering the verse, "Little children, make sure no one deceives you" (CEB). As I thought about the beginning of this passage and the truth that God loves us so much that we are called children of God, I envisioned a seesaw with God's love on one side and worldly deception on the other. As I pictured this playground component, with kids taking turns going up and down, I realized that at times I can fall into this rhythmic back-and-forth.

Some days I relish the knowledge that I am a child of God. Things are going well, issues aren't that insurmountable, the stress is manageable, and I feel pretty good about where I am in life and what I'm doing.

Then there are other days where deceit enters through the voices of others that I've absorbed over time or through my own inner critic that tells me I'm not good enough or smart enough. I suspect you might be familiar with this rhetoric too—that barrage of thoughts that peels back like a stinky onion as more and more insults and insecurities surface. The more I uncover, the stinkier it gets!

Society likes to tell us we need to own more, do more, be more. God tells us we are enough because we are children of God. Maybe your inner critic sometimes takes the stage like mine, telling me how I could be better or reminding me of how I have failed. God tells us we are good because we are children of God, created in God's image. What God creates is good.

Clarifying our identity as children of God is not about earning God's love or hiding our flaws. It's about trusting in the love of God for who we are so that we will continue to grow and flourish as God's agents of love in the world.

God, thank you for your love. In those moments where I don't feel worthy of love, where I don't feel like I'm enough, gently remind me of the truth that I am your child. Amen.

As I spent some extra moments reflecting on today's few verses, I noticed more than the (understandable) fear and doubt of Jesus' followers. When reading the stories of Jesus appearing to the disciples, we tend to focus on their reactions. But this time I was drawn to how Jesus shows them his scars, his woundedness. Jesus comforts his followers through his brokenness. The Savior of the world, God made flesh, who was betrayed, beaten, crucified, and buried, but who rose again chooses to show his scars. He encourages his followers not only to look at them but to touch the places he was wounded. That's intimate. That's real. That's Jesus. That's our God.

In this selfie-obsessed, touch-up crazed, post-your-best-self world, it's tempting to hide those wounded pieces of ourselves and show only the best. It's almost easier to wear a mask and pretend everything is okay. Unfortunately, some of us feel like this is the version our church expects us to bring on Sunday morning. We should show the world we have it all together because we're followers of Jesus.

What if we aren't meant to cover up our scars and pretend they aren't there? What if we're meant to use our very brokenness—those wounded, scarred bits—to show others more about who Jesus is, to let the love and light of a Savior who knows hurt and suffering shine through those very places?

I don't think we're called to share our wounds with everyone at all times, but I do think that erasing the blemishes doesn't give the true picture of Jesus. People need authenticity. It's hard to be real, to be authentic, when we're so skilled at hiding. Maybe Jesus is challenging us to consider a different approach.

Take a few moments to lift up your scars to Jesus.

I used to serve at a ministry location that had inmates from the local correctional institution come help with maintenance and landscaping. Volunteers would provide lunch, and we'd sit down and eat together, converse, and get to know one another. If I'm honest, it was a way we thought we were "bringing Jesus" to those who were incarcerated. One day, one of the men shared his own journey of reading scripture and trying to understand more about faith. He said, "Grace is the most beautiful word in the Bible." At that moment I realized why having conversations with those who are different from me is so important. It's not because I need to bring Jesus to the table; Jesus is already there!

When Jesus had a meal with his followers, scripture tells us that he opened their minds to understand. When I had that lunch with this group of inmates, it was as if Jesus opened my mind to understand. I was reminded how easy it is to lump people into the category of "other"—those who have different lived experiences, those who think or act in ways I might not, those who I don't agree with—because it's easiest to keep people at arm's length and make judgments about them. But when I sit down for a meal and conversation, that begins to change. I start to see Jesus in others, maybe even those I would have assumed needed me to bring Jesus to them.

We live in a fragmented and broken world. We're flawed. We have our own baggage that shapes our perspective. What if we set aside our fears and differences and break bread with those who aren't like us? What if through these acts we not only build relationships but learn more about ourselves? What if through these acts Jesus opens our minds to better understand scripture?

God, give us eyes to see people the way you see them. Give us ears to hear their stories. Give us hands that are welcoming and open. Amen.

On Loving and Being Shepherded

APRIL 15–21, 2024 • CLÁUDIO CARVALHAES

SCRIPTURE OVERVIEW: This week's readings open with a confrontation in Acts between Peter and John and some of the religious leaders. Peter speaks in harsh terms to the leaders, stating that they had killed Jesus; yet by the power of Jesus' name, a man who could not walk has been healed. By that same name, spiritual healing happens as well. The other three passages employ the metaphor of the Good Shepherd. "The LORD is my shepherd," the psalmist declares, and the shepherd cares for all our needs. In John's Gospel, Jesus declares that he is the Good Shepherd who lays down his life for his sheep. First John repeats this imagery. Jesus proved his love when he laid down his life for us. If we truly love one another, we also ought to sacrifice in tangible ways.

QUESTIONS AND SUGGESTIONS FOR REFLECTION

- Read Acts 4:5-12. When have you gotten into difficulty for exercising your Christian faith and values? If never, why not?
- Read Psalm 23. What is your first memory of hearing or reading this psalm? Has it had a significant role in your life of faith? If so, what has its role been?
- Read 1 John 3:16-24. How do your actions reflect your love for God and for your fellow children of God?
- Read John 10:11-18. What "wolves" have you faced in your life? How have you experienced the presence of the Good Shepherd with you as you faced these threats?

Originally from Brazil; professor of worship at Union Theological Seminary in New York City; author of *Liturgies from Below: Praying with People at the End of the World* (Abingdon Press, 2020) and *Praying with Every Heart: Orienting Our Lives to the Wholeness of the World* (Cascade Books, 2021).

By what power or by what name did you do this?" The disciples had to answer this question in public without much time to process and compose their answer. They had to say not what they had polished and rehearsed but rather what naturally came from a deeper place, so much so that the book of Acts says that Peter was "filled with the Holy Spirit." This question is one that should fire us up!

"By what power or by what name did you do this?" What is the source of your strength? What is the name you call upon to help you live your life? What wakes you up in the morning? What makes you never give up? We are likely not immediately facing a council of leaders, elders, and other high ranking officials who are angered by our actions. We have a minute to compose our answer to this life-shaping question.

For me, it is the love of God that provides the source of my strength. The God of life who inhabits every inch of my body is what makes me alive! The Spirit who breathes on me in every breath—this presence keeps me moving. The life of Jesus is my inspiration to work and live. When I see my children, I sense the breath of God in them and am inspired to continue my work for their sake. When I encounter nature, I see the little birds around me, and I live for them. When I see the rivers where I live, I live for them. When I see people on the street, I am moved to do something to give them honor. For to love God is first to know the love of God in me.

"By what power or by what name did you do this?" What would you say?

God of our lives, may we know deep inside of us that we can live only because your Spirit lives in us and your wondrous love holds us. Amen.

For the next four days, we will read Psalm 23, and I invite you to engage in a process of *lectio divina* as you read. Each day, read the psalm multiple times, slowly and out loud. Pay attention to what word/phrase stands out to you. Each day will be something different. Listen for what God is saying to you in what stands out.

As I do *lectio divina* on this first read, this phrase stands out to me: "The LORD is my shepherd, I shall not want." And I ponder what it even means to not want. How can we imagine this in a world where we are demanded to want everything? The very notion of what it is to be human is connected to what one can desire. We desire things so much that Brazilian indigenous leader Davi Kopenawa called us "the people of the merchandise."

What if we desire God? What would happen to us and our daily habits? Who would we be? I am reminded of Mechthild of Magdeburg, the mystic whose whole life was dedicated to pursuing this love. She wanted to have a "God-hunting heart." Once we have a "God-hunting heart," all we want is to figure out what this love might mean to our lives and how we can live off this divine love. The basics for life will follow.

Perhaps to fully know that God is our shepherd is to know that God is enough. If we understand God as our shepherd, we will realize that we are loved, cared for, healed, protected, held, fed, and embraced. And if God is translated into a community of loving people, we can give ourselves to each other and realize collectively that we do not need to desire so many things so desperately. The church has the opportunity to be a real translation of a society that knows "the LORD is my shepherd." And together, knowing that the Lord is our Shepherd, we will learn that we shall not want.

The Lord is my shepherd, I shall not want. (Repeat three times.) Amen.

As we repeat our reading of Psalm 23, another set of words comes to my heart: "God makes me lie down in green pastures; God leads me beside still waters." Let us read this backwards. The verses from yesterday said we "shall not want" because the Lord is our shepherd. This shepherd, the Lord, takes us to green pastures and beside still waters. That is why we shall not want, because we have what we need to eat and enough to drink.

Not long ago in Brazil, a poor mother of five children was put in jail because she stole five dollars worth of food for her and her children to eat. They were hungry. All she had was an empty belly and children to feed. The conditions of society prevented her from being able to be a good shepherd to her children and she was quickly punished for it. The judge who presided over her case—who earns an annual salary that in the US would be equivalent to $100,000—decided to put this woman in jail, saying that she had a "harmful character."

This woman and this judge live in a world where a few have more than they need and many must always be in need. There exists enough for all in our world. How can we who have more than what we need shift to desire what God desires and be moved share of our wealth so that everyone can have enough?

Many churches inspire their members to demand that every single person should be provided with enough food and water, shelter, and care. What more can we as followers of Christ do to ensure that every person has what they need? Through our church work, we can create places that provide for all to have enough. Every time we eat and drink, let us remind ourselves of our Shepherd and the command we have to be our Shepherd's hands and feet in the world for others.

God, make me lie down in green pastures; lead me beside still waters. (Repeat three times.) Amen.

On this third day of reading Psalm 23, my attention is caught by this: My shepherd "restores my soul." It is another reason I shall not want. I have the healing of the Holy Spirit within me. I have the balm of Gilead to be poured out on my head and over my body.

No matter what our experiences, we will always carry bruises and hurts, pain and sorrow within us. We are living in a time of losses and absences. COVID-19 took the lives of countless people. We feel the loss of societal foundations we thought we could depend on: church, democracy, respect, honor, truth. We are seeing the natural world being devoured. Agribusiness is killing everything, deforestation is everywhere, rivers are polluted, oceans are filled with plastic, animals become extinct. Climate catastrophes are happening worldwide. We are seeing the explosion of anxieties, depression, and panic attacks. We feel our world as we have known it is disappearing, and very little is being restored.

God seeks to heal our world, our brokenness, but we must first allow ourselves to be healed and restored through God's mercy and grace. Then we can turn and be tangible offerings of God's mercy and grace to the world around us. Our churches can become what Pope Francis called "field hospitals," providing the basics for those hurting and suffering out in the world. We can learn from indigenous people how to find our healing in our forests, our plants, and our relation with the earth God has gifted us. We can redeem our relationships with one another by acting with honor, truth, and respect for our fellow humans, modeling the ways God calls us to be in relationship with one another. When we are restored and embody that restorative healing for the world, we will realize that our shepherd indeed "restores my soul."

Blessed shepherd, restore my soul. (Repeat three times.) Amen.

On our last day reading Psalm 23, the words that come to me are "God leads me in right paths for God's name's sake." This is a continuation of the "Lord is my shepherd." The shepherd always chooses the best paths to take his sheep and teaches them where to go, how to go, and what to be careful of. In Christian language, this is a parable for discipleship, the art of learning how to live with God and from God. In our journey with Jesus we learn where to go, what to avoid, how to orient ourselves, and with whom we should be. The paths the shepherd leads us on are oriented by God's namesake. We cannot forget that God's namesake is love! (See 1 John 4:8). Love is what orients our lives. To learn to love is to learn the wisdom of life. Love is the art of being free.

It was St. Augustine who said, "Love God and do whatever you please: for the soul trained in love to God will do nothing to offend the One who is Beloved." Isn't this beautiful? With love as the core of our being, we cannot help but act in ways that spread God's love throughout the world. Jesus reminded us that it is by our fruits that we will be known (see Matthew 7:20). Our fruits will be our witness.

What paths do you walk? What paths does your church walk? Who are the ones who walk with you? Do they have a heart filled with love and compassion? What is the namesake you carry in your heart? What name are you called, the name that comes before your own name? To be led in the right paths, we need to carry the namesake of God in our lives: the mighty name of love!

God, lead me in the right paths for your name's sake. (Repeat three times.) Amen.

Today we continue with the notion of God's namesake: *love.* First John describes Jesus as a shepherd giving his life for the sake of his sheep. As we strive to follow Jesus' model for living, this is what we are called to do for each other: give ourselves to those who are in need and to be one another's shepherds.

God's love abides in those who see a sibling in need and move to help. This is the very opposite of what we often see in our society. We blame the poor more than help them. We shame them and curse them as lazy. The narratives of love, solidarity, and equality have quickly been replaced by hatred, detachment, and individual "freedom," which is often another way of saying,"You're on your own." We are losing the sense of a collective form of living. Instead of living like Abel, we are giving in to the question of Cain: "Am I my brother's keeper?" (Gen. 4:9)

Every day we must be reminded of John's words, "Little children, let us love, not in word or speech, but in truth and action." It is not enough to speak of love. We must keep the act of loving one another. In a time where truth has been co-opted by propaganda, we must continue to live in real truth and proclaim that as the way to live more fully. We must continue to make the Christian faith a faith that is deeply marked by actions of love and kindness. Our faith turns us inside to be transformed and then turns us outside in order to care for others, especially for "the least of these" (Matt. 25:40).

Today I call upon the name of my God: love. (Repeat three times.) Amen.

How comforting to know that Jesus our shepherd knows us and promises to be present with us, especially in times of distress. We can rest in the knowledge that Jesus will never leave us. And we are invited to know Jesus as Jesus knows us, to enter into this relationship of love and care.

But to know Jesus is not a one-time event. Rather it is a constant practice of listening to Jesus' words in scripture and God's voice in our lives. This is no easy task. Everywhere we see how the voice of our shepherd has been confused with other voices. Politicians and other leaders say they speak for God. News reporters and people on social media call on God's name. But do the words they speak and the actions they perform align with God's words? Or do their words and actions confuse our hearts and prevent us from hearing Jesus' voice?

We live in an increasingly divided world, and we are pushed harder and harder to choose a side. We struggle to listen to Jesus' voice. As we see in the other scriptures we have read this week, to know Jesus as our shepherd is to love those in our world who are in need: it is to feed the hungry, visit the sick, claim freedom for those in captivity. To be able to hear Jesus' voice is to listen to the cry of animals, of forests, trees, rivers, and oceans. Anything that takes us away from caring for each other, from receiving immigrants, from attending to the poor, the widows, the single mothers, the children in need, is diminishing our ability to listen to our shepherd.

How do we regain our ability to listen to the voice of Jesus through the presence of the Holy Spirit? How can we be a presence of transformation in the world? That is our task as people of faith. We must collectively find a way back to Jesus' words: "I am the good shepherd. I know my own and my own know me."

Jesus is my shepherd; he knows my voice. I am Jesus' sheep; I know his voice. Amen.

The Word of God Speaks

APRIL 22–28, 2024 • MARSHA CROCKETT

SCRIPTURE OVERVIEW: Two primary themes emerge from our readings for this week. In Psalm 22, we find the promise that faraway nations will turn and worship the Lord. The book of Acts provides partial fulfillment of this promise. Through the action of the Spirit, a court official from Ethiopia hears the gospel and can take it home to his native land. The Johannine readings focus on abiding in God. "God is love," the epistle states, so all who claim to abide in God manifest love to the world. The author pushes the point: If we maintain animosity toward others, we cannot claim to remain in the love of God. In John, Jesus states that we must remain in him if we want to bear good fruit for God.

QUESTIONS AND SUGGESTIONS FOR REFLECTION

- Read Acts 8:26-40. When has an unexpected encounter led you to a deeper understanding of God?
- Read Psalm 22:25-31. Recalling that Psalm 22 begins with the cry, "My God, my God, why have you forsaken me?" do these verses of praise seem surprising? When have you seen this kind of movement in your spiritual journey?
- Read 1 John 4:7-21. How does your assurance of God's love for you move you to love others?
- Read John 15:1-8. How secure do you feel about being attached to the vine? What has God done in your life to make it more productive?

Certified spiritual director and author of the recently released book *Sacred Conversation: Exploring the Seven Gifts of Spiritual Direction* (Upper Room Books, 2022).

Discerning a wise path through life is an inherent desire for most people. And for those of us who call ourselves Christians, discerning the voice of God is how we find our way. We pray to God, "What should I do in this situation? Tell me the way I should go." But we mostly encounter silence, or at most a heart-tug if we're fortunate. Rarely do we get the explicit instruction that Philip did. He practically got a road map to follow the will and way of God.

I want such a map, especially if a situation feels like I can't make everyone happy, or when it seems as if two choices are equally good. I get caught up in worrying over which is right or which is better. Yet God seems silent in suggesting an explicit path. This used to bother me until I began to meditate on Paul's words: "In him we live and move and have our being" (Acts 17:28). This helped me shift my focus from insisting on a specific path as God's will to seeing life itself—my living, breathing, moving being—as God's will.

Ordinary life is the road ahead, for there God goes before us, and follows behind us, and gathers us up in between. So, the places we go, the people we interact with, the things we choose to do or not do—these are the explicit invitations to see and know God. And here we partner with love and truth and grace living within each life, informing us of the divine road map. Sometimes it's a wilderness road. Sometimes a busy street. All I need to remember is that life is the place where God speaks.

Lord, when I'm looking for answers, I'm happy to receive your explicit direction, a road map to your will. But when the details are unclear, remind me that you are with me wherever I am. Amen.

So much of the Christian life is about being on the journey with others. Yet our church traditions have become more of a destination, a place where someone can go to be told what's important, what God wants of them, what a Christian life should look like. Church can easily become more about talking at people than entering with them on their journey.

Philip gives us a beautiful image of what it means to be on a journey with another and to hear the word of God in new ways. We see him joining the Ethiopian eunuch on his path and asking a simple question, "What are you reading?" He didn't approach the man with the attitude of "God told me to come here to tell you about Jesus," even though that was the truth. Philip respected the man more than that. He let the eunuch lead, and lead he did, by inviting Philip to sit with him, to listen to the word, and to ask the questions. Philip responded "starting with this scripture," the place where the man was meditating, and from there he shared the good news of Jesus. Even after this conversation, Philip didn't instruct the Eunuch what to do next, but allowed the man to discover his own next step. "Here is water; what is to prevent me from being baptized?"

What an impact we may have in our churches if we join others as they are on their journey rather than insisting they join our way! The Spirit of God speaks clearly in this story, but it was not only to Philip. In fact, Philip seemed to be listening just as intently to the Spirit speaking through the Ethiopian.

Lord, humble my heart to listen well to your Spirit at work in my life, and to join others, setting aside my own agenda, as I listen to the Spirit on their path as well. Amen.

I was making my way through a labyrinth alone, praising God, grateful for all creation, humbled by the interworking of life with earth, with others, and with the Divine. I sensed that "participa[tion] of the divine nature" that Peter spoke of (2 Pet. 1:4). I was awed and wooed into silent surrender, to an eternal peace surrounding me.

I had always thought of praising God as my offering to God, something I initiated and created by acknowledging the inherent attributes of God's loving presence, creative force, endless grace, and immense truth. Yet in this moment of praise, I was struck with the truth that even my praise was given to me by God. I realized that I had nothing more to offer to God than a tiny newborn baby could offer—just a living, breathing, clamoring life with arms outstretched to receive it all.

When I recognize that "from [God] comes my praise," I become the one simply seeking the Divine along with all creation turning toward its Maker. And the praise continues from one generation to another. As I enter the world of praise as a just-born infant, I proclaim my deliverance to the next generation. It is interesting that the word *deliverance* is from the same root we use for delivering a new life into the world. And the final statement is not any of my doing, or anything I have of worth to add to the immutable glory of God, but "he has done it." Everything is completed in us by the One who alone is worthy of praise.

Holy One, may I join you in creating words of praise. May I come as an infant and cry out your name. May I lift my arms in the praise that emanates from your glory. Amen.

My father was a talented singer. When he married my mother in 1952, he sang the 1940s hit "I Love You Truly" as she walked down the aisle. Growing up I could see that most days my father lived out that sentiment, frequently calling my mother his "bride" even into their old age. But even the most idyllic romance has its weaknesses. I know it couldn't have been perfect, but it was a truly faithful love.

Even with such an example to live by, these words in scripture remain difficult to grasp. Maybe this is because there is an unfathomable depth in the simplicity. Maybe it is because our culture has desensitized love to the point that it's lost its meaning. Or maybe it is because freely offering love has led to being hurt in a variety of ways. And where we experience hurt, we avoid repeating the same mistakes.

Yet, if we love one another (as imperfect as that love may be), we are born of God and know God. In other words, when we offer our small doses of love, God completes what we cannot offer. This is true especially as we consider loving ourselves, perhaps the most difficult love to appropriate well and the most resistant to grace. We're simply hard on ourselves.

God's love is perfected or completed in relationship with human beings and within the Trinity. Love is activated, fulfilled, and given a voice only when it's given away. Love is pointless except in relationship. And this relationship and this love is how God speaks into this world to complete our small acts of love.

Lord, let your love speak fully into me. When my attempts at love fall short, are misconstrued, or lack in grace, let your love complete what I cannot offer on my own. Amen.

Fear of any sort can be crippling. Even the natural fear instinct of fight-or-flight restricts and limits us by banishing peace from our minds to push adrenaline into the body, equipping us to escape harmful situations and survive.

But there is another kind of fear that diminishes and undermines the human capacity to love. This underlying anxiety forms as armor around the heart, protecting us from the possibility of being hurt emotionally. What is intended to protect from one kind of hurt can lead us to an armored existence that keeps all kinds of love at bay. It turns our intention to avoid pain into the face of distrust, or anger, or resentment.

At one point in my life, I realized I had become hard-hearted and distrustful following a painful betrayal of love. A friend pointed it out, and I couldn't deny the truth. I began to pray, "Lord, tender my heart." I didn't want to live a hardened life toward my friends, family, co-workers, or in my faith community. I didn't want to be one of those people who others avoid because they don't know what to expect when they interact with them.

Mine wasn't a miraculous healing but a slow turning toward the face of love, an opening of my heart to the way of love. I found a trusted spiritual director who walked with me through this season. I learned to rest in silence. It felt like being rehabilitated in the ways of receiving and accepting love from others, until eventually I felt more myself and more secure in the love of God toward me, which is the only path to offering love to others.

Lord, so much in this world threatens the life of love. Keep me from shutting down, turning off, or letting go of the possibility of love. Lord, tender my heart today. Amen.

I think and write a lot about the idea or discipline of abiding. I like that word because it speaks of faithfully remaining and dwelling with something or someone. I struggle the most to abide in the midst of my ordinary routines and chores—making one more meal, washing one more dish, commuting to work one more day. These simple acts become burdens unless I remember what it means to abide.

Abiding isn't always comfortable. Deepening our roots and connections to God, self, and others can call us out of our comfort zones and into the deeper waters of faith lived out in the world. Or it can mean staying to offer grace and encouragement when worldly wisdom wonders why you don't find an easier way and just move on. One who abides doesn't run away at the first hint of discord or boredom. Assuming there is no threat of physical or emotional harm, abiding is an act of faithfulness.

And abiding is often slow work for which there is no measurement for success. Just as any relationship takes time to cultivate, so too our relationship with God and self and community may grow or deepen in fits and starts, ebbs and flows. It takes time to build a spiritual history with God and with others. And it requires investments of time, attention, and energy to practice the presence of God in our lives.

Whatever experiences we find ourselves in where we feel the call to abide, the call is to deeper intimacy with God, self, and others. May God give us the courage to abide.

Lord God, I'm fickle of heart when life gets too challenging or uncomfortable, and I want to run and hide. Bolster my spirit and open the door to the place where I can learn to abide in you. Amen.

D o you ever wake up with a song stuck in your head or in your heart? The old hymn "Abide with Me" has recently lodged itself within me, calling me to pay attention to it. Just as I think it's run its course and left me, I hear it again—literally hear it. It was even sung in its entirety on a recent episode of one of my favorite PBS series, "Father Brown"!

So, I'm stopping to listen, to give pause to what feels like a prayer asking Jesus to abide with me, stay with me, as the disciples on the road to Emmaus asked, "Stay with us, for evening is approaching." I am drawn to this prayer because it isn't focused on how I can or should abide with Christ (although he asks that I do), but rather, in my ordinary life and in my persistent weaknesses, how does he abide with me and stay with me in it all? Lines from the hymn haunt me:

Fast falls the eventide . . .
the darkness deepens; Lord, with me abide . . .
Help of the helpless, O abide with me . . .
O Thou who changest not, abide with me . . .
Ills have no weight, and tears no bitterness . . .
I triumph still, if thou abide with me.

If I am still and sit with this reality of Jesus making his home in my world, I can imagine his calm presence in my sometimes-chaotic thoughts and activity, in the midst of my boredom with certain facets of my life and in my relationships and daily tasks. He becomes the host and I the welcomed guest as he opens the door to his dwelling place deep within my soul where he always meets my cry, "Lord, with me abide."

Lord, abide with me. Amen.

God's New Ways

APRIL 29–MAY 5, 2024 • JON MARTIN

SCRIPTURE OVERVIEW: The Acts passage continues to tell the story of the advance of the gospel. The Holy Spirit falls on a group of Gentiles. They believe and are baptized, thus showing God's inclusion of all peoples in the plan of salvation. Psalm 98 is a simple declaration of praise. All creation will sing to and rejoice in the Lord. The two passages from John are linked by their emphasis on the relationship between love and obedience. We do not follow God's commandments in order to make God love us. On the contrary, because God has first loved us and we love God in return, we follow God's teachings. Jesus provides the model for us, being obedient to his Father out of love.

QUESTIONS AND SUGGESTIONS FOR REFLECTION

- Read Acts 10:44-48. When has the Spirit of God brought you to a new understanding?
- Read Psalm 98. Where have you encountered "a joyful noise" in creation? How do you make a joyful noise in praise of God?
- Read 1 John 5:1-6. When have you considered God's commands as burdensome? When have you found them freeing?
- Read John 15:9-17. Are you accustomed to thinking of your relationship with Jesus as a mutual friendship? If so, what does it mean to you to be Jesus' friend?

Pastor of First Presbyterian Church, Lexington, NC; United States Navy Chaplain in Charlotte, NC.

The larger narrative of Acts 10 is the story of God preparing Peter to be part of the conversion of Cornelius. Peter was in Joppa (see Acts 9:43), while Cornelius was in Caesarea (see Acts 10:1). The linear distance between Joppa and Caesarea is about thirty-five miles. By comparison, the religious distance between Peter and Cornelius is much greater. As the narrative moves towards today's passage, God brings these two people together, and the religious distance ultimately vanishes.

I visited Caesarea as a young minister. A steady breeze off the Mediterranean Sea washed over me as I stood in the ruins of that ancient Roman city. I imagine Acts 10 beginning with a steady sea breeze moving through two coastal cities, while ending with the Holy Spirit moving through the place where Peter was speaking to Cornelius and other Gentiles. Does the author of Acts want his readers to recall the Day of Pentecost, with the sound of wind followed by the filling of the Spirit? (See Acts 2:2-4.)

When Peter sees the outpouring of the Holy Spirit, he asks, "Can anyone withhold the water for baptizing these people who have received the Holy Spirit just as we have?" In that moment, the wide religious distance between Peter and his hosts collapses.

Peter's question challenges me. Am I looking for those places where I see God expanding the community and collapsing the distances between people? What communities am I a part of that celebrate such work of the Holy Spirit? When have I been Peter in this story and moved to include people not like me into the community? When have I been Cornelius, the one who is different and welcomed? I have been both. When have you been each?

God, as you continue to work in us, insider or outsider, carry us closer to you and each other on the wind and the outpouring of your Spirit. Amen.

When my family moved to a new state, there was one particularly mundane task that took me a while to complete. The presets on my car radio no longer connected to familiar stations, and I struggled to find new stations to program. While listening to new radio stations, I realized my search was really about finding local stations that played the music I already wanted to hear.

When Psalm 98 begins with the command to "sing to the LORD a new song, for he has done marvelous things," I need to ask myself whether I am doing that. When I sing along to my radio presets and sing in church, it's not new music.

The Hebrew word for "new" in Psalm 98:1 is *chadash*. The same word is used in Exodus to describe the "new King [that] arose over Egypt who did not know Joseph" (Exod. 1:8) and in Numbers to describe an "offering of new grain to the LORD" made on the day of the first fruits (Num. 28:26). The songs I sing in church (and in my car) are not *chadash* in the sense of a new Egyptian king or new grain.

Is there a way then to obey the command of Psalm 98:1 if I am not singing new songs? What about interpreting "new" not as *original* or *new-on-the-scene*, but as *new-to-me*? A new song could simply be an old song I haven't heard before. That would make many old songs new. It would honor the idea that many old songs are worth teaching to a new generation or to people new to the faith. Isn't scripture actually full of old songs (including Psalm 98) waiting to be sung again with those who don't know them yet? What new and new-to-you songs are you learning?

God, thank you for a singing faith. Fill us with songs that are new to us, even old songs sung with new voices. Amen.

I remember how difficult it was to sing over web-based video conferencing for worship services during the pandemic. The platform is designed to focus on one presenter at a time, so when people are singing together, the software doesn't know who the presenter is. A further complication is the time delay resulting from computer networks transmitting digital signals at different speeds. I frequently consoled a congregation during a video conference by saying that our song that sounded uneven and awful was nevertheless a joyful noise to the Lord.

When Psalm 98 summons the earth to make a joyful noise to the Lord, I think about the challenges of video conference singing. The psalmist summons humans (both vocalists and musicians), the roaring sea, the creatures in the sea, the world, all the creatures who inhabit the world, and finally the rivers and the hills to make a joyful noise. What a magnificent ensemble! But how do the creatures in the sea coordinate what they are singing with the rivers clapping their hands? And how can the hills sing together for joy when they are separated by wide valleys? I can imagine the sung praises from all the earth sounding jarring, choppy, and uncoordinated.

What if, however, there is a difference between how music sounds to those who make it and how music sounds to God? Is this one of the lessons of the final verse of the psalm? God "will judge the world with righteousness and the peoples with equity." What if God hears equally each participant's uniquely joyful contribution? How beautiful would it be to imagine that God hears this global song, not as disparate or dissonant, but as righteous because God attends to each expression of praise.

God, thank you for hearing the earth's full song. Keep sending your Spirit to sustain this joyful noise. Amen.

As a Navy Reserve Chaplain, I serve with Sailors and Marines in an environment where words like "victory" and "conquer" are frequently used. So, when 1 John 5 uses "victory" and "conquer," that catches my attention: "For whatever is born of God conquers the world. And this is the victory that conquers the world, our faith."

When I hear "conquer" and "victory," my experiences cause me to picture Marines raising the United States flag on Iwo Jima, or the iconic account of Marines at Belleau Wood in the First World War. I picture the grainy, black and white photograph of President Lincoln with Union troops at Gettysburg. My country's history is full of victorious and conquering moments, so I also think about Jackie Robinson conquering a racial barrier in professional baseball in 1947, Chuck Yaeger's victory over the sound barrier that same year, and Sally Ride's victory as a crew member of a 1983 Space Shuttle mission.

There are also victories that are not singular events, military or otherwise. These are the regular, incremental efforts of faithful people. Could that be the "victory" and "conquering" of 1 John 5:1-6? The steady, faithful work of believers? Many churches collect food every week for their community food pantries. Many congregations share their fellowship halls with anyone who needs a safe place to spend the night. Many faith communities are intentional about including all people. Many churches show up after a natural disaster to bring relief. Aren't these examples of a different kind of "conquering" and "victory"? Admittedly, these are not celebrated in the same way as a singular event like a footprint on the moon, but who is it that conquers the world but the one who believes that Jesus is the Son of God and lives to carry out God's commands?

God, strengthen the faith of all your children to keep us in this Spirit-filled, conquering, shared work. Amen.

One January evening, I was finally home after a full day of ministry. My plan was to head to the couch in pajamas with a cup of hot tea. Just as I was settling in to a quiet evening, the phone rang. A church member was in the hospital. I set my tea aside, got dressed, and headed out the door. I didn't begrudge the sudden shift in my evening plans, in part because of the way love is explained in 1 John 5, "Everyone who loves the parent loves the child."

Loving God and loving the children of God is commanded of us, but John also writes that his commandments are not burdensome. John's counsel that God's commandments are not a burden is helpful for me.

Why do we need to be reminded that the command to love is not burdensome? Do we turn love into a burden when we limit how widely it is shared? Or when we think it's too much work? Or when we underestimate our God-given ability to receive and share it?

When is a burden not a burden—when it is comfortable to carry, or when others are carrying it with us, or when we eventually set it down? Once more, a burden is not a burden when God is at work empowering what we can carry.

The annotated Bible I regularly use offers two references on this text: "My yoke is easy, and my burden is light" (Matt. 11:30) and "I can do all things through him who strengthens me" (Phil. 4:13). One speaks to the burden we carry, and the other to the One who helps us carry it.

God, keep growing our love for you and your children as an expression of our belief that Jesus is the Christ. Amen.

Jesus tells the disciples to abide in his love. Apart from the New Testament and a hymn or two, the word *abide* is rare in modern English usage. I usually hear its more popular synonyms like *remain*, *endure*, and *withstand*.

Today's passage is part of an extended narrative by Jesus ahead of his arrest (see John 13-17). I hear an urgency in this text. In the hours following this extended narrative, Jesus will be arrested (see John 18:12) and handed over to the Empire (see John 19:1). The disciples will experience up close the horror of what the Roman Empire can do. They torture and crucify their enemies. Before this, however, Jesus tells the disciples to abide in his love. As he anticipates the horrors ahead, is he telling them not to be distracted from what they have learned from and experienced with him? And when they are confronted with the ugliness of the Crucifixion, is he reinforcing ahead of time the joy they already have?

If abiding in Jesus' love can see them through the worst event they will experience—the death of their rabbi, the Messiah—then as followers of Jesus it can see us through our worst experiences. More broadly, to abide in Jesus' love is to stand up to any horror or trouble that would invite us to abide elsewhere. To all such horrors we proclaim that we refuse to pack our belongings and abide in fear, worry, scarcity, estrangement, or anywhere else. We already abide in Jesus' love where our joy is complete. I am comforted by this news. How can I share that comfort and help widen the circle of those who abide in God's love?

God, when we face difficult days, remind us where we abide. Comfort us by your Spirit and help us include everyone in your love. Amen.

When I was ten, my older brother, who was twelve, taught me how to find the North Star. First find the Big Dipper, he would say, now follow a line from the two stars at the Dipper's end to a star at the handle end of the Little Dipper constellation. That's the North Star, and it never moves.

In today's scripture, Jesus spoke to the disciples about being a community of mutual love. He commanded them to "love one another as I have loved you." This love begins with the love of the Father for the Son, flows to the Son's love for the disciples, and then to the disciples' love for one another. In this Easter season, we celebrate that God's love shared with the Resurrection community is sacrificial, lasting, prayerful, and more. We are recipients of this love and are called in turn to share that love with others.

The stars of the Big Dipper share a unique relationship. Not only do they form an easily identifiable shape, but they help us find the North Star. The clarity of their position points in a similarly clear direction and has provided guidance to travelers for millennia.

Like the stars in the Big Dipper, all of us in the Resurrection community share a unique relationship. Jesus said, "Everyone will know that you are my disciples if you have love for one another" (John 13:35). Further, we point beyond ourselves to the one who shows us the greatest example of love, who is the true light which enlightens everyone (see John 1:9). Gloriously, the resurrected Jesus chooses us, calls us friends: "You did not choose me, but I chose you. And I appointed you to go and bear fruit." Jesus is the steadfast light of the world (see John 8:12) and points us to God.

God, keep forming us so that our mutual love is never exclusive. Help all who seek direction by us find the true light. Amen.

Love That Heals

MAY 6–12, 2024 • CHRISTINE ALLEN HOLDEN

SCRIPTURE OVERVIEW: Scripture tells us that in our lives, especially in our spiritual lives, we need to distinguish what is true from what is false. The psalmist admonishes us to follow the truth of God and flee wicked ideas. This week we read about Judas, who did not follow that advice—with disastrous results. In Acts, the apostles seek to replace Judas with a witness to Jesus who has not been led astray. In John's Gospel, Jesus bemoans the loss of Judas and prays that his followers will cling to his words. First John reminds us that God's words are trustworthy above all. They bear witness to the life that comes through Christ, whose legitimacy was confirmed by his ascension into heaven.

QUESTIONS AND SUGGESTIONS FOR REFLECTION

- Read Acts 1:1-11. How do you experience the power of the Holy Spirit in your life? How does the Spirit guide you?
- Read Psalm 1. Who are the people around you who exhibit the strength and fruitfulness of those described in this psalm?
- Read 1 John 5:9-13. How have you come to know the testimony of God in your heart? How do you live differently as a result?
- Read John 17:6-19. What helps you to sense God's presence and protection in your life?

Ordained clergy in The United Methodist Church; spiritual wellness coach and university teacher of contemplative studies and spirituality in reconciliation; committed to mentoring emerging adults and empowering new leaders; passionate about supporting those who have experienced spiritual abuse and trauma; mother of two children and delights most of all in her call to motherhood.

In a world that seems more and more committed to the notion of certainty—and more and more willing to do anything to get it—psalms like this one seem to be a certainty-seeker's dream. There it is in black and white: what is good and what is wicked. Yet this beatitude does more than draw lines of demarcation on a road map to heaven or hell.

Historically, early Judaism took a more formative rather than an informative approach to discipleship. To follow the Torah, to meditate on the Law, was a commitment to be a lifelong learner of the ways and will of God. It was a path or pattern for becoming more loving, just, and generous. It was not about memorizing the specific data points that lead to a binary definition of wickedness and goodness. It is what Jesus points people to over and over as he chooses to do what is right, especially on the sabbath. It is also what Paul refers to in 2 Corinthians 3:6 as he speaks of the *spirit* rather than the *letter* of the law. Interacting with God this way is being shaped by love, like water reshaping river rocks, rather than beating our heads against rocks for not rigidly following the rules.

The blessing of following the Torah is not in winning at not sinning. It is the gift of real life that comes when we allow ourselves to be fed by a continuous stream of God's love. The unloving ways in us will then die off because they are no longer necessary. We no longer need to hold ourselves or others to exacting standards. The energy we used to spend trying to do everything right can now be redirected toward learning how to love ourselves, others, and the world around us.

Holy God, show me what your love is like. I want to love the way you love. Amen.

Life in the community of faith isn't easy. Following Jesus doesn't make human beings less complicated. In fact, if anything, healthy spirituality points out more of our dysfunction as we become aware of what holy love really looks like. There is no idealism about this among the disciples after Judas' betrayal and tragic death. Sometimes we think that the church ought to be something it really just cannot be—free from hurt.

While we belong to a larger narrative in the eternal timeline of all things, we are very much a part of the imperfections that exist in our world. And that means dealing with the painful reality that human beings both do harm and have harm done to us. On top of this, harm that happens within our trusted spiritual circles often cuts twice as deep. After all, these are supposed to be folks who have our backs; but then we find out that they are, well, more human than we hoped they'd be.

For many, this incongruence can be so hard to reconcile that the pain is traumatic. In the case of the friends in today's scripture, Judas's death ended the relationship, piling grief upon grief. We experience a similar loss when we must disengage from harmful relationships, and in fact our loss is amplified when we find we need to disengage from the whole community. Our sense of belonging, place, and trust is deeply compromised. This kind of experience can have deep impacts on our mental and spiritual health, as well as our bodies.

It isn't a comfortable thing to allow ourselves to confront harm that has occurred within our faith community. But naming our hurts is often the first step in the path toward healing.

Loving God, thank you for seeing our hurt and knowing our need. Help us heal. Amen.

When deep betrayal and grief occur in a faith community, it can be difficult to decide how to respond. Any act of betrayal directly impacts some, but it also indirectly impacts a larger network of people. Judas's betrayal most directly affected the disciples, but it also affected the wider community. Peter's actions in this painful moment may give us some clues about what to do when shared trust has been violated.

First, Peter convenes the group. While individual counseling, pastoral care, or other conversations are essential components of healing, there is much wisdom in gathering the larger group together. The group can do the work of grief: listening to and comforting one another; reestablishing a collective identity; expressing anger, tears, or fears about the harm and its potential effect on the future of the community. It is important that people not feel alone in the process of this kind of healing. Gathering helps them stay connected.

Next, Peter names the hurt plainly and without gossip or interpretation. *Judas ratted Jesus out.* We hope our churches will be safe places; but when harm happens, it is critical that faith communities tell the truth. True healing can be built only on a foundation of honesty.

Finally, Peter helps the larger group discern a small next step. Moving on can sometimes feel overwhelming, especially when we try to look too far into the future. Peter's community urgently needed another leader, so he focused on this next immediate need. Notice they didn't leave that meeting with a detailed plan for the next year—they left with the nomination of one new leader. Moving forward from harm doesn't happen all at once.

What harm is your community facing? How can Peter's actions provide a pathway toward healing?

Wonderful Counselor, we're hurting and need your help. Amen.

ASCENSION DAY

Early in ministry, I worked with two young adult staffers, brilliant both in humor and intellect, who discovered a Jesus action figure in the church storage. Little Jesus got into all sorts of slightly irreverent mischief, being placed in different spots in the office, sometimes donning festive costumes, and each time with a message or a theme. My favorite was for the occasion of Ascension Day. After many months of these games, I arrived that day to find him strung on a pulley attached to my office door. We were in hysterics all day, as with each entrance and exit, Little Jesus whisked triumphantly skyward.

I get the sense that the disciples experienced the hand off of Jesus' physical ministry on earth as some kind of unfunny, disorienting version of "now you see him, now you don't." After all, they had come to depend on his presence in a particular kind of way. He was now taking on a variety of supernatural forms that might have had them called crazy by their neighbors if they had tried to articulate it. In addition, they still had all kinds of logistical questions. Surely it felt to them like an all-too-short period of training for an intense and important new job: They knew they were being given responsibilities and would from now forward have significantly limited access to their trainer. They accepted the invitation to participate in something larger than themselves. Yet what would that look like? And when would it happen?

The "when" of God's work in the world is often above our pay grade. But Jesus clearly orients the disciples and us toward the "how" and the "why." "You will get the Holy Spirit," so that "you will be able to be my witnesses." Where are you longing for the Spirit's power?

Come, Spirit, orient me with your presence and power. Give me words to meaningfully express your love to others. Amen.

I have long been a fan of the Wordsworth poem, "The World Is Too Much with Us." We constantly feel the strain of what living in this world can do to us. The racing pace ever bearing down, the press of consumerism and greed driving us always to hustle for more, the unscrupulous manipulation of humanity's ego resulting in dehumanization and violence, the fragility of our mortal bodies and of the planet, the broken record of competition and condemnation droning the message that says we are not enough—it is all relentlessly distressing.

But then, as if we can hear into Jesus' own most intimate thoughts, God's word reminds us that we do not belong to this world; we are planted in a much larger narrative. Jesus stirs up the memory for us that the world we experience now is one small part of something in which we find ourselves. This smaller piece is fraught with complications and imperfections to be sure—but it's not the whole story! And, although we don't know the timeline, we know that the larger story has different outcomes. When the pain of now is too much, we need to think beyond ourselves. This world is a chapter of our story but not the whole book.

As Jesus prays, he repeats the comparison. We do not belong to the world just as he doesn't. And sandwiched in between is a request that we be protected from evil. So what is the nature of the evil Jesus identifies? If we are like him, clearly his chapter in the world was not protected from harm or slander or injustice. However, it was marked by an indissoluble, persistent connection to the presence of love in the larger narrative. To participate in this love connection—re-presenting Christ to the people of the world—is to be made holy.

Eternal God, remind us of the persistence of your abiding love at work in us and in the world. Amen.

The word *religion* comes from a Latin root that means to *bind* or *connect*. This reconnecting seems at the heart of what Jesus desires as he prepares to finish the period of his life spent in human form. Jesus prays for us to have the same unity with God that he has. At first this may seem confusing. How does Jesus, who is himself fully God, compare the intense and complete level of union he experiences as a member of the Trinity to what humanity might enjoy? Yet how easily we forget that the *imago dei*, the image of God, is planted in each of us from the very beginning. We are made in God's image—God's love—and we are carriers of both.

Reconnection with God in a way that restores our knowledge and experience of the image of God in us is Jesus' greatest aim for humanity. I have come to believe that healthy spirituality will always pull us into deeper connection with God and in turn into deeper connection with ourselves, others, and God's creation. It is this binding of ourselves to God that lets us cherish ourselves, one another, and creation the way God cherishes us. Everything God has made is beloved and of sacred worth. Without this image, we are internally prone to self aggrandizement or condemnation. Externally we are likely to prefer division, hierarchies, and dehumanization because they make us feel safer and more powerful. The constant reminder that we belong to one another is the beginning of the New Heaven and the New Earth—the reconciliation of all things to God. It is in this sacred way of knowing God, ourselves, and one another that we are set free.

Lord, make us one with you, one with each other, and one in ministry to all the world. Amen.

As I engage the world outside my parish, I often hear the stories of spiritually curious skeptics and those hostile to all things spiritual. Folks frequently say that what they see when they look at the church from the outside is conflict. They see our conflict in interpreting the scripture, conflict between claimed values and actual behavior, conflict about what being a Christian legitimately entails, and conflict even with common sense. Let's face it, who would want much to do with that? We cannot really blame folks for staying an arms-length from the church.

Johannine literature pays a great deal of attention to the importance of witness, especially as a way of affirming that Jesus is real and that Jesus' reality is good news. A lived experience of the good news of Christ is so much more transformational than just hearing about it, particularly for those who are not engaged in spiritual practice or a community of faith. What is the special sauce in such an inspiring witness?

John helps us to understand that it isn't enough only to share what we have seen. Human testimony is good but can be unconvincing. And it is authoritative for those who believe to say that the Holy Spirit is an affirming witness about Jesus. But if you cannot trust that God exists yet, how helpful is confirmation from within the narrative?

When our witness takes on flesh, we become vessels of God in the world, much as Jesus himself did. This is when our testimony can truly make a difference. Jesus' life is profoundly marked by the inclusion and liberation of all of creation. Does our behavior show and tell that story? Does it reflect our words of witness? Is our life profoundly marked by love that includes and liberates?

Jesus, walk with me in the way that leads to life. Amen.

Stories of the Spirit

MAY 13–19, 2024 • KEVIN HENDERSON

SCRIPTURE OVERVIEW: This week's readings remind us of the powerful role of God's Spirit. For many Christians, the Holy Spirit is the person of the Trinity we understand the least. In the book of Acts, the Spirit empowers the apostles on Pentecost to speak in other languages and, in so doing, initiates the establishment and missional reach of the church to the wider world. The psalmist uses a wordplay on *ruach*, the Hebrew word for *breath* or *spirit*, to teach us that God's Spirit was present at the Creation and is necessary for the ongoing survival of all life. Paul writes that God's Spirit confirms that we are children of God and can approach God with confidence, not fear. Even the disciples feel uncertain about what will happen when Jesus leaves, so John provides Jesus' assurance that God will remain with them and with us through the presence of the Holy Spirit.

QUESTIONS AND SUGGESTIONS FOR REFLECTION

- Read Acts 2:1-21. How often do you take solace in praying in private? Or are you more inclined to move to take action in the public square without praying first? Which site is the more comfortable for you?
- Read Psalm 104:24-34, 35b. Where have you seen evidence of nature's resources being spent? How can you help?
- Read Romans 8:22-27. How consequential is it to you to acknowledge that God prays for us and the world? Why?
- Read John 15:26-27; 16:4b-15. What instructions do you wish Jesus had left for you?

Pastor at Sunrise Beach Federated Church, an inter-denominational congregation originally chartered as a federated church by The Presbyterian Church (USA), The United Methodist Church, and The Christian Church (Disciples of Christ); the congregation counts among its members those from every large US Protestant denomination and the Roman Catholic Church.

Waiting is hard. Waiting for God is particularly difficult, especially as the whole of creation seems to groan in pain. We hear of violence, political unrest, and injustice all around us. We witness continued degradation of the part of creation we inhabit. And we cry for and with that pain. In those moments, the redemptive work of God seems but a hope without a time-line—waiting for it with patience seems impossible. That is until we come to appreciate the analogy of labor pains signaling that we are waiting not for an ultimate end but for the birth of something new.

I'm reminded that we can also find ourselves in difficult times waiting for God to give us direction to a new path. In those long stretches when you wait for God, can you relate to the words of the author of Romans? Do you have moments when it seems you no longer know how to pray? In those moments, hearing that the Spirit's sighs are "too deep for words" is a source of comfort rather than despair.

The Spirit does not provide comfort by taking away all my questions or doubts. The Spirit does not always arrive with ready answers. Rather the Spirit comes along and intercedes for me to help me give a name to all of those hopes, dreams, and, yes, fears that I have while I wait for God's gracious and loving guidance.

God of eternity, may the Spirit come along beside me, inter-ceding to disrupt my impatience and inviting me to speak my greatest needs. Amen.

We often say that preaching should comfort the afflicted and afflict the comfortable. How often though do you think of the Spirit as the afflicter? We translate the Greek word *Paraclete* used in John's Gospel as *Advocate* or *Comforter*. And, at least at times, those are both apt. However, I can't help but wonder if *Afflicter* or *Disturber* are as—or even more—appropriate.

Jesus tells the disciples that when the Spirit of truth comes, they are to testify on his behalf. That would have been a rather disturbing prospect to me. After all, Jesus had been testifying to the truth of his transformative work in the world throughout his ministry. And very soon, he would be condemned and executed for it. He now wants the disciples to do the same? I'm not sure whether the disciples have become comfortable, but I am fairly confident they are going to be afflicted when the Spirit prompts them to continue that testimony.

I also wonder if the message to the twenty-first century church is that the Spirit of truth has come to disturb us. It is indeed an afflicting moment for those of us who have forgotten that Jesus didn't command us to grow our churches. He didn't require that we do everything in our power to maintain the status quo. Instead, Jesus commanded that we make more disciples by loving our neighbor. He even gave us parables to teach us just who our neighbor might be. Going further, he told us if we do not care for the least of these, we have not cared for him. Thankfully, he also sent the Spirit to encourage us when this hard work seems overwhelming.

God of mercy, afflict us for the hard work of following in the footsteps of Christ. Amen.

The psalmist says God "touches the mountains and they smoke." I grew up at the foot of the Blue Ridge Mountains, and we often visited the Great Smoky Mountains along the Tennessee-North Carolina border. The dense vegetation releases organic compounds that literally give the mountains a gray-ish-blue mist that hangs in the air like smoke.

As I write this meditation, I have recently returned from a stay in a mountain cabin in that area during the peak leaf season. The changing seasons remind me that the Spirit is always renewing "the face of the ground." No matter how many years elapse between visits to these mountains, I am always amazed at how perfectly they reflect the manifold works of creation. The area contains the largest population of black bears in the eastern United States and the greatest number of salamander species outside the tropics. It is the ancestral home of the Cherokee Nation, a people who have inhabited this land for over 14,000 years. Many who live in the area are descendants of those who remained despite the forced removal of the tribe in one of the darker periods in our American history.

Standing on the highest peak east of the Mississippi River on a clear morning, I wanted to sing "All Things Bright and Beautiful," echoing the psalmist with the resounding conclusion "the Lord God made them all." This year I noticed something different. The old-growth poplar trees at the summit are dying. Above a certain elevation there were no more leaves changing to the vivid reds and oranges of the mid-elevations. An exhibit highlighted the devastation being wrought by air pollution. It was a stark reminder that we too are called to renew the face of the ground. How we treat God's amazing creation has very real consequences.

Consider the way the Spirit may be calling you to the renewal of creation. May our meditations be pleasing to God!

Whenever I read this portion of John's Gospel, I try to put myself in the shoes of the disciples. Jesus has been saying good-bye for a while. How frightful it must have been! Their time with this charismatic teacher and healer—the worker of signs—is almost at its end. While scripture conveys that the disciples had a hard time grasping what Jesus was telling them, I suspect many must have considered the prospect that their work was coming to an end. Jesus was quite clear. What was to be their next move?

I suppose in some sense the disciples felt no different from followers of any other leader whose mission to change the world has come to an end, whether by retirement, death, imprisonment, or otherwise. The disciples had no way of knowing in that moment about the birth of a church at Pentecost. They could not have fathomed the impact this Jesus would have on the world for the next two thousand years.

So Jesus proceeds to tell them about the coming of the Advocate. Jesus will send this Advocate from God, and the Advocate will testify on his behalf. And then Jesus tells them that they too are to testify because they have been with him from the beginning. I think back to Andrew as he tells his brother Simon, "We have found the Messiah" (John 1:41). I wonder if he recalled that moment as Jesus said farewell.

The Spirit did indeed come from God. Do we live as those whose leader left the earth so long ago, or do we live as those who follow a resurrected Jesus who sent the Spirit among us? How we answer this question makes all the difference in and to the world.

Reflect on how the presence of the Spirit in our lives impacts who we are and how we live.

In wisdom you have made them all." This psalm sings to me of the diversity of creation and the diversity and inclusiveness of Pentecost. Everything and everyone created by God is one of God's creatures. To believe otherwise is to not be true to myself or my overarching sense of the love of God.

The earth is indeed full of God's creatures and God's creation—unique and wonderfully made. The psalmist says that when God sends forth God's Spirit, "they are created." In the Pentecost story in Acts, Peter, quoting the prophet Joel, says that all flesh shall have the Spirit poured out upon it (see Acts 2:17). Specifically, men and women, sons and daughters, young and old are included within this gift.

For centuries, we in the church have fought over who is included and who is not. We have waged religious warfare over who is worthy to serve and who is not. I have always found it hard to imagine how we can argue over race, sexual orientation, or gender identity. When God sends forth the Spirit, "they are created." Each and every one in God's creation is Spirit-filled.

Jesus erased a lot of lines during his earthly ministry. Our feeble attempts to redraw those lines or to draw new ones flies in the face of the stories of the Spirit. As we read passages like today's, we must remember that God's Spirit has the power to fill every single person on earth. Why do we continue to draw lines among those who have been created by the sending forth of God's Spirit?

Author and Creator of all, grant us the wisdom to see your Spirit in all those you have created. Amen.

I sometimes wonder if we focus so much on the bewilderment and amazement of the crowd at Pentecost that we do not contemplate the effect of the Spirit on the early believers gathered in that house in Jerusalem. In all of our focus on the converts, do we miss the work of the Spirit on the disciples?

In their fear and confusion following Jesus' death and resurrection, the disciples remain locked in the space where they feel safe. But the Spirit pushes them out into the crowds—into the new mission field for which Jesus has been preparing them. But they do not leave that house unprepared. The Spirit accompanies them. The Spirit allows them to speak in the languages of all those gathered in the crowd swarming Jerusalem, not as a flashy show of the Spirit's ability but so that the disciples and the crowd can connect and communicate with one another. The Spirit is showing the disciples exactly how their work will continue to be supported by the triune God.

I think particularly about Peter—brash, brazen Peter, who often speaks or acts before he thinks. This is the same Peter who had denied knowing Jesus. Peter, whose training was in fishing, not homiletics, delivers a sermon. He quotes scripture, preaches a captivating sermon, and reaches three thousand converts.

Part of the beauty of this story is realizing how powerfully the persuasive Spirit works through Peter and all the others who step outside their comfort zones. They have the conviction that the Spirit that Jesus promised them is there with them. We must remember the same Spirit is with us when we are challenged to reach out and see amazing things as well.

We thank you, God, for giving us the Spirit, who is always leading us in amazing new directions. Amen.

PENTECOST

Pentecost Sunday is the day Christians around the world celebrate as the birthday of the church. We read about "the rush of a violent wind" and the "divided tongues, as of fire," and we proclaim that this was the day the Holy Spirit arrived. But today also ushers in the season of Pentecost, the longest season of the church year, so we do not need to confine all our thinking and speaking about the Spirit to this one particular day. Yes, Pentecost is a specific holy day on our church calendar, but it is by no means the only day on which the breath of the Spirit is present and the winds blow.

We know from Jesus' first encounter with Nicodemus in John's Gospel that the wind of the Spirit cannot be contained to one time, place, or purpose. I like to think we glimpse the work of the Spirit—for which my favorite phrase is a "Spirit-sighting"—all the time. What a powerful spiritual discipline it is to remember the Spirit sightings we have accumulated in our lives.

A few years ago, I took a risk during a Pentecost sermon. I stepped out of the pulpit and, while making my way to the back of the sanctuary, asked if anyone would like to stand and share a Spirit-sighting from their life. I was pleasantly surprised by the number of people in our small, intimate congregation who were willing to share. Story after story detailed the extraordinary and even the ordinary encounters with the Spirit. These were spur-of-the-moment stories, many of which were decades old. Yet they were told with the freshness and excitement of a newly-experienced event!

Pentecost is a day; Pentecost moments are ever-present. As we begin this season of Pentecost, let us be mindful of the Spirit-sightings that bless our lives.

God, your Spirit blows when and where it will. Help us to experience Pentecost again and again. Amen.

God Loves So That

MAY 20–26, 2024 • M. KATHRYN ARMISTEAD

SCRIPTURE OVERVIEW: The scripture passages this week give us an opportunity to reflect on the power and majesty of God and what God's love, in its many forms, can mean for us. Through these verses, we get a glimpse of who God is and who we can be as God's disciples: purposeful; humble; strong; joint heirs with Christ; open to God's guidance; and recipients of peace, love, and eternal life. We read the account of the prophet Isaiah's vision and calling. The psalm describes our sovereign God's awesome voice. Paul declares that those who are led by the Spirit are children of God and joint heirs with Christ. In John's Gospel we read of the story of Nicodemus's visit to Jesus. Each scripture is compelling in its own way, but taken together, they illustrate the magnitude of a relationship with God that may be beyond our imagining but not beyond possibility.

QUESTIONS AND SUGGESTIONS FOR REFLECTION

* Read Isaiah 6:1-8. Reflect upon a time you were chosen for a special task. What helped you feel empowered to serve?
* Read Psalm 29. How have you experienced the glory of God? Through nature? Through music? Through art?
* Read Romans 8:12-17. What might it mean to God that you are a joint heir with Christ? What do you want to inherit from God?
* Read John 3:1-17. How has your life been reshaped by the Spirit? How do you share God's love with others? Who shares God's love with you?

United Methodist deacon and managing editor of *Methodist Review*, an academic, peer-reviewed journal. Her latest book is *Live Faith. Shout Hope. Love One Another: A Study Using Matthew's Gospel* (Market Square Publishing, 2022).

As a high school senior, I was busy planning for college but feeling cut off from my friends. One winter evening, after being snubbed by a classmate, I felt sad and full of melancholy. I felt alone and misunderstood. As I often did during such times, I went to my bedroom window and gazed up at the sky. It was an exceptionally clear night, and I could see a host of twinkling stars. The children's song, "Twinkle, Twinkle, Little Star" came to mind, and I remembered that Mozart had written that tune when he was five. I was seventeen. *What had I accomplished?* Then I felt a warmth like a soft blanket surround me. I felt God saying, "Trust me. I have plans for you." I felt so close and loved by God that I tried to hold on to that warmth, even as it slowly subsided. Yet I knew that God had spoken to me, and that thought sustained me through many hardships in the coming years. It led me into a deeper relationship with God. Even today if someone asks me what God's love is like, I think of that time when I was seventeen.

As a former therapist, I have heard many such stories. Every person who talked about God had something unique to say. Some felt comforted as I did. Some felt convicted to change. Some were healed. Some were forgiven or called to a new, higher purpose. Like Isaiah, many people have experienced God's loving presence seeing them through trials and tribulations. For Isaiah, his vision was a beginning of his prophetic vocation. And I'm sure it sustained him, even as it set his life's direction and his future relationship with God and God's people.

We all yearn to be known, understood, and loved by God. What is your story?

Dear God, we want to know you more clearly, love you more dearly, and follow you more nearly, day by day. Amen.

Edith struggled to find inner peace after the death of her child. She grieved that she could not have any more children, and she wanted her life to count for something more. Sure, she already had two great kids, but the death of her third child left an unrelenting gnawing in her gut. Then, one Sunday during worship, Edith heard the pastor say, "Do you need peace and purpose in your life? Let God use you." She quit listening after that because in those few words, she believed that God had spoken directly to her. She heard God say, "Edith, I need you to go for me. Go back to school. Then go to work helping others." Hearing God's call and acting with a renewed sense of purpose, Edith earned her master's degree and began what she considered her calling as a social worker. Edith found peace through following her purpose. She found her purpose—her Christian vocation—through accepting God's call. She knew that God loved her so that she could help others. With God on her side, how could she do anything else?

As Christians, we know that God is here for everyone—lay and clergy, young and old, saint and sinner, you and me. With all the power of heaven and earth at our disposal, how can we fail? When God asks us to go on God's behalf, the question becomes *how we will respond*.

In this passage, we see the Almighty ask Isaiah, "Whom shall I send, and who will go for us?" I can imagine an awe-struck Isaiah looking around and, seeing no one else there, deciding that the question must be for him. He could say no, but why would he? All the power of heaven and earth will back him. How could Isaiah fail to find his vocation in God's greater purpose? How could we?

Dear Lord, with you we cannot fail. Lead us forward with renewed purpose on those paths that you set before us. Help us say yes when you call. Amen.

God Loves So That

Reading Psalm 29 feels like the storm it describes. The phrases are short and punctuated with graphic imagery. Listening to the psalm, I can close my eyes and see the raging tempest that must have been bearing down on God's people. Perhaps they were calling out to God for help. But one thing is for sure: God's voice is powerful, and hearing it fills us with awe and inspires us to worship. Although God's voice can come as a whisper (see 1 Kings 19:12), this psalm asserts that the voice of the Lord is never thwarted. It always achieves God's purposes. On this we can depend. It speaks to God's steadfast loving-kindness.

What has been your experience with water? Do you live near it and enjoy water-related recreational activities? Perhaps you've had scary experiences with water that make you wary. Personally, I get seasick, so I avoid boats and water altogether. Whatever our experiences with literal water, we have all likely suffered from being tossed about by the metaphorical storms of life. During those times when noise surrounds us and the voice in our own head is yelling for help, it is reassuring that the God of the universe speaks to our needs and will bless us with strength and peace.

In Hebrew the word *strength* in verse 11 is a cognate for *security*, *might*, and *boldness*. In Exodus 15:2, strength is linked to salvation. Being blessed with strength in the context of this psalm means that we can boldly find our security in God's might. Likewise the word *peace* or *shalom* carries with it the meanings of safety, healing, and wholeness. The psalm is telling us that God's love will not only secure us but will do so in such a way that we are made whole. God cares for us so that with God we will not only survive but thrive.

Dear Lord, in life's storms you offer us strength and safety. As the hymn says, "A mighty fortress is our God." Thank you for reaching out to us. Amen.

"They will know we are Christians by our love." Christians should be known by how we put our love into action. God loves us so that we can love ourselves, others, and God. Yet this is not the way many see Christians in our world today. At best, Christians are seen as mistaken or misguided. At worst, Christians are seen as egotistical, hypocritical, and sometimes dangerous. People see what Christians do as a reflection of who God is, so our actions are important if we want people to know that God loves everyone.

In the early days of the church, people looked at Christians and questioned their behavior. The way they lived was at odds with the culture and often sparked curiosity, resentment, and even hatred. However, as the movement grew, Christians were spotted taking in babies who had been left to die. People saw them feeding the poor, treating enslaved people as equals, and being kind and generous to their persecutors. They even saw women in leadership roles. Followers of Christ were just ordinary people putting their love into action. Then as now, Christians can profess their faith and seek to engage the world while being open to others who are different from themselves because this openness lets others see the light of God's love in action through us.

Actions speak louder than words. We need to put love into action. But then we need to follow up our actions with words of explanation because without the words that explain our motives, our lives serve only as testimony to ourselves. If someone does not know why we live as we do, they may miss the fullness of a relationship with Jesus Christ that is available to all. To show God's love, we need words *and* deeds—just as Jesus used words and deeds—always pointing beyond self to God.

Dear God, let us be known as faithful followers who show our love for you by serving all of your people. Amen.

As long as I can remember, a large oil painting hung over the sofa in my parents' living room. For some reason, I loved that picture. So when my father died, Mother let me bring it home with me. Actually, she had never liked it—too dark for her tastes. But to me, it was magical, mysterious. The story goes that my father found the painting rolled up in a deserted barn while he was stationed in France during World War II. He couldn't find anyone to claim it, so he shipped it home. After the war, he framed it, and it went with him everywhere he lived after that. The painting was a part of my father's life—a part that predated me. It reminded me that you never know what treasure you will find if you take time to look. It was also a reminder that even in the darkest tragedy—war in this case—something beautiful can emerge. That knowledge also became part of my inheritance from my dad.

As children of God, we are God's heirs. Not only that, but we are joint heirs with God's firstborn—Jesus. So you might ask what we inherit from God. Like Jesus, we enjoy eternal life and fellowship with God and other Christians. Today's passage reminds us that we also inherit Christ's suffering. But in addition I hope we inherit God's approach to life, God's taking time to find and redeem the good and beautiful in every situation and person, God's steadfast loving-kindness.

My family tells me that I have my father's temperament; I'm sure I reflect his character because I spent so much time with him. Perhaps you are like some members of your family. As children of God, I hope we all reflect God's love. And we can if we spend time with God by studying scripture and serving God with our prayers, presence in worship, gifts, tithes, and our witness.

Dear God, help us reflect your steadfast loving-kindness and find goodness and beauty in others. Amen.

John tells us that Nicodemus, a leader of the Jews, secretly sought out Jesus at night so that he would not be seen. However, subsequently in John's Gospel, we glimpse "the rest of the story." John 19:39-42 tells us that Nicodemus accompanied Joseph of Arimathea to take Jesus' body from the cross and lay it in a tomb. We can only surmise that Nicodemus became a follower of Jesus, moving from following in secret to following openly.

I noticed something in the story that has completely changed my understanding. In verses 11 and 12, the "you" is plural. Jesus is speaking to a group, not an individual. I had imagined that Nicodemus and Jesus were conversing privately, since no one else is named. But now I believe that Nicodemus may have interrupted Jesus as he was teaching his disciples. Perhaps Nicodemus simply joined in to what was already taking place. But of course, Nicodemus couldn't just blend in. Ironically, he stuck out because of his unwillingness to live out his faith in plain sight.

We can compare Nicodemus's story as told in John 3 with the story of the Samaritan woman in John 4. Nicodemus is a consummate insider; the woman is a consummate outsider. Nicodemus's society sees him as righteous; the woman's society sees her as a sinner. Nicodemus comes at night; the woman comes in broad daylight—noon. Jesus speaks to Nicodemus as part of a group, but he speaks to the woman alone. Nicodemus becomes a secret disciple. The woman openly confesses Jesus as Messiah. Despite the differences, each has a part to play in Jesus' ministry.

For me the lesson is that no matter how you come to Jesus, no matter your motivation, no matter how you experience God's love, the important thing is that you come to him.

Dear God, thank you for loving us enough that you give us a part to play in your ministry. Amen.

TRINITY SUNDAY

These verses are some of the most beloved in the Bible. Many of us know them by heart. Yet we can always find more to unpack. Scholars suggest that when the Gospel says "God so loved," it may not mean that God loves us "so much," but rather God loves "in this way"—through the mighty act of sending Jesus into the world. God fulfills God's promises to heal, guide, sustain, reconcile, advocate for us. Through Jesus, God graciously puts God's love for us into action so that we, and others through us, may be blessed.

God's purpose is not to condemn but to save us, and in so doing give us the gift of eternal life. Through God's grace, we can say yes because God has already said yes to us through the embodiment of God's Divine "yes"—Jesus. We say yes to God when we hear and accept God's love for us. Consequently, as joint heirs with Jesus, we can participate in God's "yes" to the world through our acts of healing, guiding, sustaining, reconciling, and advocating for the world. Some of us might recognize those actions as referring to William Clebsch and Charles Jeckle's definition of pastoral care in their book *Pastoral Care in Historical Perspective*: We offer this care to others—our love for others—because it reflects the ways God cares for us.

Trinity Sunday provides an opportunity to see the ways God seeks a relationship with us. Through a deeper understanding of who God is and what it means to be in a right relationship with God, we can be inspired to ask what it means to be a beloved people of God. These verses can give us a starting point. As God's children, we are to love as God loves—graciously and without condemnation so that through us the world will see Jesus.

Dear God, we pray that you will give us the strength and confidence to receive others graciously, so that they too may experience your love. Amen.

Paradoxes of Embodied Faith

MAY 27–JUNE 2, 2024 • LAURA HUFF HILEMAN

SCRIPTURE OVERVIEW: In this week's readings, we'll explore seven ways that our embodiment manifests both the vulnerability of being human and the "extraordinary power" from Christ within—the treasure in the jar of clay. These paradoxes include the mysteries of being both fearfully and wonderfully made, how sickness and wounding makes us vulnerable to life-giving healing, how physical hunger opens us to the abundance of the kingdom of God, how our abandonment to sleep can reveal our hidden strengths, how true knowing includes not knowing, how aging can render us open to the "life of Jesus" within us, and how our mortality is charged with God's infinity. All these point to this paradox of faith: That which makes us feel vulnerable opens us up to the living God. As Paul says elsewhere, "In our weakness lies our strength."

QUESTIONS AND SUGGESTIONS FOR REFLECTION

- Read Mark 2:23–3:6. Who among the people in this passage fires an emotional response for you? The hungry? The hurt? The holier-than-thou? What is the feeling you carry toward each of these figures?
- Read Psalm 139:1-6 and 13-18. How does it feel to be so thoroughly known by and transparent to God?
- Read 1 Samuel 3:1-20. Have you ever had a dream or a vision that helped you sense God was unquestionably with you?
- Read 2 Corinthians 4:5-12. Has there been a time in your life when suffering helped reveal God's glory?

Certified spiritual director and dream consultant who works at the intersection of spirituality, sacred psychology, and metaphor; tends and teaches dreamwork through her practice Fire by Night and mentors at the Haden Institute and Wisdom Tree Collective; a member of Jonesborough Presbyterian Church; lives in Jonesborough, TN.

How easy it is to focus on the "fearful" aspects of our incarnation. True, the word originally meant "awesome" but to contemporary ears, the word *fearful* casts an anxious light. Accidents and health problems happen at any age, and despite our best efforts to exercise daily and moderate our intake of everything that tastes good, we know it could all go wrong in so many ways. Anyone else check out every little twinge on the Mayo Clinic website? Their alphabetical index is appallingly thorough: in the A's alone, they list 218 health crises you never thought of. O Lord, I can be so fearful. Search me and know me.

On the other hand, we are *wonderfully* made, regardless of your body parts that are breaking down or acting up. Today, you woke up, you got up, you are showing up, in all your incarnational body-mind-and-soul glory! Look at your clay-jar self in the mirror. Look yourself in the eye and grin. It is a psalm in itself to behold, to praise, and to bless your own body.

Years ago, I witnessed a body-blessing by lively, two-year-old twin sisters in my preschool class. One afternoon, Nell woke up early from her nap. "Sissy!" she called out. "My Sissy!" sang back Lizzie, instantly awake. Both scrambled to their feet. Then they proceeded to point out parts of their bodies which brought them pure delight: "Hair!" shouted one, clutching her raggedy mop and beaming at her sister. "Fingers!" called the other, her hands wiggling. "Toes! In my socks!" On it went, until Lizzie dramatically raised her shirt and shouted, "BELLYBUTTON!"

That was it, the ultimate in toddler hilarity: They collapsed in shrieking giggles that roused the room. It was totally worth it. The twins woke us all up to the holy delight in this serious business of being fearfully and wonderfully made.

You are the image of God. Check in with all your parts. Name them, grinning and thankful. What parts of you make you worry? Laugh?

I always read this story with compassion for the man with the withered hand. Not only because he has been incapacitated for some time, but because he was just minding his own business, going to the temple, not looking for drama, and then he walked into this charged situation between Jesus and the Pharisees.

Would Jesus cure him on the sabbath, wondered the Pharisees? Yes or no? You have to wonder what went through the man's mind in that instant, as the Pharisees lurked like jaguars ready to pounce.

His hand is the "clay jar" of being vulnerable to physical ailments. His weak spot is exactly where he is open to the power of the living Christ. And now, through that hand, he radiates the treasure of the healing power of God.

How might the healing increase his vulnerability?

The man does not seek healing; yet as the religious tension becomes political, he may wonder whether he's in more trouble now than he had been when the problem was just his hand. Now his clay jar—the fragile container of his embodied personhood—includes his willingness to do as Jesus asks him. Radical obedience to Christ implicates him in a situation that does not bode well with the establishment. He didn't mean to make trouble, but now there's no turning back.

As he leaves the temple, I wonder how life will be for him now. And for us, as participants in the story. What happens when a limitation is suddenly removed? What happens when life opens up in ways we don't anticipate? What choices do we make moving forward from our moment of healing, when spiritual freedom asks us to obey Christ over everything else?

Consider your own limitations, physical or otherwise. How is it that these very vulnerabilities are the place where you experience the presence and power of the living God?

Perhaps this passage is not only about Jesus' ongoing tension with the Pharisees and their recrimination for disregarding proper sabbath protocol, but also an invitation to consider ways that our clay-jar vulnerabilities set us up to notice the hidden treasure we carry.

The priest Ahimelech, when confronted with David's real hunger, responds with transgressive generosity. In his case, the clay jar of another's hunger opens him to grace. Sharing the bread of Presence with David and his soldiers is a beautiful act of compassion and practical problem-solving. (See 1 Samuel 21:1-6.)

Inspired by Ahimelech's open-handed freedom, we can respond to the literal hunger we see around us all the time, with monetary contributions, helping in the soup kitchen, and stocking the car with nutritious, easy-to-eat snacks for folks in need.

The Pharisees make compassion complicated. When they see the disciples plucking grain on the sabbath, they respond with criticism. In their case, the clay-jar act of eating when hungry rattles their own clay jars of outrage, and they become vulnerable to self-righteousness. But maybe they feel a kind of hunger too. Maybe they feel sabbath hunger, the undernourished howl of a soul that gnaws on the bones of tradition and misses the abundance of the feast at hand.

What if another's need activates our "treasure"? What if our need activates another's treasure? It is much easier to feed the hungry person before us than to tend compassionately the proud virtue that makes us vindictive.

Our clay-jar nature means we feel hunger not only for food but also for the feast of kingdom, body and soul. Perhaps we should take special notice of our vulnerability to our own clay and release the desire for perfection in grateful acknowledgment of our cracks.

Consider today your relationship with virtue and perfection. How does it serve you and others?

Every night, millions of us can't sleep. Stressed, unsettled, excited, wired, texted, and blue-screened beyond our limits, we might lie awake for hours. If this isn't you, be grateful. But the insomniacs may be onto something. Consider this: To sleep is to abandon consciousness and control and descend into the mercy of God and the weirdness of the unconscious. We are designed to do this for roughly a third of our lives. We're clay jars, indeed, lying in the dark, defenseless and drooling.

Samuel's story reminds me that often, in the scriptures and in our lives, we hear God best when we are in something like a dream state. Samuel hears his name in the night and runs to Eli, who offers one of the most insightful pieces of spiritual direction ever: "Go, lie down; and if he calls you, you shall say, 'Speak, Lord, for your servant is listening.'" Samuel learns to discern the surprising voice of the holy from the human voice of his expectations. These strengths will shape his life's work as God's prophet, priest, and judge.

Not everyone has the same story, but we all dream, and we may recall moments when the Holy breaks into our ordinary daylight times too. Eli and Samuel remind us that what we encounter in the world of mystery is more real than waking life. Maybe it's a feeling, an intuition, a prayer, tears, a task, a message, clarity in discernment, bewilderment that nonetheless is an assurance of Presence.

And here is the paradox: When we are literally limp and unresponsive is when God, in dreams, shows us our strengths. As we begin to understand the language of dreams, we learn who we really are in the eyes of God and how, over time, to grow into God's dream for us.

Do you recall a memorable dream, a vision, or a numinous moment? Spend time praying with that experience in gratitude and curiosity. What might be its significance to you now?

Holy humility is what the Pharisees lack as they try to trip up Jesus with their questions about the sabbath. When they harangue him about harvesting and healing on the day of rest, they seem to be speaking out of a deep human vulnerability: the need to manage the Mystery with rules that ironically obstruct their experience of the living God.

It's understandable. Jesus rearranges people in ways that disorient and reorient them all at once. Those of us whose clay-jar experiences are need, oppression, and bodily woe are more likely to abandon ourselves to the kingdom of God. Those of us who are clinging to illusions of control, preferring mastery over Mystery, show us another human vulnerability: a kind of jug-headed arrogance born of fear. Psychological comfort-seeking isn't evil. It's just an anxious safety need, located a tiny bit higher on Maslov's hierarchy, right above basic physiological needs like food and shelter.

That fear leads to a real problem, though: imagining that following religious rules ensures righteousness. Jesus challenges those rules with his iconoclastic truth telling: "Sabbath is made for humankind, not humankind for the sabbath." How weighty is that thought! Such knowledge is too wonderful—because it means ordinary people count more than lofty rituals.

The psalmist shows us that we have a treasure in our mud-molded minds that helps us respond to such disorientation. That treasure is simply awe. Our not-knowing shows that we know very well how to relate with God. Awe can pour out of us in poetry, in action, in silence, in the acquiescence to rule-breaking love, in gratitude and compassion—even for ourselves.

Loving God, it is so hard to be human! Restore us to sacred awe. Forgive our small-minded fear, and help us have compassion for ourselves. Show us how to release the drive to know it all and to simply trust you. Amen.

As a former English teacher, I occasionally diagram Paul's sentences just to see how he does it. Nobody but Paul subordinates clauses within clauses like that and consistently hooks readers for millennia. Today's reading is one of those passages that I'd send back with lots of red ink. He starts off beautifully, but by verse 10 he's deep in his mystic mind, juggling "life," "death," and "flesh" in layered rhetoric that perhaps only he can fathom.

So I will oversimplify. Being human means we suffer, and suffering can lead us to experience the vulnerability that invites God's presence in a new way. That is not to say God sends suffering, just that God's presence in our suffering is raw and strong and real, and it changes us.

We may not relate personally to Paul's descriptions of religious persecution, but our clay-jar bodies will certainly know the "afflictions and perplexities" of aging. Memory frays, bones become brittle, arteries harden, and every little thing is more difficult. Our independence is as precarious as our balance. We begin to feel irrelevant and unseen. And we mourn what we've lost.

What treasures could possibly open up through these vulnerabilities? How does Christ's light shine even and especially through trials of aging like dementia, fading sight and hearing, and the looming threat of the next heart attack?

I recall a family friend who was once full of vitality. Elderly and incapacitated, he spent months in a recliner while his wife and family tended him. He commented: "All I can do right now is sit here and suffer love."

To "suffer love" was the treasure of his aging body, offering a different kind of strength for those who loved him. That, I believe, is the "life of Jesus made visible in our mortal flesh."

Recall loved ones who allowed the aging process to create a life-giving vulnerability to God's presence. Is there a word or image that helps you name this quality you've witnessed? Hold it with you today.

Our mortality is charged with God's infinity.

The psalmist sings of the unfathomable sum of God's thoughts, as many as the grains of sand that cover the landscape of Israel. Here in Appalachia, what's all over the place are leaves, on gazillions of trees, endless and innumerable in their leafy, psalmic vastness.

I gaze at these trees all the time, how they change, how they stay. The tiny leaves unfurl in the spring light, shade us all summer long, then surrender to their flaming transfiguration in fall. Soon the brown leaves feed the soil for next year as the bare branches sketch winter upon the gray sky. "In your book were written all the days that were formed for me," writes the psalmist in verse 16. I imagine the pages of that book of days to be like leaves on the trees.

Whether or not we feel it, every day of our lives we are charged with the glory of God just as the leaves glow with living green in the rising sun. God's light pours through each of us all the time, and the holiness of the body shines through our skin, our eyes, our clay. It's dazzling.

The psalmist cannot quantify the overwhelming vision of God's presence in all things and continues, quiet with awe: "I come to the end. I am still with you."

"The end" is a threshold to endlessness. When we come to the end—of our efforts, of our imagination, of our lives—there is still treasure. The light of Christ's presence blazes through our earthly experience, now in our bodies, and forever.

When are you fully alive? Meditate on a moment of aliveness, and let your whole body resonate with that awareness.

Blessed to Be a Blessing

JUNE 3–9, 2024 • ALLEN HUFF

SCRIPTURE OVERVIEW: We sometimes struggle to believe in the power of a God we cannot see. The psalmist declares that God is greater than any earthly king and will preserve us in the face of our enemies. However, in the time of Samuel, the Israelites demanded a human king to lead them into battle. God was not enough for them. Paul admonishes the Corinthians not to repeat this mistake. We should not think that what we see is the ultimate reality. What we see is temporary; what cannot be seen is eternal. Perhaps Jesus is teaching a similar idea in this somewhat troubling passage in Mark. Jesus is not against family, but he is emphasizing that human families are temporary; spiritual family is eternal.

QUESTIONS AND SUGGESTIONS FOR REFLECTION

- Read 1 Samuel 8:4-20. How are you influenced by the culture around you? What helps you align your priorities with God's?
- Read Psalm 138. When you "walk in the midst of trouble," how do you remember God's presence with you?
- Read 2 Corinthians 4:13–5:1. How do you find yourself being renewed today in spite of parts of your "outer nature" that may be "wasting away"?
- Read Mark 3:20-35. Who is your spiritual family? Who do you identify as your brothers, sisters, mother, and father?

Pastor of Jonesborough Presbyterian Church in Jonesborough, TN.

In ancient cultures, it was customary for children to follow in the vocational footsteps of their parents. As the call stories of people from Joshua to Jeremiah to Jesus demonstrate, though, "spiritual leader of Israel" was an office too important to make hereditary. As with Eli's sons a generation earlier, Samuel's sons appear to have lacked the maturity and integrity to serve as judges.

Because of the enticements of power and control, kings and autocrats of all stripes have sought to design and implement some form of divine right of succession to keep their families in power. Aware of the dangers of monarchy, Samuel details the abuses that kings would inevitably employ to maintain control. Kings, says Samuel, will be a plague on Israel.

Determined to become "like all the other nations," though, Israel says, *No! OUR king would never do that! Our king will fight for us! He will make us like everyone else!*

In only twelve verses, the writer of First Samuel describes a paradigm shift, a watershed moment in the life of Israel. "They haven't rejected you," says God to a disheartened Samuel; "they've rejected me." God even acknowledges that Israel is only taking the next step in their long history of rejecting Yahweh and grasping at golden calves.

In an Old Testament theology class, I heard Walter Brueggemann suggest that, given the feckless nature of human kings, the titles of First and Second Kings should have question marks behind them. Brueggeman's point was that earthly kings seldom serve but never thwart God's purposes. Always padding around the edges with redemptive grace, God works around even the peskiest human leaders to continue the lineage of divine blessing on behalf of the creation.

God, grant us ever-deepening courage to follow and serve you and the wisdom to recognize when we forsake you for lesser gods. Amen.

Israel has disappointed Samuel. To him, the problems with elevating one person to the rank of king should be obvious enough to everyone. And as we noted yesterday, when he outlines the disturbing ways in which a king and his heirs would exploit them, the people dispute his claims, arguing that their king will make them like surrounding nations.

"That's my point!" says Samuel. "You'll be a mess, just like everyone else! And when, inevitably, you *'cry out because of the king,'* God won't answer."

The image of an unresponsive God doesn't exactly inspire faith, does it? Does Samuel realize he's making God sound like just another human king? Does that mean, then, that Israel faces the proverbial choice between the devil and the deep blue sea? (Or Pharaoh and the deep Red Sea?)

While Samuel could be puckered up on sour grapes, texts like Psalm 22, 44, and 88 do lament God's apparent distance and silence. And honestly, it's often tempting to feel as if God's presence is inconsistent at best. Nonetheless, the deeper and broader witness of scripture proclaims a Creator who remains faithful even when we do not.

The writer of Psalm 138 bears witness to a responsive and caring God. "I give thanks to you . . . I sing your praise . . . for you have exalted your name and your word above everything." Then, says the psalmist, "On the day I called, you answered me."

I trust that God desires and enjoys our faithfulness. When we both receive and share compassion in the midst of the creation "crying out" for redemption, we participate in the faithfulness of God who creates and blesses the faith community so that it becomes a blessing for all the earth.

God, we thank you for your timeless faithfulness. Help us to be your ears, hands, and heart for those who feel alone. Amen.

Psalm 138 opens with a defiant celebration. The psalmist looks at all other "gods" and sings grateful praise to Yahweh alone. Idols are the darlings of kings who devour the earth with violence and greed. Kings and their minions love these home-made gods because they can be made to bless self-serving power. And, as Samuel said, imposed power almost always imposes suffering on the creation.

Humbling himself before Yahweh, the psalmist acknowledges the creation's suffering. And he celebrates the Holy One, who does what idols cannot. Through "loyal love and faithfulness," God transforms suffering. "You encouraged me with inner strength . . . Whenever I am in deep trouble, you make me live again" (CEB). God answers us through empowerment, says the psalmist.

God's steadfast love and faithfulness create within us a willing awareness of "the lowly," that is, of the deep suffering around us. God's eyes see all who cry out for deliverance, justice, and peace. What seems apparent, too, is that while God may not aid "the arrogant" in their efforts to manipulate and exploit people and the earth, neither does God always hinder them. Maybe defiantly singing praise to God and offering joyous thanksgiving to God in the face of "other gods" are among the most authentic ways for us to experience and proclaim the steadfast love and faithfulness of God.

Praise and thanksgiving in the midst of injustice and suffering declare the confident "nonetheless" of our faith, the nonetheless of our conviction that, come what may, we trust and follow the responsive goodness and love of God.

God of grace, help us to sing to you our gratitude, praise, and trust, for you alone are our God. Amen.

In today's reading, Paul continues the theme with which he began his letter: Life may be full of troubles, but God empowers us to take each raw deal that life throws at us and to use it as raw material for blessing others.

It can be challenging, though, to see our pain as preparation for helping other people discover strength and courage through their own pain. It's kind of a next-level beatitude. Instead of receiving some blessing for pain endured, our trials transform us into bearers of blessing for the sake of others.

An uncomfortable question arises: Does this mean that God wills or even causes human suffering? "No, but God allows it" feels like a dodge. Sometimes there's just too much suffering caused by too much random violence, stubborn apathy, and downright meanness for me to give the Creator a free pass. This is where the great proclamation of the Incarnation helps us.

I'm writing this reflection during Advent, the season when we prepare ourselves for the news that God doesn't just fashion or allow creation. The Incarnation reveals that God, through the eternal Christ, has always inhabited and permeated the creation. In Jesus, God makes God's own self personally vulnerable to the same suffering and death that we, as human beings, experience. And we, humankind, cause Jesus' suffering and death. When Paul says, "The one who raised Jesus will also raise us with Jesus," he affirms the radical grace of God. For though we helped to kill Jesus, we will still be raised with him.

If God does not desire or cause human suffering, neither is there any suffering that God cannot redeem and transform into blessing.

God of grace, help us to embrace one another's sufferings so that we can discover the blessings of shared suffering. Amen.

Paul speaks of "gratitude," of "bodies breaking down on the outside," of those same bodies "on the inside . . . being renewed every day," and of an incomparable "stockpile of glory" (CEB).

"So," he says, "we aren't depressed" (CEB).

In 2018, my dad died of ALS. For years, we had watched his body breaking down. It was excruciating for all of us. And yet, throughout those years, Dad focused relentlessly on gratitude.

As a physician and a scholar, Dad was always reading, thinking, imagining. In his later years, he became an avid student of Aristotle. From that study, he began to formulate an approach to life that he called "practical thanksgiving." We heard about it—a lot. Even when he could no longer speak, he typed out his ever-evolving thoughts about practical thanksgiving.

Inspired by both Jesus and Aristotle, Dad said that what mattered was being grateful for the person before you at any given moment. He encouraged us to ask, "What is the good and right thing to do for the person in front of me right now?" To live with that question in mind, and to give it authority to shape one's human interactions, can create new possibilities for grace, for community, and for wholeness. It can create a "stockpile of glory" which offers blessing to everyone.

Dad had his moments of frustration and grief, but I never saw him, as Paul says, "depressed." Though his outward body eventually died, his inward being continues to call me to action, for he taught that faith is an embodied—an incarnate—practice of gratitude and generosity.

God of wholeness, help us to be faithful followers of Christ so that gratitude, healing, and blessing may abound. Amen.

In Mark 3, Jesus heals with authoritative abandon. Even the evil spirits recognize his authority. On a mountain with his inner circle, Jesus appoints twelve of them to serve as his apostles and grants them authority to do as he does—preaching, healing, and casting out demons (see Mark 3:13-19).

Jesus' obvious authority angers the "authorities." The only one with authority over evil spirits is the evil one himself, they say. Jesus' family gets worried, too, because so many are declaring Jesus to be "out of his mind." Claiming authority for oneself or assigning it to others involves a leap of faith, especially when the authority in question seems to replace some familiar or traditional source of authority.

Our religious context today is experiencing a transformation—much like the transformation that came with the arrival of the Christ in Jesus of Nazareth, as well as with the rise of the Roman Catholic Church, the Great Schism, and the Protestant Reformation. This current transformation feels like a regression. Spiritually speaking, there is a great deal of hunger and distress as paradigms shift and new understandings of authority emerge. Jesus made many people angry and afraid because he too announced a sweeping change in the locus of authority. Convinced that Jesus was destroying Torah-based tradition, the religious leaders condemned him as evil. But Jesus would not be tied up and burglarized by fear. He would continue his work as the prophet of grace, revealing to the world that creation itself is and has always been deeply and permanently imbued with the presence and the blessing of God's eternal Christ.

Doing God's will—on earth as in heaven—reveals our true relationship with Jesus and with the source of his authority. Authentic acceptance of our blessedness in Christ, then, is made evident in the extent to which we live as blessings to others.

God, grant us the peace to live as blessings in the midst of this world's upheavals and anxieties. Amen.

Blessed to Be a Blessing 195

When Jesus spoke of an unforgiveable sin, he uncorked a flow of questions and fears that continue today. It seems to me that the specter of God's unforgiveness has, in many ways, overridden Jesus' revelation of grace. Grace is a cornerstone of the Christian faith—or maybe grace sets God's cornerstone of love. For myriad reasons, though, Christians often distort this good news and use it to sow division. Fear, prejudice, and injustice remain symptoms of a house divided. In the chaos, we dismiss and forget Paul's witness that there is nothing in heaven or on earth that can "separate us from the love of God in Christ Jesus our Lord" (Rom. 8:38).

Such sins of division lead us to Friday. On Friday, we choose swords instead of confession, and we choose money over the presence of Christ. On Friday, we deny that we ever knew Christ, and we shout, "We have no king but Caesar!" On Friday, in blasphemous despair, we scream that the very gift of God is a demon to be crucified. On Friday, we, the beloved community, participate in the "unforgivable sin."

On Thursday night, though, Jesus says to his disciples and to us, "Listen, things are about to get tough. You're going to need something to sustain you when truth seems unbelievable, something to remind you that no matter how far you may feel from grace, you cannot go far enough to escape it. So here is bread and wine. They will not only remind you of me; this IS me." (AP)

And let this remain a mystery, says Jesus. For in receiving this gift, you receive and share *me*. Through this meal, you will know that even when you feel unforgivable, you are already forgiven. And, by the same grace, you are empowered to forgive.

Help us, O God, to receive your unfathomed grace and to live as grateful blessings in and for your creation. Amen.

On Receiving Anointing

JUNE 10-16, 2024 • KATE KING

SCRIPTURE OVERVIEW: The readings for this week look at the interaction between our humanity and divine kingdom power and the everyday anointing that can take place when we overlap with God's presence. The scripture passage from First Samuel tells the story of Samuel following the guidance of the Lord to anoint David as king. Then we have Psalm 20, a psalm of David, that was originally written as a prayer sung by ancient Israelites for their king. Our passage from the Gospel of Mark compares the kingdom of God to the sprouting and growth of seeds in order to expound on the beauty of small acts of faith. In Second Corinthians, Paul explores what it means to glorify God. Paul also encourages the reader that when we are in Jesus Christ, we are made new.

QUESTIONS AND SUGGESTIONS FOR REFLECTION

- Read 1 Samuel 15:34–16:13. How do you feel God's presence and anointing in your life?
- Read Psalm 20. What are the desires of your heart? Where do the desires of your heart overlap with God's desires for you? When do you feel as though you embody God's desires?
- Read 2 Corinthians 5:6-17. How can we make space for God in our physical body? Do you feel at home in your body while glorifying the Lord? When do you feel made new in Christ?
- Read Mark 4:26-34. In what small action is God beckoning you to have big faith? How is God inviting you into kingdom work through small steps of faith?

Spiritual director, mother, and writer who loves dancing, laughing, Christian mysticism, contemplation, and feeling alive.

In my days as a children's ministry leader at our small church in a suburb just outside Minneapolis, my favorite class to teach (yes, this teacher had favorites) was the preschool class. I loved the preschoolers' love for playing with blocks, the way they colored wildly, and the energy and awe that was cultivated as we circled up for a Bible story.

In that preschool room, it was so easily accepted that we have the love of Jesus in our hearts. We could talk about Jesus being and living in our heart. I knew most of the children understood this only in the literal meaning of the words. We created crafts symbolizing Jesus in our hearts and sang songs about it, and they envisioned Jesus physically existing within their bodies. Then somewhere along the way it became more comfortable as a metaphor. Somewhere along the journey of ministry with children to preteens, the idea of Jesus living in their hearts became just that: an idea. Nothing more than a phrase we use to talk about the nearness of Jesus.

Do we act as if Jesus actually wants to take up space in our physical bodies? Perhaps believing and acting as if Jesus actually lives inside our hearts would change the way we move about our day and the ways we interact with ourselves, God, and others. I can't help but believe we would reshape our words and deeds if we truly felt that Jesus was as close as our own internal organs, present with us as a part of our being.

What might God want to bless you with spiritually through the beckonings of your physical body? Does your body feel out of balance, in need of rest, or ignored? Is there a physical need God is longing to answer in your life that may help you to create more space for the presence of Jesus?

Lord, may glorifying you be at the forefront of our minds. May we treat ourselves with gentle compassion and honor our bodies as we remember that Jesus longs to make his home in us. Amen.

It is striking to me that Samuel hears God's voice so clearly. Samuel has a deep ability to experience and discern God's presence. He could have doubted the words, "The LORD does not see as mortals see; they look on the outward appearance, but the LORD looks on the heart," but he didn't. He heard them and made the next best choice to move toward the anointing he knew was going to happen. He could have second-guessed the certainty he felt when he saw David, but he didn't. He did as God's voice instructed, and the Spirit of the Lord came upon David.

Is there an area of your life you are waiting for God to bless? Is there a decision you are hoping will be anointed? Following God's plan can be challenging, and few of us enjoy the certainty Samuel experienced. But we can take steps toward faithful action, listening for God's direction. Perhaps today's reading can provide encouragement for you to keep going, keep making the faithful actions, and keep standing in watchful confidence. Miracles can happen when our faith in action aligns with God's will. Anointings happen. The Spirit of the Lord will land on us. Even as we wait, one thing we know for certain is that God is with us.

God has beautiful plans and a purpose for us. Perhaps that plan just needs a little more time for all involved to be in alignment. Perhaps, like Samuel, we may live with such hopeful expectation that we trust we will know our next best step will be made clear when we see it. Perhaps, also like Samuel, we will make wrong choices. In those too we can be confident that God is with us.

God, let us live in awe and joyful anticipation as we look for your anointings in our lives. May we feel faithful and sturdy enough to continue to stand in confidence until we see your Spirit come upon us and bless us. Amen.

Most mornings, I wake up to see my dog completely relaxed on his back, paws up, head tilted to the side, basically leaving me no choice but to offer him a loving snuggle. Then later, when I go to pick him up out of bed to start the day, he jumps slightly backward and adorably flops onto his back, requesting a tummy rub and extra nuzzles. As I reach for him again, he hops backward and back flops again. He does this countless times until I am reaching so far over onto the bed to grab him that I have really no other feasible option than to flop back onto the bed for one more drawn-out snuggle and belly rub session before the to-do lists and activities of the day take my focus.

His posture and positioning are beautifully welcoming and inviting. He sets himself up beautifully for me to simply enjoy his presence. It makes me wonder, *What is our posture and positioning toward God's presence?*

As we look at this story and notice the characteristics of the people receiving God's anointing, what do we notice? What individual qualities do we see in the people joining in the work of God? How can the characteristics of Samuel and David inspire us to be attentive to God's presence with us? I enjoy the images of Samuel standing in confidence as he waits on the anointed one to arrive and of David attending to the needs of the sheep.

May God find us tending to a wooly sheep or standing with our feet grounded and shoulders rolled back in confident anticipation as we wait for God's blessing.

May your ever-hovering presence, Lord, find us in a position of surrender and expectancy as we move about our purpose in the world. Amen.

The twentieth psalm stands out from the ones leading up to it. This psalm is written to be sung on behalf of the king in preparation for battle. It makes the psalm come alive to me to think of it as this back-and-forth between a group of people and their king. It is attributed to David, the same David we just read about in First Samuel, who was anointed and chosen by God to be king.

The chant-like use of the word *may* in this psalm stands out to me. It feels like a confident yet humble begging to God: *May* is a request, in contrast to the more absolute *will*. The word *may* in this context feels like a yearning to meet God. It is as if the worshipers in this psalm are trying to pull God's presence down into their own existence.

This psalm is complicated, though, as it is understood to be written and sung in preparation for battle. That understanding leads to the question: Where does God's desire reside within violent battle? I wonder if perhaps these worshipers didn't know either, and so they were doing their best to pray for God's presence to show them the way, hoping their king will be led into God's mysterious presence. In response to this prayerful song, the king replies, "Some take pride in chariots and some in horses, but our pride is in the name of the LORD our God."

When we fall in love with the Lord, our focus can shift from looking for God's will to embodying God's will. When our desires overlap with God's desires, we can trust there will be kingdom success because we are standing in the presence of God, knowing God in Jesus redefines our understanding of victory.

God, you are longing to join with us in cultivating love and healing on earth. May we courageously move forward in union with you, aligning ourselves with love. May we surrender our actions to the ever-moving undercurrent of love. Amen.

On Receiving Anointing   201

On the one hand, this parable feels like an invitation into purposeful work with the Lord. The man in the parable takes on the work of scattering seeds without knowing of what will take place. Any gardener knows the hope and trust required in planting seeds. We may not know exactly how the flower comes from the small seed, but we do know that the flower will never grow if we don't plant the seed in the first place.

On the other hand, Jesus is encouraging us to take the pressure off ourselves. While we do have responsibility to scatter the seeds, we are not responsible for what happens once those seeds are scattered; that is God's work. We can make life-giving contributions to God's kingdom while also remembering the growth and success of it are not in our hands. This parable reminds us of the importance of divine power over human hustle.

When attempting to do my best to balance ministry and home life, I occasionally get overwhelmed by all I have to do. Surely, you too have felt this—overwhelmed by the road ahead and wondering how everything can possibly work out when there is just so much to be done.

Thinking about the kingdom of God as a scattering of seeds feels like a practice in non-attachment and deep surrender. Jesus is inviting us to join in purposeful work for God's kingdom and then to release that work into the ever-moving love of God. Jesus is calling us to show up, share our faith in alignment with our gifts and energy levels, and then release the outcome to bloom in God's time.

God, we faithfully release our love into the world and then, in surrender, trust that your kingdom is in motion. Help us remember that sometimes we can do more with less when we trust in your power. Amen.

My mom and I always get excited when it's foggy outside. We're aware that this is unusual: Most people prefer sun and warmth to the cold and mysterious ambiance of fog. But for us fog has become a reminder because we see the fog as an acronym to *focus on God.*

The cold and mysterious feeling fog imbues can turn spirits down for the day. But I think fog is beautiful *because* it makes it difficult to see far out in front of us. Fog forces us to stand in the space we currently inhabit. It prevents us from getting out ahead of ourselves or from looking too far back. It welcomes us into being present with eyes wide open to our immediate surroundings. It's as if the heavens are, almost quite literally, hovering down even closer on foggy days to say, *I am here with you, won't you stay with me and focus on what matters most?*

Sometimes our lives can get overwhelming with the abundance of life's noises: the noise of opinions, ideas, or choices. There are countless routes and directions in life to choose from. Perhaps anointing and true success in God lie in the narrow and small spaces we find where the heavens seem to descend and almost touch the earth and bring our attention to the present moment.

The kingdom of God is like a mustard seed, Jesus said. When we are able to narrow our focus to small but certain acts of faith and love, they will grow to be so big that birds of the air will come to enjoy their shade.

God, we praise you when we are present with our small but certain immediate surroundings. May our focus on what's right in front of us feel like heaven hovering, and may our feet feel steady and secure on the narrow yet true path of life. Amen.

As a result of Jesus' death on the cross, we are able to let our false selves die as well. We don't have to look to the things that give our false selves life, but we are made new and can live as our true selves rooted in the truth of the Cross. We don't need to be concerned with how our true selves look in the world but rather focus to how alive we can be in our new lives with Jesus. The same old gospel is made new within us everyday.

Think back about your previous week, scanning with your mind's eye or moving through the days with your heart open. Was there a time that you felt you were made new in Jesus? In what moments did you feel a sense of true oneness with others or a freedom to live out your purpose? How does feeling alive resonate in your body? Can you sense Jesus with you in those moments?

When did you feel stuck in old ways of shame or rehearsing old sins and mistakes? Can you sense any spaces throughout the week where you held on to control of an outcome or felt unnecessarily defeated when there was a lack of worldly affirmation? What did you notice about how that felt in your body? How did that impact your being? Without judgment, consider your physical reactions to your experiences.

God is calling us to be attentive to the ways we show up in the world. Our showing up affects our ability to connect with ourselves and to be of service to others and to God. We can work to release ourselves from attachments to the false self so that we may live truly free. And in this feeling of freedom, we may even sense our friend Jesus holding our hand and cheering us on.

God, enliven us to step into our new life with Jesus, and embolden us to receive your invitation and anointing. Amen.

On Receiving Anointing

An On-Time God

JUNE 17–23, 2024 • GABBY CUDJOE-WILKES

SCRIPTURE OVERVIEW: When I was growing up in the church, there was a saying that I always heard from the older members: "God may not come when you want, but God's always on time." In 1994, gospel recording artist Dottie Peoples popularized this mantra in her song, "On Time God." The idea that God might not come when we want God to—but that God is never late—was a theological declaration of the *kairos* time of God. Though we may not be able to name when God will show up, and though we may even be disappointed because God did not show up when we had hoped, we still have a blessed assurance that God will come when we are most in need. We know that God will come right on time. In our passages this week we look at circumstances of dire need and experiences of an on-time God showing up just when it seemed all hope was lost.

QUESTIONS AND SUGGESTIONS FOR REFLECTION

- Read 1 Samuel 17:1a, 4-11, 19-23, 32-49. Have you ever walked into the middle of a battle that you didn't anticipate? What did you do? How did you respond?
- Read Psalm 9:9-20. When times are hard, how is your trust? On a scale of 1 to 10, how are you doing with trusting God in this current season of your life?
- Read 2 Corinthians 6:1-13. What would it mean for God to show up for you? What would that look like?
- Read Mark 4:35-41. How is your faith in times of turmoil? How do you engage God for help when you believe God is able?

Pastor, leader, innovation strategist and author; founding co-lead pastor of The Double Love Experience Church in Brooklyn, NY; has been featured in *Essence, Forbes,* and *The New York Times*; co-author of *Psalms for Black Lives: Reflections for the Work of Liberation* (Upper Room Books, 2022).

There are times when the enemies we must face have organized against us. We've all heard the saying "the enemy of my enemy is my friend." Sometimes that's not an exaggeration. Sometimes those who are against us are organizing themselves and others, and a battle is on the way. That's what we see in our text today. The Philistines are on Judah's property and are organizing themselves for battle. They are readying themselves for the fight.

But here is the good news. When you know that a fight is coming, you won't be blindsided. When you're clear that you're in a battle, you're least likely to get sucker-punched. Sometimes the greatest gift our on-time God can give us is clarity. A battle is coming, they are organized, and they are on your turf. So ready yourself for battle.

What a gift it is to have a heads-up that a battle is on the way. Yes, it may be scary. Yes, it may be daunting. Yet the clarity allows you to strategize. This on-time God that we're exploring this week has the capacity to warn us before times get hard so that we can ready ourselves. I'm not going to lie to you. In the times we live in right now, battles are coming. As politics get more partisan, the digital divide widens by the day, public health continues to be in crisis, and our personal and professional lives seem to change more than we care to admit, there are yet battles we have to face. But knowing the battles are coming gives us the fortitude to face them with courage.

God, help me not to ignore the battles that I may have to face, but rather help me to prepare. Give me eyes to see those who mean me well and eyes to see those who mean me harm. Grant me a deeper appreciation for the gift of knowing how to prepare. Amen.

Now that we've learned how to thank God for the heads-up of battle, our next lesson is to assess what we are facing. Too often our fear of the unknown keeps us from preparing and taking proper action. You know how it is: You don't want to get on the scale at your annual physical because you don't want to see how much weight you've gained. But the weight is there, and if you do not face it, you'll miss the opportunity to care for your own health before it is too late.

In the same way, once we perceive that we are about to face a battle, we often don't want to know too much about it. Once we know what we are dealing with, we have no choice but to move into action. But our passage today says exactly what the Israelites are facing: how big the enemy is, what weapons he is using, where he is from, what armor he is wearing, and more.

It was critical for the people of Israel to assess Goliath before determining who would fight on their behalf. Likewise in our own lives, we must pause to assess the opposition around us. If we do not, we might fight with the wrong tools. When life sends trouble your way, you must assess exactly what that trouble is, where it comes from, what power it has over you, and what it's connected to, before you try to fight it. If you fight without an assessment, you will have no idea if you're winning or not because you do not fully know what you are up against. I encourage you to do some bold assessments. What are you truly up against? What tools do you need to overcome the challenges you are facing?

God, give me the boldness to fully address the issues that are facing me. Before I try to fight my battles, help me to slow down long enough to assess. Then grant me wisdom and discernment so that I can respond accordingly. Amen.

Whappens when you've been called into battle? Perhaps your children have asked you to fight on their behalf. Maybe it's your co-workers. What happens when you are minding your business and someone asks you to lend them a hand in what they are facing? How do you handle it? What do you do? In today's text, David is being obedient to his father, Jesse, and going where his father says to go. David's obedience lands him right in the middle of a fierce battle between the Philistines and the Israelites. There David stands as the king and his army fights with everything they have to beat their opponents.

Sometimes we inherit battles that are not our own. The weight of showing up for someone else to help them battle what is oppressing them is no small matter. We should never take battle lightly. No matter who wins, battle takes its toll on everyone—victors and losers alike. Your favorite athlete who wins the championship of their sport might be the number one player in their league, but they still endured a battle to get there. They still have sore muscles and loss of breath, even in their victory. Battle costs something. It costs us all something.

So when you find yourself like David, brought into a battle that did not begin with you, don't forget to pray for divine endurance and protection. You will need it. But also remember that if God has called you to it, God will see you through. Our on-time God knows exactly when to tag you into this relay race of life. We need you. We need your tenacity. We need your commitment. We need your voice. Stay in the battle. When we fight righteous battles, we will come out victorious.

God, as I pick up the battles that those before me left, I ask that you strengthen me for the journey. Help me to make them proud and to advance your cause toward liberation. Amen.

When you fight, you have to do it your way. Life has prepared you for the things you are facing right now. Like David, while you may not have faced this particular battle before, you've faced some things in your past. You have a good track record, and you've learned how to walk with God along your journey. Don't ever try to show up as someone else; God has called you just as you are.

In this passage, we see Saul kindly trying to offer David his armor. But David is clear that he must fight Goliath his way, in his armor, with his tools. This is not stubbornness—this is clarity. David knows how God has empowered him to be victorious before, and David endeavors to bring that same kind of victory to this battle. David has built up a trust language with God, and therefore David has to handle this in the way that God is leading him.

Trust your history with God. Trust the ways that God has strengthened you. Trust the ways that God has spoken to you. Your trust is critical and directly connected to your victory. David cannot win without trusting that the same God who kept him while he tended his sheep would keep him against this Philistine. In your own life, you cannot win without trusting God either. Our ability to trust the on-time God that we serve is what gives us the capacity to face the giants in our lives that want to take us out.

There are giants among us that desire to keep us in our place. But when we trust our history with God, we know that God has the final say. God has the last word. And God will be our protection and our provision.

God, show me my past wins, reveal to me my best tools, embolden me for the next journey, and protect me along the way. Amen.

Through the story of David and Goliath, we have encountered the ways God leads us in battle. The on-time God that we've been talking about all week has continued to show up for us. Whether by alerting us to trouble, slowing us down to assess our problems, strengthening us to step into battles that others began, or giving us the confidence to fight it our way, God has been good. This psalm brings us into that kind of reflection. It's critical for us, in the midst of the busyness of life, to slow down enough to marvel at all the ways God has been good to us. God has been our safe and strong place. God has been our refuge and our road map.

This psalm also reminds us why we encounter battles in the first place. Any time we are challenged, it is because the world's desires are in conflict with God's desires. As God's people, we must stand up to the oppression, trouble, and affliction that we and others encounter in this world. Our battles are not for our own personal desires and needs, but for God to be victorious. And when we fight for God, we can trust in God's protection and guidance.

Because of these things and more, God is worthy of our adoration. We are all guilty at one time or another of forgetting to pause to thank God. Yet a simple act of gratitude can rightly align our entire way of life. In times of trouble and in times of joy, God is right here with us. The more we remember how present God is, the freer we become. You can't help but move freely when you know you have the protection of an on-time God.

Thank you, Lord, for always protecting me. Remind me who and what I am fighting for. Thank you for your grace and mercy that sustain me. Thank you for loving me as you do. Amen.

As we near the end of our week focusing on an on-time God, it is a good time to reflect on how we respond to God in return for God's faithfulness. Because God has shown up for us time and time again, it is only right that we show up for others. If we aren't careful, we can get caught up in receiving from God, thanking God, and letting it end there. But the true way to honor what God has done in our lives is to make the way easier for somebody else. We honor what God has done for us by helping others.

In his letter to the Corinthians, Paul is calling for this church to respond to God's showing up by showing up themselves. In our calling to advocate for God's work in the world, we must be attentive to what God is doing and ready to act with God. The long list of ways in which "we have commended ourselves" tries to cover any possible situation, reminding us that our ability to point others to God is constant and never-ending.

Imagine this: You might be the embodiment of the on-time God for somebody else. Your showing up might be the answer to someone's prayer for help. This passage reminds us all that we have standards to uphold and ways of being to embody in the world. Folks are looking to encounter God, and sometimes the closest they get to that is encountering God in us. If they were to encounter you, what would they find? What assumptions might they make? Would they walk away better? God continually shows up for us. How do we show up for others?

God, I want to honor you by engaging people how you engage me. Teach me to embody more of your characteristics. Help me to be the "on-time" support that someone else needs. Amen.

When the storms of life hit our doorsteps, how do we react? If we know that God is with us, why do we panic? It seems so logical that if Jesus is present, we have nothing to fear, and yet our humanity gets the better of us in times of crisis. When things get suddenly bad, we often forget how present God has been.

It's important to note that we react differently when we find ourselves in crises we didn't expect compared to crises we knew were coming. There are times when God gives us a heads-up that we are about to face a storm, but there are other times when chaos and calamity surface seemingly out of nowhere.

How do we remember that we still serve an on-time God when God seems late to our crisis? How do we handle the storms we face like the one in today's text? Many of us would think that because Jesus is there, we shouldn't have a storm in the first place. We must be careful, though. We cannot assume that we will be without trouble because we are faithful Christians. Trouble is not an indication that God has left us. Sometimes trouble finds us and Jesus is right there, waiting to see how we will react.

What storms are raging in your life right now? What is your faith telling you? Is it reminding you that Jesus can calm the storm? Is your faith reminding you to pray all the more? In times of unexpected crisis, we have to talk to ourselves. In the direst storms of our lives, we have to remind ourselves that God is still with us. God has not left us. God still has the power to calm the raging storms in our lives.

God, I ask that you make me attentive to your presence in my life, even when life gets hard. Let me never forget that you are in my boat. You are with me. Amen.

An On-Time God

The Grace of God Changes Us

JUNE 24–30, 2024 • CHUCK KRALIK

SCRIPTURE OVERVIEW: David is remembered in scripture as a mighty king and as a great poet. Many of the Psalms are ascribed to him. In Second Samuel we find a song of lament over Saul and Jonathan. Saul was violently jealous of David, yet David still honored Saul as God's anointed king. Jonathan, Saul's son, was David's best friend. David bemoans Israel's loss of these leaders. The author of Psalm 130, although probably not David, appeals to God in David-like fashion. The Gospel reading shows the power of a woman's faith. In Second Corinthians, Paul deals with practical matters, appealing to the Corinthians to send promised financial help to the believers in Jerusalem.

QUESTIONS AND SUGGESTIONS FOR REFLECTION

- Read 2 Samuel 1:1, 17-27. What part does music play in your prayer life? Do you sing both songs of lament and songs of praise?
- Read Psalm 130. When have you cried out to God from the depths of your despair? What was God's response?
- Read 2 Corinthians 8:7-15. How do you maintain your eagerness to practice your faith?
- Read Mark 5:21-43. What has been your experience of God's healing?

Pastor at Byers Avenue United Methodist Church in Joplin, MO; loves spending time with family and friends.

Saul and Jonathan—in life they were loved and admired, and in death they were not parted. They were swifter than eagles, they were stronger than lions" (2 Sam. 1:23, NIV).

These are only a few of the words spoken by David in his lament at the death of his friend, Jonathan, and his predecessor, Saul. David's lament has been taught throughout the ages to the people of Judah in honor of these fallen heroes of the faith. David's words seem fitting when one remembers his friendship with Jonathan. But why does he include Saul?

David had spent much of his life on the run from King Saul, fleeing for his very survival. To say that the relationship between David and Saul was strained would be a gross understatement. Saul viewed David as a threat to his kingship and strived to have him eliminated. And yet David honored Saul in his death. How could this be? Perhaps David was able to compartmentalize his feelings concerning Saul. Maybe he found a way to separate the king from the man. In any regard, David's relationship with King Saul provides us a lesson.

Many years following the deaths of David and Saul, Jesus came onto the scene, hailed as the son of David (see Matthew 21:9). He taught radical ideas, like "Love your enemies and pray for those who persecute you" (Matt. 5:44). He commanded his followers to turn the other cheek (Matt. 5:39). His life exemplified the way to love those who wish you ill: Even as he was dying, Jesus asked that God forgive those who were killing him (see Luke 23:34).

David was certainly not perfect, as we will see in future readings. But perhaps David, in his dealings with Saul, had some foreknowledge of the teachings Jesus would later make clear. At the very least, David demonstrated the grace of God that changes us to be loving of all.

God, teach me to love my enemies as Christ loves me. Amen.

There is some question around the authorship and background of Psalm 130. Many think that this psalm was written by David in response to the constant pursuit he experienced from King Saul. Another conjecture is that it is David's cry of repentance, perhaps for his sins against Bathsheba and the resulting murder of her husband Uriah. In any regard, Psalm 130 is a demonstration of the sorrow one might experience over sin and the assurance of God's compassionate mercy and grace.

The "depths" the psalmist speaks of may be of the author's own making. But whatever has led him into these pits of despair, there seems to be no way for him to get out of them through his own efforts. The psalmist realizes that "with (God) there is forgiveness" (NIV).

Psalm 130 reminds me of Psalm 139, where the psalmist states, "Where can I go from your spirit? Or where can I flee from your presence?" Truly, there are no heights or depths that cannot be reached by God's amazing grace!

This undeserved grace, as experienced by the psalmist in Psalms 130 and 139, can be experienced by each of us today. Regardless of the pit of despair we find ourselves in, God's grace is indeed sufficient for each of us. God's love finds us where we are, but it does not leave us in the depths. We echo the psalmist's words: "there is forgiveness with [God]."

Dear God, thank you for your forgiveness. Thank you for finding me and lifting me up again that I may serve you gladly. Amen.

In the second half of Psalm 130, the psalmist takes a seemingly submissive posture in waiting for God to respond in this time of need. Waiting is often thought of as a passive act. In actuality, however, waiting for God requires participation. We must engage with intentional obedience, attentiveness, and surrender—all experiences that have the potential to transform us. Perhaps this is the very reason the psalmist conveys this particular attitude in these few verses.

Indeed, it would be foolish for someone to wait for something they think is impossible. For example, no one would wait patiently for a train if there are no tracks. Likewise, it would be preposterous to wait for December 32nd when no such date exists. We wait for things we believe can happen.

The psalmist waits on God knowing that God truly exists. God is not distant, but faithfully present. God is not aloof, but caringly attentive to every need. God is indeed for us and is never against us.

And so, like the psalmist, we wait for God. Like the nation of Israel, we "hope in the LORD! For with the LORD there is steadfast love, and with him is great power to redeem." Our waiting for God is always worthwhile. When we show up in our waiting, we do not passively sit back; we become actively attentive to the ways God is transforming us into God's people.

Dearest Lord, thank you for providing the solution to my waiting and the answer to my questioning. Thank you for Jesus, my Savior and friend. Amen.

One way to understand Jesus' earthly life, death, and resurrection is sometimes called "The Great Exchange." It is the theological doctrine that equates the crucifixion of Jesus to the undeserved gift of righteousness for the believer. The idea is that a trade took place at the cross of Christ some two thousand years ago when Jesus took our sins and gave to us his holy and perfect righteousness. And then by his example we can give ourselves for others.

Paul certainly sees an exchange in his summary of the story of Christ in this verse. In this letter to the Corinthians, he frames it monetarily, as he is in the middle of urging the Corinthians to collect money for the Christians in Jerusalem. So he reminds his readers of the "riches" Christ gave up in order that we, his followers, might gain those riches.

Why would Jesus do such a thing? Why would he go to such great lengths to suffer and die to save us? Only love would do such a thing. "God is love" (1 John 4:8), and Jesus is one with God. It is therefore at the very core of Jesus' DNA to love unconditionally and to sacrifice radically. And so Jesus made the exchange with us.

Paul reminds the Corinthians of the grace they have received through Christ's actions and the way God calls them to respond. When we understand the overflowing grace that we experience as a result of Christ's love for us, how can we respond with anything but overflowing grace for others? The call to offer sacrificial love to one another is not a requirement to receive such grace from God, but a natural response. Each of us should be eternally grateful for the exchange Jesus made with us, for by his grace we are forgiven and free and can respond with nothing less than Christ's love for others.

Dear Jesus, thank you for your unconditional love. Help me to respond by sharing your love with others. Amen.

In today's text, the apostle Paul gives some practical instruction concerning the relationship between faith and good works. While faith in Christ is the ultimate avenue by which we are saved, our faith should show itself in doing good. Paul's prescription for the Corinthian church—and, in turn, for us—is that they would excel in stewardship through generous giving. Such giving proves to be one of the more difficult areas of Christian obedience.

Paul uses the phrase "grace of giving" (NIV) to describe his request of the Corinthians. Indeed, Christian giving flows from an outpouring of God's grace in Christ. In other words, when people experience the freedom of the gospel, they are motivated to give back in all areas of life. Rather than a works-based command, generosity is a gift in which Christians participate.

Moreover, the Corinthian church's obedience in this matter of stewardship will motivate others to do likewise for the common good of all the believers. Paul says, "Your plenty will supply what they need, so that in turn their plenty will supply what you need. The goal is equality" (NIV).

What a profound ideal—equality among Christian believers! Surely each of us is equal in our need for forgiveness, found through a relationship with Jesus. Likewise, each of us is equal in our deliverance from sin through the cross of Christ. May we truly "excel in this grace of giving" (NIV).

Dear God, thank you for the grace you extend through Christ. Help me to view giving as a gift in which I am privileged to participate. Amen.

Jairus' daughter's illness and subsequent death all happened so rapidly that Jesus, it would seem, had not acted quickly enough. "Why trouble the teacher any further?" Jairus's family and friends asked, their doubt leaving little room for faith. But Jesus told Jairus, "Only believe." For Jesus knew what he was about to do.

When Jesus arrived at Jairus's house, a crowd had already gathered there. These mourners were inconsolable and stricken with grief. When Jesus told them that Jairus's daughter was only sleeping, their cries of anguish turned into rumbles of laughter. *What a foolish thing for Jesus to say!* they likely thought to themselves. Jesus soon entered the girl's room accompanied only by Jairus and his wife and the disciples. The doubters and disbelievers had already been put out of the house. Their disbelief would not interfere with the miracle that was about to take place. Soon, the little girl would be healed.

At times, we too must dismiss the doubters. Otherwise, their second-guessing, cynicism, and skepticism will not allow us the room to do what is necessary. Our ambition and our dreams will be undermined by naysayers if we allow them to stick around.

Who are the doubters in your life? Who are the whiners, the wailers, and the laughers that you need to put aside? Keep them from deterring your dreams. Do not let them sway your faith.

Believe that Jesus can do what would otherwise seem impossible and that he can work through you to accomplish great things. Do not doubt his faithfulness, and do not underestimate your abilities. Believe that God can do miracles through you.

Dear Jesus, thank you for your miracle-working power. Help me to put aside those who would doubt you. Help me to believe in you always. Amen.

Jesus knows when we reach out to him in faith, and he is never too busy to provide his healing touch. Such is the case of the sick woman in today's Gospel reading.

Jesus has just learned that Jairus's daughter is sick and needs Jesus' attention quickly. But he is interrupted by a woman with the issue of blood. The status of the unknown woman contrasts with that of Jarius: She doesn't even receive a name. As a ritually unclean, otherwise unknown participant in the story, her audacity in reaching out and touching the clothing of Jesus is shocking. Surely Jesus doesn't have time for such matters. Certainly he does not care about her in this moment.

Still, the type of faith she demonstrated is the very model of faith by which Jesus would have each of us live. The woman thought to herself, *If I but touch his cloak, I will be made well*, and indeed she was.

At times, Jesus reaches out to us and intervenes on our behalf, as he does in raising Jairus's daughter from the dead. Other times, Jesus waits for us to reach out to him by faith. In either case, Jesus has the power and the compassion to heal us. Sometimes, healing takes place in this life in miraculous or conventional. Healing also occurs in the next life, in heaven, where "death will be no more, mourning and crying and pain will be no more" (Rev. 21:4). Whether we experience physical or spiritual healing that sustains us in this life, we can rest in the knowledge that Jesus is with us, responding to our needs. He may not respond as we want, but the Gospel reading shows he responds as we need.

Jesus, thank you for providing the healing we need. Thank you, even more importantly, for your presence with us, no matter the outcome. Amen.

Empowered by Grace

JULY 1–7, 2024 • SARAH MCWHIRT-TOLER

SCRIPTURE OVERVIEW: The readings from the Hebrew scriptures this week celebrate Jerusalem, the capital of the great King David, who united the ancient Israelites and built up the city. The psalmist praises Jerusalem using the image of Zion—a name used for earthly Jerusalem but also a gesture toward a future day when God's people will abide in a heavenly city. In Second Corinthians, Paul explains that even though he is an apostle, he struggles like everyone else. Speculation surrounds the "thorn" that plagued Paul; but his point is that when he is weakest, God is strongest. In Mark, we see God's power working through Jesus, who sent out others to expand God's healing work.

QUESTIONS AND SUGGESTIONS FOR REFLECTION

- Read 2 Samuel 5:1-5, 9-10. What qualities of leadership are important in this reading? How do those qualities square with your experience with those in power?
- Read Psalm 48. Bring to mind a place where you experience God's presence. What is it about that place that makes you especially aware of God's presence?
- Read 2 Corinthians 12:2-10. When have you experienced weakness becoming a source of strength and power?
- Read Mark 6:1-13. When have you discounted someone because of your assumptions about them?

Ordained deacon and Pastor of Community Life at Connell Memorial United Methodist Church in Goodlettsville, TN.

I have a dear friend who is a chronic over-packer. His wife and I enjoy laughing together as they prepare to go on trips. Recently, they were preparing for an overnight trip to see a concert, and I got the packing report: He'd laid out two different pairs of jeans, two button-down shirts, a couple of pairs of shorts, a handful of T-shirts, the sandals he would wear on the plane, a pair of sneakers, and a pair of boots. He is always prepared for every weather scenario and for any social event.

The Gospel of Mark highlights how little the disciples knew about what their lives would be like as followers of Jesus. In this passage, Jesus empowers the disciples to go out and do his work in the world. However, the details are pretty sparse. They are instructed not to take anything with them—no food, no bags—just their staffs, a pair of sandals, and a tunic.

The amount of trust they had in Jesus must have been staggering: They willfully left not only their earthly possessions behind but also their expectations about what their lives would be. Can you imagine having so much trust in God's calling on your life that you would let go of your five-year plan? Can you imagine Jesus calling you up right now, saying it was time to go and that you need nothing for the journey? What would you do?

Jesus empowered the disciples to be his servants in this world through his teachings, through his guidance, and through his love. Still today, Jesus is empowering us to do the same work—to work for love and justice in the world right now—so that earth becomes a little bit more and more like heaven.

God, empower us to do your will on earth. Invite us into your work of transforming hearts and ultimately into transforming the world. Amen.

Tennessee, my home state, released a new state license plate in 2022. The old plate showcased the rolling hills that meet the Appalachian Mountains in the eastern part of the state. The new license plate is stark in its simplicity. It is solid navy blue with an outline of the state in the top center and a recognizable piece of the state flag in the middle.

Here's where things got tricky: Two versions of the license plate were approved. Around the center of one of the plates are the words "In God We Trust." You can imagine that some people were delighted by being able to proclaim their trust in God on their state-issued license plates, and you can also imagine a similar number of people were enraged by how closely this designs dances near the line of the separation of church and state.

Psalm 48, upon a quick reading, seems like a patriotic psalm. Its grand descriptions of Mt. Zion, the holy city, are fit for singing in a crowd at a sporting event. With all this grandeur, it is easy to lose focus on why Zion is so blessed. The holy city is worthy of adoration and celebration, but the psalmist is careful to give praise not to the place itself but to God.

When the Hebrew scriptures write about Jerusalem or a holy city, very rarely does this refer to the physical city alone. Rather, the holy city is a metaphor for God's people who have been saved over and over again from destruction by God's grace and love. That is why the psalmist praises God and reminds the reader that great indeed is God who fashioned this new creation through a vision of steadfast and abiding love for God's people. God is the one in whom we trust, whether we display the sentiment on our license plates or not.

Almighty God, I put my trust in your power and humbly receive your grace. Remind me that my security, my comfort, my strength are in you alone. Amen.

Last fall, my family and I visited Rapid City, South Dakota, on a bit of a whim. The plan was to see Mt. Rushmore, hike in the Badlands National Park, and see the herd of bison in Custer State Park. On the way from our hotel room to Mt. Rushmore, we stopped at a small building on the side of the road with flashing neon signs—The National Presidential Wax Museum. As we toured, it was fascinating to see the background scene chosen for each wax figure as the most consequential moment in each president's term. I learned that since the beginning of the "television era," presidents have gotten taller and taller. Since 1981, there have been only two presidents under six feet tall, and both were only shy by half an inch.

When David was anointed king, Israel's ruling by a king was still quite a new phenomenon. In fact, when Israel's people demanded a king to match their neighboring kingdoms, Samuel was quick to respond that God was the true authority over Israel, not any kind of flawed man. By biblical accounts, Saul fit the bill of the strong authority figure that we, as humans, seem to be innately drawn to.

David was a different kind of leader. David was no world-worn soldier with a strong fist and a stronger voice. He was a shepherd, a musician, a poet, and he challenged the idea of what it meant to rule. Instead of the war-king, David was the shepherd-king, modeling God's own relationship with God's people. Instead of wielding power over us, God gathers us gently, like a shepherd leading his flock to safety.

As you might already know, David was no perfect ruler. He struggled with the temptations of the world, but God still empowered David's leadership through God's grace, freely given to this shepherd-king.

Holy God, shepherd me into your loving arms, encouraging me to follow where you lead me by your mercy and grace. Amen.

On the most recent election day, we took very seriously introducing our four-year-old to our civic duty of voting. She came with me before school and went with my spouse after work to our local polling location at a neighborhood church's recreation center. Every day on the way home from preschool, we pass that recreation center. Without fail, my daughter says wistfully, "I really wish we could stop and vote today." I guess we really nailed the importance of voting, but we need to circle back on the frequency of elections.

Although the anointing of David did not include an election, 2 Samuel 5:3 does share that David's final anointing was different than his first secretive anointing that was done in the presence only of Samuel, David's brothers, his father, and God. This new anointing is an anointing not done by a prophet but instead by the people. In this moment, David makes a covenant not only with God but with God's people represented by the elders within David's own community. It is with them that David makes a promise—an earthly covenant—that he will lead them and care for them as God's anointed leader for Israel.

All the elders participated in this pivotal moment in Israel's history. In a country that is defined by partisan politics, it is difficult to imagine any ruler being accepted and validated with such unanimous certainty.

Take a moment to imagine what it must have felt like to be King David, surrounded by those who would stand as his greatest supporters in his times of prophetic leadership. Who in your life recognizes your God-given gifts and graces and will stand with you?

God, reveal to me those in my community who support me in my journey of becoming the person God has created me to be. Amen.

If you have read much about the church community in Corinth, you know it wasn't an easy one. Some of Paul's firmest words and most famous teachings are in his epistles to them, urging them to fulfill the potential he sees within them. They wanted to learn about and love Jesus Christ and follow his teachings, but they learned very quickly that living in community is not for the faint of heart. Paul reminds them how love has guided, transformed, and changed them. I think that Paul had a particular soft spot for this community because his epistles reflect his understanding of how spiritually hungry this community is.

Reading this passage, maybe you find yourself with this same kind of spiritual hunger. It can be difficult to read accounts of these firsthand, tangible experiences with God and not be overtaken with jealousy. In a Sunday school class of preschoolers during a group discussion, a child stood up, stomped his foot, and said to me, "It would just be *easier* if Jesus came to me and told me what to do just like he did everyone else!" I certainly can't say I disagree.

Many of us have called out to God in our suffering, but most of us have not heard God answer us in a clear, audible voice that says, "My grace is sufficient for you." However, we can attune ourselves to our own spiritual needs by incorporating spiritual practices that allow space for us to listen to God's working in our lives. Practices like *lectio* or *audio divina*, the Ignatian Examen, walking a labyrinth, and breath prayers can be a way to attune ourselves to the voice of God working in our lives. Don't be afraid to try a new practice to order your spiritual life. It can be trial and error, and that's okay too! God is with you, offering you grace that is all-sufficient.

God, empower me to hear your voice in my life. Attune me to your grace working through me and within me. Amen.

Rejection is, unfortunately, a universal human experience. I certainly wish it weren't, but I bet you can think of multiple times that you've experienced rejection. Maybe it was from a romantic partner. Maybe a family remember rejected you. Maybe you did not get a job that you passionately interviewed for. Maybe the sting of being picked last for the elementary school kickball team has faded, or maybe the rejection of your great idea at work still leaves you bitter.

In our week's reading in Mark, Jesus teaches the disciples an important lesson: Rejection of the disciples and their mission will happen. This rejection might or might not be personal (like the rejection Jesus would experience in his ministry, ultimately leading to his death), but it would be present. We all can attest to the reality of the pain of rejection, and Jesus does not shield the disciples from this possibility.

Instead, he empowers them to decide when enough is enough. He reminds the disciples that we can never shove the gospel down anyone's throat and force them to respond. Regardless of how good the good news is, no one becomes a true follower of Jesus through coercion. I can only imagine that this was difficult news for the disciples to accept. After all, they were men who had given up everything to follow Jesus and share his good news of love and grace.

Similarly, we are not responsible for others' acceptance of us. Hear this lesson of empowerment that Jesus gave the disciples in your own life. Are there places in your life where you have done enough? Are there places in your life that you need to shake off the dust to care for your own heart?

Holy God, thank you for the example of Jesus and the disciples knowing even in the face of rejection that they were good enough, strong enough, kind enough, and competent enough. Thank you for calling me enough too. Amen.

When an elder or a deacon is ordained in the United Methodist Church, the resident bishop lays hands on the clergy person and says, "Take thou authority" (and I'm paraphrasing) to do the pastoral work of the church. All the years of seminary, the hundreds of pages of paperwork and the hours of interviewing melt away into this one moment.

Unfortunately, taking authority doesn't eliminate all the personal failings that pastors face. It doesn't, at least for any pastors I know, suddenly wash away fears of saying the wrong thing from the pulpit. It doesn't wash away the discomfort that comes in having to make tough leadership decisions. For me, it certainly didn't wash away my fear that I would make mistakes that would cast shame upon the church and even upon God.

Luckily for all of us followers of Jesus, we have a book full of stories of people with failings whom God chose to work through anyway. We have poor public speakers, prostitutes, adulterers, tax collectors, persecutors, and prodigal sons, and we have a God who still says to these people, *I choose you.* We have a God who proclaims, "You will be my people, and I will be your God" (Jer. 30:22). We have a God who says, *I know your weaknesses, and I will make you strong. I know your failings, and I can still work through you. I know your hearts, and I could not possibly love you anymore than I love you right now.*

The apostle Paul is honest about his own weaknesses. A modern-day reader might say that he models vulnerability. Paul's honesty gives the permission many of us need to be imperfect, to show up with our authentic selves with the confidence that God can and will use us as a part of God's work in the world.

Gracious God, give me courage to offer my whole self—with my imperfections and my failings—to you. Use me, all of me, to shine your love in the world. Amen.

Power and Ritual

JULY 8–14, 2024 • APRIL CASPERSON

SCRIPTURE OVERVIEW: The scriptures for this week focus on power and authority. The biblical narrative throughout the Hebrew Bible and the New Testament provides a framework for how humans should understand and engage with power. Power and authority belong to God, and part of God's grace and compassion for the world and for humanity includes the unmerited grace offered to all. However, humans have agency. Scriptures are full of outlines of how humans should care for others, and how those who are on the margins are not asked to give from their scarcity. In contrast, those who have abundance in resources and wealth—which includes power—are asked to give up some of their abundance so that all may have what they need.

QUESTIONS AND SUGGESTIONS FOR REFLECTION

- Read 2 Samuel 6:1-5 and 12b-19. What symbols carry power in this story, and where is the presence of God?
- Read Psalm 24. What gives us a connection to God in this scripture?
- Read Ephesians 1:3-14. What is the connection between the infinite power of God and humanity's need for grace?
- Read Mark 6:14-29. Where is God present in the life and death of John the Baptist? Where is God present in your life?

Deacon in the West Ohio Conference of The United Methodist Church; director of enrollment management at Methodist Theological School in Ohio; diversity, equity, and inclusion consultant within and beyond the UMC.

This entire narrative is one of power and celebration. We have a giant crowd that has been waiting for this meaningful event for generations. There is a symbolic ordering of the procession, the ark is positioned in the midst of a celebration, and the procession is full of music and celebration. The movement of the ark to its resting place is then situated within the Hebrew texts, showing how its presence is a fulfillment of how humans are to celebrate the work of God.

A processional would have been a common practice for many, even those who did not fully understand the meaning of the ark. The movement of symbolic items to a holy place was a community ritual, honoring the overarching power of God.

Imagine the abundant celebration of a people who had been longing for such a fulfillment. And then we end this scripture excerpt with a very realistic response from an outsider. The daughter of Saul, Michel, was watching the procession from inside a building, and she "despised (David) in her heart." What do you think motivated her displeasure? Was it the celebration? Was it David's behavior? Was it the display of power from a thirty-thousand-person procession? Was it that David's display of power symbolized the end of Saul's kingdom for good? Was it anger at her inability to harness and own the power of the ritual?

Where in your life have you been celebrating when someone on the outside sought to diminish the power of your joy? It can be heart-wrenching when someone who wants to have power over you tries to steal your joy. Fortunately, when your joy is a part of who you are and what you believe, joy cannot be taken away.

Life-giving God, help me to celebrate what you do in the world, and help me to remember the joy that comes from your presence, even when others seek to take it away. Amen.

Ritual has power, as we saw in yesterday's text. The parade and procession of the ark to its final resting place most likely took hours, if not days. In addition, the gathering of thirty thousand people would have been remarkable to behold. The community would have seen a parade of people reaching out to the horizon. Such a procession was a once in a lifetime experience for those participating and for those watching. Imagine observing the massive gathering as David entered into the tent to present offerings to the Lord.

Upon exiting the tent, David offered a blessing and then proceeded to give food to the entire gathering. The procession itself was a ritual; the exiting of the tent and the sharing of a meal with thirty thousand people was the culmination of the ritual. Rituals are powerful symbols that help remind us of God's power in our lives. And rituals are powerful when they invite us into the celebration. Could you imagine the impact of waiting generations for the placement of the ark, watching it as it found its final home, and then being invited to share in a meal that came from the offerings of the community? Can you imagine what it looked like to have a group of thirty thousand people receiving a meal?

There is power in breaking bread together. In addition, there is power in knowing that every person—not just the men— receives enough to eat. When everyone is welcome at the table and everyone is given their fair share and more, power structures are upended. Communities move from scarcity to abundance. God's desire for the world is brought closer to fruition, and the long-awaited transformation of our hearts begins to take form.

God who feeds bodies and souls, open my heart to where you are offering nourishment to my soul. May I be open to your presence in holy moments. Amen.

Psalm 24 is seen as a nod to the return of the ark and a naming of God's almighty power and authority over the entire universe. This text centers God and God's role in overseeing all of creation. Similarly, the text asks the reader to imagine who may be worthy of being in God's presence. The stakes are high for humans seeking to draw closer to God: They are an invitation to be blameless in morals and ethics, to seek God with a clean heart, and to be committed to God.

We cannot achieve this communion with God on our own. The only way someone can have access to God is through God's grace and goodness. This also means we do not control access to God. When you run into traditions, rules, and regulations that seem like they are designed to create a barrier between humanity and God, consider where those rules and regulations came from. They may be a reflection of the blessing of the Lord that is given to God's followers, or they may be a way for us to exert an earthly power upon one another.

We have all likely been in a situation where the rules and regulations felt like they were designed to keep some away from the goal, rather than to point a path towards the desired outcome. When have you been denied entry? When have you been the gatekeeper? We must always assess the power dynamics. "The earth is the Lord's and all that is in it," says the psalmist. We have no doubt at times created barriers for others who may be seeking access to a deeper faith or to a deeper connection with God. We must repent of that gatekeeping stance and seek to move aside, letting God be the one to place boundaries and offer grace.

God who welcomes all, open my eyes to the ways in which I attempt to keep others from you. Shape my witness to the world so that my life may reflect the love you have given to all. Amen.

Today's scripture reads very much like a liturgy that would be well known by a community. The narration reminds us of the infinite and powerful presence of God. When we consider that a human lifetime is just a tiny slice of years in comparison to God's presence within and outside of time, it is a humbling reminder of our role in the universe.

Liturgies are words used to create shared meaning, muscle and brain memory from specific language. If your worship experience includes liturgies, the repetition of words likely evokes certain emotions or memories in you. In my United Methodist tradition, the repetition of words at Communion, baptism, and other special occasions draws me back to similar events, linking them in importance and power. Liturgy can center us on that which we know to be true.

Liturgies can also give us concrete examples of lofty concepts. Today's reading includes images of God as a powerful warrior entering into the community. God is mighty in battle, the King of glory, and the Lord of hosts. In other words, God is over and above any conception of power we can come up with—and God even exists outside of time, before the most ancient monuments.

As a liturgy possibly used when the procession brought the ark to its resting place in the Temple, Psalm 24 proclaims God's sovereignty. In all the ways familiar to Israel at the time, God is proclaimed as the victor of battles, the King to be praised. In bringing the ark to rest, David proclaimed God's ultimate rule over the people. Psalm 24 speaks the words of the people on this important occasion: "The Lord of hosts . . . is the King of glory."

Eternal Creator, let my words praise you and remind me of your eternal nature. Amen.

This scripture moves from the cosmic infinite to the very personal, truly relational connection God has with humanity. We have insight into God's selection of humanity through Jesus Christ and through the power of the grace and work of Christ. We have relief from brokenness and access to a glimpse of God's will for humanity.

Part of this movement from the infinite to the personal includes the image of being marked with a seal of the Holy Spirit. Marking is a sign of claim, an exertion of power and possession over something. This kind of power and control can be healthy or unhealthy, welcoming or coercive. The juxtaposition of God's infinite power and adoption of humanity is balanced out by the articulation of the infinite grace that comes from the life, work, death, and resurrection of Christ. God's power and exertion draw everything in the earth to God through a sacrificial relationship that unconditionally loves.

Love can take many forms: romantic, familial, platonic and between friends, and care for others you are serving or in service to. In all of those relationships, the power between two people or two groups can be healthy or unhealthy. Healthy, abundant, unmerited love is an expression of care and protection. It is not punitive or conditional, and it embraces the whole person who is loved. Verse 14 in today's scripture turns God's love into the truth of the inheritance of redemption that is offered to all.

Being loved fully and unconditionally changes the way we act in the world. We are free to love ourselves and to share that unconditional love with others. This is the inheritance we receive as children of God.

God of power and love, may the inheritance you have given to me shape the way I move through this world, and may my life be a witness to the abundant riches of your grace. Amen.

Those in power in today's passage had very different opinions of John the Baptist. Herodias had preconceived notions against him, while her husband, King Herod, feared him yet "liked to listen to him." John had a following. John also did not fit easily within the typical boundaries of religious leaders. John attempted to upend the power structures and their obligation to keep the status quo. Also, John was pointing to Jesus, a religious leader who intersected with the poor, the marginalized, the unclean. King Herod was very aware of the destabilizing power of these two religious leaders.

Herodias "held a grudge" against John. Neither Herod nor Herodias fully understood John's power. The phrase "greatly perplexed" speaks volumes about how Herod tried to understand the new system that John was preaching about. How confusing and unsettling that must have been for someone who so deeply benefited from an unjust system!

When we encounter something new and unexpected, we often try to corral and control the out-of-bounds, dangerous thing. On the other side, when we are proponents of these new and unexpected ideas, we may be the ones corralled and controlled by those who do not yet understand. Individuals who name injustice are often suppressed by those who benefit from those unjust systems. The biblical narrative focuses on the destabilizing individuals; they are often those who point away from the world's values and point towards God's values.

God of all, help me to have my eyes opened to the systems that include some and exclude others. Give me the courage to speak up against injustice and the fortitude to follow up my words with actions. Amen.

Herod was bound in the tension between doing what was right—refusing to behead John the Baptist—and upholding the social norms and standards around keeping one's word. Both options had their own level of danger. Beheading John would have upended the uneasy, unspoken treaty that allowed the prophet to speak truth to the community. But ignoring the oath Herod had made would place his authority in danger.

After John the Baptist's death, we see a symbolic ritual of the presentation of his head to the girl. After the presentation, the disciples took his body and engaged in burial rituals. In many ways, we have come full circle with this week's readings. We began on Monday with a deep dive into ritual. The movement of the ark to its final resting place was filled with joy, and yet we had an observer who despised the joy of the gathered community. In today's reading, we encounter a tragic event—orchestrated by one who took joy in the tragedy—that ends with a burial ritual designed to bring peace to those who practice it.

Engaging in ritual acts gives us an access to the power of healing and restoration. The power of God's overarching presence in the world means that out of troubling ends we can find some wholeness, and we can also close out difficult seasons by celebrating what is now completed.

In your life, how have you used ritual to redeem brokenness or to name the end of a difficult season? What in your life right now needs a ritual? As you go into the coming week, consider what belongs under your power and what belongs to God's power. Keep yourself open to the rituals that will allow your life to be reordered for abundance.

God of Power and Might, help me to reorient myself under your care. May your power be a guiding force in my faith, and may my life be a reflection of your grace for all. Amen.

Where Does God Reside?

JULY 15–21, 2024 • LARISSA ROMERO

SCRIPTURE OVERVIEW: David was God's anointed king over Israel. He believed God desired a house, a temple worthy of God. But God wanted David to understand that only God can build things that truly last. Thus, God promised to construct a dynasty from David's family. From this line will eventually come the ultimate King, the Messiah, who will rule God's people forever. The Messiah will complete God's work of uniting all people as children of God, and the author of Ephesians declares that this has happened through Christ. All God's people—Jew and Gentile—are now part of a holy, spiritual temple. In Mark, Jesus shows that part of being a great king is showing compassion. He puts aside his own desires to help those in need of guidance and healing.

QUESTIONS AND SUGGESTIONS FOR REFLECTION

- Read 2 Samuel 7:1-14a. When have you changed your opinion on something significant? What led to the change?
- Read Psalm 89:20-37. What helps you recall God's faithfulness in times when you may feel abandoned?
- Read Ephesians 2:11-22. Where have you found Christ breaking down dividing walls between groups of people? What part does your Christian community play in bringing people together?
- Read Mark 6:30-34, 53-56. When have you had an experience of illness or accident that left you isolated from community? How did that increase your awareness of others in that situation as you moved to health?

RCA minister who has served in both UCC and Presbyterian contexts; mother to Frida Democracia Romero-Schmidt and wife to George Schmidt; raised in New Jersey by her parents, Gabriel and Darla Romero; loves to paint, garden, and build beloved community.

I do not remember the first time I heard, "Home is where the heart is." It is one of those colloquialisms that was embedded deep and early. In this text we receive a reinforcement that God always belongs with God's people, whether that be in a tent, a temple, or church building—wherever the heart of God is, God makes a home.

I appreciate that David felt the full comfort of being "settled in his house" and next assumed that God would also want to be settled. Having moved quite a lot, I recognize and sympathize with the need to feel rooted and in place. Many of us innately know the good security of a house (or apartment or room of our own) that has been made a home. We put up our pictures of sweet memories, fill the house with friends and laughter, experience shelter from the elements, allow it to reflect a certain part of our personalities. We sanctify it with the loving relationships given safety through settling. We imbue spaces with our spirits and invite in the Spirit.

Why is God resistant to have a house? God needs to reside where God's heart is. I particularly appreciate that God's heart doesn't reside in any one house or any one place. I think of unhoused folks and the deliberate solidarity God chooses to maintain with that unrooted community. We know that later on down the Davidic line, empires come in to destroy sacred places like temples and destroy houses and homes. But the destruction of temple, house, and home did not destroy God with them.

God-on-the-move, thank you for committing to meeting us wherever we are. May we remember that we need not be secure and in place to know your company and blessing. Amen.

Isee this often in the church. We, as beloved community, are full of good folk who wish to give of themselves. Sometimes, though, we get so caught up in what we want to do for God that we forget to invite God into the conversation. David and Nathan are ready to build God a house, but God says, "Actually, that's not what I need."

Volunteers of church life sometimes fall into this trap. We know we are really good at something or have an idea that must materialize immediately! We have to build it! It could be the actual church building. It could be a program. It could be a small group. Whatever it is, we're willing to work ourselves to the edge of burnout for it. Sometimes we do burn out, all the while not taking a moment to ask, or ask again, "Should I be doing all this? What is God calling me to do?"

How do we know God's needs? David was happy to be in a house and assumed God would also want the same. But how often do we confuse our desires and fears with God's? We must spend time in prayer, listening for God's guidance. Spiritual practices help attune our thoughts toward God, which makes us more receptive to God's voice in our lives. And we know from the Anointed One who comes later that God's self and needs are known through the least of these. If we're wondering whether we've brought God into the conversation and how our work needs to change, listening to the least of these may be the start. Most simply, it comes from listening to others' needs more than our own desires.

God, help me relinquish the expectation that you need what I need. Help me slow down and hear you. Help me share power and listen to the most vulnerable. Grant me the vulnerability to rely on the beloved community and the hope that rests in you. Amen.

My daughter in all her toddlerhood often experiments with the world around her. It is how she learns best. This also means that countless times a day I hear, "Uh-oh!" When I hear that "Uh-oh," I know I need to redirect my efforts—milk has spilled, a spoon has fallen, the guitar she wasn't even supposed to be able to reach has been dropped.

Almost every time, the mistake is a testing of boundaries. She turned the cup upside down to see how much liquid would come out. She tossed the spoon when I tried to help her use it. She saw the guitar was out of reach and made it her new goal to reach it. In each of these instances there is a consequence; there is something from which she can learn. While I balk at the psalmist's claim that God punishes us when we mess up, I can understand there being consequences that we misinterpret as punishment. With my daughter, the relationship is wholly about her learning; it's not about my discomfort.

God as a loving parent surely loves me as deeply as I love my daughter. I know that my toddler's boundary testing doesn't affect my love for her in the least. I love her steadfastly, even as she learns. Similarly, when we test the bounds of loving-kindness and choose to relinquish the commandments and laws God provides, God does not relinquish us. God's love remains steadfast. We are continuously tethered to the love of God through the line of covenant promise, beginning with David and made all the more full in Christ. It is incapable of breaking.

Loving Parent, when we test boundaries and make missteps, give us such a sense of your steadfast love that we feel free to fall into your grace and learn again. Amen.

Years ago for my Lenten prayer practice, I chose to paint abstract art. I had seen the work of a synesthetic abstract artist who saw colors when she heard music and would paint what she heard. This moved me, so I spent the six weeks of Lent in the basement, dripping, splattering, and scumbling. There were rules I chose to stick to. Let's call them Christ-inspired boundaries. I could use only three tools. I could use only three colors. I could paint only one layer a day.

In this practice of self-imposed limits, I became aware of a wall that I had put up internally: this idea that I had to do everything really well to do anything worthy. My prayer-painting broke through this wall. In this prayer practice, I realized that my limitations offered up a vibrant potency. I found peace knowing that my limitations didn't prohibit God from doing something wondrous with me. The Spirit of Christ gave me a tangible experience of grace as I put paint to canvas.

The writer of Ephesians talks of the boundaries that Christ broke down, specifically opening the way for Gentiles to become part of the community of faith. These divisions provided much debate for the early church, but ultimately the early followers strove to live into the expansive love of Christ. For us today, the divisions may still signify hostilities that exist between groups of people, or they may be the boundaries we put up within ourselves, the places we don't expect or don't want Christ to go.

Ultimately, that season's painting prayer practice became an outer manifestation of God's indwelling. I noticed God waiting for me at the boundaries of my self-understanding and perceptions. Sitting next to the canvas with only so many tools and colors, I found a rooted rest and the anticipated new humanity that would come at the close of the season—with resurrection.

Indwelling God, help us all to break down internal walls and be flooded with Christ's peace. Amen.

God's home can be in our very bodies. Regardless of the body, God can dwell there. Moreover, God chooses more often than not to make a home in those bodies often deemed outside the bounds of current norms, those "aliens of the commonwealth." In Christ, each body is brought near, no longer alien but intimately known and accepted and affirmed as it is. Christ abolishes the very boundaries of our norms, our laws of purity and unanimity.

A woman who spoke of her experience as a person in a wheelchair changed my understanding of how we establish boundaries in communities. She viewed herself as *differently-abled*, not *disabled*. As is true in any group of people, there is multiplicity in the community of persons with disabilities. While some prefer *disabled* in order to bring greater visibility to the community, this woman had a reason for insisting that she was *differently-abled*. She asked this poignant question: "Why stairs?" Why not only elevators and ramps? What if we had a society committed only to ramps and elevators? Suddenly, she wouldn't be at a disadvantage; she would simply have a different approach to the same point of access wherever she went. Her point was that the way we set up our communities defines who is in or out.

God in Christ chooses to make a home out of the beloved community. No one, no body, is a stranger or alien to the body of Christ. All are reconciled and made members of God's household. The community was set up to define that all are *in*. Wherever walls are abolished and norms are sacrificed for the sake of reconciliation, there God lives.

Peacemaker of the universe, you mend all things, and we ask that you mend our relationships to one another. Reconcile us to live in community so that we are all full members of your household. Amen.

Spiritual abandonment feels particularly pervasive these days. I don't have to go far to hear stories of wounds and aches from folks who feel outcast by the church community and have either left the church or have stayed but feel burdened in place. In these stories, I hear a longing to be called *beloved*, even as the church that held them did not. Where the church cannot act past its boundaries, does Christ?

Our passage indicates that Christ will go even to the boundaries of our compassion and ability to create community. I was in college when my spiritual deconstruction began. Like so many others, it unmoored me. I fortunately had the benefit of classes and professors who helped me reconstruct my faith. To be honest, I feel as though I am reconstructing my relationship to God through Christ to this day. It is an ongoing process, where I bring my mat to the center regularly to ask for a touch of the cloak.

Not everyone has this gift of a safe space to reconstruct their faith. We do not put a high value on it as a society. You often have to go to the edges of society to find that space. Many folks from the LGBTQ+ community liken the gay bar to a church, a community where they are loved, accepted, supported, and called to be their full self. I once read a challenging poem that visually described Jesus joyously dancing at the gay bar. I come back regularly to this image of Jesus dancing on the edges of what's acceptable to remind folks, "You are beloved." Wherever healing emerges, I like to imagine Jesus there in the thick of it. Even if some never return to the church, God builds them back up through the boundary-crosser Christ.

Christ of both cross and crossing, you find ever new ways of calling us beloved. Like sheep who have wandered from their shepherd, bring us back into the fold that we may be healed. Amen.

This text brims with edges and boundaries. Christ calls the faith ambassadors to a deserted place, presumably the outer edges of society, to rest. Christ then crosses over the shoreline, only to enter a flock of folk who had followed them to the margins to meet him. At Gennesaret, he once again moves from water to land, which sends people to fetch the sick. The sick were kept in one way or another away from society, and here folks travel throughout the region to bring them in. The sick are brought to the very centers of the towns and cities—the marketplaces. When there, all one had to do was touch the fringe of Jesus' cloak to be healed. Christ himself is the point where crossing these edges and boundaries brings healing.

I am Mexican-American. Stories of boundary-crossing tend to bring to mind border crossing. My grandparents came through Ellis Island, and so the crossing was more like stepping ashore than meeting a fence. Since then, our family has always flown to Mexico. We've not had to contend with the border. As many times as I've visited my family in Texas, I've never been to the border. I wonder what it would be like for me to cross that edge. Our society so often forgets that many of those who cross the southern border are asylum-seekers—people seeking home and healing from whence they flee. Would I find healing in deeper solidarity with my southern siblings?

In all instances, Christ requires those seeking healing to cross boundaries with him. God as the incarnate living Anointed One continues the precedent set back in the days of liberation from slavery: God cannot be contained and will break past any confinement or boundary to bring healing.

O God, may your steadfast love continue to uphold Christ's smashing of boundaries, that your healing may always cross over again. Amen.

Abundantly Far More with God

JULY 22-28, 2024 • JAY HORTON

SCRIPTURE OVERVIEW: The Bible is filled with the stories of imperfect people. David is a classic case. In Second Samuel he uses his power to have sex with another man's wife, tries to cover it up, and then plots the murder of her husband. How can this be the same man who penned this week's psalm, which decries the foolishness of people who act in a godless way? Like us, David was an imperfect person who needed God's extravagant mercy. In Ephesians we read of this same extravagance given through Christ, whose power can do what we cannot—namely redeem all of us who are also foolish and fallen. The Gospel author demonstrates the power of Jesus through what he describes as "signs," which Jesus performed not primarily to amaze the onlookers but to point them to his identity as the Son of God.

QUESTIONS AND SUGGESTIONS FOR REFLECTION

- Read 2 Samuel 11:1-15. Where in today's world do you see the selfishness of powerful people bringing tragedy for people with less power?
- Read Psalm 14. Do you number yourself among the wise who "seek after God"? Why or why not?
- Read Ephesians 3:14-21. How does "being rooted and grounded in love" manifest itself in your life?
- Read John 6:1-21. Where do you see yourself in this story?

Communications Coordinator, Georgia Interfaith Power and Light (GIPL), Decatur, GA; Master of Divinity, Candler School of Theology, Emory University.

Psalm 14 is a lament, a passionate expression of deep and heartfelt emotion. The psalmist says their feelings out loud. There is something special about that. It is not sugar-coated or polished; it is dramatic and emotional. The Common English Bible translation of verse 4 is especially coarse: "Are they dumb, all these evildoers . . . never calling on the LORD?" The psalmist sounds like an evening news pundit or late-night talk show host. While not inaccurate in their retelling of events, there is definitely some sensationalizing occurring.

Sometimes we think we cannot talk to God in such a manner. We are afraid to vent our deepest thoughts and emotions to the Almighty, like we might offend God. We think our prayers need to be buttoned up, censored, rated no higher than PG. As a result, we sometimes inhibit ourselves from being honest and vulnerable with God. The tone of this psalm reminds us that it is okay to talk to God through whatever emotions we are feeling. Our honesty might actually help us grow closer to the Divine.

God is not fragile or sensitive. There is nothing that God has not seen or heard before. In the psalmist's vulnerability there is strength. Instead of dismissing deep emotions, the writer gives in to their depth and breadth, and it is ultimately from this pain that the realization is born that life is better with God. Finding our way in faith begins with letting ourselves feel. God gave us our emotions for a reason, and God can receive them. Our pain and frustrations do not hurt God's feelings. Without the darkness, how would we know the abundant light?

God of our anger, God of our irritation, God of our sadness and sorrow, help us to know that we can bring our whole selves to you. No thought or feeling is too raw or disturbing for you to bear. It is in our honesty and vulnerability that we realize a bounteous life is possible with you. Amen.

Whille lament can be cathartic, it is important not to remain in a state of "everything is horrible" all the time. Lament is the release that opens the door to hope. The end of Psalm 14 reminds us who is in control—God, not humanity. "The LORD is their refuge." It is the Lord who "restores the fortunes of his people."

I used to stay up until all hours of the night worrying about the day's events. My mind would wrestle endlessly with all the ways I could have done better. Should I have told my boss this instead of that? Should I have written that sermon yesterday because the rest of my week is filled with meetings? Why did I not go to the gym this morning? Anxiety wrecked my sleep.

When I discussed this issue with my therapist (yes, you can have Jesus and a therapist too), he suggested "vomit journaling," a hideous name for a helpful task. He recommended that when my anxiety started to fester, I should just write: write all my thoughts and feelings down, give them to the paper. He suggested I forget punctuation and proper grammar and just get the words on the page. He said if I did this, I would find a new sense of calm. And he was right. I find when I journal in this manner that it frees me of the disquiet of my mind, and I am able to realize a new peace. I can see things that I never would have been able to recognize before.

Lament done properly creates space for God. It gives us the opportunity to share freely that which is occupying our mind and emotions, and then it opens us up to see the abundant life of the Divine in our midst. Lament can ultimately move us to hope.

Great Spirit, may you continually work on our souls, moving us from pain and heartbreak to hope and joy. May we find in you deliverance and a place among the righteous, now and forevermore. Amen.

The story of David and Bathsheba is a quintessential example of human desire superseding compassion and self-control. David commits adultery with the wife of one of his soldiers. Instead of fessing up to his indiscretion when she becomes pregnant, he manufactures an opportunity for her husband, Uriah, to think the child is his own. When that fails, he decides to have Uriah killed and takes Bathsheba for himself.

In the factual account of David's actions, there is much room for interpretation. Undoubtedly, David's actions are reprehensible. Before this moment, David was walking in lockstep with God. What has happened? Has his ego gotten too big? Does he think he can do whatever he wants, forgetting that it is God who has led him to his place of power? The prophet Nathan will go on to say as much in chapter 12. David was a mere shepherd boy—it was God who anointed him king over Israel and delivered him from the hand of Saul (see 2 Samuel 12:7).

This story of David is often used to show that God can still work through people who make major mistakes. David certainly made a major mistake—multiple mistakes, in fact, first committing adultery and then attempting to hide it. While we might not commit adultery or order a hit on a lover's spouse, we all on occasion make the mistake of prioritizing our desires over what is right. Sometimes we also try to cover up our misdeeds when we are caught. We think we can do life on our own, but we must remember it is God who provides all we have. Life is better with the Divine. While this story of David does show that God can still work through us even when we mess up, it also reminds us that following God from the beginning is the better way to live.

Forgive us, O God, when we think we are above admonishment. When we arrogantly act like David, remind us from whom all blessings flow. Help us prioritize your righteousness over our desires. Amen.

In this chapter of the fourth Gospel, Jesus reveals just how far the generosity of God extends. When Jesus and the disciples encounter a large crowd, Jesus sees an opportunity to facilitate a teaching moment. He challenges his disciples to come up with a solution, knowing (the scripture says) what he intends to do, no matter their response. Philip deems it an impossible task, but Andrew, if also defeated, at least acknowledges the presence of potential in the boy's five loaves of bread and two fish. Jesus sees this as ample. He gives thanks to God, multiplies the food, and feeds the five thousand. Where the disciples see resources lacking, Christ sees abundance.

Several years ago, the inner-city church where I work saw a need. People in the area were desperate for affordable housing. Several community members, in fact, had died on the front steps of our church from lack of adequate shelter. The members knew something needed to be done to fix this issue, but such an enormous task seemed impossible. Money was not flush and membership had dwindled, but they had some valuable land and a hearty faith. So, the few gathered, prayed, got creative and resourceful, and five years later saw the rise of a 320-unit affordable, work-live-play complex in the heart of downtown Atlanta. It provided not just shelter but education for the underhoused and disadvantaged.

Even when we think our resources are minuscule and inconsequential, Jesus reminds us that, with God, they are more than enough. Our God is a God of abundance. God takes what little we have, blesses it, and multiplies our gifts for the redemption of the world.

Provider God, help us to remember that with you nothing is impossible. Thank you for turning what little gifts we offer into holy miracles. Amen.

After the large crowd was miraculously fed and leftovers were still spilling from baskets, the scripture tells us the people "wanted to force [Jesus] to be their king." Jesus had fed the crowd and shown them how God provides a lot out of a little. And yet the crowd in this scene wants more. We want more.

While the crowd does not debase themselves to adultery and murder, their actions mirror those of David's we read about earlier this week—in a grim reality of humanity at its most selfish. Rather than allowing God to work and choosing to join in God's work, David and the crowd both let their personal interests take over. David's actions led to death. The crowd's actions will eventually lead to the same. They miss the point of what Jesus is doing here and instead want to shape Jesus' actions to support their own desires. They want Jesus to become the long-awaited earthly king that David was, the one to lead them out of Roman oppression. It seems they forget where David's kingship led.

The disciples, too, have a short memory. Despite having just witnessed Jesus feed an enormous crowd with only five loaves and two fish, the disciples also have yet to comprehend that God does not act in the ways they expect. If God can feed the hungry from nothing, then surely God may walk across stormy waters to meet the lonely and distressed.

God will never be the earthly ruler king we envision—a great emperor or courageous conqueror. That is too unimaginative. God will always be greater, more creative, and more compassionate than we can conceive. We must shift our expectations. We must shift our understandings of what is possible. Life with God will not look as we envision—it will be far better!

Great unsettler of the status quo, remind us that you show up in ways we least expect. Our assumptions will never do you or your world justice. Break open the creative wanderings of our souls so that we see your miracles in our life. Amen.

We live in a polarized world. With each election cycle and church council meeting it feels like more people are finding reasons to hate and separate themselves from one another. Whether it be because of political party, national origin, sexual orientation, or ideology, we would rather split over difference than celebrate what unites us. I find people have forgotten the words of the apostle Paul to the church in Ephesus, a vibrant church made of Jew and Gentile alike.

On his knees in a posture of humility, Paul gives thanks that every member "takes its name" from God. We have a common origin and a common Spirit that strengthens us all. Paul asks the people to take Christ into their hearts and to see, as he has, the great possibilities for a diverse church grounded in love.

The most profound experiences of Christian love I have had have always occurred in diverse faith communities: in multicultural churches here in the United States and in the Global South, singing with LGBTQ+ Christians in praise and worship, talking about the Bible with refugees from Africa and the Middle East. It was during such profound and varied faith encounters that I truly experienced the breadth, length, height, and depth of God.

Paul says true love in Christ "surpasses knowledge." Whatever we think we know to be true about God's love, we need to go further. Love transcends all the boundaries we create and draws us closer to one another. It is only with the full, diverse community of saints that we will begin to comprehend "the fullness of God."

Almighty, help us see our faith differences as assorted expressions of your love. Fill us with your spirit of unity until we begin to see diversity as a blessing on the path to abundant life. Amen.

The apostle Paul closes this prayer to the church in Ephesus by giving thanks that humanity is able "to accomplish abundantly far more" with God than without. Abundant life, Paul says, is available both here and now and in the future because of the work of Christ inside each and every one of us.

The locus of Christ's work is important here. At times we get so caught up in looking for hope, love, and support outside ourselves, we miss the ways Christ sustains us from within. We are desperate for comfort, praise, and redemption from the world. We long for acceptance from our colleagues and friends. We desire affirmation from our civic leaders and bosses. Yet we forget the most powerful and constant voice of worthiness comes from our Creator within—a God present yesterday, today, and in the future.

When the world fails us and our self-esteem is driven to a new low, we must look to the power of God available to us throughout the ages. You and I are enough, and more than enough is possible for us—not because some external earthly force proves it but because an eternal divine grace decrees it.

Abundant life is possible by the power of Christ at work within. Post this on a sticky note and place it on your bathroom mirror this week. Add the phrase as a wallpaper to your phone or computer screen. Then, in moments when the world tells you there is not enough to go around or you are not enough for the world, you may confidently reply that with Christ greater things are more fathomable than you would ever dream.

God of all generations, grant us the assurance of your hope this day and in the days ahead. Abundantly far more is possible with you than without. Teach us not to rely on the realities of the world when we know your truth that resides within. Amen.

A Sudden Jolt

JULY 29–AUGUST 4, 2024 • MARTHA SPONG

SCRIPTURE OVERVIEW: David thinks he has gotten away with his sins, but God sends Nathan to tell David a story. The story angers David, but Nathan reveals that the story is really about David's own behavior. Indeed, it can be tempting to condemn others' sin while we justify our own. Psalm 51 is David's appeal to God for forgiveness and restoration. If we want to please God in our own lives, what does this look like? Ephesians tells us that the signs of a redeemed life include humility, love, patience, and building up one another (the opposite of what David displayed). In John, Jesus has crowds following him because they want a free meal. The lasting nourishment they truly need, Jesus teaches, comes through believing that God has sent him.

QUESTIONS AND SUGGESTIONS FOR REFLECTION

- Read 2 Samuel 11:26–12:13a. When has someone else helped you see that you have sinned? How did you respond to that person?
- Read Psalm 51:1-12. When have you felt "unclean" before God? How did God restore you?
- Read Ephesians 4:1-16. What are your gifts? How do you use them to build up the body of Christ?
- Read John 6:24-35. How do you feed your soul?

Clergy coach; United Church of Christ pastor; co-founder and former executive director of RevGalBlogPals; editor of *The Words of Her Mouth: Psalms for the Struggle* (Pilgrim Press, 2020).

We have seen it in others: A person makes an impulsive decision, and that decision leads to another and another. One wrong turn begets a second poor choice and a third, until what seemed like the action of a moment or a lucky coincidence or a seized opportunity becomes a pattern of harm against others. And when the harm-doer has power, this route is so much easier to travel.

Nathan the prophet has seen this story unfold through David's actions. The king has taken another man's wife, used her for his pleasure, and is destroying others to keep his discretion a secret. How can Nathan stop the cycle of sexual and moral violence that has power over him and everyone else involved?

Nathan tells a preacher's story, a parable, leading David down a different kind of path with his fable about a beloved lamb. The listener's sympathy goes naturally to the injured party. Even David, who has so much, identifies with the poor man's heartbreak. No one wants to lose what they love.

Nathan is patient. He waits for David's anger to rise against the rich abuser in the story. Then he speaks the truth, jolting David into seeing his own actions from a different perspective. Only then does Nathan outline the specific case against the king. And only then does David see and confess, "I have sinned."

We may not have the power of a king, but we can still make choices, rash or planned, that harm others. And while our missteps may seem less dramatic than David's, ignoring or rationalizing them only makes things worse, for us and for others. Whose authority might we trust to show us where we have gone wrong? Whom do we respect deeply enough to receive their jolt and then believe?

All-powerful God, bring people into our lives who will disrupt our acts of harm and jolt us with the truth we need to hear. Amen.

What does confession look like? Often it is limited to the weekly collective confession we offer in worship, with words chosen by someone else. Even if time is allotted in worship for silent, individual prayers of confession, we may or may not be prepared to name our wrongdoing. And when we do, how often do the thoughts form like answers to a job interview question: What are our weaknesses? "I tend to work too hard." We end up bragging in the wrong direction, identifying weaknesses that we actually think are strengths. Consider step four of Alcoholics Anonymous's 12: "Make a searching and fearless moral inventory of yourself." Confession—real confession—asks for more.

Scholars associate this psalm with the story of David and his actions leading to yesterday's reading, seeing it as David's attempt to acknowledge his actions. The words have become a gift to the rest of humankind. It is not as specific as our own accounting needs to be, or David's for that matter. Instead it gives us a ritual framework that can inform our personal confessions. Its ancient words can open our hearts to God too. We trust in God's steadfast love and mercy, we name our wrongdoing, and we ask for forgiveness.

Yet there is a limitation here. The psalmist focuses on how the relationship *with God* has been broken, which is certainly important. But we will also want to consider the impact of our transgressions on others. The psalm helps us make a start, but it is not all that the experience of being jolted can stir up in us.

Read these verses from Psalm 51 and then take a pause. Allow time and space in silence to account for the ways you have failed God, broken relationships, or harmed others. Allow the stillness needed to feel and acknowledge regret for particular actions or inactions. Then hold on and listen for God.

Holy One, have mercy on us. Amen.

Penny had just started her position as a youth director in a town that was new to her, and she was excited about an invitation to play church league volleyball. She had played softball in college, but volleyball was her second-favorite sport—the one she played with abandon. She hyped herself up to play well and make a good impression on her new teammates. At the first game, she threw herself into it, literally, going for every point and celebrating her successes with enthusiasm.

Until someone said, "That's not how we play here."

Amped up and embarrassed, Penny grabbed her gear and stormed off. When she got to the car, she remembered that she hadn't driven herself and saw that her ride had not followed her. So she leaned against the car, and she waited.

When we have been jolted by some truth about ourselves, we have a range of options for response. We may be reflexively apologetic, or we may wall ourselves up in denial, or we may lash out to justify ourselves. Penny, waiting by the car, found herself in a particularly painful position as she cooled off enough to ponder what had happened and sat with the knowledge that she had done it wrong.

And then she prayed.

Penny's errors may seem small compared to David's, but this psalm attributed to him offers us a framework for growth no matter how we have messed things up. David knows the first step toward making things right must happen on the inside. He prays, "Therefore teach me wisdom in my secret heart." Like Penny in the parking lot with no way home, we start by assessing ourselves honestly, then we invite God to be part of the process. This is the tender space where change can occur, where new possibilities can emerge, and where healing can begin.

Loving God, we often get it wrong. Teach us a better way in our secret hearts. Amen.

This week's Gospel lesson starts in the middle of an action-packed story. A huge crowd of people are following Jesus, who had fed them all with a little boy's five loaves and two fishes. Afterward, Jesus withdraws to the mountain to avoid being forced by the crowd to be king. The disciples sail off, and Jesus walks across the Sea of Galilee to rejoin them. Now safely on the other side, they are rejoined by some of the crowd, and those folks want to know how Jesus got there.

Jesus responds with a phrase he uses when he wants to be sure people know he's not speaking in images or metaphors, but is being direct with them: "Very truly, I tell you." The 2003 movie *The Gospel of John* used the Good News Translation, and the actor Henry Ian Cusick let the edge of frustration creep into his delivery of the line: "I am telling you the truth!" Jesus is blunt. These people don't care about the deeper implications of a miraculous meal on a hillside; they just want more bread.

We may read the words and think, "Oof. How uncomfortable they must have felt if that was their real reason." Yet the people stick to a line of questioning that misses the point of who Jesus is. And maybe they are not so different from us. We too can connect with the wrong detail, make an incorrect assumption, or hold on to the simplest explanation or the answer we wish were true. As we've seen in David's story and the journey of this crowd, we can get caught up in our own desires, missing God's interests entirely. How open are we to redirection when our focus is on a false idea, our hopes are vested in an ill-advised direction, or our admiration is directed to the wrong person? What gets through to us?

Jesus offers another truth, meant to rock them again. The work they are being asked to do is just this: to believe in him.

God of all, shake our doubts with your truth. Amen.

From a distance of almost 2000 years, we may wonder why the people who saw Jesus up close seem so confused about his identity. We believe, don't we? And all we have to go on are other peoples' stories in scripture and tradition. We pledge our faithfulness at baptism or confirmation, make promises for our children, and reaffirm our faith in both liturgy and action in the world.

Had Jesus not given them signs already? He tells them the truth about who he is. In John's Gospel he makes his claim more directly than in the other three. Jesus knows who he is. God knows who he is. Everyone should know who he is! Yet this crowd of people, who ate on the hillside and traveled across the water to find Jesus just in case he had more bread up his sleeve, want something more.

What do we imagine held them back from believing?

After the last several years in which people have argued and pushed division into every angle of our society by challenging things we have believed to be true, perhaps we can understand the people seeking and questioning Jesus that day. Living under Roman occupation for decades, ruled by kings and governors and generals chosen by a distant emperor, the people who crossed the Sea of Galilee looking for Jesus wanted something they could trust. No wonder they were drawn to physical bread they could hold and taste.

When we have witnessed the unlikely, the astonishing, or the seemingly impossible, we interrogate rather than accept it. And we may, like the seekers in John 6, be shaken by the truth Jesus is telling us. The bread of life, the true bread that will sustain us always, comes from God.

Gracious God, you sent Jesus Christ to give life to the world. Give us this bread always. Amen.

In this second half of the book of Ephesians, the subject shifts from theological instruction to moral teaching. Now that we believe in Jesus Christ and have committed ourselves to following him, how must we live? The foundation of Christian community must be love of God and love of one another, and that love must be expressed with gentleness and humility.

In my work as a leadership coach, I sometimes lead group sessions. In each group's first session we think together about community guidelines, creating a covenant for how the participants will interact and treat one another. The expectations cover a range of possibilities: hold conversations in confidence, be fully present to others, give no advice unless requested. My least favorite coaching moments are the ones where I must name a behavior that is harmful to the group. I know I am delivering a jolt, often to someone who meant well.

Paul had his own experience of being jolted on the Damascus Road. He began his journey proud, zealous, and sure of himself, but ended it blinded, dependent, and stunned. When he implores us to live a life worthy of Jesus, we know he faced the challenge of learning how wrong he was and shifting not just his behavior but the direction and purpose of his life.

When we first acquire new understandings of ourselves and sit with them long enough to let God be part of the conversation, we may be ready to acknowledge our learnings—and perhaps even our regrets—in our trusted relationships. It's humbling to do it, especially because the culture around us prizes confidence and success over the admission of our limitations. Yet Paul teaches what *we* need to do *now* as much as what the letter's recipients needed to do then: to understand the qualities needed to create and preserve a community of love.

Open our hearts, O God, to hear anew the great commandment Jesus gave us: to love you and one another. Amen.

Two Tuesday nights each month, a suburban church hosted a dinner followed by a program for adults and an activity for kids. The brainchild of an associate pastor and a Christian Education director, it attracted a multi-generational crowd of both newer and longtime congregation members. The attendance grew each time, right up until Tuesday, March 10, 2020. Then they paused for the COVID-19 pandemic. The associate pastor moved to another church. By the time church leaders felt comfortable gathering in person, no one knew if Tuesday nights would attract anyone anymore. And admittedly, when it started up again in the fall of 2022, the organizers saw a diminished crowd. A few of the previous participants had left the congregation, some of the older folks had grown too frail to come out at night, some had new obligations that conflicted, and others simply did not return.

Looking around the long tables on the first night back, the senior pastor's wife felt her heart lurch as she noted the missing (and missed) people first. Would this be another loss caused by the pandemic?

Tempted to ruminate on loss, she instead pulled herself back into the moment. She noted a family who had never come before, new volunteer leaders, the engagement of more of the church staff and their families, and the joy all ages had in being together. Tuesday night by Tuesday night, the atmosphere of kind welcome brought her to a new appreciation not just of the gathering but of the gifts being shared there. Each person there, age 5 to over 85, had been "given grace according to the measure of Christ's gift" and brought something needed: gifts of pastoring (not just from the clergy!), teaching, hospitality, companionship, and building up the body in love.

Divine Parent, bless the growth of each body of your people. Help us to embrace the new lives to which you call us. Amen.

Beneath It All

AUGUST 5–11, 2024 • CHRISTAL WILLIAMS

SCRIPTURE OVERVIEW: Our readings from Second Samuel invite you to look at the cries of King David as warrior, father, child of God, and king. These readings contrast with the life and call of Jesus as the bread of life, which comes down from heaven and is gifted to all. In the psalm, we will see both the faith and frailty of a psalmist who acknowledges the need to be heard, forgiven, and rescued by God. The reading from the letter to the Ephesians calls for unity and maturity in the body of Christ. This week's reading will be bread not only for your soul but your life.

QUESTIONS AND SUGGESTIONS FOR REFLECTION

- Read 2 Samuel 18:5-9, 15, 31-33. Have you ever been afraid? Did that fear paralyze you? How does your relationship with God help anxiety to dissipate?
- Read Psalm 130. When have you experienced God's presence in times of despair?
- Read Ephesians 4:25–5:2. What is the difference between unity and uniformity? Once accepting this relationship in the body of Christ, how vital will replacing old behaviors with new ones become?
- Read John 6:35, 41-51. Have you ever had to make a declaration that seemed unpopular? What unpopular statements are you being called to make now?

Regional Minister and President of the Christian Church (Disciples of Christ) in Tennessee; author of the books *The Power of Asking; Unleashing God's Best For your Life* (West Beach Press, 2013) and *Beneath it All: A Conversation Specifically for Women* (Howard Publishing Press, 2015).

Even the most beautiful of relationships are complicated. Any parent figure knows this truth in their relationship with those they care for. It is the connection itself that can cause such friction. Adults trying to guide growing children generally want only the best for them, but what exactly is "the best" is often a point of contention.

I admit to being the cause of most of my family's uproars and disappointments as a child. I had a free spirit and semi-risk-taking attitude, and my chant growing up was often, "I can handle things on my own," even when I knew that I could not. I did not mind stressing my mother or working her last nerve, as I know I did frequently. My mother, Norma, was open and honest and did not always agree with my decisions, but she knew I would mature and leave her nest.

As David receives the news of Absalom's death, we are offered a glimpse into his spiritual, emotional, and mental state. David is living the results of his past indiscretions: sending Uriah into battle and having him not return home, being married to Bathsheba, his dysfunctional fathering to Absalom, his decisions as warrior king. At the end of this story, Absalom dies at the hands of David's men, and David is left suffering.

As parents and caregivers know, best intentions do not always suffice. Relationships with other people always have two sides, and we can only control one of those sides. As my mother knew, and as David must have wrestled with, the choices others make are outside our control. But we must not feel like we are completely removed from the relationship. Our own autonomy may not bring about the end result we seek, but it will certainly have an effect on the relationship and the other person.

Thank you, God, for being in the midst of our relationships with others. We count on your direction and guidance now and in the days to come. Amen.

Mental health is so important that we have devoted an entire month to its awareness. Although efforts are moving forward to highlight the importance of these needs, I still wonder how many folks are receiving the help they need. As the number of people dealing with mental health challenges increases and funding decreases, how will we as a society meet the need? We have experienced wars, pandemics, financial meltdowns, and political chaos in the past three years, causing fear and anxiety. We must find ways to help calm and broker our safety and sanity. We must let it be known that it is okay to seek out a mental health professional while listening for God's direction.

Have you ever heard of the "dark night of the soul"? This psalm offers a front-row seat into the life of one walking through the soul's dark night. This term derives from the title of a poem by the 16th-century mystic and poet St. John of the Cross. The poem and subsequent phrase represent the distance one feels from God during time of uncertainty. In this psalm, we witness the desperate outcries of a psalmist searching for this unknowable, unseeable God.

But the affirmation we see in this psalm counteracts the feeling of that dark night. The psalm is still framed here with an understanding of God's presence: Even when it feels like God is far away, we can be assured of God's presence with us. God hears the voices of the frail and offers mercy. God's ear is turning to the voice of those in distress, and assistance is there. At those times when God feels distant, we can recall God's grace and wait to feel such presence again.

Thank you, God, for turning on the light in our souls. May we find the peace, healing, and relief we need in this time of lamenting. Amen.

Have you ever heard the phrase, "If you are going to pray don't worry, and if you are going to worry don't pray"? This phrase implies that prayer assuages worries, and worrying inhibits prayer. I find, however, that the two do often go hand-in-hand. In Psalm 130, the psalmist is obviously distressed about Israel's sins and the depths in which the people find themselves. Their response is to call out to God.

Do you think that God answers prayers? Although I am an avid reader of scripture and practitioner of spiritual disciplines, sometimes it can be hard for me to wait, trust, and believe that God will respond. I tend to be the girl waiting by the metaphorical front door for good news. Some see this anticipation as not trusting in God or the process.

However, the psalmist says we wait on the Lord as the watchmen wait for the morning. Watchmen sat at the city gates throughout the night, anticipating danger and being prepared to raise the alarm. They stood awake and alert, focused on watching for the danger and waiting for the morning while others slept. The watchmen had faith that dawn would arrive, but they had to stay alert to make sure they made it safely until then. The psalmist has faith that God's answer will soon be revealed like the dawn. Active waiting does not indicate impatience or faithlessness. On the contrary, as the watchmen wait for the morning, the psalmist focuses on God in preparation to receive God's answer.

The psalmist calls on others to place their hope in the Lord. In our own waiting, we can call others to experience God's "unfailing love" and "full redemption."

God, we are actively waiting and ready to call upon you in trouble and in times of joy. Amen.

Beneath It All

Participating in the after-Thanksgiving sale is often a clear example of the old ways versus new ways of living cited in scripture. Somewhere on a cold Friday morning, there will be shoving, snatching, and skipping in line, hoping to claim a bargain or snag that special gift. More than a few people will return home disappointed, cold, and frustrated by the behaviors of their fellow shoppers. The joy of shopping for others and preparing for the holiday season is often a stark contrast to the reality of the anger, bitterness, and wrath on display in the stores.

This Ephesians passage calls for unity and maturity in the body of Christ. The church at Ephesus lives within the new standard protocol for being faithful followers of Jesus Christ and active participants in the church. The writer calls the community to put away the behaviors of their past lives and step into honesty, forgiveness, hard work, and kindness. The author specifically identifies truth-telling as a behavior that builds up the community of faith.

How does your community of faith address disagreements and conflict? We can take the admonishment to speak the truth in love to our neighbors while being sure not to "make room for the devil." The true testament of members of Christ's body is to speak love and honor during a disagreement. Not confronting disruption and contention breeds discord and opens the space for more anger and resentment. The words to the Ephesians are as relevant to us today as they were when first written. We, too, can put away our old ways to further build the body of Christ.

God, give us the strength to live with honesty and love. Amen.

In 1973, Revlon launched the perfume Charlie with a now-famous television commercial that sold the promise of youth and freedom. "Kinda young, kinda now, Charlie! Kinda free, kinda wow, Charlie!" said the jingle, while model Shelley Hack commanded attention and admiration in a stylish pantsuit. Women everywhere began wearing pantsuits and buying Charlie.

The fifth chapter of Ephesians opens with a call to "be imitators of God." Having a model to follow, someone to imitate, to look up to and strive to be like makes a huge difference as one seeks to grow. As humans, it's natural for us to seek to be like someone else, which is why marketing campaigns like Revlon's are so successful. But as followers of Christ, we don't look for worldly role models to follow. We seek to imitate Christ and the ways Christ modeled for us God's love.

Living in a community of faith helps us as we strive to walk in this love. As part of the family of God we have an opportunity to transmit God's love to others and inspire them to walk in Christ's love, as well. We are putting into practice the attributes of a loving God. We should exemplify loving our neighbors as ourselves while offering a true reflection of Jesus Christ. While walking the way of love, we must manifest Jesus in all we say and do. It brings about a new look and a sweet fragrance. "Kinda free, kinda wow!"

God, we offer thanks for your unconditional love and sacrifice. Jesus, it is you who continues to show us the way. We shall follow. Amen.

At age six, I declared to my family, "I am accepting my call to preach!" What an announcement for a child barely out of first grade. I was responding to a deep hunger I was feeling: the beginning of my call to ministry. Forty-six years later, I do indeed preach the gospel, but I do so in a world much different than the one of my six-year-old self. In my work I often encounter those succumbing to a life of debt, consumerism, and wishful thinking. We are inundated with opportunities to engage in costly activities that do not satisfy us.

In this passage, Jesus boldly declares, "I am the bread of life. Whoever comes to me will never go hungry." What a novel idea that one man could fulfill such hunger and unquenchable thirst! Jesus, the Bread of Life, came to reconcile humanity with God. The first of Jesus' well-known "I Am" statements in the Gospel of John, this identification as bread becomes a foundational representation of Jesus' role in the world and even foreshadows the Eucharist that will be instituted in his last days. In the second part of this verse, Jesus further clarifies that he will fulfill the basic needs—hunger and thirst—of any who come to him.

Jesus is the one who can quench one's spiritual hunger and thirst. I did not understand the fullness of my call at age six. But I am blessed with the opportunity to connect people to the one who truly satisfies. Jesus, the fulfillment of this new covenantal relationship, helps those who seek satisfaction outwardly and come up empty. Christ offers the opportunity to stretch their faith, enabling them to move past a physical loaf of bread to the eternal bread of love and life in Jesus Christ.

Thank you, God, for fulfilling our deepest longings and attending to our greatest needs. Amen.

In the seventies, American families purchased "Wonder Bread," the perfectly sliced loaf sealed in the white and multicolored plastic bag with the red twist tie. Known for its freshness, one loaf provided enough bread for sandwiches to feed a family for a week. We would often roll the tasty, gluten-filled slice into a ball and stick it to the bridge of our mouths for a fun snack.

In a variety of forms, bread has been a staple of households for centuries. It's no wonder that Jesus uses bread as an illustration to help us understand the role he is to fill, declaring that he is the Bread of Life. Physical food is essential to physical life, but it is not enough for the soul. Jesus insists there is a spiritual food that is more filling, satisfying, and sustaining than physical food. He reminds the Jews of their ancestors who were sustained in the wilderness by the bread God provided. Jesus now pronounces that he is that which is more filling than physical bread.

True satisfaction is more than any physical meal we can eat. We accept that Jesus, as the one sent from heaven, is the necessary ingredient that provides a connection to God while strengthening us in our human frailties and enabling us to live out our calling to be God's love in the world.

Having a relationship with Jesus is life-sustaining. It outweighs anything we could ever seek in this earthly life. One taste of Jesus invites us never to hunger again. We are connecting in ways that satisfy our deepest needs and most heartfelt longings. It seals our hearts forever.

Thank you, God, for the miracle of love and covenantal relationship with all of humanity. It feeds and nourishes us, just like a holy meal that offers us the bread and the cup. We want to be filled with you so that we can share your love with others. Amen.

The Beginning of Wisdom

AUGUST 12–18, 2024 • DAVID E. RAINEY

SCRIPTURE OVERVIEW: If you could ask God for one thing, what would it be? God offered this chance to Solomon, and the king asked for wisdom to rule God's people well. God honored this request by giving Solomon many other gifts too, as long as the king followed God's ways. The psalmist tells us that wisdom begins with understanding who we are and who God is. Ephesians addresses practical implications of wise living: follow the will of the Lord, be filled with the Spirit, encourage one another, and be grateful to God. The Gospel passage continues Jesus' metaphorical description of himself as the Bread of Heaven. Here Jesus anticipates the sacrament of Communion, in which we partake of his body and blood by faith.

QUESTIONS AND SUGGESTIONS FOR REFLECTION

- Read 1 Kings 2:10-12; 3:3-14. Do you hesitate to ask God to show you your call? Why?
- Read Psalm 111. Where have you seen God's faithful and just actions in your life? In the world?
- Read Ephesians 5:15-20. How do you live wisely and make the most of the time?
- Read John 6:51-58. What is the significance of Holy Communion in your life of faith? How has your understanding of this sacrament changed over time?

Husband, father of three, retired United Methodist pastor in Nashville, TN.

The scriptures this week invite us to reflect on the nature and gift of wisdom. Clearly, there is a difference between being "smart" and being wise. We may be clever, quick, knowledgeable, powerful, and wealthy, yet tragically foolish. But God would lead us into life-giving wisdom. How does this happen?

"The fear of the Lord is the beginning of wisdom," the psalmist says. As many scholars have pointed out, the Hebrew word sometimes translated into English as "fear" also means "awe" and "reverence." What a difference to understand that the psalmist is not calling for us to be afraid of God, but to be awestruck by God's power and in wonder at God's faithfulness!

Importantly, the psalmist's emphasis is not on our faithfulness to God, but God's faithfulness to us. Wisdom begins with remembering God's great deeds. God's nature is to be "gracious and merciful." Wisdom leads us into praise and thanksgiving: "I will give thanks to the LORD with my whole heart."

One pastor described a special journal he kept during the Thanksgiving season. Each day he listed three specific things for which he was grateful—not just "friends," for example, but a particular friend. Not simply "nature," but a specific experience in the outdoors. *I'll try that*, I thought, and a decade later I'm still at it. It gives me such joy! In the midst of abundant reasons for fear and anxiety, this practice grounds me every day in gratefulness and hope.

"The beginning of wisdom" suggests that wisdom originates in awe and thanksgiving but continues to grow and mature as we practice it. Let us be confident as we begin and end each day—not in our own understanding but in God's understanding of us.

O God, our Creator and Redeemer, fill us today with awe and thanksgiving. Help us to grow in your wisdom. Amen.

Our scripture today is set in a time of royal transition. King David has died after a long and respected reign. His son Solomon is now on the throne. It is a time of uncertainty and watchfulness for the people. Solomon is young, perhaps just twenty. How would he rule the kingdom which David had built? How would he use the power now in his hands? We can imagine Solomon had his own questions.

As the story is told, God appears to the new king in a dream and says, "Ask what I should give you." What an offer! Solomon answers carefully. Much depends on his answer, and God hasn't said, "I'll give you whatever you ask." This is not like Aladdin and his lamp. First, Solomon reflects on God's steadfast love for his father David. Implied is the question: Do I too have your steadfast love? Then Solomon admits he is only "a little child." He hardly knows how to go in and out of the building, yet God has made him king of this great people! It's all so overwhelming.

Few of us find ourselves in positions of such power and responsibility, but most of us can relate to feeling overwhelmed and ill-equipped. Perhaps we're in a new job. Maybe we're in a new marriage or newly a parent. Maybe we just woke up feeling unprepared for the challenges of the day. We want to do well—for ourselves and for those who are dependent on us—but we wonder if we are up to the task. Solomon offers us a model: Start by remembering God's steadfast love—for our forebears, for us, and for those we are called to serve.

Thank you, God, for your steadfast love. Equip me with the wisdom I need to meet today's challenges and to serve those who rely on me. Amen.

When God says to the newly crowned Solomon, "Ask what I should give you," Solomon ultimately responds: "Give your servant, therefore, an understanding mind to govern your people, able to discern between good and evil."

A part of wisdom is appreciating what we don't know. Members of my family are medical practitioners. They have observed that the safest providers are those who are ready to consult with others when they have questions. Solomon begins his reign with such an appreciation of his own limits. He asks God to give him understanding and to guide him in his decisions.

Solomon asks God for wisdom to "discern between good and evil." This request reflects a dilemma we often face. It's not that we don't want to choose the good. It's that we don't always know what the good is. Sometimes we are so afraid of making a wrong choice that we become immobilized. How important to remember that we live in grace! God does not expect Solomon, or any of us, to be infallible. The important thing is that we come to God seeking understanding, wanting to do the loving thing, and giving thanks for God's mercy in our mistakes.

As the dream concludes, Solomon's answer is met with divine approval. God is pleased not only with what Solomon asked for but with what he didn't ask for. He didn't seek personal glory or the destruction of his adversaries. He asked for understanding in order to serve others. God goes on to award Solomon many things, but it would not be wise for us to expect some kind of value-added bonus for seeking wisdom. Wisdom is its own reward.

O God of grace, you know my limits and my heart. Guide my decisions this day and sustain me with your grace. Amen.

This week's Gospel continues John's extended drama from last week about Jesus and bread. Chapter 6 began with an account of Jesus feeding a multitude using a boy's lunch. Then came the terrifying after-dinner sail in which Jesus appeared to his disciples walking on the water.

After telling us of these miraculous events, John turns to a different kind of drama—a spirited dialogue involving Jesus, a curious crowd, and some suspicious religious leaders. Jesus wants them all to have "true bread."

The image of bread is a powerful one. Since I started to bake bread myself, the image has become even more compelling. I want to choose healthy as well as tasty ingredients to eat and share. There are many kinds of bread throughout the world—from pita to tortilla, sourdough to corn sticks—but most people know some form of bread as "the staff of life." We need bread to fill and sustain us each day. Whether literal or spiritual, what is "true" bread? What will satisfy our deepest hungers and truly sustain our families, our congregations, and our communities?

In the world, many things are offered to us as bread. Which choices are foolish and which are wise? We can be lured by things which are in fact only spiritual junk food. Worse, we may feed on ideas which are harmful to our minds and hearts and lethal to our life together. Thus, we must be careful about our choices.

Knowing well the hungers of the human heart, filled with compassion, Jesus came offering the world "true bread," the bread of life, love, justice, and grace. Consider today your needs and your sources of bread. Which are truly satisfying? Consider how you can share this bread with others.

"Let them thank the LORD for his steadfast love, for his wonderful works to humankind. For he satisfies the thirsty, and the hungry he fills with good things" (Ps. 107:8-9). Amen.

In John 6 Jesus expresses his longing to feed the crowd with "true bread," that which will continually and most deeply satisfy their needs. But then he shifts from saying he will give them true bread to saying that he himself is that bread.

In this week's Gospel, Jesus proclaims, "I am the living bread that came down from heaven. Whoever eats of this bread will live forever." For most of those listening to Jesus, this was just wrong on so many levels! Bread was what you ate for dinner, or bread was the manna that got the Israelites through the wilderness, but Jesus calling himself "living bread from heaven" must have seemed either lunacy or blasphemy.

John presents Jesus' claim in all its jarring outlandishness and all its wondrous promise. On one hand, following Jesus would appear to be a fool's errand. On the other, it is the wisest of choices, the way of life itself. At some point, one either cautiously backs away from this Jesus or joyfully runs toward him.

In an old joke attributed to Groucho Marx, a man tells of his brother who thinks he's a chicken. "We don't try to talk him out of it," the man explains. "We need the eggs."

Most of us have times when we wonder if following Jesus is a very smart choice. But just often enough we have faith in the wisdom of it. We don't let anyone talk us out of it. We need the bread! One more time we take the bread which Jesus lovingly offers us—and taste eternal life.

"Be present at our table, Lord; be here and everywhere adored; thy creatures bless, and grant that we may feast in paradise with thee" (John Cennick, 1741). Amen.

Be careful then how you live, not as unwise people but as wise, making the most of the time."

In this week's reading from Ephesians, Paul continues to call the Christian community into a distinctive way of life, one which is loving and healthy, one which is grace-filled, one which builds up. Because foolishness abounds, followers of Christ have to be careful.

By being careful, Paul doesn't mean to be timid but to be intentional, to "take care" how we live. Otherwise, we can get distracted, be misled, lose our judgment, or simply become anesthetized.

"Do not get drunk with wine," Paul writes; and, of course, that's prudent advice. But perhaps by "drunk" Paul intends something more than the bottle. In a world where malevolent voices appeal to our worst selves, we must be wise about what spirits we imbibe. When we are spiritually thirsty, hurting and afraid, we are vulnerable. Social media algorithms can lead us into some dark places. Be careful, Paul says. Be wise. Be intentional. Be filled with "the Spirit."

Paul also urges us to "make the most of the time." It's another way of speaking about intentionality. As a cancer survivor I have been reminded of my mortality. We have a limited number of years and days. We don't want to waste them on things that don't matter, or worse, in ways which are destructive. Stated positively, we have precious resources which we can use well! Each day offers new opportunities to see and savor, to do justice and love mercy, to give thanks to God.

"Thou who hast by Thy might / led us into the light, / keep us forever in the path, we pray. / Lest our feet stray from the places, our God, where we met Thee; / lest, our hearts drunk with the wine of the world, we forget thee" (James Weldon Johnson, 1921). Amen.

Be filled with the Spirit," Paul urges. In today's passage he recommends one specific way by which people of faith can be filled: "Sing psalms and hymns and spiritual songs among yourselves."

The Methodist movement is deeply rooted in singing, of course. Charles Wesley is credited with writing 6500 hymns, many sung by Christians of all denominations. From "Hark the Herald Angels Sing" to "Christ the Lord Is Risen Today," whether in choir lofts, pews, or around a campfire, our singing has never been about everyone being on pitch. Rather, it's about the power of voices joined together to touch hearts, to connect us, to make room for the Spirit to inspire and give courage. Have you ever been surrounded by a group of singers, but did not feel like joining in? When I've found myself in that place, inevitably the music takes over. It's been put this way: Sometimes we sing the hymns and sometimes the hymns sing us!

At the end of his life my dad was hospitalized. Conversation was difficult. We both loved hymns so I began "In the Garden." To my wonder and comfort, Dad joined in: "And he walks with me, and he talks with me, and he tells me I am his own." Through music, we find we are able to give thanks to God "at all times and for everything in the name of our Lord Jesus Christ."

It's my experience that the transcendent power of music is not restricted to music written specifically for the church. The Holy Spirit works through many instruments and styles, Saturday night as well as Sunday morning. But whether it is through music, scripture, the beauty of nature, or the words of a poet, it is wise—it is good—that we find ways to be filled with the Spirit at all times.

"Through all the tumult and the strife, / I hear that music ringing. / It finds an echo in my soul. / How can I keep from singing?" (Robert Lowry, 1868). Amen.

In the Presence of the Divine

AUGUST 19–25, 2024 • DAVID DARK

SCRIPTURE OVERVIEW: God had prevented David from building a temple in Jerusalem but then permitted David's son Solomon to build it. In First Kings, Solomon places the ark of the covenant in the holiest place, and God's presence descends. The psalmist rejoices in the Temple and would rather be in its courts than anywhere else because that is where God dwells. The New Testament readings remind us that the people of God have always met with resistance. The author of Ephesians compares living the Christian life to going into battle, so we must be prepared. Jesus also meets with resistance in John. His teachings are too hard for many to accept, so they abandon him. When we face resistance, therefore, we should not be surprised; but we are also not alone.

QUESTIONS AND SUGGESTIONS FOR REFLECTION

- Read 1 Kings 8:1, 6, 10-11, 22-30, 41-43. How does your faith inform the hospitality you show to friends? To strangers?
- Read Psalm 84. How do you find joy in the Lord? Recall a recent time when you felt a deep sense of this joy.
- Read Ephesians 6:10-20. How do truth, righteousness, peace, faith, salvation, and God's word help you live boldly as an ambassador of the gospel of Jesus Christ?
- Read John 6:56-69. How do you respond to Jesus' question: "Does this offend you?" This teaching was hard for his disciples. Where do you struggle with it?

Associate professor of religion and the arts at Belmont University in Nashville, TN; author of *We Become What We Normalize: What We Owe Each Other in Worlds That Demand Our Silence* (Broadleaf Books, 2023).

When appeals to the sacred are made, we're never too far from someone's—or a group of someones'—sense of what is holy. We know the power of kneeling during a song for which people are expected to stand up. We know about the tension that is created when someone's actions don't sync up or play along with what's expected, especially in a space like a sports stadium or a church service that is considered sacred. King Solomon is playing with the fire of authority. We don't need archaeological studies to know what that looks and feels like.

But there's a necessary check on Solomon's sacred flex. God has promised to ensure David, Solomon, and their descendants as successors to the throne. Appeals to royalty as a sacred matter, however, do not suffice. The highest of heavenly appeals and the most beautiful and vast of earthly constructions will not contain the wildly free and wildly powerful God to whom Solomon makes his address. God's holiness breaks whatever chain of command we have in mind as we consider this scene, consigning prophets, priests, and kings the role of servants to God's righteousness.

Where God is rightly invoked, God hears the cry of the alleged foreigner—the one outside of Israel or whatever boundary we've conceived and established. God is too free, too holy, too welcoming for it to be otherwise. When we follow God appropriately, we receive those who are belittled and abused as our own.

Just and gracious God, help us conceive of you rightly and righteously. In the reading of your word, transform our thoughts and actions so that they are a sweet fragrance to those who feel estranged and far off from you. Amen.

God's presence can coincide with physical joy and comfort, but it isn't synonymous with it. We can, after all, experience God's presence even in grief and physically uncomfortable circumstances. We can experience God's presence anywhere. Even the most modest and mundane of spaces can be rightly thought of as the dwelling places of God.

Scripture describes the altars of God as places where every living creature can find safety. We can be those who help others find such rest in God. When we live into such a conception of the world, we live more knowingly and joyfully in our own skins. What does it mean to comport ourselves and arrange our lives as dwelling places of God?

For starters, it means regarding all other people as infinitely valuable bearers of the divine image. To undertake this imaginative, demanding, and sometimes joyous task is to begin to make wherever we find ourselves a sacred space. Yes, there are divisions all around us and even forms of desecration of these holy spaces we try to experience. But there's also the opportunity, new every morning, to live in the sacred now of God's presence. It is not, after all, merely theoretical. It's as real as the ground beneath our feet. We can recognize God's presence in all we say and do. We can embody and know it as a lived joy.

When we do this in every moment, we are giving glory to God. We undertake it in the lived-out specifics, practicing God's presence one holy human exchange at a time.

God, alert us to your presence as we negotiate our days. Enliven us to make your presence known in the ways we interact with, speak of, and characterize the living souls around us. Amen.

We build worship spaces and we design and lead worship services. We schedule stop and start times in chapels and sanctuaries. But then scripture issues a challenge, inviting us to imagine ourselves dwelling within God's courts and to imagine the space and span of our lives within God's house right here and right now in the land of the living. To contemplate our everyday lives in this way can upset our calendars, our agendas, our 11:00 a.m. worship time, and whatever it is we have planned. What would it mean to live the whole of our lives as prayer?

Start by recognizing all the ways we're prone to flee God's presence. What does that look like? We choose to live in tents of wickedness, seeking refuge in ill-gotten gain, deceit, denial, and corruption—fleeing the requirements of moral uprightness and whole-life integrity. Such spaces, however, have no power to save, no capacity to heal, and no lasting joy. Steering clear of such false sanctuaries requires discernment.

It is better to live as a welcoming doorkeeper in God's house than as a high roller in the tents of wickedness. God's righteousness will heal and restore in the long term. Perhaps we have to imagine it to sense and experience it. Amid the busy and noisy efforts of the workaday world, we have to slow down, accept silence, and gather our wits in light of the abundant goodness of God. We have to adjust our hearts and minds and bodies accordingly. This is the effort of prayer. This is the work of accepting reality on God's holy terms. This is waking up to our own lives.

Loving God, make us aware of and alive to the false signals of wicked operations, and make us alive to your righteous presence in every nook and cranny of our days. Make us doorkeepers in your abundant, soul-sustaining house. Amen.

God is gracious and gentle. God's mercy and loving-kindness are abundant. And yet we are called to be strong and stand in the strength of God's power. What kind of power is this? How do we conceive it properly?

Paul pulls out the poetry with a heavy dose of paradoxical imagery. There's armor to be had—weapons too—but it's the kind of protection and defense a body assumes beneath the skin. There are evil days, but we have good news of peace to share, embody, and make known. We can fasten around ourselves a commitment to truthfulness. We can guard and protect our centers with God's righteousness. Faith in God's goodness and the hope of the promised age to come can function as a shield against the strategies of enmity, accusation, and rancor. They are legion. But they are also doomed.

The word of God in all of this is indeed like a sword that cuts to the heart of these matters. It restores our senses, focuses our minds, and divides the real and the lasting from the false and the temporal. God's word is also relentlessly communal. We get to remain alert together, praying for one another, and drawing energy boldly to make known—paradoxically again—the mystery of this gospel, this good news.

In an age of weaponized despair, scripture invites us to know and conceive of God's power as creative, effective, longer lasting, and more definitively triumphant than steel and chemicals. God's truth and love, after all, have the final word.

God of power and glory, quicken our minds and bodies with your always-liberating, always-effective word so that we make known your love and encouragement to our sad and weary world. Amen.

When we look at one another's faces, we are beholding infinitely valuable bearers of the divine image. God's image is there, not sometimes but always. When we talk to others, however, recognizing the divine image we are looking at can sometimes prove difficult. It is easy—too easy—to mistake a person for an idea we associate with their appearance, their carriage, their positions, and their opinions. A person is none of these things. They are more than the ideas they express, push, or loudly cling to. They are more than whatever it is, for better or worse, that has hold of them.

We are too. It is easy—too easy—for us to mistake a rejection (or even a simple questioning) of an idea or a position we hold for an attack on our person or our very identity. It is easy to mistake a struggle over ideas for a bodily attack. Rightly sensing and naming the real struggle is a formidable task.

This is the task scripture calls us to. Wrestle away with ideas, with bad conceptions of self and others. Duke it out with the wicked infrastructures of crushingly awful ideas about what humans are here for. Take on the authorities. Confront, interrogate, and demand accountability of unexamined policies born of unexamined decisions, policies that belittle, malign, cage, crush, and even kill our fellow human beings. Fight the systems.

But we must be exceedingly wary of reducing others to one issue or identity. Nobody's just an operative. Nobody's just a bigot or an abuser. We absolutely must combat the traumatic actions of others. But as we hunger and thirst for righteousness in the land of the living, we must look into the eyes of those we're prone to oppose and see the image of God. It's always there.

Loving God, may your love and affection for our alleged enemies guide our interactions with them. Make us agents of your love. Amen.

Jesus is often a tough pill to swallow. His words, we are assured, are spirit and life. But it is sometimes difficult to know how to process them thoughtfully and meaningfully.

In this we are not alone. Scripture tells us that people who knew, heard, considered, sympathized with, and even followed Jesus struggled with the way he described himself and his intentions. They found his teaching too difficult to accept. *Eat his flesh? Drink his blood? Live by doing so?*

Blessedly, neither Jesus nor his followers are completely done with the matter. A dialogue ensues. Is Jesus referring to his actual flesh? No and yes. It is the Spirit, after all, that gives everlasting life. Incorporating the kind of life Jesus describes, embodies, and hands on to others across the centuries is a commitment of the whole heart, mind, and body. If we try to see it as a simple question of a literal or even figurative consuming of Jesus' life, we miss the engagement into which Jesus is inviting us. These matters require thought, meditation, and another person or two with whom we can mull—and mull repeatedly—these difficult teachings, this difficult life.

Movingly, Jesus seemed to get it. His insistence on a difficult paradox meant that he lost people. He asked those who remained if they, too, were going to move along and leave him behind. Perhaps even more movingly, Simon Peter spoke as one who, though confused, remained convinced. Jesus' words, he observes, bear eternal life. Peter was right.

Illuminating God, make us students of the everlasting life you offer, and keep us attuned to all the ways that life overcomes death here and now. Amen.

We have a phrase that gets at a movement of the heart. When a person is suddenly and discernibly prepared to make a change or own up to a bad decision, we sometimes refer to this event as a "Come to Jesus" moment. It's a lovely phrase. It's a biblical reference, but it isn't limited to the Bible. It names a mind alive to repentance, a change of heart, and a body in sync—righteously in sync—with what heart and mind have decided to do. Such moves are a very big deal. They can add up to revolution. Maybe they're the only moves that really add up to revolution.

In scripture, Jesus tells us that whenever these moves happen, we have God to thank for them. When real repentance and real revolution occur, we will know it because we know change by its fruits. The real deal is its own credential. And God deals in reality. To accept reality on its own terms in our daily life is to be in relationship with God as Jesus makes God known. The eternal life Jesus promises isn't fanciful. It is eternally realistic. Jesus calls us to a higher realism than we're accustomed to. He invites us to get real.

Jesus does so with some hard sayings. Then the Bible gives us accounts of what living according to those hard sayings looks like. We have the lived passion of Jesus: his public confrontation with the forces of evil and his mission of healing, loving, freeing, and delivering. To enter, embody, and extend his realistic eternal life is to enter into his passion in our everyday exchanges. We can do so because God grants us the power to do it. We can become more real. By God's power, we will. It is promised.

Eternally realistic God, grant us the ability to see ourselves and others as you see us. Give us the eyes of faith to see what you're showing us. Lift us up. Amen.

God's Good Gifts

AUGUST 26–SEPTEMBER 1, 2024 • ANDREW GARLAND BREEDEN

SCRIPTURE OVERVIEW: The poetry of Song of Solomon is thick with romantic imagery, and most scholars agree that these lines mean what they say on the surface; they are written from the author to the beloved. Psalm 45 echoes the refrain of admiration and desire. Such desire is not wrong if it is awakened at the proper time, as the author of Song of Solomon says elsewhere. James argues that ethical living is done not in word but in deed. True religion is not putting on a show but displaying mercy and controlling the tongue. In Mark's Gospel, Jesus rebukes some of the religious leaders on this very account because they talk of obedience to God but do not live it out. What we say and what we do should match.

QUESTIONS AND SUGGESTIONS FOR REFLECTION

- Read Song of Solomon 2:8-13. The narrative poetry of Song of Solomon invites us into scripture in a different way than other texts. How does God speak to you through this poetry?
- Read Psalm 45:1-2, 6-9. How do your relationships honor the gift of love?
- Read James 1:17-27. When do you find yourself as merely a "hearer" of the word and not a "doer"? What motivates you to act on God's word?
- Read Mark 7:1-8, 14-15, 21-23. What human traditions or rituals do you tend to make too important?

Acquisitions editor of *The Upper Room* daily devotional guide; graduate of Lipscomb University and Vanderbilt University Divinity School; lives in Charlotte, TN.

I must confess that Song of Solomon isn't a book that I devote a lot of time to reading. I never quite know what to do with it. But when I read the verses in the passage above, I am struck by the beautiful and poetic language in phrases such as "The flowers appear on the earth; the time of singing has come, and the voice of the turtledove is heard in our land. The fig tree puts forth its figs . . . they give forth fragrance." I am amazed at how sensory these verses are—flowers, the earth, the voice of the turtledove, the fragrance of the figs.

Some biblical scholars interpret Song of Solomon as a love poem from God to the Israelites with whom God made a covenant. I think this is a fitting interpretation and the one I am most drawn to because in my reading, so much of scripture is the story of God's love for God's people. The Bible is full of magnificent images and wonderful metaphors that help us relate to God and give us glimpses into God's loving character.

I find that one of the most deep and meaningful connections I have with God comes through language. Scripture is God's gift to us, and I have immense gratitude for this gift. For me, the words of scripture are where my relationship with God begins. Scripture is one of the places where I encounter God each day. Even in parts of the Bible that I struggle with and don't fully understand, I can sense God's mysterious presence in the words, inviting me into the story to challenge me, to make me think, to teach me something. Those times when I come across a particularly striking image or turn of phrase, it's almost as if I can hear God saying to me, "Arise, my love, my fair one, and come away."

Dear God, thank you for the gift of scripture and for your vast love for us. Create in us each day the desire to encounter you through your word. Amen.

Psalm 45 arose from an occasion of joy—a wedding. It is a song attributed to the Sons of Korah, who were descendants of one of Moses' cousins. They were musicians who played an important part in temple worship, and several of the psalms are attributed to this group.

This particular psalm contains many theological themes and is grounded in reverence for God. I have a deep and abiding affinity for worship music and for those who compose and perform it. I think this affinity began early on in my spiritual development. Singing hymns was an important part of the church tradition that I grew up in. A typical worship service would include seven or eight—maybe more—hymns. To this day, singing remains for me an important part of worship and something that I continue to enjoy. Hymns continue to shape my theology and my understanding of who God is.

I admire the depth and economy of a well-written hymn and the powerful emotional response that it can evoke. I admire the way a hymn's poetry and musical setting can capture thoughts and feelings in new and helpful language. Perhaps their emotive and layered nature is what draws me to the Psalms. They give me a new vocabulary for my emotions and new language for God.

I love the first verse of Psalm 45: "My heart is stirred by a noble theme . . . my tongue is the pen of a skillful writer" (NIV). It seems to me that this could be the motto of artists everywhere whose creativity points to the Divine, whose work adds richness and depth to our worship and to our spiritual lives.

Dear God, thank you for the gift of creativity and the way it enriches our lives and helps us draw closer to you. Amen.

The New International Version of Psalm 45:6 says, "Your throne, O God, will last forever and ever; a scepter of justice will be the scepter of your kingdom." If you're like me, you might be wondering what place the word *justice* has in a wedding psalm. I haven't been to too many weddings where justice is a prominent theme. However, one school of interpretation reads this psalm as an allegory for Israel as the bride of God. Viewed through this lens, I find it a good reminder that there's a relational element to justice. In one sense, justice is all about relationship—finding balance and seeking reconciliation when the scales tip too far in one direction.

When I was an undergraduate, I took a class at the Tennessee Prison for Women. Each week, a professor and a group of traditional students from my university would drive across town to the prison and have class with a group of inmates who were also working toward their college degrees. One of the goals of our time together was dialogue between the inmates and traditional students.

During the first class, the teacher asked us to define justice. We all fumbled around a good bit trying to give an answer. I'm pretty sure I never succeeded. Even today I cannot give you a succinct and articulate response. But what I could do is tell you about the friendships that I formed with many of the women, how they welcomed me—someone remarkably different from them in many ways—into their community, how the program we were part of helped them pave a new path for themselves, how the relationships we forged enabled us to break stereotypes and recognize one another's humanity, and how over the course of a semester the balance of the scales tipped, if ever so slightly, in the direction of reconciliation and peace.

God of justice, teach us to recognize the gift of being in relationship with others and to seize the opportunities that arise from those relationships to make the world more just. Amen.

When was the last time someone gave you a perfect gift? What was it? Who gave it to you? What made it perfect? Several years ago, my brother-in-law gave me an old mountain bike. I've spent many afternoons on that bike, riding along the trails at a local park. It has brought me many hours of joy and has been a welcome escape from the stress and grind of daily life. It gets me outside and away from my desk—away from the emails and calls and requests and to-do lists. It's sitting here only a few feet away from me, a reminder to drop it all and give my brain a break.

I have always loved the outdoors and spending time in nature. It is where I go when I need rest and healing. It soothes my mind, and it is where I feel most connected to my body and most like my authentic self. It is a different world from the one that I and so many of us inhabit each day—a world of screens and noise and disembodiment, a world that is increasingly disconnected and anxious, a world that is exhausted and running on fumes. I spend a lot of time outside biking, hiking, and rock climbing. I make it a point to get outside almost every day. When my workday is finished, I turn off my computer and head out. It's one of my spiritual disciplines.

Our society doesn't always place a high value on play, especially when we could be doing more "productive" things. And I think that's because society doesn't always value rest or recognize how essential it is to our health and well-being. Intervals of rest and renewal in whatever forms they might take are important to our mental and physical survival. They are gifts from God and wonderful gifts that we can give ourselves.

Dear God, thank you for the gift of rest. May we intentionally set aside time each day for rest and renewal. Amen.

Not long ago, I started writing notes to myself and placing them on the bulletin board that hangs above my desk. These messages include character traits that I want to exhibit in my life, words of encouragement that people have offered me, and reminders I know will help. One says, "It's okay to say no." Another reads, "Don't do dumb things." And one that has proven helpful time and time again and that I have been exceedingly grateful for is "Listen, and then speak." A paraphrase of James 1:19, "Be quick to listen [and] slow to speak," this is my reminder to be a good listener and also to be careful and thoughtful with my words. This verse is about attentiveness, but it is also about self-control.

The words we speak and how we speak them are serious business. They can be life-giving or life-depleting. They can make someone's day or do irreparable harm. I can remember words—good and bad—that people spoke to me as far back as my childhood. The words that others speak to us remain with us, and the words we speak to them remain with them. Our words matter. There have been more times than I would like to admit that I have spoken words that I wish I could take back, when I have said something that I wish I hadn't. And I imagine that's probably true for most of us.

Each day I try to speak words to others that give life. Some days I'm better at this than others. And it's not always easy. But I try to remind myself of the many times that someone has spoken affirming words to me and the gift that those words have been. Today we will no doubt have the opportunity to be good listeners and to speak words of affirmation and hope. This could very well be some of the most important work we do today. We never know the difference that it might make in someone's life.

Dear God, thank you for life-giving and affirming words. I pray that I will always use my words carefully and speak in a way that builds others up. Amen.

I'm inclined to side with the Pharisees here. Isn't their question innocent enough? Isn't Jesus' response a little harsh? I'm someone who appreciates tradition and can have a hard time breaking away from it, so I get it. These verses do make me pause, however, and ask myself some questions: What traditions do I participate in regularly that are helpful? Why are they helpful? And on the flip side, what traditions do I engage in that are perhaps unhelpful?

I think about the story of the man by the pool of Bethesda in John 5:1-9. People would go to this pool in search of healing. Jesus encountered the man there who had no one to help him into the pool so he was cut off by others every time he tried to enter. I imagine the man trying the same thing time and time again for years, only to have someone always make it to the pool ahead of him. This is a story about a miraculous healing. But I think it's also an invitation to take a close look at our patterns and habits and ask ourselves if any of them are no longer working for us.

Traditions can be a wonderful gift when they serve a useful purpose. Reciting prayers and ancient creeds connect us to Christians across the centuries. Rituals add depth, richness, and character to our worship. But sometimes our traditions keep us stuck in a cycle of futility, doing the same thing over and over and always hoping for a different result. They can keep us from exploring what's possible. They can even prevent our healing and the fullness of life that God offers us. Maybe Jesus is telling us in Mark that it's okay to examine our traditions from time to time. Maybe he's reminding us here that it's okay to try something new. The freedom that comes from letting go of traditions that no longer serve us well can also be a gift.

Dear God, thank you for the traditions that connect us and bring us closer to you. Give us the courage let go of the ones that no longer serve us well and to try something new. Amen.

There's a sense of urgency that comes across in these verses. In verse 14, Jesus is decidedly emphatic, saying to the crowd, "Listen to me . . . and understand." I appreciate Jesus' intensity. And I think it's entirely appropriate. Jesus is shifting the focus away from rules and toward relationships. He is placing the emphasis on the condition of our hearts and our behavior. How do we treat one another? How do we show love to our neighbor?

Recently, on a Sunday afternoon I stopped at a coffee shop on my way home from church. As I was walking in, a person approached me and asked for money to buy food. Although I had plenty of cash, I declined and went on my way. My conscience immediately started nagging me, and I felt guilty. I had just gone to church that morning. I had listened to the sermon, prayed the prayers, and sung the hymns. I had checked all the boxes. But when I was given the opportunity to act on my faith by helping someone in my community, I had chosen not to. When I got back to my car, I considered the state of my heart and sought the way I truly wanted to respond. I decided to drive around the parking lot to see if I could find the person. But I never did.

Experiences like this compel me to measure my actions against my faith. They call me to account, to take an inventory of my priorities. I don't always like the result. But such experiences are a necessary, if painful, gift. They get my attention, and, quite emphatically, force me to stop and examine my heart. They are my mandate to do better, to help my neighbors who are struggling, and to live out my Christian faith in all my relationships. Jesus' message here is clear: It's not our ability to follow rules that's important but the way we treat others that truly matters.

Dear God, thank you for the opportunities we have to show love to our neighbors. Help us never to miss a chance to serve others in your name. Amen.

The Life to Which God Calls Us

SEPTEMBER 2–8, 2024 • JAMES E. STRICKLAND

SCRIPTURE OVERVIEW: It is sometimes an uncomfortable subject for many, but God does have ethical standards. The author of Proverbs declares that those who act unjustly, particularly if they oppress the poor, will provoke God's judgment. The psalmist repeats the refrain that God blesses the righteous but is not pleased with those who choose a consistent lifestyle of rebellion against God. James challenges us practically on this point. Do we judge people by their wealth or status? This is not from God. True faith shows no partiality and prompts action. Jesus models this in Mark when he heals two Gentiles. Jews and Gentiles generally remained separate (an ancient form of racism), but Jesus did not discriminate based on their ethnicity. He cared only about their hearts.

QUESTIONS AND SUGGESTIONS FOR REFLECTION

- Read Proverbs 22:1-2, 8-9, 22-23. How has God shown you that there is no difference between persons who are rich and persons who are poor? How does this affect your actions?
- Read Psalm 125. When have you seen righteousness in someone the community (or the church) has labeled "wicked"?
- Read James 2:1-17. How do your works support your faith? How does your faith in God move you to action on behalf of others?
- Read Mark 7:24-37. God calls us to love all our neighbors. How can you be a good neighbor to those your community has excluded?

Retired Christian educator; ordained deacon; husband to Starr and father to Beth (Brooklyn, NY) and Andrea (Disney Cruise Line); active at Belmont United Methodist Church, Nashville, TN.

Proverbs, one of five Wisdom books in the Bible, is a collection of truths and sayings intended to shape our lives into contributions for the whole community, lives that are gifts to be shared. When I think of the wisdom taught in Proverbs, I think of my grandfathers. Interestingly, my family name means "tender of the cows" and, indeed, my paternal grandfather was a dairyman offering fresh milk to the community. My maternal grandfather was of Scottish descent, a man of extremely high character who loved life, his family, and his church and saw them as God's gift to him. He lived his life as a reflection of this love back to God.

As I read today's passage, I am reminded of a deeply profound Rembrandt painting *The Apostle Paul* (c. 1657) hanging in the National Gallery of Art in Washington, DC. It depicts Paul sitting at his desk deep in thought as if contemplating his life, God's love for him, and the reflection of this love as it was exhibited through his daily living.

Our lives should be a reflection of God's presence through our thoughts, decisions, and actions—remembering that each day is a gift from God to be shared with the whole community for the betterment of all creation. Heeding the wisdom sayings found in Proverbs is a way we can remember the life God calls us to and the ways we are to treat those around us, especially those who need our generosity, respect, and prayers.

Almighty God, may our lives today reflect these words of wisdom in our thoughts and our actions. Amen.

The Psalms invite us to experience our emotions and senses—joys, sorrows, adoration, prayer, strength, weakness, sights of grandeur, sounds of praise, feelings of majesty, and the sweet tastes of creation. You can find a psalm that expresses just about any emotion. Today's psalm represents a journey of trusting in the surrounding love of God.

This surrounding love of God came to life for me on a recent trip to Seattle, Washington. For three days as we traveled throughout the area, we could see Mount Rainier (originally known as Tahoma) in its full glory against bright blue skies with its jagged snow-capped peaks, all in clear view no matter where we were. While there we visited Mount Rainier National Park and experienced the grandeur of the Cascade Mountain range. We hiked through dark green forests and open meadows ablaze with wildflowers and occasionally saw some small creatures. The feeling was like being in a sanctuary completely surrounded by God's love in the majesty of God's creation. I can understand why the steadfastness of the mountain is used in this psalm to represent the constancy of God.

The transition in verse 3 provides the turning point for this psalm. It reminds the reader that the assurance of God expressed in the first two verses is not separated from the world but rather is found right in the midst of any struggle or "wickedness." My physical encounter with the holy in the mountains of northern Washington was a retreat from my ordinary life, but we are reminded through the psalm that God's presence is steadfastly with us every ordinary day of our lives.

Gracious God, thank you for the grandeur of your creation! Thank you for the steadfastness of your love. May our lives reflect your presence to all those who come our way. Amen.

Today we find ourselves in the letter of James, dealing with issues of showing favoritism, berating the poor, dealing dishonestly, and professing faith without works to support our beliefs. Martin Luther famously called James an "epistle of straw" because he did not think ethical instruction was related to salvation. However, Methodism's founder, John Wesley, believed strongly that these "warnings" were essential and would lead us to a deeper faith in Jesus Christ.

While on a mission trip to Haiti, we missioners were told our work there would help the Haitians tremendously; however, we were "to work with our brothers and sisters," respecting them, sharing with them, and listening to them. When the project neared completion we were offered a day of relaxation at a nearby American hotel complex. When we asked if our Haitian brothers and sisters could join us, the answer was "No, they are not allowed!" We refused the invitation and celebrated with the Haitians in another setting.

Throughout scripture we are reminded we have much to learn from our brothers and sisters who are poor by worldly standards but often much richer than we in their faith. Jesus proclaimed that the poor among us are also the inheritors of God's kingdom. Their faith, trust and belief show us how we are to live.

James's words invite us to put action to our words. The best way to test and build our faith is to examine our actions. We must ask ourselves, "Am I being true to my faith through good works?" "Am I honest in my responses?" "Am I judging by appearance only?" "Am I loving my neighbor as myself?"

Forgive us, O God, for our unfaithfulness. Give us strength and guidance this day. Amen.

My family attends a large-membership, multi-cultural United Methodist Church that recently made an official decision to become a reconciling congregation, meaning we commit to being a welcoming space for persons who identify as LGBTQ+. As I reflect on today's scripture, I am remembering the years of conversation, anger, hate-filled notes, and also membership loss as the congregation voted affirmatively to step out in faith in what we believed was right, following the teachings and ministry of Jesus Christ.

The decision to become a reconciling congregation came after three long years of listening to one another, carefully listing all concerns, and praying. After the affirmative vote, the next step was to create a welcoming statement that would appear on every printed publication from the church, clarifying our identity and proclaiming our commitment to be a place where all are welcomed to encounter the love of God.

Each community of faith, and each individual follower of Christ, must consider these words from James. The debate about the connection between faith and works has long raged with ardent adherents on each side proclaiming their way is the best—or the only—way. But the whole of scripture teaches that both are essential. Our faith must inform our works, and so our faith is essential. But if our works do not point back to our faith, as James says, what is the good of our faith?

For my local church, participation in local Pride events, the display of rainbow flags throughout our building, and our publicly posted welcome statement are visible signs of our ministry for *all* God's people. We dug into what we believe as a community of faith and have then allowed that faith to inform our works.

This day, O God, we pray that our faith and our works intertwine to help us live and work for your kingdom here on earth. Amen.

The Life to Which God Calls Us 297

In today's reading, a mother with strong faith approaches Jesus and begs him to free her daughter from an unclean spirit. The interchange in this story has challenged Jesus' followers for centuries. It appears that Jesus is hostile to the Syrophoenician woman before he admits defeat—two things we don't really see Jesus do elsewhere. While the struggle in the text relates to Jesus' purpose in the world and the challenges the early church faced around inclusion of Gentiles, it can also challenge our relationship with those around us today.

When I was studying for a master's degree in Christian education at Scarritt College and Graduate School in Nashville, Tennessee, my advisor recommended that I teach in the children's center that was located on campus. I felt insulted and wanted to invest my time in something that would be more worthwhile toward reaching my goal. I valued children and their role in the community of faith but did not think that working with them would benefit my intended educational path. My advisor's wisdom prevailed, however, and I spent a very beneficial year teaching four-year-olds.

How do we as Christians view those who are not perceived as valuable to our society today? Jesus at first dismisses the woman for reasons we may not know or may not be comfortable attributing to him. The woman has the wherewithal to advocate for herself and her daughter. She challenges Jesus, and he admits she is right. How have we dismissed or ignored those among us who try to speak for themselves and their communities? How do we react when we are challenged to live out our professed beliefs? What, exactly, can we learn from Jesus' experience in this story?

Open our ears, gracious God, to those among us who are often dismissed or ignored. Help us listen and respond with understanding and love. Amen.

As Jesus leaves the region of Tyre and heads toward the Sea of Galilee, word of his healing power spreads quickly throughout the area. As I read this story three words immediately come to mind: *compassion, wholeness,* and *thankfulness.*

A deaf man is brought to Jesus for healing. Notice the compassion Jesus has for this man. Notice how Jesus cares for this man who was born deaf. Quietly and alone with him, Jesus speaks a word *Ephphatha,* which means "open up." The man's ears are opened, his tongue is released, and he speaks! Imagine the joy, excitement, and perhaps even fear in what this man now experiences for the very first time in his life—the ability to hear and speak!

Have you ever experienced such joy, excitement, or fear when something changed or "opened up" for you? Did you offer a prayer of thanksgiving for this event, this blessing, this healing?

Before my senior year of college, I experienced a call from God into the ministry of Christian education. What joy and excitement filled my whole life, and yet what challenges I now faced. My future was unknown even though I knew what I had been called to pursue. New questions began emerging: *Which graduate school should I attend? How would I pay for school? How long would it take? Where would I serve after completing the required degree?*

A shift, a change, or an opening of a new path often challenges us at the same time that it excites us. Our paths in life are awesome, difficult, and sometimes hard to understand. Yet when we completely trust God, we can fully trust and follow God's guidance. Today, reflect on the new things that have challenged and excited you, and offer a prayer of thanksgiving to God for all God has done for you!

Thank you, loving and caring God, for your everlasting guidance and purpose in my life. Amen.

We are bombarded with news of violence, killings, wars, famine, climate change, fires, hunger, and separations—all hitting us like giant waves. We often want to hide from the traumatic reality of what's happening in our world. It's easy to find ourselves crying out to God, wondering just exactly who is in charge around here.

The second half of Psalm 125 acknowledges this despair. "The wicked rod won't remain," says the Common English Bible, indicating that wickedness is actually holding the controls, at least temporarily. It can certainly feel at times that wickedness and evil have the upper hand. And when that seems to be the case, it's all the more important to remain faithful to God's goodness.

When it seems evil is triumphant, we must remember the greatness of God and the psalmist's faith that we are secure in God's love and grace forever. God's love will never change. The Psalms are constant reminders of God's magnificence and grace, regardless of who or what may be trying to separate us from God's love and grace.

On a mission trip to Malawi, my team members and I were invited to bring small gifts for the children: soccer balls, bubbles, stickers, small toys, that kind of thing. I decided to bring kazoos. During a Sunday morning worship in an outside brush arbor, I gave each child a kazoo and we played them together. Such joy ensued! I was reminded of the joy there is to be had in praising God through whatever means available, in whatever situation we find ourselves. God's presence is everlasting. Thanks be to God!

Step outside, look around, count your blessings, and offer a prayer of joy and thanksgiving for wherever you are right now.

God's Wisdom

SEPTEMBER 9–15, 2024 • STEPHEN HANDY

SCRIPTURE OVERVIEW: These readings offer a common theme: God offers wisdom to the Israelites in order that they may be a people of obedience. As the Israelites continuously deny God, God's wisdom pursues them in a quiet but gentle way to keep them on the path of righteousness. God shows them signposts so that there is always graceful guidance to keep them focused on the pathway ahead. James reminds his readers that the tongue is both a giver and destroyer of life. When using words, use them wisely, so that God may be honored and people may be healed.

QUESTIONS AND SUGGESTIONS FOR REFLECTION

- Read Proverbs 1:20-33. When have you neglected God's wisdom? What caused your neglect? What will it take to wait and reconnect to God's wisdom?

- Read Psalm 19:1-14. What gets in the way of hearing God even in the silence of your day? In the midst of competing noises, how can you learn to appreciate the silence so that God can speak?

- Read James 3:1-12. How do you deprogram your mind, heart, and soul to listen and not talk so much? How do you create a practice of living out of the anatomy of two ears and one mouth versus talking twice as much as you listen?

- Read Mark 8:27-38. Who is Jesus for you? Do your words for Jesus align with your actions in the world? If Jesus is the Messiah, the Anointed One, what behaviors in your life need to change to align with what comes from your mouth?

Lead pastor of McKendree United Methodist Church in downtown Nashville, TN; associate district superintendent in the Tennessee-Western Kentucky Conference; strong advocate for racial and restorative justice, serving the poor and marginalized, and participating in life groups for discipleship, missional engagement, and accountability.

God grants us wisdom in all aspects of our lives, all parts of our being, especially when discerning how to navigate through the chaos, disorder, and disruptions in our lives. Wisdom is an undervalued and underestimated gift. Mother Wisdom comes to us upon invitation and is never forced. Think about a time you needed more knowledge than you had available, but you had the capacity for more. Wisdom bridges the gap between our ability and capability. Wisdom is best practiced when we put feet on God's knowledge.

Have you ever walked or driven somewhere new only to discover you were lost because of unclear signage? Even with modern-day GPS technology, we can get lost. What do you do when you get lost—stop and reevaluate or forge ahead?

God's first people, the Israelites, repeatedly got lost. But to make matters worse, they refused to ask for the wisdom to return to and stay on the path that God had laid out. They wanted to do things their own way, and we are often the same, wishing to build up our own sense of importance, rather than follow God's plan. The Spirit of Wisdom guides us to steps that are good for the whole community, whereas we generally seek to prove we are right, lifting ourselves above our peers. Maybe that's the compelling dilemma that keeps humanity from requesting wisdom—we want to be right, and sometimes we choose that over God's calling for us to be good for all.

Our Israelite siblings had a reputation for dismissing God's instructions for their lives, just as we do today. God would be justified in no longer sharing wisdom with us, but that's not God's nature. God is waiting to give us wisdom for this life. We simply have to ask.

God who is all-wise and all-knowing, grant us your presence and power. For in your presence, your wisdom is evident. May your spirit of wisdom consume us daily as we represent your kingdom on earth as it is in heaven. Amen.

Shhh! Be quiet! Silence is speaking! As odd as it sounds, words can get in the way of hearing. We live in a culture where speaking is the preferred method of communication. David, the prophet, military strategist, and, in this psalm, music director tells his audience to listen to the heavens speaking in a quiet gentleness. While people sleep on earth, the heavens are pronouncing and recounting the glory of God and rejoicing without using words. From the celestial introductions of each day to the closing of the night, God fills each component of the earth and all its inhabitants.

God's glory is the manifestation of holiness and evidence in the world. Holiness is unspoken and at the same time speaks volumes throughout the day and night, as each progresses and complements each other. Day and night take turns pouring constantly into each other as the stream of God's glory ebbs and flows and takes residence in the earth. God's word is gracefully embodied and embroidered in the heavens and seen across the horizons.

God's silence demands attention as the arrangements of all heavenly instruments await with anticipation the heavenly glory. Regardless of the arrangements, God is orchestrating and causing an outpouring of celebratory moments and movements. Even when we can't hear it, the heavens are pronouncing a response to the marvelous works of God's hands. Will you join the celebration in silence?

God of creation and holiness, give us insight to understand what it is to share in your glory on earth as it is in heaven. Immerse us in patterns of deep silence so we can be vessels that connect to the heavenly horizons and the faithful foundations on the earth. Amen.

Directions can be tricky, especially if you are in a new place or country and are not familiar with the culture, language, and customs. Things get "lost in translation" easily. Having the interpretative lens to translate the directions leads to a better sense of forward motion and a greater sense of competency. One of the beauties of time spent studying and learning God's directions is being confident in our path forward.

God's directions are accompanied with visible and clear signposts, as outlined in verses 8-11. God's grace invites us to pay attention to these everyday signposts. They become spiritual maps for formation and transformation as we are drawn closer to God. From signs of caution, dead ends, and detours, these signposts come with clear messages that help us adapt to dangers that pull us away from God.

When we follow God's directions, those signposts guide us away from our own foolish ways and inability to think rationally and act honorably. They help prevent material possessions, self-centeredness, and prejudices from causing us to become misaligned with God's will.

We know that God's ways are always directed toward unity in the body of Christ. If God doesn't direct us, how will we find our way into God's preferred future? We want to be humble and honorable on this journey of faith. We follow God's direction so that "the words of [our] mouths and the meditation of [our] hearts" will be pleasing to God.

God, direct us so that our ways will be your ways, our hearts will be your heart and our hands will be your hands in the world. May we never become complacent and satisfied with mediocrity, but grounded in your grace and compelled by your radical love. In Jesus' name. Amen.

Teachers can be incredible and inspiring leaders who shape and transform each generation of students. But a teacher can only do so much. Students must listen intentionally to grasp the information. Here's the challenge: No one is ever directly taught to listen. We are only taught and graded on speaking.

Opening our mouths is risky business, especially if we fail to think about our words before we speak them. Controlling our speech is critical. Once we say words, we cannot take them back. Were they harmful, the damage is done.

As we begin to tame our tongue, we can start by understanding how God designed us. God designed us to listen more than we speak: We have two ears and only one mouth. James talks about the items that control, whether a bit for a horse or a small rudder on a boat. In both cases, each controls the direction. For humans, it doesn't require a separate device. What if we simply listen twice as much as we speak? I'm sure that would bring God great joy!

We must be careful what we say and how we say it. Words can create a fire or put one out. Let's examine our words and witness. We have the responsibility and the choice to be light and salt in the world instead of darkness and bitterness.

God of mercy, forgive us when we intentionally hurt one another with our words. Help us to listen more than we speak, and to use our words to build up others rather than to tear them down. Thank you for extending grace to us when we don't represent you by our words. In Jesus' name. Amen.

Circuses and carnivals displaying animals who are tamed and trained to do amazing tricks leave us in awe of what's possible. Think about taming the lion, the king of the jungle, or the tiger, a fierce predator. Now imagine if humanity could tame and train their tongues the same way. The tongue can be extremely deceptive and dangerous, especially when it goes unchecked. The tongue can spew evil and division while also being gracious and generous. Our tongues have the ability to curse and to bless in the same breath.

God's intention for the tongue is to simply bless (or love) God and to bless (or love) our neighbors. Why deviate from God's intent and instruction? Do apple trees produce oranges or do pear trees produce peaches? James reminds us of the volatility of the tongue and calls us to use our tongues only in the way intended. If we are made in the image of God, then our tongues should affirm and give life.

Solomon writes in Proverbs 12:14, "From the fruit of their speech, people are well satisfied; their work results in reward" (CEB). Good should come from our minds because our humanity reflects the holiness of God. That good should flow from our mouths, encouraging and building up the world around us. Jesus came to earth to show us the power and impact of our words. There is truly life and death in the tongue. When we follow Jesus, goodness and mercy flow from our tongues. Use your words wisely!

God who gives us breath to breathe and words to use, remind us that our words and witness represent Jesus Christ in the world. May we choose our words prayerfully and carefully. Amen.

Identity: Who am I? Who am I becoming? Without a clear sense of identity, we can easily drift from our missional identity in Christ and community. As followers of Jesus, our identity is grounded in the person and redemptive acts of Jesus. How we respond to "Who is Jesus?" determines who we are in the moment.

Several months ago, I attended a Barna Research Group event. The presenter, Glenn Packiam, made this statement: "Our purpose is not grounded in programming but rather in a person." He referenced Jesus Christ, and his words suggested that we have too often placed our purpose (or identity) in programing. His statement caused me to pause and reevaluate the importance I have placed on programming. Around what—or whom—do we shape our identity as Christians?

The disciples answer Jesus' question "Who do people say I am?" by offering several options. Then Jesus asks, "But who do you say I am?" Peter passes the test by identifying who Jesus is and what Jesus does as the Messiah. In a surprising turn, Jesus orders the entire group gathered not to tell anyone his identity. This good news had to be internalized until the right time. Jesus' life and message help us shape our identities around him. Understanding and identifying Christ as the Messiah is the first step that allows us to begin to form our own identity in Christ.

Gracious God, you call us to be identified with you in all things. Forgive us when we forget that you are enough today and forever. Our value and blessings come from your claim on our lives. Grant us the ability to remember who you are and who we are becoming. In Jesus' name. Amen.

Most of us try to avoid suffering and rejection at all costs. However, Jesus sees suffering and rejection as necessary. As he talks about this with the disciples, what they hear is contrary to what they understand a king should be. Jesus proposes a new type of leadership that teaches the benefit of suffering and rejection. Kingdom thinkers and doers will be rejected by the powerful leaders of the day. Powerful political leaders will kill Jesus, but Jesus tells the disciples that after three days he will come back.

Peter counters Jesus' words with a rebuke. Jesus pivots and rebukes the evil spirit that has entered Peter: Get behind me and go away! Then Jesus turns to the crowd and offers a way forward for those who want to be a part of this new, glorious kingdom. "Those who want to save their life will lose it, and those who lose their life for my sake, and for the sake of the gospel, will save it." *Please follow me*, Jesus calls; *it's a matter of life and death!* Jesus reminds them that it is time to lose this life in exchange for God's paradise.

The disciples struggled, just as we still struggle, with balancing earthly glory and reward with that which waits for us in heaven. What appears to be foolish is actually a sign of faithfulness. Following Jesus can lead us into suffering and rejection but also into joy and peace in the midst of our current situation. When we follow Jesus and work for the kingdom of heaven, we experience God's peace that passes all understanding.

O God, where you lead us, we will follow. Not every day will be sunny; some will be dark, rainy, stormy, and uncertain. Remind us not to get stuck but to keep moving forward. In Jesus' name. Amen.

The Way to the Kingdom

SEPTEMBER 16–22, 2024 • CRISTINA DINOTO

SCRIPTURE OVERVIEW: Proverbs describes the noble wife and sets a standard that can seem impossible. This woman is capable and respected and also generous and wise. She serves but is not weak. Is she a "superwoman," and do all women need to be "superwomen"? No, she is noble because she follows the counsel of the psalmist and is deeply rooted in the teachings of God. Therefore, she represents a standard for everyone to emulate, not just women. James, another teacher of wisdom, encourages believers to show these same characteristics by following the wisdom given by God. In Mark's Gospel, the disciples display a lack of wisdom by arguing over who is the greatest. Jesus reminds them that greatness in God's eyes comes through service, not through seeking recognition.

QUESTIONS AND SUGGESTIONS FOR REFLECTION

- Read Proverbs 31:10-31. How have societal expectations shaped your life? How do you allow them to shape the ways you interact with others?
- Read Psalm 1. What fruit are you yielding in this season?
- Read James 3:13–4:3, 7-8a. In what ways does your life reflect "gentleness born of wisdom"? How are you gentle with yourself and with others?
- Read Mark 9:30-37. How do you seek to serve others in your daily life?

Pastor, Christian educator, and writer from Argentina; author of *De Camino por La Vida* (*On the Way Through Life*), *Encuentro en El Camino* (*Encounter on the Way*), and *Bajo Cielo Estrellado* (*Under the Starry Sky*); member of the National Liturgy Commission; contributor to *El Aposento Alto* (the Spanish edition of *The Upper Room* daily devotional guide).

Serving means subjecting ourselves to another by doing what they desire or request. As Jesus tries to teach his disciples a revolutionary, upside down understanding of God's kingdom, he reaches for a child. Welcome this child, he says, and you welcome me. How I love the place that Jesus gave to children (and women), to the point of identifying the kingdom of God with them. This teaching of Jesus is tough and demanding, but it is also necessary and beautiful. Jesus asks us to appreciate serving others without thought for our place. A humble servant is greater than one who serves no one.

Many children in Jesus' time as today were lucky: They were loved by their families and did not want for anything. But children as a group—then even more than today—were powerless. They were vulnerable and at the very bottom of society's power structure. By placing a child in the midst of his disciples, Jesus is saying that the kingdom of God is not received just any which way, but by being last. The Kingdom of God makes the little things great.

How am I serving others in Christ's name? What does God see when God looks at my heart—am I a good disciple? Do I commit myself to my brothers and sisters according to what they need, or according to what I want, what is easier and more comfortable for me? The gospel is only gospel when it goes out from us to others, when it is lived by those of us who follow Christ. Jesus reminds us that we are servants of all those whom the Lord puts in our path, just as Jesus served those who needed his grace, love, and healing.

Dear Jesus, teach us to love with a heart willing to serve. May your grace surround us, may your teaching speak to us, and may your life be lived through us as the genuine gospel of love. Amen.

The disciples were hearing from Jesus things that they would never have wanted to hear. I too would have felt sadness, worry, and fear if I had been there.

The disciples' fear silences them. We can speculate on what they were afraid of: Were they afraid their questions would anger Jesus? Were they afraid of Jesus' death and didn't want to ask so as not to probe that conversation anymore?

Fear is a tricky emotion, especially when it comes to a fear of death. Instead of allowing my fear to freeze me, I want my fear and concern over the end of my life to motivate me, move me toward completing the actions I want to complete. I want to leave this life without regrets. I do not want to die not having contemplated serene sunrises or starry night skies. May I not miss one last walk by the seashore, the feel of the autumn sun, or the delight in the September flowers or the colors of April. May no one pass through my life without having heard the word of God flood their soul and give them the peace and security of an all-powerful Creator because that word made me live always in love. May no debt of love remain unpaid by me. May the "I love you" I have not yet said not remain unsaid for long, as well as the smiles that I kept in reserve or out of shame. May I leave no forgiveness of others undone nor offers of forgiveness from others unreceived.

What are you afraid of? How can you—in healthy and safe ways—let your fear prompt you to action that glorifies God?

Dear Lord, I want to live following your steps. Thank you that in your paths I came to know laughter and tears, but also comfort and sharing in your infinite grace. May I continue to live by your side until the end of my days. Amen.

Many women of our time are like the woman in today's text. They work both inside and outside their home, they take care of the children, they support their partners. In many cases, however, women are not as highly valued as this text suggests: Women receive lower salaries than men and are subject to a greater number of violent acts than men.

For several years I worked in organizations that help women who are victims of violence. I am filled with sadness and indignation when I hear the statements of those women who have experienced verbal, emotional, or even physical violence. The saddest are those whose deaths are caused by those who say they "love" them. The World Health Organization estimates that one in three women has experienced some form of physical violence by an intimate partner.

It is therefore encouraging to see couples collaborating together both inside and outside of the home, working together to complete chores, provide income, and create a home without thinking about what traditional roles should be filled by the man or the woman. Healthier relationships lessen the likelihood a woman will experience violence from her partner.

Verses 10 and 11 speak of a unique trust that can only come from a relationship held in the hand of the Lord. In such a relationship, husband, wife, and children can live where pure and renewed air exist inside and outside the house, where true affection and well-being abide. I believe that not only will the woman who loves the Lord will be praised, but the whole family will be blessed.

God of love! Bless the life of each of the women who work inside and outside their homes for the good of their loved ones. May they feel that love returned when kind words, caresses of love, and sweet currents of fresh air flow through all who live there. Amen.

Whithe tree planted on the banks of the river, and then I begin to daydream of an autumn or spring day, when the air is warm and the sun is radiant and all creation invites me to spend the day outdoors. In Argentina, this would include drinking "mate," a traditional warm beverage, enjoying something delicious to eat, and listening to some joyful music in good company or alone. I envision an ideal day to rest, to forget the sorrows of life and experience true communion with nature among all the beautiful things that the Lord gives us.

And if I read the psalm again, I realize that what God wants is for us to be that tree that offers rest and peace to those who need it. That tree is us rooted and sustained by the sap that is the grace of God that nourishes our spirit every day. Like a tree that gives shade or a stream that carries fresh water, we are called to yield fruit for the sake of God's love.

The psalmist says, "Happy are those . . . [whose] delight is in the law of the LORD, and on his law they meditate day and night." I invite you to be that tree planted on the banks of the stream, to meditate on the word of the Lord, and to feel safe and secure in God's hands. Wait like the tree to serve others as their rest, as their respite.

Thank you, God, for comparing us to that tree that provides rest. May we bring the shade of the tree and the coolness of the water to all who have lost their way back to your loving embrace. Amen.

The image of a tree on the water's edge always makes me think of times of peace. The word of God brings me to times of peace from a convulsed, violent world that gets lost in fights and greed, in wanting to be first or having everything at the cost of others being left with nothing. God is in the middle of God's creation showing us how to live, teaching us through that creation—through observing the trees, hearing the birds sing, feeling the water of rivers flow—what coexistence would be like if each person occupied their place accompanied by others, without wanting to be out in front of anyone.

I live in a desert climate that human hands have turned into a true orchard. Throughout the city, between the sidewalks and the streets, small channels allow the water that comes down from the mountains to run through and water the trees that have been planted in all the streets and squares. The intense heat of summer is mitigated by so many green trees. Instead of sweltering under the hot desert sun reflecting off of concrete and pavement, it is a delight to walk under the shade of leafy branches.

When I look at the trees in my city, I think of the trees in the psalm: Some are old, many younger ones are growing, but all of them have in their hearts the intention of growing larger to give respite and shade to the traveler. Perhaps you often walk along tree-lined streets not realizing that the trees that are there offer you the best they know how to do. They give you fresh air, they offer you their shade in exchange for nothing, and you can even sit under them to rest. How much we have to learn from creation!

Thank you, Lord, because your creation is perfect. Nudge us to contemplate your beauty through an awareness of the trees that give us shade and air. You did everything well! Amen.

When we talk about the wise or wisdom, I always remember a young lady from Sunday school who would say, "Wise is he who always knows what he does and does it well."

In today's scripture, James speaks to us about the wisdom of God and the wisdom of the world. I wonder how many times when making decisions we confuse our desires for God's and believe that we are doing what God wants, then yield to our will by doing what we want.

We must ask ourselves how to know if God is giving us the wisdom to resolve a situation. The wisdom of God comes wrapped as a gift along with a life of intimacy with the Lord. That life is cultivated and, like everything that is cultivated, grows if it receives care. The closer we draw to God and God's word, the more assuredly we can trust the wisdom we believe we are receiving.

As we return to scripture, we recognize God's wisdom as that which provides peace, honesty, gentleness, and love. "The wisdom from above is first pure, then peaceable, gentle, willing to yield, full of mercy and good fruits, without a trace of partiality or hypocrisy." We can trust this wisdom to help us make decisions that are for the good of all.

Furthermore, we must remain capable of changing our opinions as we listen to one another. It is not wisdom to reject one who is right only because of rivalry or our own desire to be right. That is where evil begins; that is where we stop being wise in the eyes of God even when we want to believe otherwise. Our awareness of God's word and our willingness to listen to others are helpful ways for us to check our wisdom and make sure it is truly from God.

God of love, help us to love with the wisdom that comes from above, which does untold good for us and others. In the name of Jesus. Amen.

The director of a college asked me to preach at a worship service designating the college a "School of Peace." I thought
about what to say so that the younger children at the elementary level would also participate and understand how to live in
peace, how to make peace. I began by saying that Jesus brought
peace. Even though there were people who did not want him,
he loved everyone and always took them into account. I asked
everyone present to hug those around them, even if they were
not their closest friends. Then everything turned into a party.

How good it is when seeking peace to look at each other
with the eyes of the heart! As we build peace, we can take time
to stop and think about what we are going to say: will my words
speak goodness or will they hurt the other person? We must
learn to build God's peace day by day among all because peace is
not an individual structure but a collective, community one. This
selfishness is what James warns against in today's last verse. We
must seek peace for the betterment of everyone we encounter,
not just for ourselves.

Like wisdom, we gain true peace by drawing closer to God,
and we can best experience that peace when we put it into action
in our relationships. We need to heal ourselves from believing
that we must always be in a hurry and from making our relationships temporary. We need to get rid of focusing only on our own
concerns so we can see the concerns of others. We need to be
honest with ourselves, understand that we are not alone, empathize with people, and above all to listen to the quiet call of God.

We learn peace alongside learning the love of God. If we
love God, we will be able to build peace.

*God, we ask that your peace enter the corners of our being
where it has not yet penetrated. We pray for all those who cannot find peace in their lives, and we ask for them and for us to
experience your peace. In the name of Jesus. Amen.*

Speak the Truth

SEPTEMBER 23–29, 2024 • CYNTHIA JOHNSON-OLIVER

SCRIPTURE OVERVIEW: The Jewish people have faced possible destruction numerous times. The story begins not with the Holocaust in Europe but far back in history during the time of Esther. The wicked Haman plots to wipe out God's people, but God saves the people through Esther's courage. The psalmist praises God for this kind of salvation from seemingly impossible circumstances. Although we may not face genocide, we have our own struggles. James encourages us to pray with faith, believing that God can and will answer. Our prayers are powerful, James assures us. Jesus teaches us the importance of letting nothing stand between God and us. Using vivid hyperbole, he admonishes us to put the pursuit of God above everything else and to support others in that same pursuit.

QUESTIONS AND SUGGESTIONS FOR REFLECTION

- Read Esther 7:1-6, 9-10; 9:20-22. When have you chosen to speak out in a way that made you vulnerable in order to help someone else?
- Read Psalm 124. Recall a time when you had a strong sense of God's being on your side. What was the situation? How did that assurance come?
- Read James 5:13-20. How do the members of your faith community pray with and for one another?
- Read Mark 9:38-50. Whoever is not against you is for you. How can you share God's love with those outside your inner circle?

Founder, FaithJustice Foundation; founder and president, Bishop Joseph Johnson History Project; ordained elder, Christian Methodist Episcopal (CME) Church; author of forthcoming book *The Soul of the Bishop: The Remarkable Life of Bishop Joseph A. Johnson, Jr.*

The book of Esther is one of only two books in the Bible that are named for women. Written in the style of a Jewish novella, it presents the story of the eponymous queen who is in the right place at the right time to save her people. It is a compelling tale of divine providence at work in the lives of God's people. But it is also a tale fraught with difficult issues. The story begins with gender objectification and oppression (what happened to Vashti?!) while also exemplifying the dangers of racism and antisemitism as Haman endangers the lives of the Jews to seek revenge on Mordecai.

As is often the case, God chooses an unlikely hero, a young Jewish woman, who would have had no power in the Persian empire. Yet she rises to the occasion when justice requires it. According to court rules, Queen Esther would have had no guarantee of safety in approaching King Ahasuerus. Nevertheless, she puts her life in danger to save her people. She speaks truth to power. And because she does, love and justice win out over hatred and oppression.

We may not confront such a pivotal moment with stakes as high as those confronted by Esther. But many of us will face important moments when our call to do justice is put to the test. These moments may take place in corporate boardrooms, church committee meetings, or courtrooms. They may take place at city council meetings, local protests, or around holiday dining tables.

Esther is a reminder that one does not have to be wealthy or powerful to be used by God; one need only be available and willing to take a stand in the important moments of life. To speak up may involve taking a risk, but perhaps we are present in the room for such a time as this.

Lord, help us have the courage to speak truth to power. Give us the boldness to take a stand for justice in both the big moments and in everyday life. Amen.

The stress of the beginning of the pandemic coupled with the normal ups and downs of life left many feeling over-whelmed, myself included. During 2021, I lost three close family members within three months, had a medical misdiagnosis, and took my oldest daughter to her first year of college. I was overwhelmed. During that time, I remember dreaming about a tsunami coming to shore as I ran to seek higher ground.

The psalmist similarly must have remembered feeling over-whelmed. This passage recalls an enemy that would have swal-lowed them alive, a flood that would have swept them away, and a torrent that would have gone over them. This imagery could refer to the dangers confronted as Nehemiah rebuilt the wall. But it also recalls the stories of Noah and the flood, Moses parting the Red Sea, and the chaos-to-Creation story itself.

The writer praises God who helped them escape their enemies. It is a psalm of thanksgiving for deliverance that comes only from the Lord. The psalm exhibits that familiar juxtaposition of human humility and divine exaltation. Humility involves an acknowledgment that there are some problems that cannot be solved with human faculties. It confesses a vulnerability to the vicissitudes of life. Exaltation or praise, on the other hand, acknowledges that God's presence is powerful enough to rescue us from difficult circumstances. God can do the seemingly impossible. Thus, "if it had not been the LORD who was on our side," who knows where we would be!

Like my dream, challenging times force us to seek higher ground. We can do so through prayer, meditation, therapy, or other self-care. Then, like the psalmist, we can testify about the God who is our help.

Lord, we thank you for the times you rescued us from the floods of life, and we ask you to help us testify to your saving help to encourage others facing challenging times. Amen.

One of my favorite times during worship is the communal sharing of joys and concerns. Mixed among the earnest prayers are those that elicit a chuckle, like when individuals request prayer for their favorite sports team. It generally signals that, while they are physically at church, they are mentally already at the game that follows. These requests, though, raise a serious question: What does it mean to say that God is on our side?

In this text, the psalmist boldly declares that if it had not been for the Lord on their side, calamity and destruction were certain. The writer attributes victory to God's presence and protection. Knowing that God was on their side must have strengthened their faith during difficult times.

But what about when this notion takes an unexpected direction? How is it that the name of God has been used to sanction war, violence, and terrorism while also used to motivate freedom, democracy, and civil rights? In our public square today, people of all shades of faith make religious claims to undergird their policy positions. Should the one who wins claim that God was on their side and not on the other?

Rather than seeing the image of God in others, many create an image of God that looks a lot like themselves. If your vision of God looks like you, that may be a sign that you have fashioned God in your image.

Rather than claim that God is on our side, shouldn't we take steps to make sure we're on God's side? In the biblical tradition, God is always on the side of love and justice (see Micah 6:8), God protects widows and orphans (see Psalm 68:5), and God sets free the oppressed (see Luke 4:18). Before we claim that God is on our side, let us be sure we are on God's side.

Lord, help us to always to be on your side, not by creating you in our image but by seeing your reflection in others, especially those in need. Amen.

Igrew up in a Black Methodist church in the South. We had a clear understanding of what it meant to wear your "Sunday best." It was quite a sight to behold the church mothers outdoing one another with their colorful hats and handbags or shoes to match. I must confess, however, that when I became a pastor at a predominantly White church, I embraced the more casual dress code. I still enjoy dressing up sometimes, but I also don't mind the come-as-you-are atmosphere. I appreciate the culture of both.

Writing to the early Christian community, James promotes an atmosphere in which people are encouraged to bring their authentic selves—whether cheerful or suffering, whether healthy or sick. James's call to meet people where they are likely extends beyond these basic categories. The epistle writer is traditionally believed to be James, the brother of Jesus, a leader in the early church and the "first bishop" of Jerusalem. It was James who made the decision that Gentiles need not become practicing Jews to join the young Christian movement (see Acts 15:13). It was that fateful decision that aided Paul on his missionary journey and ultimately led to the spread of Christianity.

At a time when the contemporary church finds its tent growing smaller, maybe James's ministry is a reminder that we are called to meet people where they are. No matter how they dress, the color of their skin, the amount in their bank account, who they love, or the assistive technology they use, all are embraced by the love of God and should similarly be welcomed by the church.

James encourages the early church to choose authenticity over conformity, compassion over judgment. Aren't we called to do the same today?

Lord, help us embrace the beautiful diversity of the church today, whether represented by pink hats, khaki pants, wheelchairs, or rainbow flags, and help us welcome everyone with open arms of love. Amen.

The epistle of James addresses the unfortunate reality that sometimes we wander from the truth of who God is and even from the truth of who we are. How painful it is to realize that we have wandered from ourselves.

Written like the wisdom literature of the Hebrew Bible, James outlines directives for moral living for the Christian community. As the brother of Jesus and head of the Jerusalem church, James not only had a front row seat to the early church, he was also among its architects. Concerned with communal ethics, James appears to address his epistle to those who are prone to wander. He encourages praying for wisdom, balancing faith and works, resisting temptation, taming the tongue, and more.

By chapter five, James shifts his attention from the wanderer to those who have stayed. How should the church respond to those who have wandered? Bring them back! Seek them out with the concern of a shepherd who has lost a sheep. Run out to meet them like a father whose child was presumed dead but comes home alive.

Sometimes the tension created in this call can be destructive instead of life-giving: Either we seek to pull in those whom we deem "lost" so fervently that we scare them (and others) off, or we rest back and wait for people to find us, failing in our call to seek out those who have wandered far from home. It is a delicate balance, one we must continue to struggle with, and perhaps one that will never have a clear answer. Our task is to authentically offer the love of Christ to all we meet. The church is called to be a place of beloved community, where all are greeted not by condemnation and judgment but by the welcoming arms of the community. We continue to struggle to offer God's grace to all.

Lord, grant us grace-filled hearts and courage to reach out well to those who need to experience your grace and love. Amen.

I admit it: I used to have a sweet tooth. I was a chocoholic. It became a rather expensive habit as I developed a preference for the more luxurious candies. And what I wouldn't give for chocolate cheesecake! I'm getting hungry just thinking about it.

But it became clear to me in time that this "addiction" was not serving me well. In fact, numerous health complaints seemed to point back to too much sugar. I realized that it was time to let go. First, I gave up sugar during Lent. The benefits were unmistakable. Although it was quite difficult, I eventually eliminated added sugar from my diet altogether.

But even my challenging decision pales in comparison to the tall order given by Jesus in this passage: "If your hand causes you to stumble, cut it off." It is a troubling directive with high stakes—missing a hand, he scolds, is better than missing out on the kingdom of God.

We don't believe Jesus is encouraging literal amputation, but he is illustrating the importance of letting go of whatever causes us to stumble. I do not think this is limited to official sins. Rather, Jesus is challenging us to identify those bad habits, addictions, and distractions that lead us away from God's plan for us to experience the abundant life—mind, body, and soul.

In this passage, I believe that Jesus is asking us to be honest with ourselves. What is holding us back? What is distracting us from following Christ? How can we begin to let it go?

Today, I don't even miss sugar. I also don't miss the ailments it caused. That's the thing about letting go. We learn to replace that which causes us to stumble with that which helps us grow stronger, and we become better versions of ourselves. Then we can bring our best to God as we serve in the community of faith.

Lord, help us to be honest enough with ourselves to let go of what causes us to stumble, and help us embrace practices that bring out the best in us for your glory. Amen.

During March of 1930, Mahatma Gandhi led a march from his ashram to the Arabian Sea, a 240-mile journey, to make salt in defiance of the British Salt Act. The law prohibited Indians from making and selling salt and instead required them to purchase it from British rulers, who levied a heavy tax. During this act of mass nonviolent civil disobedience against the law, 60,000 Indians were arrested, including Gandhi himself. Nevertheless, like Queen Esther, Gandhi spoke truth to power, and his efforts eventually led to Indian independence.

Salt is an essential element. It plays an important role in human health, promoting fluid balance and muscle function. In food preparation, salt has long been used as a preservative and to enhance flavor. Today, salt is plentiful, and our U.S. society struggles with the ill effects of overuse. But historically, salt has been scarce and expensive. Roman soldiers, for example, were paid with "salt money," the literal meaning of the Latin word for *salary*. In religious contexts, salt was used in offerings as a sign of the salt covenant.

In Mark's Gospel, Jesus encourages his disciples to have salt in themselves. Believers, he means, are called to add value to society. Disciples should be among those who preserve life rather than hasten its demise. Followers are called to be essential, to be among those who leave circumstances better than they found them. In sum, we are called to be different. Otherwise, we risk losing our saltiness and not being useful in the kingdom.

Some people are called to add value in big ways like Gandhi, to make major sacrifices to create a more just society. But everyone can find ways in everyday life to add positive flavor in our homes, churches, and communities.

Dear Lord, give us the courage to have salt in ourselves, to be a positive force of love, justice, and truth in the world. Amen.

Faithfulness Isn't Easy

SEPTEMBER 30–OCTOBER 6, 2024 • MOLLY VETTER

SCRIPTURE OVERVIEW: This week we read about Job, an upright man who faces severe trials but never loses his faith. Job's story brings us face-to-face with the fact that living a godly life does not make us immune to suffering. Like Job, the psalmist wonders why he suffers, even though he lives according to God's standards. Hebrews presents Jesus as the ultimate example of unwarranted suffering, yet because of his perseverance he is ultimately glorified. In Mark, some Pharisees test Jesus on the interpretation of the law concerning divorce. Jesus makes strong statements about marriage, but his larger concern is that their hearts have become hard. He contrasts them with little children, who model faith by receiving God with an open heart.

QUESTIONS AND SUGGESTIONS FOR REFLECTION

- Read Job 1:1; 2:1-10. What helps you to live with integrity?
- Read Psalm 26. Do you feel free in your prayer life to honestly share with God all that you are feeling?
- Read Hebrews 1:1-4; 2:5-12. In what ways does God speak to us in our day?
- Read Mark 10:2-16. What qualities found in children do you try to cultivate in your spiritual life?

Senior Pastor at Westwood United Methodist Church in Los Angeles, CA; ordained elder in the California-Pacific Conference of The United Methodist Church.

One of the great gifts of the book of Job is that it tells the story of an experience too many of us know all too well: Choosing to be faithful to God doesn't mean your life gets easy. Or, conversely, the fact that everything is hard and nothing seems to be going your way does not indicate a lack of faith.

I invite you to read this text from Job devotionally, sharing compassion at the experience of a good human who lost it all. From the top of his head to the bottom of his feet, Job is covered in sores. What a wretched and visceral description of misery! I immediately imagine how other people looked at him with pity and contempt and likely gratitude that they didn't have it so bad. Being in such a horrific physical state is itself an indignity.

I have sympathy for his wife, who wanted to relieve him of such misery. I sympathize with her deep desire to be saved from watching her loved ones suffer. It is agony.

It's easy to fall into the trap of believing that our successes in life come because of our faithfulness. There are even preachers who preach this message. We like to think that we have earned our good fortune. And while I value hard work, I also see that I cannot control many of the things that matter most. I cannot prevent all harm from coming to me or my loved ones. I cannot take the credit for the many gifts I have inherited through power and privilege that is beyond me.

Job's witness and experience of Job is one that prepares us to earnestly pray for sanctification: It helps open our hearts to be ready to pray for perfection in love.

God of love, remind me that no matter how hard it gets I am your beloved. May I be perfected in love enough to speak this covenant prayer: "Let me have all things, let me have nothing." Amen.

Some prayers, like "Mercy!" and "Bless you," are easy to hear in varied contexts, pronounced in different ways and with diverse meanings. As I read Psalm 26, I wonder *why this prayer, why today?*

This psalm, attributed to David, begins with a description of the integrity of the one offering the words to God. I confess that I am tempted to point out David's moral failings and dismiss the psalm on those grounds. Besides that, I was formed in churches that value humility, and I'm generally too cautious to begin a prayer by trying to tell God how good I've been. I'm happy to talk about how I've tried to be faithful, but I'm fearful of how easy it is to cross over from confidence to smugness. I hope I don't need to convince God about my well-intentioned heart.

What if instead of petitioning God to believe in my righteousness these words become a prayer meant for my formation? With each breath in and each breath out, I repeat, "I walk with integrity," because I need the help. It's hard to live with integrity; it requires ongoing self-examination, humility, and openness to change.

These words can be a gift to guide firm steps and provide level ground for me, reminding me of my call as I walk through life. As I remember my integrity, I know that I am beloved. As I pray for mercy, I dare to believe that divine grace saves me from being judged by my worst choices. I remind myself again and again not to seek power by going along with evil or giving in to fear, but to be filled by God with daring courage to stand with the oppressed, to speak truth to power, to bravely offer compassion to others.

Lord, help me walk with integrity. I want to be faithful to you with every breath and in every moment. Amen.

We are invited to praise God "in the great congregation." Faith is meant to be lived out together in community; we stand on the shoulders of generations who've gone before us, and we live in the hope that our faithfulness will become a stable foothold for the generations who will come after.

Scholars who try to uncover the context of the Psalms have suggested that these words might have been written as a prayer to be spoken in preparation for worship. I'm drawn to imagine ways that these words have given voice to generations and generations of people who were eager to enter into holy places, to worship in the presence of God. I find it inspiring to remember that my sung prayers to God are a part of a much longer and larger hymn of praise, sung by a great choir.

My college choir sang through an incredible repertoire of worship music that continuously stretched me to improve my musicality. I depended on the strong voices of others in my alto section, from whom I learned the rhythms. I tuned up my pitch to match theirs and to harmonize with the whole of the ensemble. What a gift to be a part of a great choir!

Even more so, what a gift to be a part of the living tradition that is the church of Christ. In this great choir, this gathered assembly, this large congregation, I'm saved from isolation. I find a sense of belonging in a community that stretches through time. I find inspiration in my ancestors in faith, who have showed me what faithfulness and integrity can look like. Together, each of us takes our place, testing our integrity next to the faithfulness of our neighbors, building on the witness of our ancestors, and embracing our responsibility to generations yet to come.

May my life proclaim blessing to you, Lord, as I stand in the great congregation. Amen.

The beginning of the book of Hebrews offers us a beautiful hymn of praise to God. It reminds us of the gift of salvation we have received from our God. The hymn-like beginning of this epistle recalls how God spoke to our ancestors, as told in the Hebrew Bible. It honors the prophets and leaders who listened for God's voice. It reminds us of the foundational Christian theology that is described so clearly in the first verses of the Gospel of John: Christ has been present from the beginning, participating in the work of Creation, and offering salvation to the world. I am grateful for the reminder of God's creating, redeeming, and sustaining power. It is a gift to wake up each day belonging in the love of God.

When Hebrews was written in the first century, Christ's death and resurrection were in contemporary memory. We read about them millennia later, knowing not only the glory that was embodied in Christ Jesus, but also the glory that has been visible in the church. I think of the many witnesses who have boldly lived toward compassion, justice, and love; their lives have been an ongoing proclamation of divine glory.

You are invited to add your own verse to this hymn today, singing the story of salvation that continues through the lives of the people of God. I encourage you to call to mind your ancestors of faith, those who've inherited this same salvation and who have conveyed it to generations after. Who are the people who shaped your own life of faith? Whose stories would you add to this hymn to give further testimony of God's continued speaking and sustaining power?

Thank you, God, for the generations who have reflected your glory in this world. May I live in such a way that I convey your glory so those who come after me can see and know your power. Amen.

A "pioneer" of salvation, Christ shows us what the path is going to be like if we want to practice Christ-like love. There's going to be suffering.

Part of this is because we are human. Borrowing poetry from Psalm 8, these verses contrast God's majesty to our earthiness: We are mortals, and yet, wondrously, we are recipients and participants in divine salvation. Christ connects us to God, claiming us as siblings and showing us holy love that isn't easy. Being human means experiencing limitation, vulnerability, and grief.

Besides all this, following Jesus tends to get folks in trouble. Like Jesus, we make people uncomfortable when we build community with those who've been excluded. Folks get uneasy when we are quick to forgive, fearless in choosing nonviolence, and persistent in tending the sick.

The Wesleyan tradition describes the process of "Christian perfection." We are made perfect in love as we practice love in the world. Rather than granting us a ticket out of suffering, deep faith gives us the courage to persist with love whether it brings suffering or joy. Sometimes, even, by divine mystery, the two come together, as we endure the struggle with a joy that is possible only through God. With Christ as our model, we let love be perfected in us. As we get more practice at offering compassion, as we extend grace, as we learn to see God's presence in everyone around us, we get better at it. This is the path that Christ pioneered for us that guides us toward beloved community.

Help me practice love in all circumstances, O God. When I suffer and when I experience joy, may I do so for the sake of love. Amen.

I find it impossible to read this passage without thinking about what it means for people I know. As I read Jesus' response to a question about divorce, I think of those who have experienced it. I would like to be able to offer some words of solace to people who are immediately on edge when they read these words. Marriage and divorce have changed since Mark's Gospel was written. We live in a world where both women and men can own property, work outside the home, and participate freely in the life of the community. Divorce no longer necessarily leaves one partner without any security. In so many ways, this passage isn't about those who have chosen to end a marriage.

It is, however, about the religious leaders who bring a question to Jesus. At first, it seems to be a general question about what is "lawful" for "a man." Immediately, Jesus makes the question personal, replying to them directly with a question for "you." I suspect this subtle shift might just be key to making sense of this passage for today.

As he directly addresses the questioner, Jesus invites a leader in his religious community to take seriously the responsibility for those in his care. These verses about marriage and divorce are followed immediately by teaching about welcoming children. The Gospel just keeps pulling our focus to the vulnerable and the powerless. Instead of asking us to feel pity or embarrassment for the presence of these powerless children, Jesus brings them front and center asking us to welcome them. We are expected to learn from them. They are the ones with access to the kingdom.

Read together, these two passages invite us to be shaken loose of our own individualistic attempts to define our own righteousness, so that we can see an invitation to beloved community in our belonging with and for each other.

God of love, help me see past my present questions so that I can receive your salvation as a little child. Amen.

I love the priority Jesus places on welcoming children. In moments when I'm aware of my own failings—aware of things I've done and left undone that have caused harm—I find blessing in knowing that little children have access to the kingdom of God. They are welcome, beloved, and valued simply because they are.

As I read again these verses, I'm struck by the tension between the behavior of the people who brought their children to Jesus and the behavior of the disciples. The disciples, who had chosen to give up their lives and follow Jesus, did not want Jesus to spend time with these children. But the people—the ones who brought their children out to be blessed by him—saw a compelling enough possibility in Jesus that they bothered to show up with their children.

It ought not surprise me that the disciples, who stood to lose so much if Jesus' project went astray, would object to Jesus spending his time with little children. These verses don't tell us exactly what was objectionable, so we're left to assume that the disciples thought Jesus was wasting his time on people who hadn't yet amounted to much. I can empathize with their misguided desire for Jesus to be strategic about whom he spent time with; after all, they had given up a lot to follow him.

At their objections, Mark tells us, Jesus got angry. With the indignation of a protective parent, Jesus insists not only that they are welcome but that the disciples themselves cannot access the kingdom of God unless they become more like them. We need not only to allow for their presence but to honor the ways they already have what we need. If we want to receive the blessing that Jesus has to give, we need only to receive it humbly.

Open my heart to receive the blessing you offer, O God. May I welcome your presence in all your children. Amen.

Where Did You Go?

OCTOBER 7-13, 2024 • MEG LASSIAT

SCRIPTURE OVERVIEW: Faithful people still have questions for God. Job wishes he could sit down with God and plead his case because he wants God to justify what has happened to him. The psalmist also feels abandoned by God and wonders why God is not coming to his aid. God can handle our questions. Job wanted an advocate, and Hebrews says that Jesus now fills that role for us. He is our great high priest and understands our sufferings, so we may boldly approach him for help. In Mark, Jesus deals with the challenge of money. It is a powerful force and can come between us and God if we cling to our resources instead of holding them loosely with thanksgiving for God's provision.

QUESTIONS AND SUGGESTIONS FOR REFLECTION

- Read Job 23:1-9, 16-17. When have you, like Eliphaz, attributed your own suffering or that of others to wickedness on your part or on theirs? How often do you find yourself blaming others for the situations in which they find themselves?
- Read Psalm 22:1-15. How could your prayer life be more honest and transparent? What feelings do you hold back?
- Read Hebrews 4:12-16. When God shines the spotlight on your soul, what does God see?
- Read Mark 10:17-31. How do you square your "wealthy" life with Jesus' call to discipleship?

Ordained deacon and a member of the Indiana Conference of The United Methodist Church; served United Methodist agencies and in independent consulting related to leadership development; lives in the Indianapolis area and attends Meridian Street UMC.

Job 23 is midway through the chapters where Job's friends offer many (unhelpful) ways for Job to understand and end his suffering. Job's friends toss out ideas and solutions but don't empathize with Job's pain. In Job 22, Eliphaz claims Job caused his own suffering because he drifted away from the Almighty. Therefore, all Job needs to do is "agree with God" (Job 22:21) and all will be fixed. Hearing this, Job lines up his arguments to present to God. But then . . . God doesn't even show up for the conversation—wow!

Maybe it's okay that God chooses not to participate in this conversation. Eliphaz's latest idea for how Job can "fix" his suffering is misguided at best and harmful to many who have heard similar suggestions from well-meaning friends. We live in a broken world; we will experience pain. And just as it's wrong to blame the victim of a crime, it's unfair and hurtful for Eliphaz to claim Job can end his suffering by "simply" returning to God.

Job's response illustrates his deep frustration with God. Life is not a well-planned series of events where we do the "right" thing and God rewards us. Tragedy strikes. We explain all our reasons that it shouldn't have happened, and yet we still must live through its aftereffects. Tragedy cannot be explained or brushed away. Answers aren't easy—and often don't exist.

It's difficult to sit in the pain of not knowing why, but that's where we are today. The fact that bad things happen does not necessarily mean we did something wrong. And our source of hope does not rest in our own ability to be righteous before God. One thing I do know, however: God is with us as we walk through the pain.

Be with me in my suffering, O Lord. Hear my prayer as I shout out to you. Instill in me your grace. Amen.

When I served as a youth minister, our group went spelunking in southern Indiana. There is an extensive underground system there, so we experienced almost everything caving offers: squeezing through narrow caverns; crawling through deep, sticky mud; marveling at the beauty of the stalactites and stalagmites stretching toward each other. At one point, we paused and our guide asked us to be as quiet as possible. Once we were quiet, he instructed us to turn off our headlamps on the count of three.

"One, two . . ." Our lamps went off, and the world went dark.

We heard nothing and no light seeped in. I waved my fingers in front of my face—saw nothing. I lost all sense of the people standing inches from me. It felt as if a thick, dark blanket constricted around my chest. The longer the darkness lasted, the tighter the blanket squeezed. Our guide warned us we would "stay dark" for about a minute, and in those sixty seconds my thoughts floated from awe to reassurance that this was temporary to holding my breath as I counted down the last few seconds. We audibly exhaled as we flipped on our headlamps.

I wonder if that's what this darkness felt like for Job. Job's confident arguments from yesterday's reading shift quickly to fear. As darkness settles and he can't find God, I wonder if he felt that same sense of disorientation I felt in the cave. Once the darkness settled, did he hold his breath and wait for the light to return? I believe he had faith his relationship with God would be restored. I'm just not sure he knew yet how he would get there.

Even when I can't see the next step, O God, I trust that you walk behind me and before me to guide the way. Show me the way to you. Amen.

Psalm 22:1 is most often heard on Good Friday, for these are Jesus' last recorded words before he "breathes his last" (Mark 15:33-37). So it can seem unseasonal to read these words today, with Good Friday far behind us and the Advent season soon to begin.

The word *forsake* means to completely abandon or desert someone or something. It conveys a sharp or extreme break in the relationship and leaves the one who was forsaken feeling powerless to repair the relationship. It is not to be taken lightly. Being forsaken has lasting effects.

We cry out, and sometimes our prayers seem to go unanswered, even to the point where we feel forsaken. We wonder if God is even listening. A partner sits by the bedside and prays for their beloved's healing when healing doesn't come; a parent prays for their child's recovery to no avail; we lose our job after years of faithful service; we face retirement with the fear of too few resources; life does not go as we hoped, and tragic pain continues. Where is God when these things happen, and how do we come to terms with feeling forsaken?

Psalm 22 does not give easy answers. But in these verses, we see a person who continues to pray, even when feeling completely abandoned. We see a person who boldly names their needs before God and continues to search for God. I wonder what gives the psalmist the motivation to stay connected to God. I wonder how this person has the strength to remain faithful even when they think God has not been. And I stand in awe of the strength and faith it took to name their grief at being forsaken while continuing to trust that God would heed their prayer.

What might you need to proclaim boldly to God today?

God, even when there are no easy answers, I cry out to you. Hear my prayer. Amen.

Time and again Jesus tells his disciples he is not the Messiah they expected. And here, again, Jesus challenges tradition and religious teachings in surprising and difficult ways. Chapter 10 is filled with the unexpected from Jesus. In the middle, it is anchored by the encounter with the rich man.

Jesus confronts the status quo and his disciples' posturing to earn easy rewards for doing the right thing. Throughout the Gospels, we read how Jesus beckons us to change our expectations of what is right, our priorities for what is important, and the very way we live. I'm certain the disciples did not fully realize this when they left what they knew to follow him. I imagine them huddled together thinking of different angles and questions to pose to Jesus about what following really means. In the middle of this scene, a rich man walks up and asks how to earn eternal life.

Jesus shows his love for the rich man and responds, "You lack one thing." Even with the rich man following all the rules, other priorities got between him and his relationship with God. It is easy to blame the rich man. But even if we aren't rich, aren't we a lot like him? Other priorities interfere with our relationship with God. We justify to ourselves that we always do what's right and good. And we hold on to the "one thing" that gets in the way—even grieving its possible loss.

Our relationship with God depends on us and on God. This week we wrestle with that relationship, the times we feel forsaken, and the times when we have stepped away. Where do you find yourself today? Do you feel forsaken, or is there "one thing" keeping you from God? Or is it a little of both?

Holy God, even when our relationship is strained, we walk this road together. Help me see the next step for growing closer to you. Amen.

Flying from Johannesburg to Atlanta takes sixteen hours and forty minutes on a 296-passenger plane. Two of us occupied the window and aisle seats in our row and waited for the unlucky person who would sit in the middle. The flight was filling up, but that seat stayed empty. Flight attendants announced the door would soon close and we prepared to leave. We dared to marvel at our luck of having an empty seat between us. Seconds before the door closed, the 296th passenger boarded. When he sat beside me, my vision for the flight switched from mildly tenable to cramped and uncomfortable.

Then he shared how lucky he was to be on the flight. He had been on standby with many ahead of him, all who had bags to check. But he carried only the small duffel now stowed beneath his seat. The plane had been near its weight limit, and the airline could only add a passenger who had no checked bags. He hadn't seen his family for three years, and that morning he learned his daughter was critically ill. Rushing to make this flight, he packed a few items and hurried to the airport.

A persistent interpretation of today's passage dating at least to Thomas Aquinas says that Jesus is referring to a small, winding security gate in Jerusalem called the "Needle." To pass through the Needle, the camel's handler must remove its bags, steer the camel through the gate's twists and turns, and reload its bags afterwards. It's time-consuming and inconvenient. The camel's only way through is without wearing bags.

It's easier to travel without added baggage. What baggage do you need to shed so you can travel more easily? Even when it is time-consuming and difficult, we are assured that we don't do this work alone. Jesus accompanies us, and Jesus reminds us that with God all things are possible.

God, help me get rid of extra baggage so I can travel more easily with you. Amen.

High priests are the people God chooses as liaisons between the things pertaining to God and the needs of the people (see Hebrews 5:1). Jesus, as our high priest, has struggled and been tempted but remains without sin. Jesus has always walked with us; he knows the intentions of our hearts and understands our weakness. Jesus knows all of who we are and all we are called to be, and he invites us with all our strength, all our sin, and all our weakness to leave our baggage behind and travel with him in our faith journey. How exciting is that? We are fully known, we are fully called, and we are fully loved. This reassurance gives us the strength we need so we can be bold in our faith as we ask God for mercy and grace, even in the times when we don't know where God is.

Job showed boldness and courage when he claimed God would understand his arguments. The psalmist was bold to question why God had forsaken him, yet remained secure that God would hear his needs. The rich man's boldness forced him to reckon with his understanding of living a faithful life. And the disciples were bold enough to continue following Jesus even when their faith was tested more than they ever imagined it would be.

Living a faithful life is not for the faint of heart. We will be tested, we will feel separated from God, and we may cry out. But today's passage reminds us that even when we fall short, even when we can't find God, even when it seems that God has forsaken us, we are called—even compelled—to be bold in our faith, to seek God's grace, and to be assured that help is available in our time of need.

Thank you for your reassurance and invitation to boldness, O God. I rest in your peace. Amen.

Have you ever walked into a room and felt like you were interrupting a conversation? When a passage begins with the word "indeed," that's what I think about. "Indeed" is used to strengthen an earlier point. Something was said, and, indeed, that statement needs emphasis.

Immediately preceding this passage, the author of Hebrews highlights the importance of entering sabbath rest. As this week ends, we recall that scripture has challenged us and asked us to examine how and when and why we've been disconnected from God. Our reflections have been relentless in exploring the dark places of our faith and acknowledging the times we have been, or still are, separated from God.

When I first learned to cook, my father taught me to always use the sharpest knife possible. That confused me—it felt counterintuitive. Why would I use the sharpest knife possible? What if it slipped toward my finger? Wouldn't that hurt? Wouldn't a dull knife protect my hands better?

The more experience I gained, though, the more I understood. A dull knife couldn't cut like it should. I needed to push too hard for the knife to slice properly, and that increased the chances it would slip. The only time I seriously cut my hand was when I was rushing and using a dull knife. Three stitches later, I indeed felt the wisdom of my father's instruction.

Just as a sharp knife slices with precision, the word of God pierces into the kernel of our being and helps reveal all of who we are. It rights us where we go astray and affirms us where we align with God. Given a week of reflecting on what it means to be separated from God, I find reassurance and sabbath rest in being fully known, being fully loved, and being offered mercy and grace. Indeed, it is time to rest.

Dear God, thank you for fully loving me, even when you fully know me. Amen.

Did you know that you can enjoy
The Upper Room Disciplines
in multiple formats—digital or print?

The Upper Room Disciplines is available in both regular and
enlarged print, but are you aware that it is also available in
digital formats? Read *Disciplines* on your phone, computer, or
e-reader. Whatever your preference, we have it for you today.

The Upper Room Disciplines is available in a variety of formats:
- Print (regular-print and enlarged-print versions)
- eBook
- Digital subscriptions (website, email, and app)

For more information, visit Store.UpperRoom.org or
call 800.972.0433.

Need to make changes to your account?

Call Customer Service at 800.972.0433 or email us at
customerassistance@upperroom.org. Customer service
representatives are available to help you with any updates.

Decisions and Authority

OCTOBER 14–20, 2024 • SKIP ARMISTEAD

SCRIPTURE OVERVIEW: These four passages lift the primacy of God as the author of all and thus the greater authority over all. God questions Job about his authority and ultimate knowledge of God's creation. The psalmist affirms God as the author of creation. The Hebrews writer affirms that God, the author of life and the ultimate authority, chose Jesus as the great high priest. Jesus demonstrates God's authority to determine positions of authority and status in God's kingdom of Heaven to his disciples. When we decide to praise God, trust God's authority, and serve, we help others and grow in faith.

QUESTIONS AND SUGGESTIONS FOR REFLECTION

- Read Job 38:1-7, 34-41. How do you continue to hold on to belief in God's goodness when you are in a period of anguish?
- Read Psalm 104:1-9, 24, 35. Take a meditative walk or find a clear space to view the night sky. Reflect on God's authorship of creation as reflected in these scriptures. How do you share in the creativity of God?
- Read Hebrews 5:1-10. In what ways does the understanding of Jesus' willing vulnerability while serving as high priest affect the way you interact with others?
- Read Mark 10:35-45. Reflect on times you and others wanted a special position or promotion—perhaps the same one—that provided status and symbols of success. Where do you see genuine examples of servant leadership in your community?

Retired from over 50 years as a United Methodist pastor; serves as a Stephen Minister, men's Bible study leader, and a Stop Predatory Gambling advocate; Master of Divinity from Christian Theological Seminary; enjoys woodworking, video editing, and gardening.

THANKSGIVING DAY (CANADA)

Pastor Joe grew up in a very poor family during the Great Depression. One day, he asked his mother how she and his father got by with six children. His mother said, "Son, when things got depressing, we decided to count our blessings, naming them one by one. It took a while, but once we counted our blessings, there was no Depression." Pastor Joe learned the value of simply deciding to be grateful.

The word *enthusiasm* comes from the Greek *en* (in) *theos* (god). Some say that enthusiasm and gratitude emerge after the decision to throw oneself (en) into a goal, activity, or relationship with (god).

Today is Thanksgiving Day in Canada. While many feelings of thanksgiving emerge naturally from a grateful awareness of the blessings one receives, the decision to be thankful and grateful to God, especially during adversity, enables the transformation of a negative perspective into positive gratitude.

When Joel says, "Do not fear," and "O children of Zion, be glad, and rejoice in the LORD your God," he advises them to decide to focus on gladness, joy, thanksgiving, and blessings, despite their circumstances.

When Jesus tells us to seek God's kingdom first, he encourages us to focus intentionally on the author of all blessings, which will result in our experiencing the blessing of a deepening relationship with God.

When I realize that I'm moping, disgruntled, or even angry, one of my antidotes is to decide to focus on my blessings. As a result, not only do my emotions shift toward encouragement; my thinking becomes clearer.

Most loving and gracious Lord, please help me count your many blessings. Amen.

In my first theology class, we studied various theologians, which excited me because these people provided answers to questions I had not considered. Then, we explored other theologians who contradicted the previous ones. So which theologians gave the right answers? Confused, I questioned all my answers about God. I wallowed in doubt. On our midterm exam, the professor asked us to describe Ludwig Feuerbach's theology and give a critique. Feuerbach believed that God did not create humanity in God's image; rather, we fashioned God from our idealized image of a perfect human. Confused and exhausted, I wrote, "Feuerbach must be right. If God existed, our understandings would not be contradictory and confusing." I turned in my exam and went home for a nap.

Later, I drove back to school to withdraw from seminary. Why be a minister for a God who did not exist? At a traffic light, I felt an overwhelming presence of God. I didn't hear voices, but thoughts flashed across my mind: *Are you saying that all the times I've been with you never happened? Are you saying that all those I have helped through you never received my help? Are you saying that I'm nothing but a psychological-sociological figment of your imagination?* Instantly, my doubts, questions, and answers evaporated, and my faith became grounded in a relationship with God, not facts. While I still have more questions than answers, my faith is based on a relationship, not knowledge.

The story told in the book of Job is challenging, but throughout Job engages in a relationship with God, and God engages back. We, too, can struggle with knowledge, can ask the unaskable questions, can challenge everything we've ever been taught and still rest assured in our relationship with God. God's love for us is larger than any struggle we can endure.

Lord, just as you came to Job through his questions about you, may we receive your assurance and presence amid our questions and doubts. Amen.

An employee at a church where I once worked proved to be a morale problem for the entire staff. She constantly criticized individuals, decisions, and policies but claimed innocence when confronted about these issues. Before we decided to dismiss her, she resigned. A year later, I saw her in a store and felt an intense, sickly feeling mixed with anger. I didn't want to talk to her, yet I felt a nudge to reach out to her anyway. I approached and greeted her and engaged in some small talk.

After a few minutes, I felt a nudge to praise and acknowledge the good things she had done. So, I spent the next five minutes sincerely praising various things she initiated, some we were continuing. Amazingly, her demeanor toward me changed, and even more amazing, my attitude toward her changed too. God was authoring a growing reconciliation between us. I was grateful I had followed the leading of the Spirit to praise and affirm her.

David praises and affirms God's mighty acts in Psalm 104. David praises God, proclaiming God's greatness because he was inspired to do so. In other psalms David praises God despite the struggles and difficult people he encounters,

God creates a positive power in praise that affects the giver of praise, not just the recipient. Just as Job blessed God despite losing everything (see Job 1:21), when I praise and affirm the greatness of God through the gracious acts of others, it changes, empowers, and transforms my unhealthy attitudes and feelings into positive energy. While this positive energy does not make struggles or problems disappear, it provides calmness and assurance in the face of adversity, enabling me to respond more effectively to a situation instead of merely being reactive.

Thank you, Lord, for creating the gift of praise and the power that emerges from praising you, others, and ourselves. Amen.

Authority is important. Before many of us make major purchases or investments or seek medical care, we consult with an authorized and experienced person. Authorities are credentialed.

I debated on my high school and college debate teams. In every debate, my colleague and I not only expressed a point of view but also had to support that position with a quotation from a credible authority on the subject. Otherwise, it was considered "only an assertion" or a possible lie. We may have been knowledgeable, but we were not credentialed as authorities.

Today, we have plenty of debates over fake news, alternative facts, and conspiracy theories that create confusion in the medical world, news media, politics, and the church. We have many self-appointed authorities who present assertions as facts. We must be careful—more careful than generations before—who we choose to listen to, whose facts we believe.

Jesus had authority. Jesus taught as one with authority (see Matthew 7:29); forgave sins to validate his authority (see Matthew 9:6); received challenges to his authority (see Matthew 21:23); gave his disciples authority (see Matthew 10:1); and authorized us to make disciples of all nations (see Matthew 28:18-20). The writer of Hebrews even states that God validated Jesus' authority as our Great High Priest.

As the noise and access to talking points and information increases, we must become even more diligent in our efforts to listen closely to the authorities who can guide our lives well. While many earthly authorities may contradict each other, there is only one authority who can guide us through life toward and into eternal life—Jesus Christ!

Lord, because you are the author of perfect truth, please guide us toward the truth that sets us free. Amen.

Each week, my second-grade teacher, Mrs. Darden, chose a student to be room monitor for the week. There were enough weeks that everyone would have one turn. The room monitor's job was to lead the class line and to help maintain calm in the classroom by raising their hand, signaling silence. I anxiously awaited my turn.

When spring approached, Mrs. Darden was away for three weeks. I convinced the substitute teacher to choose me to be the room monitor for those three weeks. I loved the power of raising my hand and leading the lines. But when Mrs. Darden returned, she was unhappy with me because it meant that two of my classmates would not have a chance to be our room monitor. I was embarrassed. Not only had I usurped the opportunity from two of my classmates, I had missed the whole purpose of being a classroom leader.

James and John have a similar desire to be the teacher's pet as I had in elementary school. They ask Jesus to appoint them the seats at his right and left, meaning they wish to be second only to him when he takes his rule, as they expect him to do. Jesus challenges them, not denying the request but asking instead if they truly understand what kind of "rule" he anticipates taking on. When word spreads throughout the rest of the disciples, Jesus must confront all their expectations of glory, telling them instead that they, like he, are called to serve.

In reprimanding me, Mrs. Darden reminded me that greatness comes in serving, not in being raised up above others. That year I began my understanding of servant leadership and the ways that true leaders can think of others before thinking of themselves.

Lord, please transform our lives as leaders who serve you and others. Amen.

The war in Bosnia (1992–1995) was horrific, killing at least 200,000 people and displacing two million. The danger was so severe that the United Methodist Committee on Relief (UMCOR) was one of very few organizations that continued providing aid to Christian and Muslim victims. During a truce, the Methodist bishop from Germany went to Bosnia for the church's annual conference. About twenty-five people were expected, but over five hundred people, mostly Muslim, showed up. Why? They were so grateful, they wanted to learn about the God of UMCOR—a God who loved them too.

The author of Hebrews shows how God reaches out to us through Jesus, authorized by God to be our great high priest, according to the order of Melchizedek. Who was Melchizedek? After Abram finished his war against the five kings, Melchizedek, the king of Salem and priest of the "most high God," ministered to Abram, providing bread and wine. Also, Melchizedek blessed Abram. In response, Abram was so grateful that he gave Melchizedek a tithe of everything (see Genesis 14:20). Abram saw, through Melchizedek's ministry, the hand of God reaching out to him.

I have served in many ministry capacities, from volunteer to pastor, for fifty-five years. There are plenty of people who can tell stories about my fallibility and inabilities. Yet I also stand amazed at the number of people who tell me that God made a difference in their lives through me. It is humbling to know God can use any of us to make a difference in another person's life. It is also an instructive reminder to focus on Christ, our ultimate authority, and not on our personal, imperfect wills.

When we serve others with a focus on God, they will want to know more about the love of Christ, our perfect High Priest.

Lord, imperfect as we are, help us love others so they want to know you. Amen.

During my teenage years, I heard a preacher talk about a young man who climbed the corporate ladder to become CEO by the time he was thirty. Feeling burned out, he surprised everyone by giving up, selling all he had, and moving to a monastery in Asia. Months later, he sent his worried family a letter, explaining how he was experiencing a new life of serenity and peace. He valued getting away from the "rat race," competition, and backstabbing to get to the top. "Life is so much better now!" he said. "I'm doing so well; the head monk says I'll become the best monk here in a relatively short time!"

James and John wanted seats of power and positions of authoritative status and success. Many of us do too! It is difficult to let go of the desire to be on top.

While preaching one Sunday morning, I placed a ladder in front of the chancel. While slowly climbing, I talked about the ladder of success, explaining that there is nowhere to go but down once you have reached the top. It is also dangerous to stand at the top because it is easier for the ladder to topple.

Next, I placed a giant cross beside the ladder and said, "Healthier status and success comes not through climbing an earthly ladder but by carrying a cross of service and sacrifice." While the top rung is the highest step one can climb on the ladder of success, the cross of service has no limits.

When Jesus talked to his disciples about greatness and the best seats at the table or being with him in God's kingdom, instead of pointing to a worldly ladder of success he pointed to a cross, saying that greatness is in serving, lifting others, and even dying for another. Which seat offers the most prestige? One where we can best serve others.

Lord, please help us sit in the seat that best serves you. Amen.

Sacred Worth

OCTOBER 21–27, 2024 • PAUL W. CHILCOTE

SCRIPTURE OVERVIEW: Sometimes we can look back and see why challenging things happened to us, but this is not always the case. Job never fully understood his story but finally submitted his life to God in humility. In Job's case, God restored with abundance. The psalmist also rejoices that although the righteous may suffer, God brings ultimate restoration. The reading from Hebrews continues celebrating Christ's role as the compassionate high priest. Unlike human high priests, who serve only for a time, Christ remains our priest forever. A man without sight in Jericho knows of Jesus' compassion and cries out for it, despite attempts to silence him. He asks Jesus for mercy and physical healing in his case, and Jesus grants his request because the man has displayed great faith.

QUESTIONS AND SUGGESTIONS FOR REFLECTION

- Read Job 42:1-6, 10-17. What are your happy and unhappy endings? How do you acknowledge both?
- Read Psalm 34:1-8, 19-22. How does God deliver you from your fears? Recall a recent experience of this.
- Read Hebrews 7:23-28. What distinction do you draw between sacrifice and offering?
- Read Mark 10:46-52. How do you respond to Jesus' question, "What do you want me to do for you?"

Award-winning author and retired Methodist historian and theologian; involved in theological education on three continents: Africa, Europe, and North America; author or editor of over thirty books, including *Praying in the Wesleyan Spirit*, *Making Disciples in a World Parish* (Upper Room Books, 2001), and, most recently, *The Quest for Love Divine* (Cascade Books, 2022); frequent speaker and workshop leader in applied Wesleyan studies.

The empathetic narrator of the book of Job plumbs the depths of perennial mysteries about life. Rather than answering the many perplexing questions—particularly the mystery of suffering—the story itself opens up spaces in which we can experience and know God as we empathize with Job. The final chapter opens with a poetic reflection on humility that leads to repentance as Job ponders the profound relationship between himself as a creature and the Creator.

Rudolf Otto, in his classic book *The Idea of the Holy*, uses the phrase *mysterium tremendum* to describe God. God is an awe-inspiring mystery. God often seems to be infinitely far beyond us—the Wholly Other. When Simon Peter experienced God in Jesus, he responded in the way any normal human being would. "He fell down at Jesus' knees, saying, 'Go away from me, Lord, for I am a sinful man!'" (Luke 5:8). The prophet Isaiah had the very same experience in the Temple as he encountered God. "Woe is me," he cries out! "I am lost" (Isa. 6:5).

If we are honest with ourselves, we have only one response to God when we truly comprehend who we are in relation to who God is: repentance. "*Kyrie eleison*," we cry. "Have mercy." John Wesley defined repentance as true self-understanding, an image he drew from the parable of the prodigal son. The lost son "came to himself" (Luke 15:17), and that discovery was two-sided. He realized just how far he was from his father. But he knew simultaneously that nothing could ever strip him of his primary and eternal identity. His repentance was an act of contrition and a reclamation of identity. With Job he could exclaim, "Now my eye sees you."

Forgiving God, you sometimes seem so far beyond me. I fall on my knees before you. Do not overwhelm me, but embrace me with your unbounded love. Amen.

The story of Job comes to an end. On one level it feels something like a storybook ending, but we know there is much more to it than that. Job's heart must still ache. Despite the material restoration and a new family to carry forward his legacy, the holes in his heart can never be filled completely. The wounds linger. While much healing must have taken place, the scars remain as perennial reminders of the pain he endured in his life. Despite new discoveries about God and the ways of God, trust in God does not remove questions. Restoration cannot resolve everything.

The most stunning aspect of this conclusion to the book of Job has to do with Job's three daughters—the only children named in the narrative. The author gives them an identity and leaves Job's sons without names. In the ancient world, women inherited nothing. Job's provision of continuous support for his daughters as well as his sons was a gracious and prophetic act. Those who heard or read this story in ancient Israel—or in the time of Jesus for that matter—would have been shocked and mystified by the unexpected ending.

Perhaps Job discovered through his suffering that every person is precious and that no one should ever be excluded. Every person has an identity. Each person is unique and of sacred worth. While we cannot verify Job's motivation, we are able to see the consequences of his actions. He secures an identity for his girls. He treats them with dignity and honor as individuals of value and worth. Perhaps this story foreshadows what the author of First Peter would proclaim to future generations: "Once you had no identity as a people; now you are God's people" (2:10a).

O God from whom every family in heaven and on earth takes its name, we give you thanks for the identity into which you call us. Amen.

O taste and see that the L ORD is good." The eighth verse of the psalm states the central theme of this hymn of individual thanksgiving. I have quoted this statement many times in courses I have taught on mission and evangelism. For me it functions as the foundation of our witness in the world. God's actions flow from this essential affirmation about God's character.

Just ponder for a moment the verbs associated with God's actions in this psalm. They speak volumes about who God is. With regard to our ardent prayers, God hears and answers. The verb "keeps" in verse 20 is so rich that it really can't be contained in one word alone: It means *protects, guards, preserves, watches over*. God delivers, saves, rescues, and redeems. And what is the response of the one delivered by God? The redeemed bless and praise God. They magnify, exalt, and boast in God's name. What God has done for us and how we respond both define our identity as God's beloved children. Our praise of God gives us our identity.

While this psalm is focused particularly on the individual, the singer exhorts others to join the chorus of praise. In his lyrical paraphrase of this psalm in his manuscript poetry, Charles Wesley extends the same invitation to those who seek to taste and see that God is good:

All humble followers of the Lord,
With me exalt God's praise,
Join humankind with sweet accord
To glorify God's grace.

Blessed are you, Lord our God, Sovereign of the universe, through whose word everything good comes into being. Restore our identity through our exaltation of your name. Amen.

The author of Hebrews refers to Jesus throughout this letter as a great high priest. The Old Testament portrait of the high priest, Melchizedek, foreshadows the perfect priesthood of Jesus Christ. Jesus perfects this holy office by his obedience and suffering (see Hebrews 5:8-10). As the pioneer of salvation, he not only offers sacrifice for his people but serves both as the priest and the victim. "He has no need to offer sacrifices day after day, first for his own sins and then for those of the people; this he did once for all when he offered himself."

The author distinguishes his understanding of sacrifice from those of others in the ancient world. He does not view Jesus as an innocent victim who purposefully endures the sufferings merited by the guilty. Such a concept of substitution was rather foreign to the Hebrew mind. Rather, Jesus' sacrifice consists in his obedience and perfect fulfillment of the redemptive will of God. This once-for-all sacrifice atones for sin by virtue of Christ's role as mediator between God and fallen humanity. He freely surrenders his life and dedicates it to the recovery of all people. Through this priestly act, he restores fellowship for all with a gracious and loving God. The vicarious death of Christ—the priest/victim—is the fundamental note in the teaching of this letter.

The death of Jesus also gives us a new identity. We are those for whom Jesus has died. As a consequence of Jesus' obedience we are forgiven sinners whose relationship with God has been restored. We no longer need to live under the tyranny of disobedience and sin. We are set free to live in and for the purposes of love.

Forgiving and restoring God, we are thankful for the way Jesus gave himself freely and once-for-all that we might all live, and live abundantly. Help us embrace our identity as a forgiven people. Amen.

Jesus and his disciples pass through Jericho, a city known for its religiosity. Despite all the religion, however, the needs of the people are great. On Jesus' way out of town he encounters Bartimaeus. You can sense the blind man's heart begin to race as he learns that Jesus is coming near. The son of Timaeus cries out to the Son of David, not just once but twice, with the earnest plea, "Have mercy on me." He acknowledges his need. And Jesus loves him for it. Those standing around, however, rebuke Bartimaeus, just as the disciples chased away the children in an earlier scene (see Mark 10:13-16).

The account of Bartimaeus provides a case study about identity, the power of words, and the impact of narratives laid side by side. Earlier in Mark we have Jesus' encounter with a rich man who ran up to Jesus with some important questions (see 10:17-22) Jesus reminds his disciples about the pending disaster in Jerusalem (see 10:32-34), then James and John demonstrate their cluelessness about Jesus' way (see 10:35-45). Finally, we come to Bartimaeus. This story comes in the context of deep questions about life, the quest for power, and Jesus' way of self-sacrifice. The question of identity looms large.

The rich man was happy with the identity he had earned. He had done everything right. He had adhered to the law. And Jesus loved him for it. He didn't need anything, at least in his mind. But he could not throw off his wealth or the power that came with it. He did not follow Jesus even when invited to do so.

The rich man was unable to acknowledge his need, and parted from Jesus. Bartimaeus, however, began to discover his true identity through acknowledging his need for mercy and love.

Loving God, in acknowledging our need for you we begin to understand that our identity is inseparable from our relationship with you. Help us to embrace our need for you. Amen.

As the story of Bartimaeus unfolds, note the change in the tone of his detractors: "Take heart; get up, he is calling you." Two important aspects of his identity surface in the scene. First, Jesus calls him. Most of his life Bartimaeus had called out to others, often with little or no response. But now Jesus calls *him*. He is the object of someone else's interest, no longer nothing but someone.

Second, in Jesus' day, most people viewed blindness as a curse. The blind, they thought, must have done something wrong. Sin had caused their loss of sight. This attitude isolated the blind from others and the community. They had no way to support themselves, so they were given cloaks—their license to beg. More than likely, the cloak was Bartimaeus's only possession. His identity was all bound up, therefore, with that cloak. He was defined by this symbol of his brokenness.

But even before he is healed, Bartimaeus throws off that cloak. He throws off his old identity. He relinquishes all the baggage associated with that piece of cloth. As the cloak hits the ground, a new identity begins to emerge in his heart and soul. Note the language. He "throws off" and "springs up." These are powerful action words. He springs up and finds his way to Jesus. No longer defined simply as a blind beggar, he waits expectantly for something special to happen.

Are there aspects of your own self-definition that you need to throw off? Identify just one element of your self-understanding that stands as a barrier to your true self. Put on a piece of clothing, associate it with that piece of who you are that you need to throw off, and then remove it, letting it drop to the floor, praying: "Blessed Jesus, I wait expectantly for your transforming grace. Shape me anew. Amen."

In the story that immediately precedes this one in Mark's Gospel, James and John, in their quest for power and glory, told Jesus what they wanted. "Teacher," they demanded, "we want you to do for us whatever we ask of you." And Jesus asked, "What is it you want me to do for you?" We know what followed. They wanted him to honor them above their fellow disciples.

In this new scene, having already witnessed the transformation that was happening in the life of Bartimaeus, Jesus poses the same question to him, "What do you want me to do for you?" "My teacher," he responds. It's interesting that this is the same greeting in Aramaic that Mary Magdalene uses when she encounters the risen Jesus—the affectionate greeting of a faithful disciple. And it only appears in these two instances in the New Testament. "My teacher," he says, "let me see again." Done.

Jesus' conversation with the rich man ended with the words "Come, follow me," an implicit invitation to take up a new identity, to become his true self (see Mark 10:21). Despite the fact that Jesus' final word to Bartimaeus is "Go," as Mark tells us, "He regained his sight and followed him on the way." He embraced his new identity as a beloved child of God. He did not even need an invitation because he was home.

And what about our identity? Where do we discover who we really are? Through the water of baptism we find that we are all the beloved children of God. And whenever we gather at our family table to receive Holy Communion, God proclaims, "You are my child. Receive my grace. Embrace my love. Share this love with all."

As you wash your face each morning, remind yourself that you are a beloved child of God and pray, "Loving God, thank you for creating me in your image and claiming me as your beloved child. Amen."

Where We Bury Our Umbilical Cord

OCTOBER 28—NOVEMBER 3, 2024 • RAY BUCKLEY

SCRIPTURE OVERVIEW: In some indigenous traditions, mothers will bury each child's umbilical cord to symbolize the child's connection to the roots of their community and tradition. The passages this week ask us to consider our faith roots and connections. Ruth leaves what she knows to build community and connection in a new land, eventually being adopted into a new family of faith. The psalmist's praise for God's care for the poor, the oppressed, and the foreigner calls us to live out our inherited faith by doing God's work in the world. The scribe's encounter with Jesus in Mark invites us to consider what we have inherited as the most important law guiding our lives. And the writer of Hebrews reminds us that Christ's work was greater than any we could ever do on our own. Ruth, the scribe, the psalmist, and Jesus the Christ are examples of those, named and anonymous, who have come before us in the faith.

QUESTIONS AND SUGGESTIONS FOR REFLECTION

- Read Ruth 1:1-18. When have you left the familiar behind to set out into the unknown? Where did you experience God's presence and help in that situation?
- Read Psalm 146. When have you witnessed God at work in the world in a way that gave you hope about an otherwise seemingly hopeless situation?
- Read Hebrews 9:11-14. How does the redemption offered in Christ's death free you to worship the living God? What form does your worship take?
- Read Mark 12:28-34. What does it mean to you to love your neighbor as you love yourself? How do you act on that commandment in your everyday life?

Director for the Center for First Nations Spirituality and a faculty member of The Academy for Spiritual Formation; author who makes his home in the Matanuska-Susitna Valley of Alaska and is a traditional basket maker and wood carver.

When my body dies and my soul goes home, I want my ashes to be placed upon the earth. They will not linger there long before finding their way into the life of other things. It is the way of some who have given me life, and although I'll never know their names or stand at a stone commemorating their presence here, I will find them. They will be in the soil itself, the heartwood of the trees, the moss among the rocks, the berries, blown by the wind back into crevices. They would have known this as a sacred thing; not preservation, but creation. This is our deep spiritual birthing place, the place-where-we-have-buried-our-umbilical-cord. This is our ancestral heritage. Our home.

I attended a gathering at which each person was given five small blank pieces of paper. We were asked to identify five of the most important things or people in our lives and write each one on a piece of paper. We were then instructed to select one piece of paper to live without and hold it up for a volunteer to collect. The internal struggles were evident on the faces of many in the crowd. The instructor then asked us to repeat the process, explaining that we were going to give up one of the five each time. On the third time, however, the volunteers walked briskly through the room, sometimes ignoring what was being lifted and instead taking one or more pieces of paper that had not been offered from each person.

When famine, war, political violence, racial genocide, natural disaster, or disease destroy our countries, killing our families, we—like Naomi and Elimelech—choose life, leaving behind the place-where-we-have-buried-our-umbilical-cords. We hang our harps on unfamiliar trees, wondering if our sacred songs make sense in the places and situations in which we have been forced to live.

O God, you have been our home. Be the place-of-our-umbilical-cords. Amen.

At a very young age, my mother was abandoned in an empty house by those who abused her. Her early life was a frightening journey toward safety. As an adult, she was known for her kindness and compassion, with a remarkable capacity to turn any place into a home.

Home, like family, actually has very little to do with the people or places of our birth. Even the words *home* or *family* can bring fear to the many people who live their lives without knowing either. Our collective testimonies seem to say that homes and families are intentional creations, and we are drawn to seek and create them for ourselves and others.

When we say we have "found a home," we are often speaking of the place and people where our worth is affirmed by love. They are the places where we are given permission to edit what others have attempted to name us (or we have named ourselves), and where our sacredness is affirmed. Home is the experience of covenantal relationship, where the bone marrow of spirit can be informed and edited.

Generations before Elimelech, Naomi, and their two sons immigrated to Moab, the Moabites had refused to offer food and shelter to the desperate Israelites. By religious law, the Moabites became a hereditary, unredeemable, spiritually-alien nation. Naomi, her husband, and their children were famine refugees; a small family fleeing to Moab to be able to eat. For a time, Moab would be a home, the sons finding love and marriage among the Moabite people. But as circumstances changed, Naomi and her two daughters-in-law were all that remained. This, then, becomes not only the story of Naomi and Ruth but a spiritual story of who becomes our family—and a richer lesson in "home."

O God, you have led us from famine to the homes of the "unre-
deemable," where we made our home too. May we always be
grateful to them and to you. Amen.

We are preparing to move. For my part, there are boxes of books in several languages, each one feeling like an old friend. I have not seen some in many years, and when I do, there is a sense of celebration. Carefully, though, I am giving them away. I am aware, as are most who teach, that we often find ourselves quoting each other or the same large pantheon of wise men and wise women. As my older brother reminds me, "Pass the books along. There will be others written. These will stay in your memory." Our experiences—what we value, what we trust—will stay with us throughout our life.

The psalmist begins this song with *hallelujah*, "Praise the LORD!" This is a declarative invitation for everyone within hearing distance to testify to the goodness of God. It is not a learned response of worship or cultural expression of excitement, but a *Yes, I have seen it. I am a witness.*

There is a beautiful Ojibway love poem that speaks of the blood of one, flowing toward their beloved like red streams during the moon-of-ripening-strawberries. It is the almost indescribable feeling of connectedness with another. It is holding an infant next to your heart, the grasp of its hand around your finger, feeling that your heart could not possibly hold any more love and protectedness. It is inhaling the fragrance of a sweater when the wearer is away. It is wrapping your arms around someone you love and feeling your physical hearts begin to synchronize, or, as do the Māori's of New Zealand, pressing noses and foreheads together, "sharing breath." It is to walk on the sand of a beach fitting your feet into the footprints of those walking with you, wondering about this gift. This is what it is to praise God, to experience the justice and rightness of God's reign.

Lord, we praise you. May your wisdom which we have embraced go with us wherever we go. Amen.

Hallelujah is an invitation, an open-ended shared interactive expression for all who hear it to immediately participate. It is an "us" word. The writer abandons the "I" of personal expression to speak out of the collective memory and experience of God's people.

In many languages of the world, there is no tense; past is spoken of in the same voice as present. The effects of action and event, both past and present, are concurrent in the retelling. In a sense, it is a celebration of physics, that to every action (or word) there is a reaction, the effect of which is continual movement.

The faithful character of God in history is almost without tense, being present/active in the past and present, continually into the future, doing always what God has committed God's character to do. The wronged are being defended, prisoners are being freed, and the hungry are being fed. The blind are at this moment receiving sight, and those who have been forced into subservience are being lifted up. The character/actions of God that we have witnessed in the past are reflected in the character/actions of God now as well as in the hoped-for future we look toward when our reality contrasts with this vision of justice.

In this moment God is involved in the minutiae of human experience: God is loving people and influencing the evil toward goodness. God is protecting aliens and strangers. God is taking the sides of orphans and widows and is squashing the wicked exploiters. We are led into the story, compelled by the Spirit of God to participate in both the character and actions of God.

Spirit of God, open my eyes that I may see you. Open my spirit that I may do your will. Amen.

ALL SAINTS DAY

Among Native bead-artists, the best and most enduring work comes from those who sew only one bead at a time, securing it into its place and then linking it to those surrounding it. The work is tight, strong, and secure. From the Kiowa and Crow nations come bright, often free-form, artistic compositions. To wear a piece is to take upon oneself a testimony of heritage translated as art.

In the middle of a very hot Oklahoma summer, the late Steve Littleman was the master of ceremonies for the Kiowa Black Leggings Society. As the dancing slowed, he brought the community's attention to a deep, cultural event: A child was receiving a spiritual name.

Many of the child's family members wore Pendleton blankets over their shoulders, ready to be given as gifts. The spokesman for the family began, pulling from his memory the names of at least two hundred and fifty years of ancestors. The child heard, and the community remembered, the names of men and women, punctuated with deeds, events, or virtues. Through the recollection, names became living people. Some had been known for living in such a sacred way that they had been woven into the oral history of a people. Names became continual spiritual witness. From one of those lives, a life associated with holiness and faithfulness, a name was given to the child.

We wear upon ourselves, like blankets, the testimonies of those who have walked ahead of us. Their names and deeds, woven tightly, become our encouragement and adornment to be given away to listening ears. They are the Lord's, and they lead the way for us up the hill of the Lord.

You are great and good, O God. You are humble and strong. In the voices of our generations, we are your witnesses, woven together one bead at a time. Amen.

On the bookshelves in my room are volumes that I try to read at least once a year. The paperbacks are worn and falling apart. The bound copies are often the books whose titles are worn away, the gilt simply a memory. They are radically diverse: the works of artists and painters, scholars, musicians, great thinkers, and the thoughts of comedians and preachers (sometimes both). I love Buber's historic *Tales of the Hasidim* and Noah benShea's parables of *Jacob the Baker*, where students, scholars, and desperate souls like me bring questions to wise persons, hoping to gain spiritual truth.

My heart is weary when the work of the gospel becomes strategy in the guise of holiness or the desert experience of spiritual formation needs to fit a business model and marketing plan. As Kathleen Norris reminds us in *Amazing Grace*, we find ourselves in times when some who raise questions do so to expose, embarrass, and entrap.

A religious scholar who had been listening to Jesus asks a deep and simple question (the deepest insights often come from the simplest of questions): *What is the greatest commandment?* Jesus, recognizing the sincerity of the scholar, removes the legalism of all the law and commandments. At that moment, debate about nuances ceases, and the schisms are immaterial. In a few sentences, legalism becomes relational, and love becomes both the behavior and measurement: Love the Lord your God with everything you have, and love your neighbor (all those God places in your path) as yourself. It was enough for the religious scholar, and it is enough for us. *Love.* And our brother Mark reminds us that, after that, no one spoke.

O God, we fluff our feathers, parading our own inflated size. Then the rain comes, and we are left puny, dripping until we are dried by our neighbors flapping their own wet wings. Amen.

Among the Amish, one of the most egregious sins is that of "speaking for God." We do it so easily, don't we? In an effort to perpetuate our "rightness" and the control that comes with it, we create denominations (and destroy them); we bloody history (and people groups); we suppress and enslave whole races, genders, and the poor. We recollect that God has not granted us the opportunity to stand in judgment, and that seems to take all the fun out of our faith. What are we, we think, if not the keepers-of-rightness? We look around and discover that we have become religious hoarders who cannot live without our collection of holy words and souvenirs. When God tells us that our sacrifices and burnt offerings are an affront and offense, we still breed the doves and hang on to their cages "just in case." Others who look at us see the piles of continually growing debris that we use to buttress our positions and in which we find comfort. Somewhere around us is the place-where-we-buried-our-umbilical-cord; the place of our spiritual birth; our honest-to-God, honest-to-self place; *our home.*

God walks through the great divergent piles of spiritual refuse we keep accumulating. Has this worked? Was this enough? Were the places of worship you made in the desert sufficient? Were the lambs and doves good enough? What else would you like to add? What is the language I AM should speak to you?

The language and love of Christ are all that we need.

Holy One, you did not require a sacrifice to forgive us. It was all we knew. You walked to our altar. Certainly, there must be more that we must do. You pat down the earth-soil. Here you have buried your umbilical cord. Amen.

God Provides

NOVEMBER 4–10, 2024 • KIMBERLY TYREE INGRAM

SCRIPTURE OVERVIEW: Ruth's story forms part of the background of the family of Jesus. The son of Ruth and Boaz, Obed, is David's grandfather. The women of Bethlehem rejoice with Naomi at the birth of her grandson, and the psalmist declares that children are a blessing from God. In the scriptures, children are spoken of only as a blessing, never as a liability (unlike some narratives in our culture). The writer of Hebrews builds upon the eternal nature of Christ's sacrifice, proclaiming that his death was sufficient once for all. In Mark, Jesus warns his disciples not to be fooled by appearances. Those who put on a big show of piety do not impress God. God wants us instead to give from the heart, even if no one but God sees.

QUESTIONS AND SUGGESTIONS FOR REFLECTION

- Read Ruth 3:1-5; 4:13-17. Who are the people in your community who lack the basic provisions for a safe and healthy life? How do you try to help meet their needs?
- Read Psalm 127. In what ways do you invite God to be part of your work?
- Read Hebrews 9:24-28. When have you eagerly waited for something? How did that feel?
- Read Mark 12:38-44. How do you practice generosity in the way you allocate your resources and time?

Director of Ministerial Services and conference secretary of the Western North Carolina Conference of The United Methodist Church; active participant in her local church; spends time with children and youth; serves on the Racial Healing and Reconciliation Team; loving grandmother to Laurel Ann.

Each New Year's Eve, many people discuss and plan their resolutions. I've heard of a twist on this activity, where friends or family gather and each person present writes down a resolution for something they want for themselves or for someone else. The group then puts all the resolutions in a bowl, and each person draws one out as their commitment for the new year. The resolutions might be "the kitchen sink will be empty of dirty dishes each night before bedtime" or "I will send one text of gratitude each day." Each resolution is meant to enrich the lives of the participants and/or their communities. Each person adopts the "resolution" identified by a loved one who wants the best for their family and friends.

In this text Naomi is resolved to make life secure for Ruth, and subsequently for herself. Naomi calls Ruth her "daughter," but actually she is her daughter-in-law. The deaths of the men in their lives has left them vulnerable, but Ruth has stayed by Naomi's side in their loss, cementing their connection to one another. Naomi gives Ruth instructions for connecting with Boaz, and Ruth obediently follows them. It turns out to be good advice. Ruth and Boaz marry, and the futures of Naomi and Ruth are secure.

Who speaks into your life with wisdom? To whom are you obedient? There are many voices in our lives telling us what to believe, what to think, whom to trust. Sometimes we commit without considering agendas or motives. Are the voices to which we listen looking to improve our lives and our community? Are they encouraging us to show God's love to others?

It is good to be surrounded by people we can trust, who will help us to become faithful disciples, better citizens, and bearers of love.

God, thank you for the voices in my life who seek to make the world better for me and for my community. Help me to be discerning, and when your voice is clear, to be obedient. Amen.

While the book of the Bible is named "Ruth," the main character in these verses is Naomi, Ruth's first mother-in-law. Ruth gives birth to Obed, but the community names him and identifies him as "Naomi's." The women celebrate Naomi's good fortune, praising God!

Naomi's life has gone from secure to empty and then back to secure and full. Her life was full with a husband and two sons. Then all three died and she and her two daughters-in-law had no one to look after them, no long-term security. One daughter-in-law left Naomi and returned to her family of origin to seek a new path to security, but Ruth stayed by Naomi's side. When we get to these verses, Naomi has navigated a plan that resulted in long-term security once again. Not only that, but we learn in these passages that Obed will be the grandfather to David, the greatest king Israel ever had.

My mother-in-law has been in my life for over thirty years. She has always been faithful and kind. She lost her husband when he was only forty-five years old. Though I didn't know Carol during these most difficult days, I have witnessed the results of her strength and courage. Her four children have flourished. Today, Carol has nine grandchildren, four grandchildren-in-law, and two great-grandchildren. My mother-in-law's life has gone from full to empty and back to full.

I guess it's true for most of us. We have seasons or experiences that are full of joy and hopefulness. But then we hit bumps in the road—financial stress, divorce, job loss, death of loved ones, medical challenges—and despair threatens us. In the midst of life's ups and downs, may we give thanks for the ways God loves us through it all.

God, remind us that no life is perfect. We all have ups and downs. Give us courage in the emptiness and gratefulness in the fullness, knowing that you travel with us through it all. Amen.

In *The Message,* Eugene Peterson translates verse two of today's reading this way: "It's useless to rise early and go to bed late, and work your worried fingers to the bone. Don't you know [God] enjoys giving rest to those he loves?"

During the height of the COVID-19 pandemic, we were forced to stay home. In North Carolina, where it begins to warm up by April, people spent as much time as they could outside—one weekend we took our kayaks to a lake only to head right back home because we couldn't find a place to park. Our lives slowed down. Activities ceased. We worshiped in pajamas on the couch. As the world opened back up, we committed to continuing some of the priorities and practices we adopted during the pandemic. We wouldn't go back to being overcommitted. We would focus on relationships. We would slow down.

It didn't take long, though, for the frenzy to reappear.

We "work" to put food on the table for our children, to provide for the needs of our aging parents, to fulfill an internal need, or because our employer expects it. We are exhausted. The psalmist is telling us to STOP. It is not our role to carry the weight of the world on our shoulders. God is inviting us into a partnership of creation. A partnership of blessing. A partnership of care.

The days are getting shorter in the northern hemisphere. More darkness allows us to get the sleep we need. Take advantage of the shorter days and leave the office before night falls. Use this season as a time to distinguish between the "musts" and the "shoulds." We can't do it all.

God, we work our fingers to the bone to provide, to care, and to minister. In this season of longer nights, help us to commit to right-sizing and refocusing our commitments for our sake, the sake of our families and friends, and for the sake of your kingdom. Amen.

The beginning of Hebrews, chapter 9, describes the first covenant God made with Israel at Sinai, including regulations for worship, the role of the high priests, and rituals of sacrifice. The letter to the Hebrews shifts to the new covenant made through Christ, "the mediator of a new covenant, so that those who are called may receive the promised eternal inheritance" (9:15). No longer are God's people expected to give an annual sacrifice; the "once for all" sacrifice of Jesus atoned for us and reconciled us with God.

I was having breakfast with a clergy friend recently. We were talking about current issues in the church and he suggested that each follower of Christ, including me, would one day have to stand before Jesus and give account. We were disagreeing about a particular viewpoint, and he implied that while he believed that I was wrong, it wasn't up to him to judge—that would be left to God. It wasn't a contentious conversation, and I left thinking about accounting one day to God for my actions, decisions, and beliefs. For me, love always prevails. I cannot imagine that being a problem with God. As long as another's differing opinions are not harming others, I believe we can peacefully co-exist and even work together in our disagreement.

The good news of the text today is the promise that in the end we don't have to worry about where we went wrong. "Christ, having been offered once to bear the sins of many, will appear a second time, not to deal with sin, but to save those who are eagerly waiting for him." We are called to faith and faithfulness. We follow Christ to the best of our ability, looking to God for guidance. God will take care of the rest.

Jesus, help me not get hung up on what I've done wrong. Forgive me and help me to forgive myself, knowing that you died to save us from our sin and to reconcile us with God. Amen.

In youth Bible study at our church, one of the senior boys asked, "If you could only have one kind of grace, which one would you choose?" It was an interesting and exciting question for so many reasons. On this particular night, I was participating in the study as an adult helper while my husband led the study. I had taught these same youth in Sunday school for many of their middle and high school years. I knew from years of experience as a youth minister that you never know what will stick. It seems that these youth had learned about Wesley's understanding of grace (prevenient, justifying, and sanctifying) enough to initiate a conversation.

One youth said, "prevenient grace, because everyone, regardless of their beliefs, receives that grace." Another said, "sanctifying grace, because our connection to God is established for the long haul." Thankfully, we don't have to choose only one kind of grace. In Wesleyan understanding, God's grace is present before we even are aware of it and continues working in us even after death.

This passage in Hebrews helps us understand God's justifying grace. Christ atoned for our sins through offering his very life. When we acknowledge God's grace and respond, we experience God's justifying grace. God is constantly seeking a relationship with us. When we say yes to that relationship and commit our lives to following God, we are justified. We place our lives into God's hands and become willing to follow where God leads, being led by God to work in the world for God's purposes.

God, thank you for the gift of salvation. Help me respond again and again to your justifying grace which atones for my sins and keeps me in right relationship with you. Amen.

The "scribes" are scholars of Hebrew law who interpret and instruct religious expectations. They are among the religious leaders with privilege and status, profiled by what they wear (long robes), a preferred response (respect), and deserving of "the best seat in the house" (places of honor at banquets).

In the Gospel of Mark, the scribes are often seen in opposition to Jesus. Chapter 1 distinguishes Jesus' authority as different from the scribes. In chapter 2, the scribes had "questioning in their hearts" (v. 6) and debated why Jesus ate with tax collectors and sinners. In chapter 11, the scribes doubted Jesus' authority. If we look up the Pharisees and elders, we find even more references to the "church" leaders in opposition to Jesus.

We must be careful with such one-dimensional caricatures, however, as these images have been used to support two thousand years of antisemitic views. When we understand the complexity of these persons, we can understand the multitude of challenges they faced as they encountered a Jew named Jesus of Nazareth. For whatever reason, Mark shows us that they did not recognize the priority of love that is incarnate in Jesus.

In Martin Luther King Jr.'s description of the Montgomery Bus Boycott, *Stride Toward Freedom*, he tells the story of the Black community's effort to integrate public buses. King indicated that no one in the White community worked to help others in the White community prepare for the needed changes. Not even the White church leaders.

It's easy to look backward through the lens of history and identify where opportunities to embody the love of Jesus were embraced and where they were overlooked. The world pressures us in numerous ways to choose what's best for ourselves over others. Jesus chose a different way. Where in your life and community is God calling you to embody the love of Jesus even when it might not be the easiest or most popular choice?

God, help me to be more like Jesus. Amen.

The story of the poor widow who gives her two small copper coins is familiar to church-going folks. It is more about kingdom living than how to use our money. The poor widow teaches us what it means to trust, to have faith.

My friend Andrea pastors a relatively new church start. Originally, they were a second campus of a large United Methodist Church, but after a few years, they got their own charter. Recently, they started a new online ministry that reaches young adults in their twenties and thirties. It is exciting to see the way they reach "nones and dones" in their community. After Andrea had shared her church's story in a webinar, I emailed her to express my thanks for the work she and her church are doing. But Andrea's response voiced her concern over the church's finances. For the first time in their history, the church was at risk of not making payroll or fulfilling their commitment to connectional giving. In the midst of such uncertainty, however, Andrea was grateful I had reached out. "Your email brings hope," she said, "in a week where there seemed to be very little. So thank you!"

The ministry of this church reminds me of the poor widow. We give what we have out of a response to God's grace with hope for what is to come. God places a call on each of us. We respond in faithfulness. We trust God for the rest. By the time you read this devotion, it will all have worked out, one way or another. I don't know how, but I am certain that whatever path lays ahead, that church will move forward with faithful steps and expectant hope for the future to come.

God, help us to give of our time, gifts, and resources as a reflection of our faithfulness, that thy kingdom will come. Amen.

The Gift and Grace of Dependence

NOVEMBER 11–17, 2024 • FREDERICK W. SCHMIDT

SCRIPTURE OVERVIEW: The inability to have a child brings pain to many today, and this was equally true in ancient times. In that context it was sometimes even worse, for Peninnah openly ridicules Hannah for being unable to conceive. But as a result of Hannah's desperate, heartfelt prayer, God blesses her with a son, Samuel, who will become a powerful prophet. Hannah then rejoices in a God who exalts the poor and needy. Hannah provides an example of the boldness with which we also can approach God now because of Christ's sacrifice. The destruction of Jerusalem is the focus of the passage in Mark. Jesus here predicts the demolition of the Temple and the city, which the Romans executed in 70 C.E.

QUESTIONS AND SUGGESTIONS FOR REFLECTION

- Read 1 Samuel 1:4-20. How do you persist in prayer when your prayer seems unanswered for a long time?
- Read 1 Samuel 2:1-10. How do you express your joy and thanks when God answers your prayer?
- Read Hebrews 10:11-25. What helps you to persevere in the practice of your faith?
- Read Mark 13:1-8. What signs make you anxious about the future? What helps you to hold on to hope?

Senior scholar and inaugural holder of the Rueben P. Job Chair in Spiritual Formation at Garrett-Evangelical Theological Seminary, Evanston, IL; Vice Rector at the Episcopal Church of the Good Shepherd, Brentwood, TN.

The story of Hannah draws us into a conversation about our dependence upon God and our capacity for trust. Appearing at the beginning of First Samuel, Hannah's plight is not just a story of personal anguish; it provides an account of Samuel's role in the history of Israel and foreshadows the plight of Israel as it looks for a king and deliverer.

Hannah's circumstances mirror the predicament of Israel, both of whom are surrounded by hostility and incomprehension. Her situation is hopeless. She is surrounded by detractors. Her husband and ally, Elkanah, fails to appreciate her plight, and initially even Eli, the priest, mistakes her prayers for drunkenness.

Despite her apparently hopeless situation, Hannah is delivered from her distress and finds peace before Samuel is conceived. This does not happen magically or through manipulation but by turning to God. Her lament is a frank confession of her distress, her unqualified dependence upon God.

Faith is about having convictions—ideas, beliefs, certainty—about God, but it is more than that. Faith has an active component that includes dependence and trust. Hannah's story and that of Israel's early history challenges us to expand our capacity for that kind of faith. Hannah's story begins with a prayer for a child that ultimately leads to an answer to prayer that shapes the nation's future. Through both stories we learn that the journey of dependence and trust often entails allowing God to name the prayer and also its answer.

Gracious God, I confess my hopelessness. In the face of circumstances beyond my control, I am overwhelmed. I cry out for relief. You, alone, can turn mourning into joy. I place myself back into your hands. I invite you to shape my prayers. I long to hear your voice. Amen.

Our approach to prayer is often transactional. We lift a concern in prayer. We wait for an answer, and we test the value of our prayers against the quality of the response that we receive. Our approach also expects instant gratification. In the meantime, our confidence in God hangs in the balance. The promises of God are only as good as God's last performance, and God had better hurry.

The spirit of the narrative near the end of the first chapter of First Samuel runs counter to the modern temperament. Eli offers a parting benediction of peace that Hannah accepts, and with that we are told she "went her way and ate and drank with her husband, and her countenance was sad no longer." It is only later that Samuel is conceived, and—read as the beginnings of Samuel's ministry and the fortunes of Israel under Saul and David—it is years later that the full significance of Hannah's prayers is realized. In fact, the outworking of Hannah's prayers covers decades, and she could not have anticipated the implications of her prayer, particularly if one keeps in mind the promise of a messiah or "anointed one" yet to come from the house of David (see 2 Samuel 7:4-17).

What kind of prayer and what kind of spiritual life is this? It is, from all that Hannah has said, a life of absolute dependence upon the fact that God "is," and that God is merciful. When—in her pain and grief—she comes to grips with these two realities, she finds peace or *shalom*, a life centered in and on the will of God, a peace that arises from a place of deep dependence upon and trust in God.

Gracious God, grant me a peace that surpasses all understanding, a peace that is grounded deep in my knowledge of you. Help me to trust you more and more each day. Amen.

Hannah's prayer in the second chapter of First Samuel and the poetry of David at the end of Second Samuel (22–23:7) provide thematic bookends to the stories of Samuel, Saul, and David. Both passages emphasize the truths that inform the writer's critique of that history. They outline the path of dependence upon and trust in God, and they provide a picture of kings and deliverers that will shape the messianic expectation of both the Old and New Testaments.

In more didactic form, Hannah's prayer and David's oracle underline these truths: God is God, and we are not. God alone makes and keeps covenant. God alone anoints and empowers. God alone delivers those who are without hope. Those who forget these facts place themselves under God's judgment.

For ancient Israel and for us as individuals, the temptation to self-sufficiency is constant. The stories of Saul and David illustrate this point. Gifted and anointed by God, their lives and their efforts come to grief when they forget their dependence upon God: Saul in the wake of his dishonesty and disobedience, David in the wake of his exploitation of Bathsheba and the murder of Uriah. However, the books of Samuel go even further to sketch the perils of self-sufficiency: Israel's desire for a king is itself threaded through with those perils. As such, the prayer of Hannah and the poetry of David serve as a word of caution to both the individual and the nation, pointing to the God who alone can deliver us.

Gracious God, I confess my hubris, my pride, my need for control. I confess the harm that I have done to those who depend on me. Teach me to depend on you. Free me from the primal desire to be my own god, and lead me into the future that only you can give. Amen.

The book of Hebrews was written to a Christian congregation sometime after 70 C.E. when the Temple in Jerusalem was destroyed. It is an exhortation or a sermon to a congregation. In it the writer compares the person and work of Christ with the angels and Torah (chs. 1–2), Moses and the Promised Land (chs. 3–4), the priests of ancient Israel and Melchizedek (chs. 5–7), and the sacrifices in the Temple and God's covenant with Israel (chs. 8–10).

Each comparison describes the way the person and work of Jesus is a "filling out" of expectations that are deeply rooted in hopes described throughout Hebrew scriptures. There was a pastoral concern at the heart of the writer's message. Christians were undoubtedly troubled by the loss of the Temple.

Among those concerns, it may be that his readers wondered if forgiveness was still possible. Drawing on the prophet Jeremiah (see 31:33-34), who foresees a day when the law will be written on the hearts of the nation and the sins of the people will be forgotten, the writer of Hebrews asserts that hope has been realized in Christ.

The Temple's destruction does not have the same significance for us today—in large part because of the book of Hebrews—but we still struggle with the possibility of forgiveness. We revisit and rehearse our sins. We find it hard to believe that they have been forgiven.

We know we need to forgive ourselves. But the ability to break the power of sin has never been something we can accomplish. The solution lies in depending upon a power beyond our own.

Holy God, it is more accurate to say that we need to embrace the gift of forgetfulness. Help us lay down our sins and leave them behind. Remind us that in Christ our sins have been forgiven and forgotten. They have no hold on us. Amen.

Forgiveness is not a private transaction. Together we are members of the household of God, "sprinkled clean" by the waters of baptism. Even the grammar of the exhortation in today's passage is cast in the first-person plural—"let us"—and emphasizes the collective nature of our spiritual journey.

This has always been difficult for us to grasp, and the language of the letter to the Hebrews suggests that it was a problem then. But the problem is even more acute today, particularly in the West.

Those who think of themselves as "spiritual but not religious" outnumber mainline Protestants. That may be the spiritual path of some, but it is not the Christian path. The Savior who "fills out" the hopes and expectations of the prophets creates a new redemptive and healing world reality for the people of God. In ancient Israel, the high priest entered the Holy of Holies on behalf of the nation, symbolically carrying the tribes of Israel with him, wearing an *ephod* (or sleeveless tunic) adorned with twelve stones. Now, the writer explains, our proximity to God has been made immediately available by a new high priest.

So, if by "religion" one refers to the communal life of Christ's body, then it is impossible for us to be spiritual without also being religious. Our experience of God's household is, by definition, not a personal possession or private experience. Baptism is not a once-and-done transaction, and its impact upon us is not confined to our relationship with God. It transforms our relationship to one another, and we depend upon it. Our experience of it "stirs us up and encourages us."

Gracious and loving God, teach us how to participate more fully in your life, that we may be forever changed, more readily available to your purposes, and remade in you. Amen.

Some years ago, I served as Canon Educator at Washington National Cathedral, and I frequently met guest speakers at the airport. On one occasion our guest was a New Testament scholar whose original discipline was archaeology. Driving to the Cathedral, we threaded our way up along the tidal basin, passing the various monuments that dot the District's landscape. "You know," he said, "I've often thought that this will make a fantastic ruin one day." It was a startling observation.

I have no doubt that the disciples were similarly taken aback when Jesus told them that one day the Temple would be a ruin. That, no doubt, is why they began pressing Jesus for reassurance the moment they were alone.

It is natural for us to become dependent upon our surroundings: the homes we were reared in, the towns we live in, the churches we worship in, the nations where we share life with our neighbors. The roots of that dependence run deep, and from them we draw a sense of belonging, identity, security, and control. This is both necessary and natural.

But as we grow and mature spiritually, we begin to realize that ultimately the weight of our well-being cannot rest there. All the things that we hold dear are subject to change, and the demands that they make on us are often in conflict with one another. As the good gifts of God, they are not God; God alone is able to order the things that we love in a way that is life-giving. The spiritual journey is a matter of learning this lesson, over and over again, until it takes a deep hold on our hearts.

Gracious God, grant me the wisdom to receive the good gifts of life without depending upon them, knowing that you and you alone are never-changing and worthy of devotion. Amen.

The Gift and Grace of Dependence

Anxiety can be driven by unrest and violence, the loss of old certainties and the rise of new ones, accelerating change and the dis-ease that seems to arise spontaneously when times are good. Anxiety can be a product of social, political, and historical forces. It can be a function of growth and maturation, a feature of life's milestones, and a dimension of aging and illness. Our need to have a sign can also be driven by our personal history and temperament. Whatever its cause, anxiety often causes us to look for signs to provide reassurance.

But signs can be misleading. On the wall of our library is a sign that says, "If you've been looking for a sign, this is it." When looking for signs, we see what we want to see, which then means we can misinterpret their meaning or draw the wrong conclusions about them. We can attribute a significance to them that is, in truth, completely missing. And, as Jesus notes, we can be deceived by them.

More deeply, the desire for signs can lead to a largely magical approach to the spiritual journey. The exceptional becomes a fixation. The mundane becomes a burden. As a result, we can lurch from god-sighting to god-sighting, little realizing that God is as much or more present in the moments in between.

Signs themselves can also become our god. I have known more than one person whose confidence in God waxes and wanes with what they counted as the miraculous, leaving them vulnerable to events that are shaped by chance and choice, not by God.

Gracious God, free me from the need for a sign. Instill in me a faith that needs one thing—you—and a sense of hope that rests on a confidence in your love and mercy. Through Christ our Lord. Amen.

Belonging to the Truth

NOVEMBER 18-24, 2024 • L. ROGER OWENS

SCRIPTURE OVERVIEW: Second Samuel records the final words of David. David takes comfort in the covenant that God has made with his family, which must be continued by kings who will honor God and rule justly. The psalmist sings of this same covenant with David's family and the same necessity to follow God's decrees in order to rule well. Revelation opens with a vision of Jesus Christ, the fulfillment of the Davidic covenant, the King to rule over all kings for all time. Many expected Jesus to set up a political kingdom. Yet in John, Jesus tells Pilate that his kingdom is not an earthly one. This week let us thank God that the kingdom is based not on the exercise of power but on Jesus' example of serving others.

QUESTIONS AND SUGGESTIONS FOR REFLECTION

- Read 2 Samuel 23:1-7. What characteristics would you include in a description of a just leader? Where do you see those characteristics in world leaders today?
- Read Psalm 132:1-18. What is your vision of Paradise? Who will be seated at the table with you?
- Read Revelation 1:4b-8. How do you bear witness to the "Alpha and the Omega"?
- Read John 18:33-37. What is your understanding of what it means to live in God's kingdom?

Hugh Thomson Kerr Professor of Pastoral Theology at Pittsburgh Theological Seminary and author of *Everyday Contemplative: The Way of Prayerful Living* (Upper Room Books, 2022).

These verses offer us an image for just, faithful leadership: "One who rules over people justly, ruling in the fear of God, is like the light of morning, like the sun rising on a cloudless morning, gleaming from the rain on the grassy land." The night may be dark, cloudy, and rainy, but when morning comes the darkness disappears. How refreshing and enlivening is the clarity of such a morning!

You need only to think of a world leader like Nelson Mandela to understand this image. After the long, stormy night of apartheid in South Africa, Mandela's leadership, marked by a commitment to justice and reconciliation, was like the light of a new day. However, political leaders are not the only ones called to this ideal of just leadership. These verses speak to parents, pastors, and principals as well—all who hold positions of authority and leadership. How can each of us exercise authority in ways that are just, so that clarity like that of a new dawn will be their hallmark?

King David in these verses speaks of his own reign, which had its dark, stormy periods. When we remember that aspect, we can hear his words as ones of hope. When we fall short of this type of leadership, we know that with God, renewal is possible.

When we lead with justice, in the "fear of God," we become signs of the reign of Jesus himself, the heir to David's throne, who, as the book of Revelation says, is himself the light of the city of God.

Lord, help me see where you are calling me to leadership today, and give me the wisdom to lead with equity and justice. Amen.

This psalm begins with the celebration of King David's oath: "I will not give sleep to my eyes . . . until I find a place for the LORD." A few verses later the writer calls on God, "Rise up, O LORD, and go to your resting place." What is the relationship between David's promise to find a place for the Lord and the psalmist's cry for the Lord to come to a resting place?

After my lecture on Christian spirituality, a student asked me, "Where is the place for God in my life?" I replied, "There is no place for God in your life." Even though David finds a "place for the LORD," God's presence is never under our control. A better question might be this: "Where is my place in God's life?" God is present not because David found a place for God but because of God's promise to be with the people.

The divine decision to be with people finds its fulfillment in Jesus, in whom God rests. In freedom God chooses to live among us. And God's place continues to be among us in the Spirit of Christ, who makes the church Christ's body, the ongoing incarnation of God in the world. We need not find a place for God in our lives but, instead, perceive the shape of God's sovereign presence and activity already at work in our lives.

The spiritual life entails discerning God's activity in our lives. Sometimes we imagine that our prayer practices are our work of making a place for God. But we should consider them ways we glimpse God's sovereign presence and redemptive activity in our lives, remembering that God has chosen us as God's resting place.

Lord, help me remember that it's not my job to find a place for you. Instead, may I find the places where you are already at work in my life. Amen.

The sixteenth-century reformer Martin Luther said that the gospel comes to us in the form of promise: God has acted and will act to save us. The God of the Bible is a promise-making, promise-keeping God.

This psalm celebrates the promise God made to continue the line of David's rule and to make Zion God's ongoing home, a freely given promise based on gracious desire: "For the Lord has chosen Zion; he has desired it for his habitation."

When we forget that God relates to us on the basis of gracious promise, we may be tempted to turn our relationship to God into an if-then relationship. If I am good, then God will love me; if I study my Bible, then God will listen to me; if I tithe, then God will bless me; if I serve the poor, then God will reward me.

Whenever we take this approach, we are reshaping the gospel. Gospel comes as God's promise, expressed in this psalm by the word chosen. The promise to David is not a response to David. God's promise of salvation never comes as a response but as a free, unconditional gift.

Christians see God's promises fulfilled in Jesus Christ, the Son of David and the new Zion, the one whom God has chosen to embody divine saving presence in the world.

When you feel tempted to believe that you have to pressure God to keep the promise or coax God to be present with you, reconsider that temptation. In Jesus, God offers an unconditional promise: I am with you always, even to the end of the age.

Gracious God, give me the faith to receive your promised gift of love, and free me from the belief that I have to earn that love. Amen.

Some of us attend faith communities where we call the pastor a priest, and it's his or her role to celebrate the sacraments and pronounce God's forgiveness. Others of us go to churches where we call the minister "pastor" or "preacher," but it's still easy for us to imagine that he or she has a privileged relationship with God—a relationship we think we could never have.

During the sixteenth-century Reformation, a renewed understanding emerged of a concept called the "priesthood of all believers." That phrase doesn't mean that we don't need human pastors and priests to lead, teach, and guide the people of God. It means that the whole people of God—the church itself—is a priestly community. Clergy and laypeople together make up this priestly community. This community serves God by serving as a priest to its neighbors, offering a sign of God's presence to them.

Some people believe that the term "priesthood of all believers" means that each one of us is our own priest, that we don't need others to help us in our relationship with God. Rather, it means that in baptism we become priests for one another precisely because we do need to help one another relate to God. We need to announce God's forgiveness to one another. We want to intercede in prayer for one another. We desire to allow our voices to carry words of praise on behalf of others when their own voices can't. We need to be the kingdom of priests God has made us.

And in our priestly praying, we will thank God for those pastors and priests whom God has given to guide us and equip us as we grow into our own priestly role as bearers of God's love, forgiveness, and presence in the world.

Almighty God, as a member of your priestly people, help me see how I can make your presence and grace known to my friends and neighbors. Amen.

Dietrich Bonhoeffer, the German theologian and martyr during World War II, once said that the most difficult thing for human beings to come to terms with is the reality that we were not in the beginning. We struggle with being in the middle, with being creatures.

Today's passage clearly states that God alone is the beginning and the end, the Alpha and the Omega. God is the one "who is and who was and who is to come"—not us. We are in the middle.

Often we think of sin as actions and behaviors prohibited by God. But a broader concept of sin involves the human tendency to chafe against our creaturely place in the middle, to be beset by dreams and aspirations of being more than creatures and then trying to live them out those dreams.

I prefer to think of the Christian spiritual journey as the journey of learning to be creatures with limits. Creaturely limits don't constrict us except when we rebel against them. Within our limits as creatures we find our truest freedom. Saint Irenaeus noted, "The glory of God is the human being fully alive." Being fully alive implies embracing the reality that we are human beings, not God.

In Jesus, God entered the middle to show us the beauty of creaturely life, to restore us as the image of God in creation, and to show us what "fully alive" means for being human. Salvation from sin does not mean that we are no longer creatures. It means that we will embrace being creatures in the appropriate way and flourish within our human limits.

God of our Lord Jesus Christ, help us embrace ourselves the way you created us—limits and all. Give us patience when we get frustrated with our creaturely limits. Amen.

Earlier in John's Gospel the crowds try to make Jesus king, but he slips away. In truth, Jesus is already king—just not the kind of king the people desire. And so Jesus tells Pilate, "My kingdom is not from this world."

We often interpret Jesus' words to mean that his kingdom is otherworldly, merely spiritual, which is why we often hear people say that the church should stay out of politics. Saying God's kingdom is spiritual gets us off the hook. Then we don't have to be held accountable for how we engage in what the world calls politics.

When Jesus says this to Pilate, he's not referring to a spiritual kingdom. He means that the realm that acknowledges his rule is not governed by the coercive social conditions of worldly kingdoms. If his kingdom were from this world, he states, his followers would resort to violence to protect him.

We take it for granted that violence and coercion are a necessary part of life, but Jesus doesn't think so. He came to introduce a new social reality that we call church—real people in real relationships who have discovered that because Jesus chose to die rather than fight, we can live together without coercion or violence. Thus, we can signal to the kingdoms of this world—whether local communities or national governments—that alternatives to violence exist.

Jesus does not rule a merely spiritual kingdom. He rules over a kingdom in but not of the world. In Jesus' kingdom, the practices of forgiveness and reconciliation have overcome the practices of threat and coercion. God invites us to enter this reign and let it shape our lives and the communities in which we live.

King Jesus, help me to live today in a way that witnesses to your kingdom of love and peace. Amen.

Reign of Christ Sunday

"Everyone who belongs to the truth listens to my voice." We send our children to school hoping they will learn things that are true. We go to Sunday school and study our Bibles believing they offer us truth. Some people believe that to be a Christian you have to assent to a certain set of propositions about God, that you have to believe these principles are true. In each case, we believe that the truth of what we read, learn, or believe corresponds to "the way things really are."

When Pilate interrogates Jesus, Jesus makes a statement that upsets our conventional notions of truth: "Everyone who belongs to the truth listens to my voice." What does it mean to belong to the truth?

Maybe Jesus is saying that truth involves more than believing certain propositions are correct, something we do with our minds. Truth involves a relationship. In this case, truth is the relationship of learning to belong to Jesus. So truth isn't just in our minds—what we believe; it's in our lives as they become conformed to Jesus' image. And this process occurs as we listen to him.

We let Christ the king reign in our lives when we let our lives be conformed to the life of him who is the Truth. Spiritual disciplines help us do this. They help us listen to Jesus and thus belong to him as we learn to obey what we hear. Through the spiritual disciplines we learn to listen to Jesus, receive him, and respond with our lives. The more we do this, the more we will find ourselves belonging to the truth. And this belonging might actually change what we believe.

Lord, help me grow in my relationship with the truth—with you—as I seek to listen to your voice this day. Amen.

Let's Hope So

NOVEMBER 25 – DECEMBER 1, 2024 • STEVE HARPER

SCRIPTURE OVERVIEW: As we prepare our hearts for Advent, the celebration of Jesus' first coming, we remember in Jeremiah that the birth of Jesus has a deep background rooted in God's promise to David. Psalm 25, traditionally credited to David, speaks of God's faithfulness to those who follow the paths of the Lord. David asks God to teach him to follow God's paths even more closely. The New Testament readings actually point us toward Jesus' second coming. Paul encourages the Thessalonians to excel in holiness and love while they wait. In Luke, Jesus discusses the coming of the kingdom in a passage that some find confusing. We note that he focuses not on the exact time frame of the arrival of the kingdom but on our need to be alert.

QUESTIONS AND SUGGESTIONS FOR REFLECTION

• Read Jeremiah 33:14-16. How have you experienced the promises of God in your life?

• Read Psalm 25:1-10. How has the Lord taught you and led you in the path of your life?

• Read 1 Thessalonians 3:9-13. Is there a faith community for which you pray in joy? How else do you express your gratitude for that community?

• Read Luke 21:25-36. How are you approaching Advent this year? What will you do to prepare your heart?

Retired elder in The United Methodist Church and retired seminary professor; married to Jeannie since 1970; father of two children and grandfather of three.

We write these meditations about two years before you read them. If you recall, two years ago hope was in short supply. Nationally and internationally, civically and religiously, it was easy to feel hopeless, or at least easy to be numbly ambivalent about the future. When someone asked, "Do you think things are going to get better?" I found myself saying or thinking, "Let's hope so."

I have reflected on this week's passages with that "hope so" spirit, and I have found that the readings give us reasons to be hopeful. We read them moving toward the first Sunday in Advent, the beginning of the Christian Year, a Sunday whose theme is hope. Are things going to get better? Let's hope so.

That's the tone of Jeremiah's words. He all but says it: "The time is coming." He wrote when it had not come, in a time when the word *wasteland* seemed the best description for the day. It was easy to believe things would only get worse. Jeremiah had his reasons to think that way, but he did not actually think that way. He lived into a future in which God would give the people "a future filled with hope" (29:11).

Today we call it *liminal space*, the "time between the times"— the time, as Paul described it, when old things are passing away in order that new things can come. It is a time of disorientation and disorder, a painful time. Jeremiah would understand this time because he lived in one like it. If people had asked him if things would get better, he would have been quick to say, "Let's hope so."

God of the in-between times, we hope things will get better. Give us grace to hang on to that hope. Some days it's all we have. Amen.

We have a friend and conversation partner in Jeremiah. He gets us because he looked for hope the way we do, seeing through hopelessness initially but then seeing beyond it. He found hope in a vision.

Visions are not things too good to be true; they are things too good *not* to be true. Visions are things that ought to be so, even if they are not so right now. As such, visions inspire us and instill convictions in us. Visions ignite actions that God uses to bring the hoped-for thing to pass, or at least to move us closer to the fulfillment of our desire.

Prophets move us by means of visions. They do not ignore hard things, but they understand that challenges do not define us. Hope defines us, and it often comes by way of a vision. In Jeremiah's case, it was the vision of the restoration of righteousness in the land. The restoration, Jeremiah said, was a fulfillment of God's gracious promise. The vision was not of Jeremiah's making. He was only sharing what he had seen. The vision came from God's nature and with God's promise. The rest of the chapter reveals that the vision rests on God's covenant commitment, which God will honor.

We have this vision more than two thousand years later—the vision of justice restored, a time when fairness, equity, inclusion, and concern for the common good will define and direct us. We long for the restoration of these qualities. Thankfully, we have prophets in the land today, visionaries who point to better days, more humane days, and in doing so give us hope.

God, you are just. You seek fairness, equity, inclusion, and the common good. You give us prophets that cast this vision. They give us hope. Thank you for them. Amen.

In our quest to live with hope, the psalmist adds an important piece to the picture. From David, we learn that hope is not an amorphous idea. Hope is trust. And more than that, hope is trust in God. The psalm begins with this truth, and then David says twice that he puts his hope in God. The validity of our hope lies in what, or in whom, we put our trust.

Misplaced trust misdirects hope because we expect things and people to give us what they cannot. In Christian history, people have put their trust in three areas: materialism, hedonism, and power—all of which fail us over the long haul. Instead of ending up hopeful, we become cynical. We go downhill, not getting better but rather becoming bitter. David alludes to misplaced hope as the psalm moves along. We see it all around us today, and we see people deformed in their character and conduct because they misplaced their trust.

At the same time, David describes a hope that delivers, that provides: hope in God. Our trust is in Someone, not some things or some people. We refuse to make golden idols of pseudo-saviors, and we give messianic status only to Christ.

Putting our hope in God means putting our lives in God's hands. As we do so, we find that "all the ways of the Lord are loving and faithful." In offering ourselves to God, we discover that no matter which way we turn, God is with us. Surrounded by God, we have reason to hope.

God, I am hopeful because of who you are. I trust you. I believe you know what you want the world—and my life in it—to look like, and I am confident you are at work to bring what you want to pass. Amen.

Thanksgiving Day (USA)

Today in the United States we celebrate Thanksgiving Day. Sixteen other countries have a similar holiday sometime during the year. As a human family, the instinct to give thanks runs deep.

Gratitude and hope go together. The things for which we are most grateful are the things we hope to continue or have restored. We reminisce, but our remembering is not only recognizing our past but also recommitting to our future. We gather with the intention to keep going.

Jesus was most grateful that God has provided a life that is abundant and eternal. He called it "the kingdom of God." He gathered apostles to share his hope in God's reign, and he constructed his message in relation to it. His words taught it and his deeds modeled it.

But notice that Jesus' gratitude became his invitation. He wanted people to seek the kingdom of God. He was filled with hope as he saw people orienting their lives in relation to it.

In this sense, we hope to see the thing we long for becoming real in people's lives. Gratitude is our response when it happens. Jesus' hope that people are made for kingdom living gave him the strength to see his mission through to the end when he could say, "It is accomplished."

So today we gather together literally and in our hearts to express our gratitude for things that have been and our hope that they will continue even after we are gone. We give thanks.

God, in giving thanks, I am expressing my hope. I am grateful for the life you have in mind for everyone. I want to live in ways that will help others seek the kingdom. Amen.

Winding their way through the readings this week are the virtues of faith, hope, and love. They intertwine in our conviction that we are living in a time of awakening—a time filled with formidable challenges but also with amazing opportunities. Today and tomorrow we will use Paul's words to zero in on love and see its place and significance in a theology of hope.

We note first that we have hope because love is the means and motivation for improvement. Rooted in God's love for us (see John 3:16), we love each other and are motivated to increase that love. There is no better definition of hope than the increase of love. Where love increases, the things we hope for increasingly come to pass because love is not only a sentiment; it is an incentive to act.

Paul began by praying for an increase of love among fellow Christians. Love is the tie that binds and the bond that commences in the Christian community. Who can deny that we need love within the body of Christ today? We have been torn asunder by divisions of all kinds. The restoration of love in the church is the necessary first step in a larger renewal of hope. Simply put, people will never believe we love them when they see us not loving one another.

We see in today's reading that love increases where it already exists. We love more by taking the love we have and enlarging it. We need to gather around our common loves, not around our differences. If we are willing to do that, we might find the life together that is necessary for us to live with hope. Are things going to get better? Let's hope so, and ground our hope in love for one another.

God, gather us, connect us, and renew us in love. Amen.

Yesterday we looked at Paul's intercession for the Thessalonians, praying for their love for each other to increase. Paul recognized that this increase would spill over onto others. That's one of the qualities of love; it does not remain turned in on itself. It moves outward. But to whom? Paul answered the question: Love spills over to "everyone in the same way." These few words tell us two significant things.

First, it is universal love. We love everyone just as God does and Jesus did. And because of the nature of the covenant (see, for example, Genesis 9:9-17), it is love for the whole creation, not just human beings. In short, we are to love everyone and everything. All means all.

Second, it is unconditional love. We are to love everyone and everything "in the same way." And what way is that? Again, we see the answer in God's love and Jesus' love. We are to love completely. We do not love some in one way, and others in another way. We love everyone and everything to the "nth degree."

Before Paul wrote these words, Peter experienced the meaning of them in Cornelius's house. The Spirit came upon the Gentiles, and that meant universal love. Further, the Spirit came upon the Gentiles in the same way as upon the Jews. That's unconditional love. Witnessing this, Peter realized that God shows no partiality; God loves everyone in the same way (see Acts 10:34-36). A little later, the Jerusalem Council met and made this universal, unconditional love the hallmark of the church. It still is. There is no greater reason to be hopeful than this.

God, everyone and everything is included in your love in the same way. What amazing grace! But then, that's just like you. Make me like that too. Amen.

FIRST SUNDAY OF ADVENT

The readings this week bring us to the first Sunday of Advent, the first day in the Christian year. We have seen how the texts address the question, "Are things going to get better?" And they have given us reasons to say, "Let's hope so" with confidence. The first Sunday of Advent is about hope.

This Gospel lesson is also about hope, although it is not always read from that vantage point. The passage is about the consummation of hope, summed up in the phrase, "Stand up straight and raise your heads, because your redemption is near." While some Christians interpret passages like this as warning about being left behind, Luke says Jesus' words are about being gathered up. It's about redemption.

This is the trajectory of the gospel. We begin the Christian year with the message of the consummation of hope. Paul described this as God's plan "for the climax of all times: to bring all things together in Christ, the things in heaven along with the things in earth" (Eph. 1:10). Again, all means all. Paul made this clear: "In the same way that everyone dies in Adam, so also everyone will be given life in Christ" (1 Cor. 15:22). Everyone means everyone.

We are dealing in Mystery. We do not know how this will happen, but we are told that it will. And that is how the Christian year begins—with hope. With confidence that all things are reconciled to God in Christ (see Colossians 1:20). Are things going to get better? Let's hope so!

God, I am filled with hope. Thank you that, through Christ, the redemption of everyone and everything in heaven and on earth is accomplished. Living in Luke's words, I stand up straight and raise my head because our redemption is near. Amen.

Mandatory Rejoicing

DECEMBER 2–8, 2024 • MARY AUSTIN

SCRIPTURE OVERVIEW: The prophet Malachi speaks of a future day when God's messenger will come to prepare the way for the Lord. The Lord will then purify the people and restore proper worship of God. Christians believe that John the Baptizer was this messenger, preparing the way for Christ. In Luke 1, the Holy Spirit fills Zechariah, John's father, who proclaims that the fulfillment of God's promises to their descendants has begun. Luke continues the story of John in chapter 3, describing John's ministry of calling people to repentance. They need to prepare the way of the Lord in their own hearts, thus fulfilling Malachi's prophecy. Paul in Philippians focuses not on the advent of Christ but on the ongoing power of Christ's presence to make us blameless and righteous in God's sight.

QUESTIONS AND SUGGESTIONS FOR REFLECTION

- Read Malachi 3:1-4. How have you encountered the refiner's fire? What was your experience?
- Read Luke 1:68-79. In what ways have you experienced God's tender mercy in your life?
- Read Philippians 1:3-11. How do you make expressing your gratitude for others a daily habit?
- Read Luke 3:1-6. How are you preparing the way of the Lord? What crooked paths are you helping to make straight?

Presbyterian pastor serving at First Congregational Church of Kalamazoo, MI; served churches in Maryland and New Jersey; former hospice chaplain.

The jacket I wore to my mother's funeral is still in my closet. I have never been able to bring myself to wear it again. Whenever I reach for it, the grief of that day washes over me again, and I pull my hand back. Putting in on again feels like putting on all that sadness again.

Baruch offers an invitation in the other direction. "Take off the garment of your sorrow and affliction," the author writes, in a word of consolation. Take off the mourning clothes, the torn garments, the items stained with ashes, all carrying the sorrow of the past.

Patterned after the prophets in the Hebrew scriptures, Baruch gives voice to God's word of hope. Writing during one era of national distress (probably between 200 and 60 B.C.E.) the author uses another time of upheaval (the exile in Babylon) to frame his message. For us, the message to shed the trappings of sadness is a timeless word.

Most of us are carrying layers of sorrow. The deaths of loved ones, shifting friendships, children with challenges beyond our ability to help, and financial worries that pile up with the years. Our country's political fractures wear away at us, and our technology isolates us from other people.

Baruch summons us to "put on forever the beauty of the glory from God" in this Advent season. God adds divine hope to all the sorrows of the past. Look up and see what God is doing! God is ready to lead us with joy, adding a deep measure of rejoicing to our sorrows.

God of love, help us to hear your call into joy this Advent season. May we put on your gift of joy each Advent day as we lay down the burdens of sorrow. In the name of the Christ child we pray. Amen.

Some years ago on his birthday, writer Ross Gay challenged himself to find something delightful each day during the year. He eventually compiled his findings in *The Book of Delights*, sharing the pleasures he found. Most of them were things like time in his garden, an encounter with a teenager in a coffee shop, ripe fruit, colorful socks, and other small joys.

At the beginning of the book, he says that he thought it would be hard to find something each day. Instead, looking for these small moments of blessing brought more of them to mind. Once he started looking, they multiplied.

Some people find similar joys with a gratitude app or a journal that chronicles moments of thanksgiving. A colleague once reached into his shirt pocket and took out a small notebook. He explained that he wrote down his prayers and was always amazed when he read them later to see how many God had answered. Even when he had forgotten, God remembered.

The daily practices we take on shape and prepare us. In Malachi, the prophet tells of one who will come to prepare the way for the Lord, for Christ. We are again preparing for Christ's coming today. We can be the messengers who help make space for Christ to enter our world anew. By allowing ourselves to be shaped by daily practices we shape our perspective to be on the lookout for the joy of Christ's coming.

The religion of my childhood had a strong emphasis on being good. There was duty, service, and fear, but no mention of joy. It's a delight in itself to hear Malachi proclaim the delight God has for the "messenger of the covenant." This Advent, what if we look for joy, and take note where and when we find it? We can search for joy in these weeks and cultivate it as part of our Advent preparation.

God of restoration and hope, your presence is a joy to us. We give thanks for all of the joys that fill our days, seen and unseen, remembered and forgotten. In Jesus' name. Amen.

Mandatory Rejoicing   401

There's always a vendetta, and sometimes a romance, on a silent retreat. So says spiritual teacher Daniel Thorson. And all the drama happens completely in people's minds as they go through their days in silence and project their own longings and rage onto other retreat participants. Someone is coughing too much. Breathing too loudly. Someone is too good-looking.

Did Zechariah experience the same projections during his months of silence? In this case, the people around him can talk. They can speculate about why he's so quiet and why God is punishing him. They can pile all their worries and ideas about God onto him.

Even if we belong to a community of faith, Advent is a individual journey for us—a chance to meet up with God again and to renew our faith in this season of waiting. It's easy to spend all our time thinking about other people. How will we get our kids to study? Get our church community to do something? Get our siblings to communicate? Nudge our friends to get together?

Like Zechariah's private season of silence, we're invited on an individual journey this Advent. God calls us to look at the places where our trust in God has become thin, where we're too certain of ourselves, where we're too attached to a certain outcome. Zechariah is a good guide for us this Advent as he moves through his own season of waiting, quietly turning more and more toward God each day. We are invited to observe the season without fear, in holy longing and divine hope.

God who is always present, may we see you clearly this Advent, and see ourselves truthfully. Help us to let go of our raging thoughts and focus on your presence. Amen.

Zechariah finally gets to speak! For months, he has been living in enforced silence, left to brood after he doubts the news that his wife, Elizabeth, is having a baby. In doubting, he's challenged what God is able to do.

We have so little silence in our lives that I can barely imagine these long months of quiet for Zechariah. Elizabeth could still talk—did the conversation dwindle after a while? Did they go through their daily routines in companionable silence? Worried silence? Anticipatory silence?

When we get our rare moments of quiet, how do they feel—like a relief or a burden? Being silent is a skill that we are losing, with our devices always available to distract us. We have to deliberately choose to be silent and to work hard to make it happen. If we don't practice, we forget how to sit with our own thoughts. Our attention spans grow shorter all the time.

Somehow for Zechariah, I imagine the silence was restorative, a time to marinate in God's promises and renew God's presence in his life. He emerges from the silence a wiser man. For most of us, our first words would be a complaint. Finally! Finally we get to talk! But Zechariah has used his time off wisely. His first words are a prayer of thanksgiving. "Blessed be the Lord God of Israel," he proclaims, giving thanks for God's goodness. He looks ahead to his son's future, and proclaims, "And you, child, will be called the prophet of the Most High, for you will go before the Lord to prepare his ways."

This Advent, we can find space to give ourselves this gift of silence for a few minutes at a time, or even a few hours. Advent invites us into the blessing of silence, and hopefully we too will emerge with praise for God on our lips.

Dear God, may we find the silence fruitful—even pregnant with hope—this Advent. Amen.

Some years ago, I found myself slipping into a long depressive time. Rationally, I had a wonderful life—a wise and witty husband, beautiful child, interesting work, kind friends. Still, the gloom of life seemed much closer than the good things. I could feel myself sinking into it.

In an attempt to remind myself to be grateful, I framed a bunch of family pictures and put them on my dresser. To my surprise, it helped. Getting ready in the morning and winding down at night, I could see that I was surrounded by love. "I hold you in my heart," Paul writes to the believers in Philippi. I experienced that same kind of holding every time I looked at my dresser. I could look at the pictures and hold my beloved people in my heart. And I knew was held in their love as well. We had a past together. Future adventures were in store. That clarity made it easier to find my place in the deeper love of God.

Of course, this is not a remedy for severe depression. If you are experiencing depression, consult a mental health professional. The tools and support received through counseling and other interventions are ways to allow our love for ourselves to overflow with the "knowledge and full insight" of which Paul speaks.

Paul finds that love for himself and for others across time and distance, and we can too. During Advent, as we wait for God to be born into the world again, our waiting is a reminder that God is already holding us in love. God holds us in divine love, and that loves flows out from us and to us. Distance and time are no match for the love of God.

God of abundant and lasting love, may our love for you, for each other, and for the world overflow more and more in this Advent season and beyond it. Amen.

John's call in the wilderness is the T-shirt, the Tweet, the slogan for Advent, all distilled into one word: *Prepare.*

John knows that the presence of Jesus is a tectonic shift in the world, and he means for his original listeners and for us to know it too.

Every huge life event is really beyond our capacity for preparation. Even when a loved one is sick for a long time, we still grieve when they take that last, tiny breath. Even the most wanted baby brings incredible disruption. We can only prepare so much before going off to college or to the military.

In the same way, God's entry into the world transcends our ability to prepare.

John summons us, calls us again, to the one change we can control—and the hardest change of all. "Make straight what is crooked," he calls out to us, and he means within us as well as in the world. Prepare a path for the coming of God.

We can straighten out the crooked parts of our hearts, the petty grudges and carefully held resentments. We can make room for God in all of our careful plans. We can clear out the rocky places where we need to be in control, the dips in the road where we fail to trust, the rough places of our rage. We can fill in the valleys of our fear and bring down the mountains of our pride.

Prepare, John says, and the preparation is within us.

Road-making God, help us to see clearly our own crooked places and to acknowledge the hills and valleys that keep us from meeting you completely. Help us to open the way for you this Advent. Amen.

SECOND SUNDAY OF ADVENT

Luke carefully locates John the Baptist in time, moving down through the line of rulers from the most powerful to the lesser powers. The word of God comes zipping into the world, and passes right by all the significant people and comes to . . . John, a nobody son of no one special. The important people are all silent in Luke's telling, and John gets to speak for God.

Watch out, Luke says; the word of God is on the move, going where you least expect it.

This Advent, are we expecting the divine presence in our midst? Perhaps we are so beaten down—by the election season, by persistent poverty, by racism, by church politics—that it's hard to anticipate God's coming. There's plenty of wilderness in our lives, too.

John the Baptist is nutty enough to believe that God is coming into his world and into ours. God is zipping past politicians and celebrities, past media influencers and Tik Tok stars, and coming to us in the middle of our own wilderness. John makes a bold promise that "all flesh shall see the salvation of God." Important people are invited, too, because the message is for all of us. But God's message doesn't start or stop with them. It is for exhausted teachers and nurses, for weary school bus drivers and restaurant workers, for worried grandparents and sleepless parents. John claims the presence of God for all the ordinary people—for all of us.

This Advent, John's message comes to us: God is on the move, coming into the world where we are.

God of surprises, we rejoice in your presence this Advent. May we perceive you in our midst and respond with joy. Amen.

Accepting the Invitation

DECEMBER 9–15, 2024 • O. WESLEY ALLEN JR.

SCRIPTURE OVERVIEW: Reviewing the scripture passages for this week, the hymn title "Rejoice, Give Thanks and Sing" might come to mind. The writers of this week's texts advise us to do all these things. At this time of year, these responses often seem to come naturally for many of us. The prophet Zephaniah exhorts his audience to sing aloud and rejoice. The prophet Isaiah calls on the people of Judah to "give thanks to the LORD." In the letter to the Philippians, Paul advises his audience to "rejoice in the Lord always." The tone of the Luke passage for this week is more somber; through the words of John the Baptist, Luke challenges his audience to maintain right relationships with God and humanity. Taken together, these passages provide a number of life lessons.

QUESTIONS AND SUGGESTIONS FOR REFLECTION

- Read Zephaniah 3:14-20. Recall a time when you have experienced joy in the midst of trouble. Give thanks to God for your joy.
- Read Isaiah 12:2-6. How does your trust in God enable you to overcome fear?
- Read Philippians 4:4-7. Are you able to release your worries to God when you pray, or do you tend to hold on to the worry even after you have prayed about it?
- Read Luke 3:7-18. Where in your life are you being nudged to do the right thing? How will you respond?

Lois Craddock Perkins Professor of Homiletics, Perkins School of Theology, Southern Methodist University; ordained elder in the Indiana Conference of The United Methodist Church.

Zephaniah's oracles fill up only three chapters—our reading for today is the conclusion to the book. Most of the book focuses on judgment against Judah coming on "the day of the LORD" because of corruption in the government and the complacency of the populace. The purpose of these pronouncements of judgment is to call for repentance (see Zephaniah 1:14). "Seek the LORD . . . seek righteousness, seek humility; perhaps you may be hidden on the day of the LORD's wrath" (Zeph. 2:3).

The book of Zephaniah, however, does not end in gloom. Our reading for today is the exclamation point of hope following oracles questioning Judah's fate. Now the invitation is to praise because God "has taken away the judgments against you." Notice this is the past tense. But most of the oracle is in the future tense: God "will rejoice" over you, "will remove disaster," and "will bring you home."

Both past and future salvation, however, are rooted in the present. The prophet uses the present tense twice, both times to express the same theological rationale for praise and hope: God "is" in your midst.

Advent is the season of expectation and waiting for the coming of the Lord. It is a paradoxical season. We await the coming of Christ (future) before celebrating that Christ came in the form of an infant (past) because we know and experience Christ in our midst now (present).

Past, present, and future. Judgment and salvation. All these overlap in our lives in messy ways to bring us closer to the God who is, has been, and always will be with us.

God of our past and future, offer us both judgment and grace in the present, that we may experience you and the life you offer in the fullness you desire for us. Amen.

In yesterday's meditation on Zephaniah, we noted the change of verb tense in the oracle. Today we want to attend to a different shift in perspective. In the first five verses, the prophet is speaking to his audience about God. The oracle functions as a liturgy that calls the people to praise and give thanks to God for the salvation they have experienced and hope to experience. Throughout this opening section, the prophet speaks of God in the third person—what God has done and what God will do.

Then, without any notice, the pronouns change in verse 18 from third person to first person. If Zephaniah had been writing with a word processor instead of on parchment, he might have fixed this awkward transition. But, as it stands, God interrupts the prophet who is talking about God and starts speaking words of salvation directly to the people. "I will deal with all your oppressors." "I will save the lame and gather the outcast." "I will bring you home."

This shift from the prophet's to God's voice signals a key dynamic of religious experience. In our pain, sorrow, and struggles we sometimes wish God would speak to us directly—just pop into our living room and offer us words of guidance, forgiveness, and hope. Instead, it is in our talking about God and our listening to others speak of God that we hear God's voice. God may not speak (literally), but God will not be silenced!

Advent is paradoxical. We wait for Christ to come to us when we know Christ is already with us. While that may not make sense rationally, it does experientially. We *know* God is with us, but we don't always *feel* God's presence. If we cease worrying, keep talking, keep listening, God will pop in and speak to us.

God, you promise your word will not return to you empty.
Speak to us a word of your salvation. Amen.

In the place of a psalm, the lectionary for the third week of Advent substitutes an oracle from the opening chapters of Isaiah that resembles the form and function of thanksgiving psalms (such as Psalms 34 and 118). In thanksgiving psalms, Israelites gave thanks for deliverance from some internal crisis (such as illness) or external threat (usually warring enemies).

Today's passage imagines a day in the future when the people of Judah will give thanks for God's deliverance from the threat of Assyria in the eighth century B.C.E. The oracle draws on language from Exodus 15, where Moses leads the Israelites in singing praise to God for the deliverance they experienced in crossing the sea. Indeed, verse 2 quotes that song: "The LORD God is my strength and my might, and he has become my salvation" (Exod. 15:2). The next line, then, reimagines the water through which the Israelite slaves were rescued from the Egyptians as water drawn from the wells of salvation.

The water of the Exodus, remembered by Isaiah as water from the wells of salvation, foreshadows the early church's understanding of baptism as pictured in the stories of John the Baptist. Indeed, Advent, like Lent, originally developed as a season of preparation for baptism. Lest we think of our baptism only in individualistic terms (*my* salvation), Isaiah 12 reminds us that the wells of salvation result in God being known "among the nations" and "in all the earth." The salvation we experience through the identity that baptism bestows on us is a sign of God's will to rescue the whole of humanity from internal and external suffering.

O God, we give thanks for the deep waters of your salvation and pray that all may be refreshed by them. Amen.

The Third Sunday of Advent is traditionally known as Gaudete Sunday. *Gaudete* is the Latin imperative, "Rejoice." In its early development, Advent was more like Lent, a time of preparation for baptism, and was longer than our current four-week season. Gaudete Sunday functioned as a sort of hump day in the middle of the season—a day of celebration that the period of fasting and abstinence is halfway over. Many churches that do not celebrate Gaudete officially still mark this day with a rose-colored candle in their Advent wreath.

Another remnant of this celebration is the reading from Philippians 4. Paul's call to rejoice has been read on the third Sunday of Advent for centuries. It provided the opening line of the traditional introit sung on Gaudete: "Rejoice in the Lord always; again I will say, 'Rejoice.'"

Paul says that in our rejoicing we need not worry because we can take anything to God in prayer. Strikingly however, Paul does not then say something like, "And if you have enough faith, God will give you what you ask for." In other words, Paul does not offer the Philippians a heavenly Santa Claus.

Instead, he concludes that when we pray about anything, God will give us God's peace. This is no naïve theology that God will make any and all of our woes disappear. This is the "already/not yet" that is particularly clear when we are waiting for Christ to come in Advent (part of Christian existence). While we do not yet see the reign of God manifested in a way that alleviates all suffering and erases all sin, we do already have access to God's peace in the midst of the flawed and finite world. That is reason to rejoice that fits with the reality we know and experience.

Gracious God, we rejoice in the peace you offer us as we walk through the ups and downs of our lives. Amen.

This is the perfect Advent passage. Paul invites us to rejoice, but, as we said yesterday, not in a naïve manner. His is an "already/not yet" worldview. In the present age we have already experienced the salvation God gives us through Jesus Christ, but it is not yet manifested through creation. In other words, God has saved us in the midst of Caesar's corrupt reign, but we remain in hope that God's salvation will result in God's reign replacing that of Caesar.

Paul names this "almost/not yet" worldview in this passage most clearly in a short line in verse 5 that is easily overlooked. We should rejoice (in part) because "The Lord is near." Not here, but near. If we could ask Paul, "Do you not think God is omnipresent and with us always?" he would certainly say yes. But then he might add, "However, it does not always *feel* like God is with us."

Paul's language of nearness takes this feeling seriously. We can compare our existence and experience of the nearness of God to driving at night on a lonely country road with no street lamps. With no oncoming traffic, you put your high-beam lights on and ease toward the center of the road a little. But then as you begin to rise up a slope, you see headlights coming from the other side of the hill. You move back into your lane and turn off the high beams. The car is near and has influenced your behavior before it has fully arrived. We Christians live, always, at that moment of our life being affected by the nearness but not yet fully arrived presence of God-in-Christ.

Christ, draw near to us now and every day, that we may rejoice even in the not-yet of life. Amen.

The Gospel readings for the Second and Third Sundays of Advent have for centuries been dedicated to John the Baptist as the one who prepares the way for Christ to come, reminding us that Advent is not simply a time of preparing for Christmas.

Last week's Gospel lesson was Luke 3:1-6, in which Luke introduced John's ministry as a fulfillment of Isaiah 40:3–5. This week we turn to the passage that follows. In verses 7–14, Luke presents John's preaching as a precursor to Jesus' ministry.

Starting off calling his audience a "brood of vipers," John seems to be quite the fire-and-brimstone prophet. Luke, however, makes clear that John's goal is not to condemn those who came out to the Jordan to hear him preach. It is to invite them to "bear fruits worthy of repentance." We often think of repentance in terms of feeling bad about something we have done. But that is not the case for Luke's John the Baptist. So far as this passage is concerned, John has no interest in our feelings.

Instead, John says repentance must be shown in the fruits of our actions. It is a U-turn in our life. There is no resting on our laurels as children of Abraham (or members of the church). Those who have abundance must share with those who are lacking. Those in positions of power must use that power justly.

Too often, we think of calls like this to repent as a burden—something difficult we must do. Repentance, however, is a gift from God. Through it, God frees us from being defined by our past and being stuck in self-centeredness. God gives us the chance to share our extra coat and treat others with dignity.

Gracious God, accept our repentance and lead us to bear the fruits of that repentance. Amen.

THIRD SUNDAY OF ADVENT

Yesterday we meditated on the first half of this passage, John the Baptist's prophetic call for repentance. Today we turn to verses 15–18, in which Luke presents John as giving witness to the coming of the Messiah.

One of the early theological problems that the church had to deal with was that Jesus' baptism by John makes him look like a disciple of John. The church wanted to assert clearly that Jesus was the greater of the two. In doing this, Luke goes so far as to speak of John being imprisoned before recounting the story of the Holy Spirit coming upon Jesus after his baptism (see Luke 3:21–22).

In today's passage, Luke has John himself make clear that he is not the Messiah. The one who comes after him is the more powerful one, the one who will baptize not simply with water but with the Holy Spirit and fire.

This is why the church has traditionally read passages about John on the Second and Third Sundays of Advent each year. We read about John, who points us to the coming of Jesus. But the picture of Jesus that John paints is not one of a lovey-dovey Messiah. It is a picture of a Messiah-judge who burns the trees that don't bear good fruit (see Luke 3:9).

Still, this is a picture of one who brings salvation. For Luke, salvation is a reversal of the status quo—the corrupt are brought down and the downtrodden are lifted up. In other words, for Luke "judgment" implies "justice." John invites us into the justice that the Christ brings in turning the world upside down. Accepting this invitation is what Advent is all about.

God who judges the living and the dead, make us instruments of your justice. Amen.

Yearning for Emmanuel

DECEMBER 16–22, 2024 • BETH A. RICHARDSON

SCRIPTURE OVERVIEW: As Christians we understand that our faith is rooted in the ongoing story of God's faithfulness to God's people. Micah celebrates this story, prophesying that the true king of Israel will one day come from the small village of Bethlehem, Jesus' birthplace. Luke features women prominently throughout his Gospel. The two readings from Luke this week highlight the prophetic insights of Elizabeth and Mary. Mary visits Elizabeth, who is pregnant with John, God's messenger. After Elizabeth identifies Mary as the mother of the Lord, Mary breaks into song, understanding that her story is tied to the fulfillment of God's promises going back to Abraham. Little does she know that her son will one day offer his body as a sacrifice for all, as Hebrews tells us.

QUESTIONS AND SUGGESTIONS FOR REFLECTION

- Read Micah 5:2-5a. What small beginnings have yielded great results in your life?
- Read Psalm 80:1-7. What is your song of praise to God today? How will you share it?
- Read Hebrews 10:5-10. How does your body help you to experience God?
- Read Luke 1:39-55. How has God spoken to you through a joyous meeting with another person?

Dean Emeritus of The Upper Room Chapel; retired elder in the Mountain Sky Conference of The United Methodist Church; writer, photographer, artist, gardener, worship nerd, and lover of dogs; lives in Nashville, TN with her family.

O come, Emmanuel, and free us from our fear and despair, busyness and distraction.

These days I find myself yearning for the coming of God-with-us. I long for the one who will bring peace to this hurting world; for an end to fear, suffering, and injustice. My heart sings this Advent hymn, "O come, O come, Emmanuel, and ransom captive Israel." (This ancient hymn will be the soundtrack of our week. Take a moment to sing it or listen to a recording.)

The prophet Micah tells of a leader who is to come. This child, born in Bethlehem from the lineage of David, will be both a shepherd and peacemaker. Micah brings words of hope to a people who are overwhelmed by threats from the Assyrians, fearful that the life they know will be taken away from them.

As we enter this final week in Advent, it becomes more difficult to protect our spirits from the distractions of our society's Christmas culture. We remember the Gospel readings in the first week of Advent that called us to guard our hearts against "the worries of this life" lest we miss what is coming (see Luke 21:34). We are called to turn away from self-centeredness, injustice, and hardened hearts and to turn toward the realm of the Holy One—toward kindness and peace, prayer and contemplation, justice and compassion for a broken world and its suffering people.

What would it be like to turn away from thoughts and actions that keep us separated from God and one another? As we approach Christmas day, we become more aware of the yearning of our hearts for Emmanuel. Our attention to that yearning allows us to focus on gratitude, to listen more than talk, to replace judgment with compassion, to pray for those with whom we are in conflict.

God-with-us, we yearn for your presence in our lives, our communities, our world. Help us to turn away from busyness and toward you. Amen.

O Come, Emmanuel, and fill our world with peace.

The prophet Micah lived in Judah in the eighth century B.C.E. Israel was under assault from the invading Assyrians, and its army was no match for the assault. Micah prophesied that a leader, a shepherd, would be coming to bring peace. This One would bring an end to fighting, would proclaim righteousness where there is injustice, and would replace hardened hearts with hearts of love and compassion.

The time of upheaval for God's people was not unlike the chaos we face today. Despite our advanced societies, we cannot get along with our neighbors. There is war between countries, hatred in communities, and conflict in families. We have taken so many of our earth's resources that we have imperiled our fragile planet. We have failed to protect the vulnerable among us—those in generational poverty; persons of color who are not even safe in their own homes; refugees and victims of war; our LGBTQ+ siblings, especially the young ones.

This time of year, I find myself yearning for the coming of Emmanuel, longing for the One who will bring peace to this hurting world. My heart sings the Advent hymns: "O come, O come, Emmanuel, and ransom captive Israel" and "Come, thou long-expected Jesus, born to set thy people free; from our fears and sins release us, let us find our rest in thee." I hunger for a holy light that will illuminate the shadows of prejudice and fear. I long for peace in the midst of war and discord, for love to replace hatred, for justice to prevail over injustice.

Micah foretells the birth of one who will be born in the tiny village of Bethlehem. Today, watch for the presence of the Holy One in unexpected places—the face of Christ in a stranger, the certainty of God's presence in a difficult situation.

O come, Emmanuel, and show us the path that we are to follow.

Today's passage describes new rules for discipleship that Christ has ushered into the world. God no longer desires offerings as a symbol of our faith, but requires, instead, obedience to God's will. Christ's followers turn away from the old precepts and follow the one who upset the status quo. He ate with tax collectors and sinners. He saw and talked to the lowly ones and the outcasts. He gathered food on the sabbath and upset the tables in the Temple. He was obedient to the will of God even unto death.

As we read this text, the voices of other scriptures inform our hearing. The prophet Micah outlined what God requires of those who would follow the Holy One—"do justice, love kindness, walk humbly with your God" (Mic. 6:8) To turn away from the ways of the world and toward the ways that lead to life. The psalmist offers this, "The sacrifice you accept, O God, is a humble spirit" (Ps. 51:17, URWB, 276). Jesus was faithful to the Creator. The writer of Hebrews quotes him saying, "I have come to do your will, O God."

We yearn for Wisdom to teach us how to live in faithfulness. In these days of polarization, we walk around in our little worlds anchored in conflicting realities, alternate truths. Family gatherings, if they are still happening, are awkward and full of minefields. Community dialogue is broken. Our institutions —governmental and churches—have broken down in dysfunctional deadlock. We hunger for the Spirit to guide us through the confusion to the path that God wants for us, if not for the leaders of the world, at least for us in our day-to-day lives.

God of Wisdom, clear out the obstacles that confuse our minds and hearts. Teach us how to be obedient to your will. Keep us on the path you have set before us. Amen.

O come, Emmanuel, and guide us through our wilderness.

Psalm 80 is a communal lament. Commentators are not certain about when this psalm was written. It could have been from the same period as our Micah passage, or it may have been later, after the fall of Jerusalem and the Babylonian exile.

A lament is a prayer for help that comes from a place of pain or despair. The people of Israel were not afraid to call out to God during difficult times. They expressed their distress, fear, hopelessness, and anger at the Holy One for not rescuing them from their difficulties. God had led the people out of captivity in Egypt, through forty years of wilderness wanderings, and into the Promised Land. They had the kind of deep relationship with the Holy One that could withstand the honest talk of lament. Despite their complaining, their confrontations, and even their disobedience, God did not abandon them.

Lament is a spiritual practice for all of us in our wildernesses. Through lament, we share our deepest longings and wounds with the Holy One who holds us and provides comfort. God is present with us—in broken relationships and difficult diagnoses, in fears about the future or regrets about the past, in those days when it seems almost too hard to get out of bed. God is here and is listening for us to speak our deepest longings.

Think about your wildernesses. Rewrite this psalm, expressing to God your yearnings for restoration and wholeness. When you have finished, read it out loud and then listen for the stirrings of the Spirit. End your meditation with the affirmation, "Restore us, O God of hosts; let your face shine, that we might be saved."

O come, Emmanuel, and let our spirits leap for joy at your promised coming.

I love this story of Mary and Elizabeth, cousins descended from King David, both pregnant in miraculous ways with miraculous timing.

Elizabeth is the wife of Zechariah, who has his own story in Luke 1:5-25. You'll remember that he is a priest in the Temple and is childless at the beginning of the story. An angel visits him and announces that he will have a son. Zechariah's incredulity leads him to spend the majority of Elizabeth's pregnancy mute.

Elizabeth, of course, doesn't have all of this information when she becomes pregnant. Into her house comes her cousin Mary who is also carrying a child. The child within Elizabeth leaps for joy. Elizabeth recognizes Mary's child and exclaims: that the One who is to come is here now, growing in his mother's womb. The Savior will be born as a tiny child here on earth.

This auspicious beginning for both of these babies sets up their future relationship. Elizabeth's son will prepare the way for Jesus' ministry as Messiah. This story is full of unexpected surprises—an old woman who becomes the mother of John the Baptist. A young virgin who becomes the mother of Jesus the Christ. The joyous leap of an unborn child. The recognition of miracles. As we wait for the coming Christ, may we look and listen for the miracles that leap into our lives.

Emmanuel, open our eyes and hearts to watch for the unexpected during these last days of Advent. May our spirits leap for joy at the recognition of your presence in our lives, in this world. Amen.

O come, Emmanuel, and illuminate the shadows in our hearts, in our world.

Here in the northern hemisphere we have arrived at the winter solstice. After sunset tonight, we enter into the longest night. Tomorrow, the sun begins to rise a bit earlier, just a few minutes each day. Some of us with Seasonal Affective Disorder have been spending a few minutes each morning in front of a light box designed to counteract the sadness that comes from the lack of light. Others of us carry the sadness of loss and despair during these days. In this culture where it's assumed that we all are happy at Christmas, this can be a very lonely time.

Some of us are grieving the loss of family members. We may be watching someone we care deeply about struggle in an uphill battle with illness. We wrestle with the painful memories of how things used to be. There are so many reminders of how broken things are, regrets about things that we said or did, wounds from the hurtful things done to us.

The psalmist says it this way, "You have fed them with the bread of tears, and given them tears to drink in full measure." Sometimes it seems that we are bogged down with the weight of grief, fear, and uncertainty. We wonder why God has fed and watered us with tears. We cry out in lament to the One who comforts and heals.

And then the psalmist offers this refrain of hope: "Restore us, O God of hosts: let your face shine, that we might be saved." Like tomorrow's sun, God's face shines into our lives, illuminating the shadows in our lives and in our world.

Emmanuel, God-with-us, hold us close as we grieve or worry or weep. Restore us and let your face shine upon our shadows. Amen.

FOURTH SUNDAY OF ADVENT

O come, Emmanuel, and turn us toward Love.

Whenever I read this song of Mary, I hear the musical setting of the Magnificat by Rory Cooney. The chorus of "The Canticle of the Turning" declares, "The world is about to turn." Every time I hear this song, I am captivated by that phrase.

In these days filled with war and poverty, droughts and storms, hatred and injustice, we yearn for "the turning" that Mary's hymn proclaims.

Mary sings about this world that is turning toward Love. God "has brought down the powerful from their thrones and lifted up the lowly; [God] has filled the hungry with good things and sent the rich away empty." God has come to the aid of God's children.

Mary declares that the world is going to turn! Everything that we have known will be turned upside down. And God is coming to this earth in the most surprising way ever – born to teenage girl. Born into human form as a vulnerable, defenseless infant.

We anticipate this coming of Love. This opportunity to give up everything we have known and follow in trust, follow in faith, follow in love. We are invited to get ready to open our hearts, our minds, our spirits, our lives—to a Love that will change us and transform our world.

Watch for the signs. Keep watch. Stay awake! Get ready! Make space in your hearts and minds and spirits. Love is coming. And the world is about to turn.

Find a recording of "The Canticle of the Turning" by Rory Cooney and listen to it today. Let your heart listen to the yearnings within you. What are you yearning for—for your life, for your family or community, for this world? Invite the Holy One to clear out the corners of your heart so that there is more space for love.

All Is Not Lost

DECEMBER 23–29, 2024 • LARRIN ROBERTSON

SCRIPTURE OVERVIEW: The boy Samuel worshiped and served God from a young age. He grows in stature and favor, the same description that will later be applied to the young Jesus in this week's reading from Luke. The psalmist praises God for raising up a "horn" for the people. This "horn" is referred to elsewhere in the Psalms as being the True King from the line of David, identified later by Luke (1:69) as Jesus. Paul encourages the Colossians to let love rule in their community and to praise God with songs and hymns (such as the Psalms). The additional readings for this special week focus our minds on the Advent of the Lord, the amazing truth that "the Word became flesh and lived among us" (John 1:14), as the prophets had prophesied long ago.

QUESTIONS AND SUGGESTIONS FOR REFLECTION

- Read Isaiah 9:2-7. Where in your world do you see darkness? What lies within your power to dispel it?
- Read Psalm 148. How do you experience God's creations worshiping and praising God? How do you join in that worship?
- Read Colossians 3:12-17. How are you clothing yourself with love during this season?
- Read Luke 2:41-52. When has a not-as-usual occurrence generated anxiety in your life? How was it resolved?

Pastor of WORD For Life Church Ministries, Fort Washington, MD; PhD Candidate in the African American Preaching and Sacred Rhetoric program at Christian Theological Seminary; Baptist minister.

Facilitated by the priests, Israel's sacrificial system of worship impacted how people conceived of God. The loss of trust in the leader of the system, caused by Eli's corrupt sons, could well produce a loss of trust in the system itself and potentially lead to a declining faith in God. However, "Samuel was ministering before the Lord." Samuel was just one person, but there was at least one. All was not lost.

Hannah, Samuel's mother, "used to make for him a little robe" to wear as he fulfilled his duties. His linen garment was not gaudy; it was not embroidered with fine jewels or royal features. The young servant grew up dressed in humility, portraying a trustworthy image within the system of worship. For persons for whom moral clarity matters as part of a vocational call, Samuel is a symbol of how it might look to reject the trappings of ego and self-interest to rightly stand before the Lord. All was not lost.

People form opinions about God, the church, and religion and its adherents by their interactions with persons in positions of trust. When that trust is betrayed, such associations often crumble. However, where these interactions remind God-seeking persons of responsibility, faithfulness, and humility, such associations are readily received.

Samuel and his family benefit from his faithful ministry. As a symbol of God's favor, Eli pronounces a blessed benediction on the life of Samuel's parents, Elkanah and Hannah. One of God's graces is to remind us that the impact of our service extends to our village. Because of their faithfulness to the Lord and to each other, all was not lost.

Lord, guide and guard my heart to serve you with integrity. May I be a blessing to those who seek you through their interactions with me. Amen.

Eli's sons, Hophni and Phinehas, were priests at Shiloh. They are synonymous with worship gone wrong. They commodified worship and used their authority to take advantage of women temple workers. When priests or trusted spiritual leaders pervert and thus prevent worship, what hope do the people have that God remains accessible and available?

This is now the second time that Samuel is interjected into the account of the degradation of Israel's priesthood. While the priesthood is being defiled, Israel is not without hope. Indeed, Samuel is growing "in favor with the Lord and with the people." He has yet to reach the age of maturity, but the response to his presence differs from the reports concerning Hophni and Phinehas. So while hope may be difficult to locate in the sons of the priest, the future holds the promise of something better. Samuel's appearance is a reminder that no matter the weight of hopelessness, sources of hope remain.

This one verse contains the power of God to make right what has gone so far astray. That Samuel is still growing implies that the remedy for worship gone wrong is not a quick fix. Just as Samuel requires time to mature, so too does setting aright the matters of priestly affairs. Still, God is on the case.

Human history is replete with God's actions toward hope, inspiring people to also live, dream, and act hopefully. We must be willing to look beyond persons of privilege and places where power is traditionally brokered. Hope is a multifaceted and inviting enterprise. Hope appears on plantations, in sharecropper fields, in clapboard homes, on reservations, in ghettos—even in mangers! In places we often neglect to look and people we have looked over, God provides sources of hope.

Lord, help me to resist the urge to cling so closely to the ills of the world around me that I am unable to recognize how you will see us through. Amen.

All Is Not Lost   425

CHRISTMAS

One of the difficulties of hope is it can seem like an abstract, future occurrence. Today's demands prevent far too many people from knowing the privilege of dreaming that far ahead. Hope finds few tangible expressions and ceases to be hope. That which is hoped for, then, becomes obsolete because it seems unattainable.

Israel appears to have reached the point of an obsolete hope when the prophet Isaiah announced good news. He foretold of God's activities to liberate and provide hope for Israel. Yes, these were to be future occurrences, but with this good news came concrete actions to begin constructing hope. While Israel's remnant awaited their future, Isaiah's prophecy illuminated the way to reach for and live in hope in the present. Therein is the power of hope: Those who have it can determine to live expectantly.

Living in hope now is connected to the child that has been born. The birth of a king's heir induces rejoicing among the people of a kingdom. The child becomes an iconic figure upon whom rests the kingdom's future. Hope lives as long as the child lives. Isaiah prophesies of a far-off occurrence, but the effects of this birth resonated immediately and resonate today. Especially today.

Finally, hope has come! Live expectantly. Receive God's gifts. Embrace the child born for us. Live this future today.

For your present hope, O God, thank you. With joyful expectation, may we ever anticipate the day when the fullness of hope is realized. Until then, may our trust in such hope be sufficient for our needs today. Amen.

Something was terribly wrong with the makeup of the traveling party. For Mary and Joseph, the festive occasion, focused travel, and familiar companions all conspired to prevent their recognition that "the boy Jesus" was not with them. He was God's unique gift to them, unlike anyone else ever born! Of course, they had to go back. Searching for Jesus was a parental and sacred duty. By searching, once again Mary and Joseph say yes to their own charge.

It matters where we search for Jesus. Jesus was right where he needed to be. It was, after all, his Father's house. Jesus was not admonishing them for coming for him. Rather he meant that no *search* was necessary. Where else would he be? Such is the question for us today. We search for Jesus—and indeed may encounter him—in the marketplace, public square, schools, boardrooms, and at kitchen tables. The one place where Jesus should always be found, however, is the "temple" of our day. Do we earnestly search for Jesus there? Perhaps Jesus might ask again: "Where else would I be?"

Something greater is at work in this story than simply embarrassed parents and a precocious preteen who discovered his purpose. We see it in the second part of verse 51: "and his mother treasured all these things in her hear." It almost seems to be a throwaway line, but how tragic it would be for something so life-changing to be lost. As with Mary, may we treasure in our heart all the things we experience during our quest. They remind us that God is at work in the world. And just as we have found Jesus, so too will many others who discover that Someone is missing from their lives.

Thank you, God, for Jesus. I pray to always remember his impact on my life. Help me to be gracious to those who are also remembering. Amen.

It's easy to overlook the fact that Jesus had to grow up. The Son of God who would become the Savior of the world, performing miracles and transforming hearts and minds along the way, was first a child who grew up. The divine orchestration of his birth did not preclude the human experiences of his life. He learned, he listened, he asked questions; some might say he had a little sass (see Luke 2:48-49). We relate to Jesus in many ways, just as he relates to us.

The "increase" of which Luke writes calls to mind pioneers or trailblazers. On the journey, trees are cut and cleared, and brush is removed so travelers can make their way forward. Moving forward—or growing and increasing—requires the work of cutting, clearing, removing, and continuing momentum. We do the same as we grow—as we increase. We cut, clear, remove, and continue forward. With every step and stage of life, fresh insights, increased skills, and new strength become available to us. The same was true of Jesus.

Jesus' increase was not only in the wisdom gained through experience. His increase was balanced with the fruit of relationships. Never far from God and never too big for people, Jesus grew because he remained connected. He stayed in God's will by staying in touch with people. The commitment of disciples; the company of Mary, Martha, and other friends; and even the benevolence of silent partners all worked together to bring Jesus to his life's purpose. To get there, he had to increase.

All journeys start somewhere. As we make our way through life, blessed increase becomes available and personal growth becomes possible. Whatever else is captured in our biographical sketch, may we find this note—increase!

Lord, the wisdom of experience and the fruit of relationships are your gifts for my good. Be with and bless those with whom I journey through life. May we all know your grace. Amen.

I grew up in a Baptist church known locally for our rich musical tradition. There was a senior choir, a male chorus, a women's choir, a youth choir, and a children's choir. My favorite, however, was the mass choir, which consisted of anyone who wanted to sing together. With everyone singing and all the instruments playing, the three- and four-part harmonies produced big, soul-stirring sounds saturating the sanctuary with anthems and hymns. But there was more to this choir than music. The choir members ministered to one another through fellowship, frustration, laughter, and tears. When we sang, all of who we were and what we had been through came through the song.

This is the command of the psalmist. Within one psalm, praise is called forth thirteen times: The heavens, angels, celestial bodies, natural elements, topographic features, animals, and people of all persuasions are called to praise the Lord. From every place, among all creation, God's praise resounds. Celestial bodies and heaven's angelic inhabitants "join with all nature" and earth's human inhabitants "in manifold witness" to God's praiseworthiness.

Praise of God isn't just about our outward behavior and spoken witness. Praising God is imbued in every part of our being—every thought, every action, every encounter. Like my church's choir, the end result is only part of the equation. Praising God is not a performance; it's a way of life.

For what reasons is God to be praised? Consider the majesty of the sun, moon, and stars. Tremble at the oceans clapping at the mountains' feet. Be refreshed by the innocence of the infant's smile. The reasons to praise God are endless and new each day.

My Lord and my God, you deserve all praise. Thank you for the consistent reminders of your presence and care for us. May I live a life of praise to you. Amen.

First Sunday after Christmas

"So, now what?" That was the question asked at a recent new member's orientation. The question silenced the room as more than one person seemed to think the same thing. Namely, what are we to do now that we are here?

In the room were people from various backgrounds and experiences. A few had experience in or around church settings, but most had not. It would be unfair to single out any person by naming their specific "what." So, it seemed, the facilitator covered them all: "Now, you put on some new clothes."

In Colossians 2:12, Paul associates believers with the burial and resurrection of Christ through faith. In Colossians 3:1-2, Paul writes that those who associate themselves with Christ's resurrection are to "seek the things that are above" and "set [their] minds on things that are above." I suspect the apostle Paul anticipates the "So, now what?" question and preemptively responds: "Clothe yourselves."

Paul commends a list of no fewer than fourteen articles that believers should add to their spiritual wardrobe. Christ has designed each article. None of these articles can be bought with money, but they all come with some cost. Each article requires more thought about how others will receive them than how we might look when we put them on.

Wearing these new clothes should remind us that we have a moral and spiritual duty to live well with one another. They should remind us that we are enabled by and are reflections of the Lord Jesus, who has called us to new life in him. After all, the wearer of these new clothes wears the uniform of Christ.

Oh, for grace to wear it well!

God, thank you for my new clothes. As I engage with the people I meet along the way, may I reflect well the Christ in whom I have found new life. Amen.

Songs for All Seasons

DECEMBER 30–31, 2024 • WHITNEY R. SIMPSON

SCRIPTURE OVERVIEW: Jeremiah delivers happy news, a promise from the Lord of a brighter future day. God will bring back the scattered peoples from everywhere to their homeland, and their mourning will turn into joy. The psalmist encourages those in Jerusalem to praise God for all that God has done. God gives protection, peace, and the law to the children of Israel. The author of Ephesians encourages his readers with confidence in God's eternal plan. God's will was to send Christ and adopt us into God's family. We have been sealed with the Holy Spirit. The opening to John helps us understand the eternal scope of God's plan. From the beginning, the Word has been with God but then became flesh and lives among us to reveal divine glory.

QUESTIONS AND SUGGESTIONS FOR REFLECTION

- Read Jeremiah 31:7-14. Consider those who live in exile from their home or from their family relationships. How can you share Jeremiah's words of God's comfort?
- Read Ecclesiastes 3:1-13. In what season of life do you find yourself? What are you praying for this season?
- Read John 1:1-18. What does it mean for you that the true light enlightens everyone?
- Read Ephesians 1:3-14. How can you live your daily life from the perspective of God's cosmic time? How will you praise God?

Deaconess in The United Methodist Church; passionate about embodied spirituality at the intersection of spiritual direction and yoga; author of *Holy Listening with Breath, Body, and the Spirit* (Upper Room Books, 2016) and *Fully Human, Fully Divine: An Advent Devotional for the Whole Self* (Upper Room Books, 2022).

Sing joyfully! Shout! Raise your voices! This invitation may sound like a memory of Christmas morning with your overly excited siblings, children, or grandchildren. But this passage invited the people of Israel to praise at an unexpected time—after exile. To sing, shout, and raise their voices to God, yes! But, after exile?

While few of us may have experienced exile from our own country, we have experienced less extreme exiles that have disconnected us from our family, home, church, friends, or neighborhood. Pause and ponder from whom or what you feel separated in this season of life. How does this make you feel? Our scripture passage today says God will offer companion-ship for these people in this way: God will lead them by quiet streams so they don't stumble, keep them safe, rescue them, make them stronger, and comfort them.

I long for safety in my relationship with God. I am grateful for a God who rescues me, makes me more robust, and brushes me off when I stumble. Yet even with God's companionship in this way, great faith is required to sing with joy to God in trou-bling times—whether or not we have lost everything.

Great faith may be required for you to remain connected to your faith after separation from something that matters to you. It may feel impossible to sing to God, but maybe you can start with simply humming for God. Notice what it feels like to take a deep breath and breathe out a sound that only God understands, no words needed.

How is God inviting you to embody this passage today? From what have you been separated, and how can you cling to God today using your voice?

Holy God, keep me safe and give me comfort. Help me feel close to you as I hum or sing, offering you my praise and thanks-giving. Amen.

Yesterday we pondered what it means to rejoice in troubling times and what that may look or even sound like. Today we continue our reading in Jeremiah with the invitation to sing with special notice of one particular word. Depending on the version you are reading, the Hebrew word *nahar* in verse 12 is translated as *radiant, flowing, jubilant,* or *rejoice.* It also means to *shine.* "They shall come and sing aloud on the height of Zion, and they shall be radiant over the goodness of the LORD."

Ponder what this scripture could be inviting us to do today. We are asked to again sing to our Creator and are called by God to be radiant, find our flow, and shine bright in this world. I am excited to consider this humbling request of us as God's people. We get to shine because of God's goodness in us!

The word *flow* is often talked about in the land of productivity. I know when I'm in my flow and when I'm not (writer's block is real). But I think of this *flow* in a spiritual sense. When I find my flow with God, the words come, the passion rises, and the work has meaning.

Recall the feeling of being in your flow with God. This memory of finding your flow could be in your work, service, hobby, worship, or relationships. Ponder that moment of presence and how it feels in your body. Recognize that you are connected to your Creator and can always shine God's light. When we recognize God's light, we shine, remain connected to God, and even remind ourselves of our humility. This light is not ours; it is a gift from the One who created us. Ponder what moments and experiences are gifts you can rejoice in from this past year.

Creator, thank you for allowing me to shine your light. Help me to find my flow in the new year and to continue shining bright in the year to come. Amen.

The Revised Common Lectionary* for 2024
Year B—Advent / Christmas Year C
(Disciplines Edition)

January 1–7
BAPTISM OF THE LORD
Genesis 1:1-5
Psalm 29
Acts 19:1-7
Mark 1:4-11

> **January 1**
> **NEW YEAR'S DAY**
> Ecclesiastes 3:1-13
> Psalm 8
> Revelation 21:1-6
> Matthew 25:31-46

> **January 6**
> **EPIPHANY**
> *(may be used on January 1)*
> Isaiah 60:1-6
> Psalm 72:1-7, 10-14
> Ephesians 3:1-12
> Matthew 2:1-12

January 8–14
1 Samuel 3:1-10, (11-20)
Psalm 139:1-6, 13-18
1 Corinthians 6:12-20
John 1:43-51

January 15–21
Jonah 3:1-5, 10
Psalm 62:5-12
1 Corinthians 7:29-31
Mark 1:14-20

January 22–28
Deuteronomy 18:15-20
Psalm 111
1 Corinthians 8:1-13
Mark 1:21-28

January 29–February 4
Isaiah 40:21-31
Psalm 147:1-11, 20c
1 Corinthians 9:16-23
Mark 1:29-39

February 5–11
TRANSFIGURATION
2 Kings 2:1-12
Psalm 50:1-6
2 Corinthians 4:3-6
Mark 9:2-9

February 12–18
FIRST SUNDAY IN LENT
Genesis 9:8-17
Psalm 25:1-10
1 Peter 3:18-22
Mark 1:9-15

> **February 14**
> **ASH WEDNESDAY**
> Joel 2:1-2, 12-17
> Psalm 51:1-17
> 2 Corinthians 5:20b–6:10
> Matthew 6:1-6, 16-21

February 19–25
SECOND SUNDAY IN LENT
Genesis 17:1-7, 15-16
Psalm 22:23-31
Romans 4:13-25
Mark 8:31-38

February 26–March 3
THIRD SUNDAY IN LENT
Exodus 20:1-17
Psalm 19
1 Corinthians 1:18-25
John 2:13-22

March 4–10
FOURTH SUNDAY IN LENT
Numbers 21:4-9
Psalm 107:1-3, 17-22
Ephesians 2:1-10
John 3:14-21

March 11–17
FIFTH SUNDAY IN LENT
Jeremiah 31:31-34
Psalm 51:1-12
Hebrews 5:5-10
John 12:20-33

March 18–24
PALM/PASSION SUNDAY

Liturgy of the Palms
Psalm 118:1-2, 19-29
Mark 11:1-11

Liturgy of the Passion
Isaiah 50:4-9a
Psalm 31:9-16
Philippians 2:5-11
Mark 14:1–15:47

March 25–31
HOLY WEEK

Monday, March 25
Isaiah 42:1-9
Psalm 36:5-11
Hebrews 9:11-15
John 12:1-11

Tuesday, March 26
Isaiah 49:1-7
Psalm 71:1-14
1 Corinthians 1:18-31
John 12:20-36

Wednesday, March 27
Isaiah 50:4-9a
Psalm 70
Hebrews 12:1-3
John 13:21-32

Maundy Thursday, March 28
Exodus 12:1-14
Psalm 116:1-2, 12-19
1 Corinthians 11:23-26
John 13:1-17, 31b-35

Good Friday, April 7
Isaiah 52:13–53:12
Psalm 22
Hebrews 4:14-16; 5:7-9
John 18:1–19:42

Holy Saturday, April 8
Job 14:1-14
Psalm 31:1-4, 15-16
1 Peter 4:1-8
Matthew 27:57-66

Easter Day, April 9
Acts 10:34-43
Psalm 118:1-2, 14-24
1 Corinthians 15:1-11
John 20:1-18

April 1–7
Acts 4:32-35
Psalm 133
1 John 1:1–2:2
John 20:19-31

April 8–14
Acts 3:12-19
Psalm 4
1 John 3:1-7
Luke 24:36b-48

April 15–21
Acts 4:5-12
Psalm 23
1 John 3:16-24
John 10:11-18

April 22–28
Acts 8:26-40
Psalm 22:25-31
1 John 4:7-21
John 15:1-8

April 29–May 5
Acts 10:44-48
Psalm 98
1 John 5:1-6
John 15:9-17

May 6–12
Acts 1:15-17, 21-26
Psalm 1
1 John 5:9-13
John 17:6-19

> **May 9**
> **ASCENSION DAY**
> Acts 1:1-11
> Psalm 47
> Ephesians 1:15-23
> Luke 24:44-53

May 13–19
PENTECOST
Acts 2:1-21
Psalm 104:24-34, 35b
Romans 8:22-27
John 15:26-27; 16:4b-15

May 20–26
TRINITY SUNDAY
Isaiah 6:1-8
Psalm 29
Romans 8:12-17
John 3:1-17

May 27–June 2
1 Samuel 3:1-20
Psalm 139:1-6, 13-18
2 Corinthians 4:5-12
Mark 2:23–3:6

June 3–9
1 Samuel 8:4-20, 11:14-15
Psalm 138
2 Corinthians 4:13—5:1
Mark 3:20-35

June 10–16
1 Samuel 15:34–16:13
Psalm 20
2 Corinthians 5:6-17
Mark 4:26-34

June 17–23
1 Samuel 17:1a, 4-11, 19-23, 32-49
Psalm 9:9-20
2 Corinthians 6:1-13
Mark 4:35-41

June 24–30
2 Samuel 1:1, 17-27
Psalm 130
2 Corinthians 8:7-15
Mark 5:21-43

July 1–7
2 Samuel 5:1-5, 9-10
Psalm 48
2 Corinthians 12:2-10
Mark 6:1-13

July 8–14
2 Samuel 6:1-5, 12b-19
Psalm 24
Ephesians 1:3-14
Mark 6:14-29

July 15–21
2 Samuel 7:1-14a
Psalm 89:20-37
Ephesians 2:11-22
Mark 6:30-34, 53-56

July 22–28
2 Samuel 11:1-15
Psalm 14
Ephesians 3:14-21
John 6:1-21

July 29–August 4
2 Samuel 11:26–12:13a
Psalm 51:1-12
Ephesians 4:1-16
John 6:24-35

August 5–11
2 Samuel 18:5-9, 15, 31-33
Psalm 130
Ephesians 4:25–5:2
John 6:35, 41-51

August 12–18
1 Kings 2:10-12; 3:3-14
Psalm 111
Ephesians 5:15-20
John 6:51-58

August 19–25
1 Kings 8:1, 6, 10-11, 22-30,
 41-43
Psalm 84
Ephesians 6:10-20
John 6:56-69

August 26–September 1
Song of Solomon 2:8-13
Psalm 45:1-2, 6-9
James 1:17-27
Mark 7:1-8, 14-15, 21-23

September 2–8
Proverbs 22:1-2, 8-9, 22-23
Psalm 125
James 2:1-17
Mark 7:24-37

September 9–15
Proverbs 1:20-33
Psalm 19
James 3:1-12
Mark 8:27-38

September 16–22
Proverbs 31:10-31
Psalm 1
James 3:13–4:3, 7-8a
Mark 9:30-37

September 23–29
Esther 7:1-6, 9-10; 9:20-22
Psalm 124
James 5:13-20
Mark 9:38-50

September 30–October 6
Job 1:1; 2:1-10
Psalm 26
Hebrews 1:1-4; 2:5-12
Mark 10:2-16

October 7–13
Job 23:1-9, 16-17
Psalm 22:1-15
Hebrews 4:12-16
Mark 10:17-31

October 14–20
Job 38:1-7, 34-41
Psalm 104:1-9, 24, 35c
Hebrews 5:1-10
Mark 10:35-45

> **October 14**
> THANKSGIVING DAY,
> CANADA
> Joel 2:21-27
> Psalm 126
> 1 Timothy 2:1-7
> Matthew 6:25-33

October 21–27
Job 42:1-6, 10-17
Psalm 34:1-8, 19-22
Hebrews 7:23-28
Mark 10:46-52

October 28–November 3
Ruth 1:1-18
Psalm 146
Hebrews 9:11-14
Mark 12:28-34

> **November 1**
> ALL SAINTS DAY
> Wisdom of Solomon 3:1-9
> Psalm 24
> Revelation 21:1-6a
> John 11:32-44

November 4–10
Ruth 3:1-5; 4:13-17
Psalm 127
Hebrews 9:24-28
Mark 12:38-44

November 11–17
1 Samuel 1:4-20
1 Samuel 2:1-10
Hebrews 10:11-25
Mark 13:1-8

November 18–24
REIGN OF CHRIST
2 Samuel 23:1-7
Psalm 132:1-18
Revelation 1:4b-8
John 18:33-37

November 25–December 1
FIRST SUNDAY OF ADVENT
Jeremiah 33:14-16
Psalm 25:1-10
1 Thessalonians 3:9-13
Luke 21:25-36

> **November 28**
> **THANKSGIVING DAY, USA**
> Joel 2:21-27
> Psalm 126
> 1 Timothy 2:1-7
> Matthew 6:25-33

December 2–8
SECOND SUNDAY OF ADVENT
Baruch 5:1-9
Luke 1:68-79
Philippians 1:3-11
Luke 3:1-6

December 9–15
THIRD SUNDAY OF ADVENT
Zephaniah 3:14-20
Isaiah 12:2-6
Philippians 4:4-7
Luke 3:7-18

December 16–22
FOURTH SUNDAY OF ADVENT
Micah 5:2-5a
Luke 1:46b-55
Hebrews 10:5-10
Luke 1:39-55

December 23–29
FIRST SUNDAY AFTER CHRISTMAS
1 Samuel 2:18-20, 26
Psalm 148
Colossians 3:12-17
Luke 2:41-52

> **December 25**
> **CHRISTMAS DAY**
> Isaiah 9:2-7
> Psalm 96
> Titus 2:11-14
> Luke 2:1-20

December 30–31
SECOND SUNDAY AFTER CHRISTMAS
Jeremiah 31:7-14
Psalm 147:12-20
Ephesians 1:3-14
John 1:(1-9), 10-18

A Guide to Daily Prayer

These prayers imply worship time with a group; feel free to adapt the plural pronouns for personal use.

MORNING PRAYER

In the morning, O LORD, you hear my voice;
    in the morning I lay my requests before you
    and wait in expectation.

        —Psalm 5:3

Gathering and Silence

Call to Praise and Prayer
    God said: Let there be light; and there was light.
    And God saw that the light was good.

Psalm 63:2-6

God, my God, you I crave;
    my soul thirsts for you,
    my body aches for you
    like a dry and weary land.
Let me gaze on you in your temple:
    a Vision of strength and glory
Your love is better than life,
    my speech is full of praise.
I give you a lifetime of worship,
    my hands raised in your name.
I feast at a rich table
    my lips sing of your glory.

Prayer of Thanksgiving

We praise you with joy, loving God, for your grace is better than life itself. You have sustained us through the darkness: and you bless us with life in this new day. In the shadow of your wings we sing for joy and bless your holy name. Amen.

Scripture Reading

Silence

Prayers of the People

The Lord's Prayer (ecumenical text)

Our Father in heaven,
hallowed be your name,
your kingdom come,
your will be done,
on earth as in heaven.
Give us today our daily bread.
Forgive us our sins as we forgive
those who sin against us.
Save us from the time of trial,
and deliver us from evil.
For the kingdom, the power, and the glory
are yours, now and forever. Amen.

Blessing

May the light of your mercy shine brightly on all who walk in your presence today, O Lord.

I will extol the LORD at all times;
    God's praise will always be on my lips.
                                    —Psalm 34:1

Gathering and Silence

Call to Praise and Prayer

O LORD, my Savior, teach me your ways.
My hope is in you all day long.

Prayer of Thanksgiving

God of mercy, we acknowledge this midday pause
of refreshment as one of your many generous gifts.
Look kindly upon our work this day; may it be made
perfect in your time. May our purpose and prayers
be pleasing to you. This we ask through Christ our
Lord. Amen.

Scripture Reading

Silence

Prayers of the People

The Lord's Prayer (ecumenical text)
    Our Father in heaven,
        hallowed be your name,
        your kingdom come,
        your will be done,
        on earth as in heaven.

Give us today our daily bread.
Forgive us our sins as we forgive
    those who sin against us.
Save us from the time of trial,
    and deliver us from evil.
For the kingdom, the power, and the glory
    are yours, now and forever. Amen.

Blessing

Strong is the love embracing us, faithful the Lord
from morning to night.

My soul finds rest in God alone;
my salvation comes from God.
—Psalm 62:1

Gathering and Silence

Call to Praise and Prayer

From the rising of the sun to its setting,
let the name of the LORD be praised.

Psalm 134

Bless the Lord,
all who serve in God's house,
who stand watch
throughout the night.

Lift up your hands
in the holy place
and bless the Lord.

And may God,
the maker of earth and sky,
bless you from Zion.

Prayer of Thanksgiving

Sovereign God, you have been our help during the day and you promise to be with us at night. Receive this prayer as a sign of our trust in you. Save us from all evil, keep us from all harm, and guide us in your way. We belong to you, Lord. Protect us by the power of your name. In Jesus Christ we pray. Amen.

Scripture Reading

Silence

Prayers of the People

The Lord's Prayer (ecumenical text)
> Our Father in heaven,
>> hallowed be your name,
>> your kingdom come,
>> your will be done,
>> on earth as in heaven.
> Give us today our daily bread.
> Forgive us our sins as we forgive
>> those who sin against us.
> Save us from the time of trial,
>> and deliver us from evil.
> For the kingdom, the power, and the glory
>> are yours, now and forever. Amen.

Blessing
> May your unfailing love rest upon us, O LORD,
> even as we hope in you.

This *Guide to Daily Prayer* was compiled from scripture and other resources by Rueben P. Job and then adapted by the Pathways Center for Spiritual Leadership while under the direction of Marjorie J. Thompson.